## DATE DUE

| | | | |
|---|---|---|---|
| | | | |
| | | | |
| | | | |
| | | | |
| | | | |
| | | | |
| | | | |
| | | | |
| | | | |
| | | | |
| | | | |
| | | | |
| | | | |
| | | | |
| | | | |
| | | | |
| | | | |
| | | | |
| | | | |
| | | | |

DEMCO 38-296

# Necessary Madness

# Necessary Madness

## THE HUMOR OF DOMESTICITY
## IN NINETEENTH-CENTURY
## AMERICAN LITERATURE

Gregg Camfield

*New York     Oxford*  *Oxford University Press   1997*

Oxford University Press

Oxford    New York

Athens   Auckland   Bangkok   Bogota   Bombay   Buenos Aires
Calcutta   Cape Town   Dar es Salaam   Delhi   Florence   Hong Kong
Istanbul   Karachi   Kuala Lumpur   Madras   Madrid   Melbourne
Mexico City   Nairobi   Paris   Singapore   Taipei   Tokyo   Toronto   Warsaw

and associated companies in
Berlin   Ibadan

Copyright © 1997 by Gregg Camfield

Published by Oxford University Press
198 Madison Avenue, New York, New York 10016

Oxford is a registered trademark of Oxford University Press

Library of Congress Cataloging-in-Publication Data
Camfield, Gregg.
Necessary madness : The humor of domesticity
in nineteenth-century American literature / Gregg Camfield.
p.    cm.
Includes bibliographical references and index.
ISBN 0-19-510040-9
1. American wit and humor—19th century—History and criticism.
2. Literature and society—United States—History—19th century.
3. Man-woman relationships in literature.   4. Marriage in
literature.   5. Family in literature.   6. Home in literature.
I. Title.
PS437.C36   1997
813'.309355—dc20       96-26019

1 3 5 7 9 8 6 4 2

Printed in the United States of America
on acid-free paper

*To Eileen Kogl Camfield*
*and Isabella Helen Camfield*
*for making me laugh*

# Preface

In *My Opinions and Betsey Bobbet's*, Marietta Holley, America's first overtly feminist humorist, has her heroine, Samantha Smith Allen, discussing suffrage with a women's rights lecturer. Samantha describes this lecturer as "one of the wild eyed ones" with whose motives she often disagrees. The two have it out over their visions of feminism, with the lecturer deriding "tyrant man" and Samantha suggesting that women ought to ground their quest for power in something more positive than animosity:

> She went right on without mindin' me—"Man has always tried to dwarf our intellects; cramp our souls. The sore female heart pants for freedom. It is sore! and it pants!"
>
> Her eyes was rolled up in her head, and she had lifted both hands in a eloquent way, as she said this, and I had a fair view of her waist, it wasn't much bigger than a pipe's tail [Samantha, as she tells us repeatedly, weighs over two hundred pounds, with principles weighty enough to match]. And I says to her in a low, friendly tone. "Seein' we are only females present, let me ask you in a almost motherly way, when your heart felt sore and pantin' did you ever loosen your cosset strings? Why," says I, "no wonder your heart feels sore, no wonder it pants, the only wonder is, that it don't get discouraged and stop beatin' at all."

> She wanted to waive off the subject, I knew, for she rolled up her eyes higher
> than ever, and agin she began, "Tyrant man"—
> Agin I thought of Josiah, and agin I interrupted her by sayin' "Men haint the
> worst critters in the world, they are as generous and charitable agin, as wimmen
> are, as a general thing."
> "Then what do you want wimmen to vote for, if you think so?"
> "Because I want justice done to every human bein'. Justice never hurt nobody
> yet, and rights given through courtesy and kindness, haint so good, in the long
> run, as rights given by law. (343)

In this passage, Holley, as usual, uses humor to cut several different ways simultaneously, making her usual gentle fun of her own narrator's pomposity and literal mindedness, attacking the nineteenth-century's version of anorexia, all while promoting a just franchise.

Such is the kind of humor that made Holley a best-selling author, one of the most popular humorists of her day. While humor is usually bound to time and place, Holley is still funny to many readers; my students, for example, find her stories to be among the most entertaining by nineteenth-century American humorists. What is funny-strange about this passage is that its comedy is virtually unaccountable by almost any theory of comic literature currently popular. It can't usefully be considered in Freudian terms because there is nothing veiled about it. Holley displaces little; the comedy comes more from contrasts in style than from any displaced aggression or any economy of affect. It also is difficult to explain in Hobbesian terms, the terms so common to so much current political criticism, because the animosities do not run in the obvious directions. Holley explicitly resists anger at the patriarchy, and in so doing makes her explicitly political comedy grounded not in ironic negation of perceived proviolege, but rather in an exultation in possibilities for self-satisfaction and improvement by expanding the range of privilege. Holley's humor embraces the enemy without smothering him.

My fascination with this constructive potential motivated my work on this book. Granted, one leg of comedy is made up of destructive, hostile, or antagonistic elements; in the passage I cite above, much of the fun is predicated on conflict, though not between the expected two sides in the battle. Still, I was early convinced in my critical reading on American humor that analysts tend to miss the other leg on which humor stands. Perhaps that has been the case because so much of the comedy written by women has been ignored in the critical histories, and without the counterpoint between humor written by women and men, it is sometimes difficult to see how humor very often cuts across the grain of obvious antagonisms in order to find common grounds for agreement as well as for disagreement. This book is an attempt to reconstruct the humorous dialogue between men and women over their shared ground, that is, home ground, in order to try to understand how humor, known since antiquity for its cutting edge, can as often be genial and creative.

In introducing this large new field, I've tried to balance the investigation between cultural history and the works of a few selected authors. Chapter 1 reconstructs two crucial aspects of nineteenth-century culture. It recovers the nineteenth-century understanding of humor, an understanding that put a premium on the genial aspects of comedy. It also examines the nineteenth-century ideology of domesticity that is the subject of the humor I will explore in depth. The conjunction here is particularly fortuitous in that domestic ideology and a widespread belief in the possibility of an "amiable" humor arose simultaneously out of the same intellectual and social traditions, yet the thrust of domestic ideology was oppressively serious, so serious as to seem to call forth a particularly aggressive kind of humor. Thus, chapter 1 shows the tensions in the culture that test the very limits of its understanding of comedy.

With this background in mind, I develop a series of paired test cases in four chapters, each of which treats a male and a female humorist who confront a complementary set of problems in the practice of humor that confronts domesticity. Thus, in chapter 2 I examine how Washington Irving and Fanny Fern use the comic sketch as a way to express disappointment in domesticity. In each case, their frustrations reveal the degree to which they accept the basic value of domesticity, and in each case, they find in humor a way to humanize a system that they detest in direct proportion to how much they value it. In chapter 3, I show Harriet Beecher Stowe and Herman Melville trying to explore the psychology of sexuality through humor; Stowe hopes that humor may contain and guide the forces of sexuality into constructive channels, while Melville uses humor as a way to liberate our understanding of the forces of sexuality to prevent us from becoming monstrous in ignorance and repression.

In chapter 4, on Mark Twain and Marietta Holley, I show the limits beyond which amiable humor could not go and remain effective. For both Twain and Holley, the gender definitions of the sexual spheres were both opportunity and threat to humor, with both swapping humor for satire when they began to take gendered ideas of morality too seriously. In chapter 5, which looks at the writings of George Washington Harris and Mary Wilkins Freeman, I show the capacities of humor to expand definitions of humanity. Harris and Freeman, in radically different ways, account for the virtual anarchy of humor, and while each appreciates some aspects of conventional domesticity as an answer to the dangers of anarchy, each is willing to confront the fact that creativity is closely allied to destruction, and that any act of creative will entails a limiting of certain other possibilities. Both use humor as a way to turn limitation into liberation, and simultaneously to recognize that the greater the freedom of individuality, the greater the losses of human connection.

Only after amassing the evidence of a number of humorists working in an atmosphere that was generally congenial to a creative and amiable humor am I in a position to move to the final, synthetic part of the book. In the final chapter, I look to recent research into the neuroanatomy of laughter and humor, and combining this with the understanding of the socially constructed aspects of humor, I discuss the dynamic interplay between individual psychology and social patterns in channeling the creative and destructive aspects of comic perception into works of literary art.

But this book is as interested in the cultural and psychic work of laughter and humor as it is in comic artifacts. That work is to liberate people from the strictures of normalcy. To the sane, laughter is a kind of madness. Certainly it has long been associated with abnormality, being the product of fools and folly. The very term *humor* comes to us, sanitized by eighteenth-century liberalism, from a model of madness; that is, a "humorist" is one whose humors are so out of balance that they cause eccentric or insane behavior. Under the spell of humor, though, "sanity" shows its limitations, and to show the limitations of reigning orthodoxies of thought and behavior is precisely the value of humor. In the nineteenth-century humor of domesticity I discuss in this book, humor allowed both men and women to manage their ambivalent feelings about the new ideology of domesticity. Not only did humor vent conflicted feelings, it served as a technique of exploration and creativity, a source of renewed vitality and flexibility in the face of relentless sanity. It was a necessary madness.

※    ※

Our interest in interdisciplinary work notwithstanding, literary scholars rarely cross C. P. Snow's "two cultures" divide into the sciences. Many humanists are still skeptical of the value of such a multiculturalism, and indeed, I found myself surprised at the course the investigations took as this study unfolded. But as a philosophical Pragmatist who follows the implications of William James's radical empiricism, my method is not to shut out possibilities, but rather to follow where the inquiry leads.

More specifically, a synthetic Pragmatism as developed by James, and more recently and cogently articulated in Richard Rorty's *Philosophy and the Mirror of Nature*, does not privilege one mode of discourse over any other. Instead, it sees any such privileging as a recourse to the myth of transcendental objectivity. Pragmatism resists the possibility of any transcendental objectivity because it recognizes that human consciousness is always mediating, that there is no raw perception without it being filtered through the paradigms of the conscious and unconscious mind. The critical task is to become not merely conscious of the limitations of a single paradigm, but to find the strengths of it as well, to see each particular model as developing some portion of the totality of experience. Critical pluralism in these terms requires self-consciousness of the limitations of paradigms not for the sake of self-consciousness nor to draw a false conclusion of superiority or objectivity through self-consciousness itself. It is, rather, to synthesize models by seeing how they answer different questions. As James puts it in *The Meaning of Truth*, "The pragmatist view . . . of the truth-relation is that it has a definite content, and that everything in it is experienceable. Its whole nature can be told in *positive* terms" (314–15; my emphasis).

James insists on the positive content of experience in opposition to the impulse of what he defines as "rationality." James sees "rationality" as a reduction of experience into aesthetically pleasing categories. Because organization of experience by reduction is so satisfying, "rationality" can easily reverse the center of ontology from experience to category, denying the truth of experience itself in favor of a transcendental ideal, always reductive, always negating experience itself. To avoid this trap of privileging categories over what they categorize, says James, one must first interrogate the purposes behind any system of thought: "Every way of classifying a thing is but a way of handling it for some particular purpose. Conceptions, 'kinds,' are teleological instruments. No abstract concept can be a valid substitute for a concrete reality except with reference to a particular interest in the conceiver" ("The Sentiment of Rationality" 321). Thus he insists on first finding the subjective purpose behind any theoretical position in order to discover the concrete, positive purposes it serves. In this way, Pragmatism becomes not a relativistic battleground between simply competing subjectivities, but a synthetic interpretation of multiple points of view. It makes a full pluralism possible.

It is important not to confuse "pluralism" for relativism in either of its popular guises, positivistic or solipsistic. In solipsistic relativism, the assumption that truth is completely contingent on perspective leads to fragmentational hermeneutics like those of Stanley Fish or Walter Benn Michaels. Such practitioners do not really work so much as radical empiricists in the Pragmatic tradition as they do as Pyrrhonian skeptics. They privilege their own putative knowledge of the impossibility of knowledge, a claim that could not be made consistently in the face of complete doubt. In this way, relativism is "rationalistic" by James's definition, that is, it reduces the world to a single transcendental category of total doubt, a category known a priori rather than experientially.

While skeptical relativism is built on a paradox, the kind of relativity used in the physical sciences and metaphorically in other disciplines is not, but both rely on a promise of transcendental knowledge arising out of the category of "relationship." Theories of relativity in the physical sciences promise that objectivity is still possible if one merely accounts for contingent circumstance, for point of view. A transcendental perspective allows one theoretically to account for anomalies in perception and thus right them, returning the world to full, monistic, categorical order.

Pragmatic pluralism stands in opposition to these two kinds of categorical analysis precisely because Pragmatic pluralism denies the ontological privilege of categorical—that is, reductionistic or atomistic—thinking. Pluralism begins with the assumption that we can know holistically that analytical reductions have their place as part of a synthetic and provisional approach to experience. That is, if we abandon linear thinking for recursive, layered, interlocked, networked thinking, then larger pictures appear in which synthesis of component parts, always based on models, always based on fragments, becomes possible. Modeling, then, becomes not a search for a single transcendent objectivity, but serves rather to find contingent approximations, always in flux, always corrigible, always mediating between order and chaos.

My love of humor as a source of creativity is probably my aesthetic motive for adopting Pragmatism, and my experience teaching humor is that humor facilitates pluralistic thinking. Humor juxtaposes ostensibly incompatible systems of thought to inspire a different order of viewing. That is what I hope this book will do, too. It is a series of radical juxtapositions to explore a complex topic. I took one line through this material to hold it together, but other lines are possible, even likely. I hope this book's structure will encourage discoveries substantially outside of the range of those I describe along the way.

In such a pluralistic spirit, there is no reason not to interrogate humor through a "scientific" model of consciousness. There is, on the other hand, plenty of good reason to do so. My effort in this study to do justice to the material, to use a structure that forces radical juxtapositions of paradigms in order to reveal their fundamental assumptions, kept turning up a few perplexing questions. Specifically, why do our critical paradigms duplicate some of the most extreme forms of gender difference postulated in the nineteenth century? The answer partly is that most of our current critical paradigms operate through classical binary oppositions, as if Ramistic logic, breaking into the fabric of Enlightenment philosophy through Bacon's *Novum Organum*, never lost its grip on Western consciousness. How could this be the case? How could such simplification persist in spite of an ostensible revolution in hermeneutics?

In studying humor, I found that the answers to these questions were buried in "science" anyway, or rather were buried in outdated models of mind that once had scientific currency, but now persist merely as subterranean footings for a philosophical discourse that refuses to examine its foundations. As Rorty makes clear, the model of mind we inherited from the early years of the Enlightenment persists in analytic philosophy. What is less clear from his study is that the same model of mind hangs on in almost every other discipline; it is a common basis behind almost every branch of the Western intellectual tradition.

The way critics react to humor reveals this quite clearly, perhaps because the gap between humor's unsettling potentials and the reductionistic model of mind oftern used to explain away those paradigmatic challenges is so great as to be obvious. This was brought home to me again recently at a conference when I participated in a discussion of Ernesto Galarza's *Barrio Boy*. After a panelist had broached the issue of Galarza's tone and the political implications of his autobiographical narrative, audience members debated whether or not Galarza capitulates too easily to the hegemonic Anglo voice or if there is a crisis of authority, of identity, *repressed* in the text. A Freudian model of mind rises quickly to formulate the mental processes of an author whose works challenge rather than support simple political paradigms.

Because Galarza expresses cultural tension through humor, many of the panelists and audience members found no tension in the book at all! Their models of power struggle could not account for the book's levity. I suggested that the book's humor might be a sign that the author found pleasure in the crisis of identity as he negotiated the conflicting pulls of Hispanic and Anglo cultures, mastering the latter not only in order to be able to speak for the former, but also because mastery of multiple cultural codes, rather than entailing loss of identity in a zero-sum game, can actually expand identity and agency. I suggested that we need not assume that all crises are marked exclusively by angst, that the author may have creatively challenged univocality through humor. A panelist responded something to the effect that, yes, the humor shows that Galarza was not a collaborator because, as everyone knows, "biologically, humor is attack." None present challenged this positivistic assertion; body language suggested general agreement.

In this context, it becomes necessary to challenge those archaic models of biology and the resultant model of mind, all the more so since humor theory in particular returns compulsively to outdated psychological theory, theory that sees the mind as a simple recording device. Even in the late twentieth century, the Cartesian model of mind hangs on; it remains "normal" to imagine the mind as a theater of consciousness in which the action that takes place can be viewed objectively by a single eye. True, that homunculus viewer of all that happens in the theater of the mind has been removed from the pineal gland where Descartes located it. True, we no longer have the Enlightenment's comfortable idea of consciousness as nature's simple looking glass; after Freud, it looks more like a distorting fun-house mirror. Nonetheless, the hope of objectivity and monistic explanation persists. If we can, the hope goes, account for the distortions of subjectivity, then we can "unmask" real motives, either by uncovering individual compulsions or even by revealing a "political unconscious." To find this putatively objective transcendence, critics often adduce the authority of Freud and move on.

It is necessary, then, to challenge these root assumptions on their own ground, to see how current work in neurology challenges older assumptions about how the brain works, how brain becomes mind. Granted, there is a persistent reductionism in the work of some analysts of contemporary neuroscience, such as in the work of Patricia Churchland or Daniel C. Dennett. But the field tends toward holism, toward seeing the mind as a complex process of networks, of homeostatic balance between degrees of order and disorderliness. In particular the work of Gerald M. Edelman and of Stuart A. Kauffman suggests a profound challenge to older models of the mind as a simple mechanism that can be accounted for in linear, atomistic terms.

Such holistic models simply take into account growing understanding that atomistic or reductionistic explanations do not explain what happens in complex systems. To use the chaos theorist's favorite analogy, a closed system such as the earth's weather is understandable in all of its particulars. No processes of heat exchange are beyond the easy ken of traditional physics, but the system itself is so variable through sheer size alone, that prediction beyond a narrow range is impossible. Too many variables in the interaction of even simple processes lead to a chaotic complexity that can be grasped holistically, but cannot be predicted. That is, a system rises beyond the sum of its component parts into something much more complex, much less predictable, much less determined, much more chaotic.

How much more unpredictable, then, is the mind that arises out of the brain. The individual components of consciousness in the brain—neurons—are beyond simple understanding in their own rights, but their combined interaction defies predictability. The number of physical connections between neurons in the human cerebral cortex alone is a million billion. Furthermore, as Edelman puts it, "if we consider how connections might be variously combined, the number would be hyperastronomical—on the order of ten followed by millions of zeros. (There are about ten followed by eighty zeros' worth of positively charged particles in the whole known universe)" (*Bright Air* 17). And neurons communicate not only by electrochemical impulse along synaptic connections, but also by a large number of chemical transmitters, transmitters that act at different rates, act selectively on different target neurons, communicate reciprocally with every part of the human body. This is not to say that the brain is a chaotic system, only that its order of complexity is so great that it defies reductionistic analysis. In an attempt to understand the dynamics that generate order in the face of such complexity, holistic models hold much greater promise.

My final chapter applies some of this new science through a provisional alternative model of mind in order to challenge reigning orthodoxies in humor studies. I fear, however, that any new theory will become again a reductionistic prison. Therefore my method, here, relies not on one paradigm, but instead approaches the problems of humor through different lenses: historical, analytical, structuralist, poststructuralist, psychological, and social.

The theory comes at the end precisely because I want first to destabilize regnant commonplaces of humor theory, and secondarily because my theorizing here is provisional. The last chapter has more implications than can be managed in a book of this sort. I do not make claims to a new hermeneutics based on a new psychology, partly because I do not wish to privilege the psychological over the social. More importantly, I do not want to privilege the theory over the experiments. But I do suspect that neurology's newly unfolding model of mind will unsettle much critical theory by demanding that we become fully conscious of assumed linearity, of an assumed promise of transcendental objectivity packed into the remnants of Descartes's model of the mind.

Peculiarly, then, the sciences lead back to a more humanistic approach to knowledge than does philosophy as it has been practiced since the scientific revolution began. A Pragmatism that embraces empiricism fully finds that science itself is moving beyond the physicist's atomistic reduction to the biologist's holism. At stake is how we understand both representation and interpretation, which always entail a model of mind. A revolution is taking place in how human beings understand the mind; it's not too early for humanists to begin to grapple with the implications of that revolution.

# Acknowledgments

As I finish this project, I find myself thinking of the enthusiastic support I received from many quarters, and while I will here and in notes try to acknowledge many of those who helped me, I know that simple thanks cannot convey the depth of my appreciation. This project has not been an exercise in reasoned argument alone, but also an exercise in pleasure. I do not think I could have pulled it off if others had not agreed that the joy of humor is worth thinking, talking, and writing about.

First among these fellow partisans of humor are my students at the University of Pennsylvania and at the University of the Pacific. They seem to enjoy turning comedy into a subject for examination even though I warn them that it might at first seem that comedy dies under scrutiny. They take on faith my claim that study eventually enriches one's sense of humor. Whether such is true for each of them, I know *my* sense of humor has been enriched by the privilege of spending class time with them all.

Special thanks must go to Elisa New and Robert Regan for reading draft after draft. Each gave not only invaluable criticism, but also even more valuable encouragement. Similar thanks go to colleagues who read some or all of the manuscript at least once: Mitch Breitwieser, John Bryant, Jim Cox, Fred

Crews, Vic Doyno, Shelley Fisher Fishkin, Bob Hirst, Bruce Michelson, Dana Nelson, and Eric Sundquist. I appreciate, too, the interchanges I had at conferences where I presented early versions of various chapters, and in particular I want to thank Lou Budd, Cathy Davidson, Susan K. Harris, Karen Oakes, Carol Schilling, Dave Sloane, and Kate Winter for their reactions to my ideas about Mary Wilkins Freeman, Marietta Holley, and humor theory.

Most of my time drafting and re-drafting this book was spent in the company of family and friends, who have been, if possible, even more supportive than my students and colleagues. I want particularly to thank Bill Dorland for his vibrant interest, and my in-laws, Dorothy and Dick Kogl, for reading the entire manuscript in next-to-last draft. Most thanks go to Eileen. She read aloud the works of Holley and Freeman with me, she discussed ad infinitum the most trivial details of my argument, and she read the entire draft early on. While I thank her for these labors, their value is as nothing in comparison with her good humor, which is both my inspiration and my reward.

# Contents

# Necessary Madness

## ONE

# Humor in a
# Heartless Haven

Sudden glory is the passion which maketh those grimaces
called laughter.

—Thomas Hobbes, *Leviathan*

The history of our race, and each individual's experience,
are sown thick with evidences that a truth is not hard to
kill, and that a lie well told is immortal.

—Mark Twain, "Advice to Youth"

### I.

I find it hard to tell some truths about nineteenth-century American literary
comedies of domesticity, or for that matter about any comedy, because
Hobbes's lie about laughter shows signs of being well told. It's not that he lies
completely in suggesting that laughter can contain hostility; his art lies in his
use of a partial truth to disguise the rest. Nor is it that he originated the idea
that laughter is aggression on a picnic, but his art also lies in his remarkable
ability both to encapsulate Western culture's classical theories of comedy as derision and to anticipate modern comic theory's shift from ethical to psychological grounds. Nor is it that his lie has gone unchallenged, but while it may have
been buried temporarily in the optimism of the Enlightenment, it arose from
the grave, or rather to its gravity, about one hundred years ago in fin de siècle
angst. In the last years of the nineteenth century and the first years of the
twentieth, it found persuasive advocates in the likes of Sigmund Freud, whose
naturalistic theory of jokes as repressed aggression exfoliates the bud of
Hobbes's lie into full flower. Now, in our own fin de siècle, an era once again
dominated by the idea that human actions are nothing more than power nego-
tiations, the idea that all comedy is naught but hostility, either sublimated
from a position of weakness or voiced from a position of strength, lives.

As I approach this study of literary comedies of domesticity, I find the longevity of Hobbes's lie a touch discouraging. After all, I write at a fortuitous moment when for the first time our critical paradigms are allowing us to see a rich, extensive body of humorous writing by women, but when the paradigms that allow that new vision have nonetheless done nothing to challenge reigning orthodoxies of humor studies. Regina Barreca, for instance, fails to follow her own advice when she sounds a "challenge of providing new patterns and strategies to characterize women's . . . comedy and humor" (9). In saying that "[t]he interpretive applications for comedy written by women have been narrowed by the inherited critical structures which do not provide for the particularly insurgent strategies used by women writers" (9), her insistence on "insurgency" alone forces her into citing Freud, and worse, paraphrasing without attributing the naturalist psychologist Albert Rapp, whose "A Phylogenetic Theory of Wit and Humor" out-Hobbeses Hobbes. Says Barreca, "[T]here exists a general theory that suggests that laughter and smiling arise out of a primitive response to anger and fear; the baring of teeth to the enemy" (7–8). Perhaps she did not cite her source because she didn't know it, but it is strange that she keeps such conservative company in her effort to find an analysis that is capable of exploring a comedy that is "characterised by the breaking of cultural and ideological frames" (9).

Not that the act of discovery of so much humor by women is not in itself extraordinarily important. I owe much in this study to those critics who have worked energetically to uncover so much lost writing.[1] But their discovery has been remarkably conservative in its treatment of humor itself. In Zita Dresner and Nancy Walker's anthology of humor, *Redressing the Balance,* for instance, the editors cite as authority for their treatment of women's humor that "most humor theorists consider the venting of aggression to be a major function of humor" (xxi). Walker's book-length study of American humor by women, *A Very Serious Thing: Women's Humor and American Culture,* elaborates this observation into a large-scale theory of how women wrote their own form of subversive aggression. In the process, she may have redefined the boundaries of American humor, but she has done nothing to reexamine the spirit of humor itself as it may have been practiced by a significant portion of the American populace. I think such conservatism sells women's humor short and wastes a valuable opportunity to see whether or not much other American humor has also been sold short. So at the outset of this study, I want to hold myself to the difficult task of studying this body of literature in a different spirit, a non-Hobbesian one. I begin, then, not with comedies of domesticity per se, but rather with a meditation on method, on how to read comedy without reducing it to a lie.

It is a commonplace of humor that a joke explained is a joke destroyed, and that any analysis of humor is therefore impossible. I disagree, obviously, for if I felt that humor disappeared when studied, and that therefore humor analyzed is analogous to reality as defined by Ambrose Bierce's *Devil's Dictionary*—"that which would remain in the cupel if one should assay a phantom"—I would not have written this book. But serious study of humor has great difficulty understanding the comic spirit. The serious approach to life simplifies experience to make sense out of it; the humorous approach complicates experience to make nonsense. Of course, the very structure of the word *nonsense* entails the dominance of *sense*, which is always abstraction from experience. Perhaps humor is not so much the complication of experience as it is the refusal to reduce experience to those abstractions that we control and name "sense" or "order." Humor takes pleasure in the chaotic exuberance of life. Trying to make "sense" out of humor risks, indeed, a destruction of the essence of humor itself.

Without a humorous perspective, then, the critic can see but one piece of any comic vision, can see only one possibility in one of those ink-blot tests of perception that shift their meaning depending on whether one sees the black as foreground and the white as background, or vice versa. To shift the metaphor, the critic of comedy who sees it seriously is like the one-legged cynic in Melville's *The Confidence-Man*, and comedy walking on one leg usually veers toward either bitterness or sourness. Or, to change the metaphor again, trying to run comedy to ground with a dog that can smell only the serious scent of comedy is likely to fail, because such a dog will keep getting crossed up by other game and in following false trails will miss the essence of humor.

That, I think, is what happens in Walker's book on comedy. The one dog she uses is the Hobbes-Foucault terrier, the dog that sniffs out power games, that runs comedy down as either the oppressive machinery of the hegemonic voice or as the sound of subversion undermining the oppressor from within his own discourse.[2] According to Walker, women's humor is essentially subversive, marked by "the common theme of women's desire to claim autonomy and power" (4). Furthermore, "[W]omen's humorous expression is almost never purely comic or absurd. Even when, as is frequently the case, it points to the myriad absurdities that women have been forced to endure in this culture, it carries with it not the lighthearted feeling that is the privilege of the powerful, but instead a subtext of anguish and frustration" (xii). Explicitly, then, Walker denies to women the possibility of happiness, even in laughter, for a woman's laughter is nothing but vented hostility over imposed anguish and frustration. Implicitly in this distinction between male and female humor, Walker suggests that happiness can come only from power, and that therefore male humor might just support a kind of malevolent glee in the unjustified exercise of power.

Walker's serious analysis of comedy reads as a revolutionary manifesto celebrating resistance, but her resistance itself traps her in the terms she wants to resist. She asks her readers to reside in resistance rather than use it as a temporary tool, to deny to ourselves the possibilities of construction and rapprochement that ideally follow revolution. She asks us to entrap ourselves in the dialectical rhetoric of liberation, to compensate for this loss by attenuating our very sense of happiness to the happiness of resistance itself.

Thus does Walker follow in the footsteps of Hélène Cixous, whose "Laugh of the Medusa" seems to be the fundamental text in this regard. Cixous justifies the action of women's writing as a act of creation—"Woman must write herself"—but defines that creativity in terms of a destructive revolution. Creativity in these terms is a product of negation: "There are no grounds for establishing a discourse, but rather an arid millennial ground to break." Granted, she sees a woman's writing in "her inevitable struggle against conventional man" as a double move, one that has "two aims: to break up, to destroy; and to foresee the unforeseeable, to project." But notice that this admirable creativity is merely the second part of a binary project, a serious project that looks to the future and is defined by a serious past made up simply of the oppressive action of a masculine culture that has denied women the right to write themselves, "from which they have been driven away as violently as from their bodies" (279). The implication is that nothing in the past can contain anything but oppression, that *joi de vivre*, *Lebensfreude*, or, in the tepid English, happiness is the pleasure of action toward the millennium rather than pleasure *in* time or *of* the moment. Such a perspective reduces laughter to a simple weapon that articulates the joy of resistance, not the joy of being.

The problem may be larger than a political one; it may be part of the very language we use to register pleasure. Notice how we tend to attach to "joy" some prepositional phrase describing an activity—the joy of sex, the joy of cooking, the thrill of victory. Humor need not be confined, indeed, in its fullest, most active manifestation cannot be confined to activity. If this is true, then women's humor of any period may provide avenues to creative pleasure, and even "masculine" humor, which Walker implies will be nothing more than a manifestation of the thrill of victory, may contain a truly liberating joy, an appreciative perception of nonsense that may include, but does not require, aggressive hostility.

Aggression theories of humor are quite compelling, compelling enough to have dominated humor studies from classical antiquity to the present, with only the exception of parts of the eighteenth and nineteenth centuries giving greater credence to other theories. From Plato to Freud and to our own time, we critics have taken comedy seriously as a manifestation of power politics. Yet in doing so, we sell humor short. We miss its potentials to address and manage ambiguity, to step outside binary opposition. We miss its creative and playful as opposed to its destructive sides. From the outset, I will have a difficult time proving that comedy is often *not* a manifestation of power politics, because it is so difficult to prove a negative. Let me try by citing a few examples from the nineteenth century that may cast doubt on Walker's idea that women's humor is such a serious thing or that men's need be such wicked glorification of power. I will spend much of the remainder of the book showing that the humor of men and women often occupies a shared ground, that women and men both used humor to manage shared ambivalences about gender roles and domesticity, but first I need to clear some ground.

To begin, consider Katherine Kent Child Walker's single comic sally, a piece that proved inordinately popular. A daughter and wife of clergymen, writer of two volumes of sacred poetry and of several books for children, and an altogether respectable woman not known for joking around, Walker published in the *Atlantic Monthly* (September 1864) a parody sermon titled "The Total Depravity of Inanimate Things," which, as much as anything, was an excuse to rattle off a series of loosely connected anecdotes. The article was widely loved and often quoted by her contemporaries, male and female. By stretching the imagination, one can find in her article various forms of feminine resistance to masculine authority, but the stretch will make a rather thin argument. It is more useful to see in these anecdotes a pleasure in the disruption of idealistic visions of human behavior, usually by some physically inspired happenstance or mistake. Both wordplay and physical comedy are central to Walker's comedy—power has little room for an appearance. To take an anecdote as an example:

> A certain good bishop, on making a tour of inspection through a mission-school of his diocese, was so impressed by the aspect of all its beneficiaries that his heart overflowed with joy, and he exclaimed to a little maiden whose appearance was particularly suggestive of creature-comforts—"Why, my little girl! you have everything that heart can wish, haven't you?" Imagine the bewilderment and horror of the prelate, when the miniature Flora McFlimsey drew down the corners of her mouth lugubriously, and sought to accommodate the puffs and dimples of her fat little body to an expression of abject misery, as she replied, "No, indeed, sir! I haven't got any—skeleton!"

It is possible, indeed easy, to see the comeuppance of the clergyman as a protofeminist attack, but the reference to Flora McFlimsey, the main character of William Allen Butler's "Nothing to Wear," a mildly misogynistic attack on fancy dress, forces a conservative reading on the anecdote, *if* one takes it seriously. But if one holds seriousness in abeyance, the fun in the piece appears in the child's inappropriate seriousness and wonderfully descriptive error in calling a whalebone corset a "skeleton." In other words, comedy can skirt seriousness merely to disrupt it, opening an apparent battle to an altered and uncategorizable perception.

Perhaps a better example of humor's refusal to fit into any narrow scheme of power politics comes from Marietta Holley, whose comic Samantha Allen novels are explicitly and deliberately feminist. What is remarkable, then, in Holley's work is how often she drops her explicitly serious agenda for a little play at the expense of her feminist narrator, Samantha, often through the development of a delightful bathos, as when in *My Opinions and Betsey Bobbet's* Samantha and Betsey miss their train for home from New York City:

> After I left Horace, I hastened on, for I was afraid I was behind time. Bein' a large hefty woman, (my weight is 200 and 10 pounds by the steelyards now) I could not hasten as in former days when I weighed 100 pounds less. I was also encumbered with my umberell, my satchel bag, my cap box and "What I know about Farming." But alas! my apprehensions was too true, the cars had gone. What was to be done? Betsey sat on her portmanty at the depott, lookin' so gloomy and depressted, that I knew that I could not depend on her fur sukker, I must rely onto

myself. There are minutes that try the sole, and show what timber it is built of. Not one trace of the wild storm of emotions that was ragin' inside of me, could be traced on my firm brow, as Betsey looked up in a gloomy way and says,

"What are we going to do now?"

No, I rose nobly to meet the occasion, and said in a voice of marbel calm, "I don't know Betsey." Then I sot down, for I was beat out. Betsey looked wild, says she, "Josiah Allen's wife I am sick of earth, the cold heartless ground looks hollow to me. I feel jest reckless enough to dare the briny deep." Says she, in a bold darin' way,

"Less go home on the canal."

And they do, after debating the terrors of going by canal when sticking to land and the train would be safer. There, of course is part of the comedy in the conception: the trains were dangerous and canals ridiculously safe by comparison. But mostly, the sequence is funny because both Samantha and Betsey are inappropriately grandiose in their "grief" over a minor impediment—Samantha, as befits her size, is always heavy. If Holley is moralizing at all here, it is to moralize for the value of a lighthearted perspective. I don't doubt that it can be done, but I do not see how this sequence ought to be made to reveal "a subtext of anguish and frustration." On the contrary, it mocks anguish and frustration as inappropriate responses to life's challenges.

Two examples of nineteenth-century "male" humor, both of which build their humor on a shared understanding of gender roles, may cast some doubt on the validity, though not the beauty, of Nancy Walker's serious understanding of humor, and at the same time begin to reveal the difficulty of hunting down humor at all. Consider first the following piece by one of America's earliest humorists, George Derby, an officer in the Army Corps of Engineers who, under the penname and comic persona John Phoenix, wrote some miraculously silly tales, including:

Sewing Machine—Feline Attachment.
Circular: To the Public:
By John Phoenix.

Permit me to call your undivided attention to an invention lately made and patented by myself, which is calculated to produce the most beneficial results, and prove of inestimable value to mankind. It is well known that the sewing-machines now so generally in use, are the most important invention and greatest blessing of the age. Every lady considers this instrument indispensable to her happiness; it has completely usurped the place of the piano-forte and harp in all well-regulated families; and she who once purchased materials for clothing by the yard, now procures them by the piece or bolt, to enjoy the rational pleasure of easily making them into garments.

In the humble cabin of the laborer, and in the halls of the high and great, now resounds from morning until night, the whir of the sewing-machine. The result of this universal grinding, although eminently gratifying to the sellers of dry goods, and the philanthropic fathers and husbands who discharge their bills, has not been of a favorable nature to our ladies in a physical point of view. It is found that the constant use of the crank has brought on rheumatic and neuralgic affections in the shoulder, and a similar application of the treadle has a tendency to produce hip diseases and white swelling of the knee-joint, accompanied by nervous complaints of a painful character. The undersigned is acquainted with a most estimable single lady of middle age, who, having procured one of the fast-running machines, was so enchanted with it, that she persisted in its use for thirty-six hours without cessation, and found, on endeavoring to leave off, that her right leg had acquired the motion of the treadle in such a painful manner, that it was impossible to keep it still, and her locomotion therefore assumed a species of polka step exceedingly ludicrous to witness, and particularly mortifying to herself. I regret to add that she was compelled, by a vote of the society, to withdraw from the Methodist Church, on a charge of dancing down the broad aisle on a Communion Sunday. A more melancholy instance was the case of Mrs. Thompson, of Seekonk, a most amiable lady, beloved and respected by all around her, but who, by constant use of the crank, lost all control of the flexors and extensors of her right arm, and inadvertently punched her husband in the eye, which, he being a man of suspicious and unforgiving disposition, led to great unhappiness in the family, and finally resulted in the melancholy case of Thompson vs. Thompson, so familiar to most of the civilized world. A turn for mechanism, and an intense desire to contribute to the happiness of the female sex, have ever been distinguished traits in my character. On learning these facts, therefore, I devoted myself to a thorough investigation of the subject, and after a month of close application, have at last made an invention which will at once do away with everything objectionable in the use of the sewing machine.

This beautiful discovery is now named

"Phoenix's Feline Attachment."

Like most great inventions, the Attachment is of great simplicity. An upright shaft is connected with the machine by a cog-wheel and pinion, and supported below by a suitable frame-work. Two projecting arms are attached to the shaft, to one of which a large cat is connected by a light harness, and from the other, a living mouse is suspended by the tail, within a few inches of the nose of the motor. As the cat springs toward the mouse, the latter is removed, and keeping constantly at the original distance, the machine revolves with great rapidity. The prodigious velocity produced by the rapacity of the cat in its futile endeavors to overtake the mouse, can only be imagined by one who has seen the Attachment in full operation.

It is thus that man shows his supremacy over the brute creation, by making even their rapacious instincts subservient to his use.

Should it be required to arrest the motion of the machine, a handkerchief is thrown over the mouse, and the cat at once pauses, disgusted.

Remove the handkerchief, and again she springs forward with renewed ardor. The writer has seen one cat (a tortoise-shell) of so ardent and unwearying disposition, that she made eighteen pairs of men's pantaloons, two dozen shirts, and seven stitched shirts, before she lay down exhausted. It is to be hoped that the ladies throughout the land will avail themselves of this beautiful discovery, which will entirely supersede the use of the needle, and make the manufacture of clothing and household materials a matter of pleasure to themselves, and exciting and healthy exercise to their domestic animals. I present [see Figure 1.1] an elevation of the "feline Attachment" in operation, that all may understand its powers, and none fail to procure one, through ignorance of its merits. The Attachment will be furnished, to families having sewing machines, on the most reasonable terms and at the shortest notice. Young and docile cats supplied with the Attachment, by application at 348 Broadway, New York—office of the patent Back-Action Hen Persuader.

Is this comedy hostile? Yes, in the sadism of torturing cat and mouse, in the image of the battle between man and wife, and in the humiliation of the former Methodist. Indeed, it shows aggression even in the Luddite satire of technology, which, coming from an engineer, suggests the author's hostility toward his own calling. But the attack on Enlightenment progressivism is a relatively minor part of the fun of this piece. In fact, I would say that the real fun comes from the commingled impracticality and absurdity of the invention on the one hand and the exhilarating imaginative genius of it on the other. In simply imagining such a machine, Phoenix makes it seem to be realizable, and yet no sooner does one get caught up in the possibility by imagining it for him or herself than the absurdity comes home with a laugh. The narrator's bland seriousness is wonderfully convincing, adding increased spice to the contrast between the "maybe" and the "no way" that flit past one another in the reader's mind in quick, delightful alternation.

Thus, this parody is a grand gesture of both/and, of both realistic mockery and the pure play of the imagination in defiance of all possible bounds. Phoenix's mock advertisement has the liberating power of a truly imaginative animated film. As such it is emblematic of humor in its largest sense: given free reign, comedy is an opening into possibilities. If so, then the tangle of humor is impervious to Occam's razor, to the search for elegantly simple explanations of complex phenomena. If humor works by contradictions and confusion, by multiplication of possibilities in simultaneous acceptance and defiance of reality, then it may be impossible to abstract the "essence" of humor except to see the essence as monumental yet ephemeral complexity.

Fortunately for the analyst of humor, comedy is rarely given completely free rein. Indeed, there is no doubt that those who make comedy often constrain its imaginative possibilities, using the liberating element of comedy for little more than the venting of frustrations, turning a potentially creative force into a merely aggressive one. But even in cases where an analysis of power is obviously appropriate, it is important not to generalize that analysis into clear-cut binary oppositions: comedy rarely allows itself to be constrained that narrowly, even when its use of stereotypes suggests that its creators are at least attempting to utilize such binary oppositions. Often the apparent target of hostile comedy is merely a deferral from the real target, and often aggressive humor masks deep ambivalence.

Consider the second of my examples of "male" humor, Robert J. Burdette's "She Had to Take Her Things Along"—a comic piece that appears at first glance to be promoting the stereotype that young women are obsessed with clothes, jewelry, and so on, and that they don't know how to "travel light." I

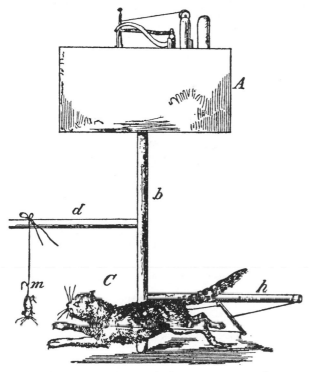

ELEVATION OF 'PHŒNIX'S FELINE ATTACHMENT.'          FIGURE I.I

know my students usually read the piece this way, and there is much in the piece that plays on the stereotype. But the attack on women is mainly a red herring; the author has hidden behind the usual misogynistic stereotype the conflict that drives the humor, namely, the competition between men for women, wealth, and power.

Erasmus T. Ruggleson, a young man of Saxon lineage, worked on a farm out here in Yellow Spring township. He was not rich, but he was industrious, and just too pretty for anything. So was the daughter of the farmer for whom he worked. She was wealthier than Erasmus, but she was not proud. When the chores were done in the winter evenings, she went with him to the singing school, and she walked by his side to church. She loved him; she had rather sit at her casement in the gloaming and hear him holler "poo-oo-sy!" in long-drawn, mellow cadences, at the hour of the feeding of the swine, than hear Campanini sing "Macaroni del Vermicelli" from "Handorgzanhandi in Venezuela." And he—he was clean gone on her. Mashed past all surgery. When they foolishly let the old man into their plans for each other's happiness and half the farm, the wrathful agriculturist said if he heard one more word of such nonsense, just another word, he would lay that farm waste with physical havoc, and blight its winter wheat with the salt tears of his only child, and that was the kind of father-in-law he was inclined to be.

Naturally, the young people determined to fly. Their plans were laid; the night was set. So was the ladder. At its foot waited the ardent Erasmus Ruggleson, gazing at the window for the appearance of his love. Presently the window opened softly, and a face he loved appeared.

"Rasmus!"

"Florence!"

"Yes, dearest. Shall I drop my things right down?"

"Yes, love; I will catch them. Let the bundles fall."

The glittering starlight of the clear March night fell on Erasmus's glad and upturned face. So did a trunk, four feet high, four feet wide, and about eight feet long. It weighed about 2,700 pounds. It contained a few "things" that no woman could be expected to travel without, and Florence had spent three weeks packing that trunk for her elopement.

Erasmus Ruggleson did not scream. He did not moan. He couldn't. He had no show. Florence came down the ladder, having first, with a maidenly sense of propriety, requested her lover to turn his back and look at the barn. He was busily engaged in looking at the bottom of that trunk, and thinking how like all creation he would yell if he ever got his mouth outdoors again.

Florence reached the foot of the ladder. "Did you get my trunk, Erasmus?" she said, looking around for him.

"Oh yes!" said a hoarse mocking voice at her elbow. "Oh, yes, he got it! Got it bad, too!"

She turned, knew her papa, shrieked once, twice, again, and once more for the boys, and fainted away.

"I never worried about it a minute," the heartless old man told his neighbors the next day, "though I knowed well enough what was goin' on all the time. I've been married twice, an' I've married off four daughters and two sons, an' if I don't know what baggage a woman carries when she travels, by this time, I'm too old to learn."

And Erasmus Ruggleson! The jury brought in a verdict that he came to his death by habitual drunkenness, and the temperance papers didn't talk about anything else for the next six weeks.

The tone of the tale suggests contempt for every character. The young man is a fool, the old is cruel, and even the jury and the temperance society seem perverse. Within the story, too, we see characters who seem to hold one another in contempt—particularly the father, who scoffs at the boy who "got it bad," and seems to think little of his own daughter. Yet he does want to hang on to her, and he takes the young man seriously enough to laugh over his death. The ridicule within the story stems from triumph indeed, from a vindication of superiority, from a successful effort to hang onto his most important possessions, his farm and his daughter. Notice he calls her his only child, even though he later says he has married off four daughters and two sons. Clearly, he sees his children as possessions that, once married, he no longer owns, so his remaining daughter is his only daughter.

The reason for his possessiveness shows in the contrast between the rustic setting and language and the daughter's pretensions toward gentility. The fact that the piece is set on a farm suggests an older economic order at work, yet her "things" suggest that she has been gentrified, that while her father may have worn out two wives with farm work, he is now rich enough that his youngest and only remaining daughter needn't work at all—she has become the symbol of his economic power. He is not going to part with her if he can help it, and certainly not for a field hand. She, on the other hand, is fully "modern," fully democratic, preferring personal charms to wealth, though not scrupling to ask her father to continue to support her in her acquisition of this most desirable of jewels. The father sees it differently, as the usurpation of his position, of the surrender of his goods to a poor man who has superior looks and youth on his side. It becomes, for him, an economic and generational battle, a displacement into the realm of his economic power of the old man's attraction to his daughter.

The young man does seem to be a poor match in two ways. For one, he is literally poor, but equally importantly, he fights the battle on weak ground: a romantic fool, he allows his sexual drives to get in the way of economic realities. Notice that he is "mashed" before he gets smashed. The temperance societies lecture on his demise, because they misinterpret the word "mashed," but perhaps their complaint is nonetheless true. Like alcohol, love is an intoxicant that deprives men of the ability to think straight enough to secure the economic security of themselves and their families. Still, in showing his love regardless of worldly concerns, the young man demonstrates his modernity; he strives to build a family on affectional rather than economic ties. But the story suggests that this modernity is a deception because love is, literally, unable to support a family, or rather, the moment the lover has to support his bride, the moment she is to become his wife, he is crushed by the burden. Love may be stronger than death, but not than "things." The fact that the girl has so many things attests to the economic power of her father. His victory is that *he* has weighted his daughter down with so much baggage that she cannot leave the family without her father's consent, without him choosing an appropriate replacement for his authority and economic power.

This sketch suggests that the economic realities of raising a family according to the ideology of domesticity provoked extreme anxiety in young men of the nineteenth century. They were supposed to be romantic suitors, each able to support his romantic fair in a position of idleness and opulence without her having to do any productive economic labor. Her organization of the household was to require no more than the "respectable" labor of supervising servants. The phony gentility that borrowed liberally from medieval romance and suggested that men were to be merely women's servants while women etherialized the household, added to the tension. Told constantly that their business pursuits were corrupting, that they were to labor for their women, that their women were to control through gentle influences of love the corrupt passions of male ardor, all of this easily promotes a psychic reaction that vents itself in attacks on women. And Burdette's piece does exactly this.

More to the point, it turns the real villain of the piece into the older generation itself. Represented by the crafty, greedy, controlling, and victorious old man, age is able to prey upon youthful ardor, able to thwart the possibilities of love through economic power. But humor rarely lets us have simple feelings of virtuous resistance to authority or of triumph. This piece works the other way, too, in expressing admiration for that power, in longing for it. To be the victorious observer of a victorious battle that was fought through the proxy of material possessions—to beat an enemy who had a facile sense of his own youthful power, to crush him without touching him, to have done so through prudent foresight without any need to rise to the particular occasion, in short to beat another man more easily than flicking away a pesky fly: what a fantasy of strength! The laughter, then, comes from anxiety about weakness and a release of anxiety in a fantasy of power. All of this is possible only because humor enables simultaneous viewing of the same circumstance from multiple points of view.

If this analysis accurately describes the primary conflict as between old and young men, then perhaps a simple rhetoric of power is still appropriate for analyzing humor; it merely needs to be deployed with a deft sense of when stereotypes hold the key to aggression and when they merely deflect aggression onto a "safe" object. But if this analysis is also right in suggesting that a nineteenth-century male reader of this piece would identify simultaneously with the old man and the young, then a clear binary opposition fails and a rhetoric of power needs to be supplemented by other analytical tools. Indeed, some of those tools are now being developed in the biological sciences in which the physiology of laughter and the feeling of pleasure that we call humor is being revealed to be much more than the simple displacement of aggression. Physiologically, it may be that the biological purposes of laughter are diametrically opposed to aggression. I'll have much more to say about that in the final chapter after I've adduced enough evidence to make some theoretical claims. For now, this example suggests some of the fundamental issues for the ensuing study, issues both about comedy and about domesticity.

For one, this example suggests that comedy works in ways much more complicated than by a simple binary opposition between desire and repression, or between oppressed and oppressor. Those who laugh may often have divided sympathies, and laughter itself may be a way of managing the tension created by such internal divisions. It is important to recognize that these divided sympathies are common to female humorists as well as to male humorists, as the subsequent discussion will show. Secondly, this example suggests that the ideology of domesticity is the source of many of those divided sympathies as it calls out different kinds of emotional responses depending on the roles it demands of each member of a family, as in this intance, the tensions between gender identification, generational identification, and romantic attachment. In order to chart these tensions and how comedy responds to them, it is necessary first to trace the broad outlines of domestic ideology as it was articulated in the nineteenth century.

## II.  "Haven in a Heartless World"

Literary comedies about home life and love are, not surprisingly, as old as literature. Family life is psychically stressful—using "stress" as a neutral term to describe heightened awareness stemming from pleasure, fear, curiosity, or other intense emotion—and any stress will provoke comic, as well as other, responses. But the particular kinds of domestic comedy with which we are now familiar were born in the eighteenth century and blossomed in the nineteenth in America with the demise of a strictly patriarchal ideology and the rise of the ideology of the sexual spheres. Much work has been done on this ideology, so I will only briefly recapitulate what so many books and articles have explained in depth.

Briefly put, beginning in the late eighteenth century in America and developing through the nineteenth, a new ideology of how family life should be constructed came to dominate American culture. Predicated primarily on sentimental liberalism, it was a direct challenge to Calvinist patriarchy and the belief that God had established a rigid social hierarchy in which each individual had to obey his or her superiors and be responsible for his or her inferiors. According to sentimental ideology, each individual was a free agent because morally equal to all others. Therefore, the only appropriate social controls were those based on affectional bonds. Families were to be built on the love between man and woman, and child rearing was to be an exercise in writing wholesome lessons on the blank slate of a child's character.

This middle-class ideology was both a response to and a stimulus to modern modes of commercial organization. Justifying the free movement of labor and the ability of individuals to contract their work for short periods, it encouraged modern industrial production and went along with the gradual shift of economic power and population to cities. By stressing that the affectional bonds of social organization were strongest at closest range, it exalted the nuclear family as the primary social unit on which republicanism would rely for the development of an educated and morally trustworthy populace. Furthermore, as labor shifted gradually from domestic production to factory production, domestic ideology was able to articulate a legitimate noneconomic use for domestic space and time by postulating it as a haven from commercial competition, as the counter to the psychic damage that individualism in a capitalistic society could inflict on the men who worked, as they called it, "in the world." As women's work decreased in apparent economic (i.e., cash) value, domestic ideology redefined woman's role from inferior but economically productive laborer, to that of equal partner in marriage, but occupying a separate "sphere." This sphere was defined as one of influence rather than power, of kindness and love rather than work, of educating children, of developing spiritual values in the face of the declining power and importance of church, of maintaining cultural continuity in the home in the face of change in the market—in general, of providing "a haven in a heartless world."[3]

In spite of a widespread consensus on when domestic ideology arose—in concert with the rise of industrial capitalism—and what it entailed, spirited debates flourish about what the sexual spheres meant, especially to women. Was the ideology merely a prison, a deflection of demands for equality into a false belief in influence? Or was the women's sphere an ideological critique of capitalism, a last gasp against the alienation of modernity, an emotional and experiential subversion of masculinist politics?[4]

To say both might seem facile, but it is a quick way of saying that the social ideology of the sexual spheres was contested ground from the beginning. First systematically postulated by the eighteenth-century British philosopher Francis Hutcheson in his *A System of Moral Philosophy*, the sexual spheres were designed to ameliorate the abusive power of patriarchal control in order to maximize individual freedom. While Hutcheson's target in part was the control fathers had over their sons through powers of contracting their labor, of choosing their mates, of determining their legacies, and so forth, he also was quite concerned about the tyrannies imposed on women both as daughters and, especially, as wives. In order to maximize freedom, he asserted a fundamental human equality and thus limited individual freedom by articulating the social limits necessary to maximize it equally for all. To Hutcheson, the primary natural limitations on individual freedom were those of procreation, and the social bonds necessary to raise and provide successfully for children became the primary realm for individuals to limit contractually their natural rights through marriage. Because he so stressed individual freedoms as the moral ground on which such important contracts can be made, he limited the realm in which children were to be raised to the nuclear family. Indeed, he may be the first thinker to flesh out the implications of Locke's philosophy for family structures, both legal and conventional, and his book marks the beginnings of radical changes in the way families were constituted in the English-speaking world.

His ideas about marriage are worth quoting at length here, not only because they are so influential, but because they lay out the ground of freedom and equality in the family that would be contested so vigorously in both England and America right up to today. This ground became contested not only because Hutcheson postulated a liberalization of family structure against which conservatives could and still do react, but also because the liberal family as Hutcheson envisioned it contains so many paradoxes. Such paradoxes are not immediately apparent in the strong statement of equality with which Hutcheson's description of his ideal of marriage begins: "The tender sentiments and affections which engage the parties into this relation of marriage, plainly declare it to be a state of equal partnership or friendship, and not such a one wherein the one party stipulates to himself a right of governing in all domestick affairs, and the other promises subjection" (163; bk.3, ch.1, sec.7). Here he is absolute in his conviction of an equality of rights in which free consent makes partnership morally and economically viable.

In the very next line, however, Hutcheson shows the extreme difficulty he had in following his conception of equality to its logical end. He believed in natural rights constituted by the equivalent powers of *moral* perception in men and women, but in practical affairs, he believed in general differences between the sexes, granting to each their separate kinds of superiorities as well as particular exceptions to general rules:

> Grant that there were generally superior strength both of body and mind in the
> males, this does not give any perfect right of government in any society. It could

at best only oblige the other party to pay a greater respect or honour to the superior abilities. And this superiority of the males in the endowments of mind does
not at all hold universally. If the males more generally excel in fortitude, or
strength of genius; there are other as amiable dispositions in which they are as
generally surpassed by the females. (163)

Here he shows his tendency to describe "dispositions" as natural traits divided
unequally between the sexes.

Arguing from nature, then, Hutcheson sets up a contrast between just laws
by which a state can legitimately govern marriage as a contract, and reasonable
behavior by which men and women partition labor into a harmonious partnership:

> The truth is, nature shews no foundation for any proper jurisdiction or right of
> commanding in this relation; and, previous to some positive laws and customs,
> there is no presumption that the parties would stipulate about any. Where posi-
> tive laws and customs have long obtained, and settled forms of contracting are re-
> ceived, no doubt there is an external right of superiority constituted to the hus-
> bands. But this shadow of right is no better than those which any insolent
> conqueror may extort from the vanquished; or any unjust sharper may obtain by
> some imperfection or iniquity of civil laws; or by the weakness, or ignorance, or
> inadvertence of one he is contracting with. To take advantage of such laws or
> forms, without regard to equity and humanity, must be entirely inconsistent with
> an honest character. . . . Domestic matters indeed seem to be divided into two
> provinces, one fitted for the management of each sex, in which the other should
> seldom interfere, except by advising. (163–65)

Hutcheson sees a putatively natural balance between marriage as "friendship"
based on "tender sentiments and affections" and marriage as a contractual economic partnership. He also, as his legalistic treatment hints here and the structure of the third book of his moral philosophy makes clear, sees marriage as a
fundamental political unit, the basis of just and wise civil government. As
such, questions of "propriety" in marriage take on both meanings of the term,
namely that of socially proper action and of ownership. The ownership interest
each partner has in the marriage, coupled with inevitable tensions in how to
direct that interest, lead to fundamental tensions and disagreements.

Hutcheson tries to reconcile potential disagreements in two ways. For one,
he divides the empire of responsibility and of labor between male and female,
postulating natural superiorities that make such a division practical both to secure harmonious governance and to secure economic success. Not denying
that such tensions might break out of the neat bounds of "provinces" of "management," Hutcheson argues further that "affairs of importance should rather
be committed to both jointly" (165) because "[c]ommitting to the husband the
whole power over the whole stock of the family, including the wife's portion, is
unjust and imprudent, as well as contrary to nature" (165). While he saw himself arguing for practical balance between economic interests, what he did instead was to point out with clarity what grounds would be contested—namely,
"[a]ffairs of importance" relating primarily to the economic health of each

family—and how they would be contested—that is, in a struggle between the terms of "nature," which he sees in part as the differential attributes of men and women, and of "justice," which he sees in part as fundamental equality.

He also points out that his understanding of "nature" and "nature's law" is at odds with what he calls "monstrous" (165) customs and "positive laws." He thus argues for substantial change, but the change for which he argues resides primarily in the realm of the "affections" and of personal character. An "honest character" will use no such accidental benefits to secure unjust power, but he does nothing to challenge the fundamental contractual basis of marriage. Hutcheson does clearly call for gradual changes in law, but he stakes his primary hope for changes in manly "honesty," for "[t]o exercise any such power, or even that of any corporal punishment, must be tyrannical and unmanly" (165). Thus, the just exercise of power must finally reside in character, not in law; the basis of prosperity and happiness, not only for wives and children, but finally for governments themselves, then, resides in the development of the "proper" character of men. As the proprietors of the sphere of child care, women were to influence power by developing the character of children.

Significantly, in spite of his assertion that intellectual powers were not universally and necessarily apportioned by sex, Hutcheson still acceded to the realities that as long as he was supporting the nuclear over the extended family in order to strengthen his case for individual freedom, he had no choice but to relegate to mothers the home sphere and the charge of nursing and teaching children. The smaller the social unit, the greater the freedom for individuals to contract their responsibilities, but, paradoxically, the greater the constraints within that very closed small family unit once under the contract of marriage. Responsibilities become fixed narrowly in the spheres of free *individuals*.[5]

Hutcheson found such an arrangement intellectually and morally beautiful, for it prescribed order even as it valued freedom. But the strains between social responsibility and individual "rights" that he helped foster were not to be settled by such a simple formula. Once set in motion, individualism was not to be checked so easily by any social group, no matter how small. Paradoxically, then, the very rhetoric that extolled the family as the preserve in which individual freedom could be responsibly nurtured carried with it the idea that the family is the essential organ of social control that the individual must resist.[6] So, too, each individual in the nuclear family group, ostensibly tied by the bonds of affection, is, in seeking autonomy, going to personalize resistance to authority by ascribing the authority of the family unit to particular individuals, described by role, within the family. The family, which should ideologically be the haven of love in a competitive world, merely focuses that competition between spouses, between parents and children, between siblings.

So in the very origins of domestic ideology lie some of the reasons for our continuing difficulties in evaluating it. It was an ideology both of liberation in comparison to those that went before and, by its own standards of equality, of oppression. Further, insofar as it ascribed to nature fundamental differences between men and women that are often merely cultural accidents, it provided its friends and enemies alike with innumerable anomalies to explain away or to attack. But still, I find myself unable to step out of the language of oppositions to suggest that these tensions are the very essence of domestic ideology—indeed of the continuing debate over how to secure both individual liberty and social responsibility in both public policy and private lives. These issues are resolvable not by ideology itself but by the complex collision between individual psychic needs, the ideas by which such needs are channelled, and the realities of life in a world that never is fully describable by intellectual constructs. One typical reaction to confusion is rage—another is laughter, and the latter, while it may merely mask rage, may also be a way to explore and acknowledge the absurd conflicts between ideology and more complicated realities.

Consider, for instance, the development of Caroline Kirkland's *A New Home—Who'll Follow?* up through chapter 18. Laughing a little in virtually every chapter, Kirkland's narrator slowly reconciles herself to the crudities of life on the frontier until, by chapter 17, she is lecturing a new and genteel neighbor on how not to appear stuck-up. She concludes the chapter by calling her genteel friend narrow-minded, only to realize that in so doing she is surrendering her hard-earned gentility to the leveling impulses of the frontier. A quick turn in chapter 18, then, recovers Kirkland's sense of disgust at the frontier's lack of respect for individuality, with the narrator mocking communal ideas of property:

> "Mother wants your sifter, and she says she guesses you can let her have some sugar and tea, 'cause you got plenty."
> This excellent reason, "cause you've got plenty," is conclusive as to sharing with your neighbors. Whoever comes into Michigan with nothing, will be sure to better his condition; but wo to him that brings with him any thing like an appearance of abundance, whether of money or mere household convenience. To have them, and not be willing to share them in some sort with the whole community, is an unpardonable crime. . . . [W]ithin doors, an inventory of your plenish of all sorts, would scarcely more than include the article which you are solicited to lend. Not only are all kitchen utensils as much your neighbor's as your own, but bedsteads, beds, blankets, sheets, travel from house to house, a pleasant and effectual mode of securing the perpetuity of certain efflorescent peculiarities of the skin. . . . For my own part I have lent my broom, my thread, my spoons, my cat, my thimble, my scissors, my shawl, my shoes; and have been asked for my combs and brushes: and for my husband, for his shaving apparatus and his pantaloons. (67–68)

Usually considered an attack on the barbarism of the frontier and the difficulty of a woman's role in a male-dominated setting, this piece is perhaps best looked at from the point of view of individuality as defined by property. The narrator here is appalled by the virtual communism of the frontier. Notice that she describes her family as the individual unit of ownership through the pronoun "my." Clearly, the property stands not for economic power alone, but for the borders one puts up between self and other, for the concept of individual dignity. Part of the comedy comes from a sense that property stands between one person's body and another's, as having one's own blankets, sheets, and beds keeps one from getting vermin. Further, the possibility of sexual sharing is raised when the list runs from "my" things to "my husband," implying, for a moment, that it is the husband himself who has been borrowed, reinforced by the synecdoche of her husband's pantaloons for what is in them.

The chapter continues by describing the domestication through pregnancy of one of the narrator's neighbors, "termagant" Mrs. Doubleday. Doubleday becomes softened and more reasonable in her efforts to keep house, and becomes gentle and feminine in "owning" a child. The relevance of this domestic image to the preamble about borrowing becomes clear when a neighbor urchin comes on the scene to say that "her mother 'wanted Miss Doubleday to let her have her baby for a little while, 'cause Benny's mouth's so sore that'—but she had no time to finish the sentence. 'Lend my baaby!!!'—and her utterance failed. The new mother's feelings were fortunately too big for speech, and Ianthe wisely disappeared before Mrs. Doubleday found her tongue" (71–72). What Kirkland does here is to promote the idea of privacy within the family, that individual happiness is possible only when one can make clear distinctions of individuality, and such distinctions are possible only within a small enough social unit that ownership is a meaningful marker of self and of affection for others. Indeed, the operative word for happiness is "my," whether it applies to a sifter or a husband or a baby. In supporting domesticity, Kirkland is arguing for the bourgeois individualism of the nuclear family at the expense of the cooperation necessary on the frontier. Nonetheless, this chapter, in contrast to the one immediately preceding it, stands as a comic gesture against her own growing comic wisdom that the realities of her circumstances dictate ideas far different from those she cherishes as a literate, genteel, bourgeois woman.

Unlike Kirkland, many other comedians, looking at the tensions between social demands and individual freedoms, comically reject marriage and domesticity altogether. Consider, for instance, one of the early tales that defined a minor genre of antidomestic satires for the rest of the century, Joseph C. Neal's "'Tis Only My Husband." Drawing on the ideas of hierarchy that sentimental individualism supposedly rejects, Neal says:

> If some are born to command, others must certainly have a genius for submission—we term it a genius, submission being in many cases rather a difficult thing. That this division of qualities is full of wisdom, none can deny. It requires both flint and steel to produce a spark; both powder and ball to do execution: and, though the Chinese contrive to gobble an infinity of rice with chopsticks, yet the twofold operation of knife and fork conduces much more to the comfort of a dinner. Authority and obedience are the knife and fork of this extensive banquet, the world; they are the true *divide et impera*; that which is sliced off by the one is harpooned by the other. (18)

These metaphors are retailed with an ironic tone that makes it clear that he doesn't really like this state of affairs. Since marriage, in these terms, requires the dominance of one partner or the other, and since men in Neal's story are outgunned in power by the influential tears and tantrums of womankind, bachelor independence is, suggests Neal, preferable to the dangerous inter-connection of marriage. How different really, then, is Kirkland's plea for do-mesticity from Neal's attack on it? Both insist on the importance of indi-vidual freedom against social constraint even though they reach radically different conclusions about the desirability of married life.

Echoing Neal, Fanny Fern often drew the same antimatrimonial point in many of her satires, such as "Aunt Hetty on Matrimony." Attacking the senti-mental idea of affection, Fern tells her feminine readers that sentiment is only for courtship:

> "Now girls" said Aunt Hetty, "put down your embroidery and worsted work; do something sensible, and stop building air-castles, and talking of lovers and honey-moons. It makes me sick; it is perfectly antimonial. Love is a farce; matri-mony is a humbug; husbands are domestic Napoleons, Neroes, Alexanders,—sighing for other hearts to conquer, after they are sure of yours. The honey-moon is as short-lived as a lucifer-match. (*Ruth* 220)

Neither Fern's attack nor Neal's similar attack needs much commentary, since versions of such comedy, if it deserves the name, are all too common still.

What does need commentary is not the way men and women often hold one another responsible for the failures of ideal visions of love, but the way in which male and female humorists share the same point of view. Comedians at-tack marriage precisely because they see spouses as a fundamental limitation of individuality. As much as women's humor attacks husbands as sources of power (as indeed they were politically), so men's humor attacks wives as the authori-tative centers of families (as indeed ideologically they were). Law versus cus-tom, individuals versus groups, men versus women, children versus parents—competition runs wild in the haven from competition.

The tension between individualism and communitarianism as expressed in the structure of the sentimental family was far from the only significant tension the ideology of the sexual spheres developed. Insofar as the ideology described woman as moral paragon and man as morally tainted by the commercial world, it pushed men toward the role of breadwinner and women toward the role of caretaker. But, as Thorstein Veblen compellingly argued nearly a century ago, "caretaker" is easily synonymous with "spender," especially as the role of the servant-wife in the capitalistic household is to display the economic power of the working man, and in so doing, to imitate the economic power of the leisure classes. The tension between Christian and republican virtues of simplicity and the aristocratic ideology of conspicuous consumption, both of which were necessary to the development of industrial capitalism, is formidable and be-came another shared focal point for comedy.

Consider, for instance, "Our New Livery," from George William Curtis's satiric *Potiphar Papers*. Written from the point of view of the ignorant but pre-tentious Mrs. Potiphar, the piece ostensibly attacks a woman's obsession with conspicuous consumption from the point of view of republican simplicity, as when Mr. Potiphar tells his wife that a livery is inappropriate for anyone in a republic, but Mrs. Potiphar, under the influence of the Rev. Cream Cheese, a High Church Anglican, wishes to be "so elegant and aristocratic" (62). Nonetheless, the dialogue between spouses after they have thrown a ball in their house suggests a more complicated masculine reaction to conspicuous consumption. In explaining why he refuses to have any more balls at his house, he says:

> "I tell you, Mrs. Potiphar, I am not going to open my house for a crowd of people who don't go away till daylight; who spoil my books and furniture; who involve me in a foolish expense; for a gang of rowdy boys, who drink my Margaux, and Lafitte, and Marcobrunner, (what kind of drinks are those, dear Caroline?) and who don't know Chambertin from liquorice-water—for a swarm of persons, few of whom know me, fewer still care for me, and to whom I am only 'Old Potiphar,' the husband of you, a fashionable woman. I am simply resolved to have no more such tomfoolery in my house." (58)

As much as anything, Potiphar expresses not that he is against consumption of "fine" things but rather that he is jealous that he cannot enjoy the fruits of his own labor, or at best, that he must share them with those who understand quantity and price alone and who therefore judge him by his net worth rather than by his taste. He laments that his truly aristocratic cultivation is lost in a world of economic competition.

His wife makes clear the real reason and ultimate necessity for such competition:

> "Dear Mr. P.," said I, "you'll feel much better when you have slept. Besides, why do you say such things? Mustn't we see our friends, I should like to know: and, if we do, are you going to let your wife receive them in a manner inferior to old Mrs. Podge or Mrs. Croesus? People will accuse you of meanness, and of treating me ill; and if some persons hear that you have reduced your style of living they will begin to suspect the state of your affairs. Don't make any rash vows, Mr. P.," said I, "but go to sleep." (Do you know that speech was just what Mrs. Croesus told me she had said to her husband under similar circumstances?)
>     Mr. P. fairly groaned. (58–59)

Here Curtis reveals the belief that keeping up with the Joneses is an economic necessity in order to support business. A business that is not growing is, according to the absurd vision of economic competitors, dying. As his household is the extension of his apparent success, Potiphar feels he has no choice but to persist in allowing his wife to spend what she will. But Curtis sarcastically suggests that such consumption is not really a part of business, but is merely a part of domesticity. He suggests that women, selfish and ignorant, conspire to use images of affection in order to force men to work beyond their powers and to sacrifice their own happiness to the accumulation of material goods. The wellspring of this comedy is double. One, relying on republican ideas of virtue, it attacks consumerism as morally debilitating. But two, from the angle of domesticity itself, the male voice is one of anger at being left out, of feeling abused by the ideology of domestic comfort and love.

Such a critique from a Christian, as opposed to a republican, perspective is readily found in the works of many female humorists of the period. Frances Miriam Whitcher, for instance, satirizes through the man-chasing, money-chasing, status-chasing Widow Bedott the power of social competition to overshadow the affectional foundation of family life. While Whitcher seems to locate the source of the problem in the un-Christian character of social climbers themselves, the woman who most effectively built on Whitcher's work, Marietta Holley, would shift the blame to an economic system that allowed women no alternative but dependence on men to provide for themselves. Still arguing from Christian principles, Holley's attack on domesticity strikes at the disparity at the heart of the domestic division of labor. As I will show in subsequent chapters, while less inclined to blame women, Holley, Stowe, and Freeman often shared with male writers like Curtis—or for that matter, Irving and Melville—feelings of disappointment that money so often governs the emotional center of the nuclear family. That is, they attack the manifestations of domesticity in the capitalist world from the point of view of the ideal of domesticity itself.

As the importance of getting money was vexed by the internal strains in domestic ideology, so was the importance of begetting children, in part because the model of sentimental domesticity as it developed in the nineteenth century was contingent on an argument from nature, that sexual dimorphism, more extensive than was superficially obvious, extended into a sexual dimoralism. Men supposedly had not only different strengths, but also different appetites, both physical and moral. Not to put too fine a point on it, men were supposed to be lusty because earthly; women were emotional but passionless because more nearly inclined to the divine.[7] Given the massive sexual repression such an ideology entailed, and given that sentimental ideology was displacing Calvinism, and that other, competing ideologies simultaneously tried to displace Calvinism—including various utopian socialist movements ranging from the materialistic to the religious—the "natural" validity of sentimental family organization was easily challenged by alternatives. Most of these postulated different organizations of labor, child rearing, and sexuality than the sentimentalists prescribed. And, of course, the rise of an active feminist movement in the first half of the nineteenth century further challenged the "naturalness" of the sentimental home. Not surprisingly, then, the collision of such alternative ideologies inspired much comedy.

Consider, for instance, the case of the Mormons, a group that comes under the frequent scrutiny of American comedians precisely because the presence of Mormons challenged not only the tenets of Christianity by extending them in what could be considered a parody of Christian revelation, but also the tenets of domesticity by extending, through polygamy, the argument that marriage is salvific. Given the crucial nexus in domestic ideology between salvation, political stability, economic power, and the nuclear family, any challenge to the central component—the nuclear family—calls into doubt the entire vision. Of course, Mormonism could also have been attacked for its apparently conservative patriarchalism, and indeed, Twain's well-known treatment of Mormons in

*Roughing It* does suggest that the antidemocratic nature of the religion does detract from individualism. Mainly, though, comedians, like so many other social commentators on Mormonism, talked mainly of polygamy and the violence of the Mormon avenging angels. The subtext of all of these treatments is that polygamy lets sexual passion loose, and once loose, it turns individuals into animals, freedom into anarchic license. The frantic corollary is that murder and free love are effect and cause respectively.

One would expect such hysteria from the conservative Artemus Ward (Charles Farrar Browne), especially as he was seeking common enemies to weld the feuding North and South together immediately prior to the outbreak of the Civil War. Browne's *Artemus Ward: His Book,* for instance, includes chapters that paint Mormon men and feminist women as "unnatural," both trying to have too much male privilege in a world that needs a delicate balance between masculine and feminine spheres to hold it together. It is less clear why Marietta Holley, whose works are explicitly feminist, would use arguments much like Browne's. She equated Mormons with those feminists who argued that divorce laws should be liberalized and that love should be sanctification enough for marriage without the intrusion of church or state. In her fictionalized encounter between her narrator, Samantha Allen, and Victoria Woodhull in *My Opinions and Betsey Bobbet's,* Woodhull advocates "free divorce, free love, freedom in everything." Samantha replies vehemently, "'That is what burglers and incendiarys say,' says I, 'That is the word murderers and Mormons utter,' says I 'that is the language of pirates, Victory Woodhull'" (329).

The common ground between two comedians with such radically different political agendas is that sexual desire is politically dangerous. In the words of Samantha Allen:

> [W]hat a condition society would be in, if divorces was absolutely free[.] The recklessness with which new ties would be formed, the lovin' wimmen's hearts that would be broken by desertion, the children that would be homeless and uncared for. When a fickle man or woman gets thier eyes onto somebody they like better than they do thier own lawful pardners, it is awful easy to think that man, and not God, has jined 'em. . . . When a man realizes that he can if he wants to, start up and marry a woman before breakfast, and get divorced before dinner, and have a new one before supper, it has a tendency to make him onstiddy and worrysome. (326–27)

Clearly worried about male sexual desire, Holley uses the same moral brush to tar feminists who advocate changes in the rules of marriage as she uses on Mormons here.[8] When talking of a woman's sexual desire, she uses the conventional code of spiritual desires rather than physical passion, but suggests that she knows that the code is merely a deflection of physical appetites into the language of spirit:

> Says she [i.e., Woodhull], "When a woman finds that her soul is clogged and hampered, it is a duty she owes to her higher nature to find relief."
> Says I, "When a woman has such feelin's, instead of leavin' her lawful husband and goin' round huntin' up a affintee, let her take a good thoroughwort

puke." Says I, "in 9 and 1/2 cases out of 10, it is folkes'es stomachs that are clogged up insted of their souls." (327)

While her antisentimental humor usually promotes economic and political changes, it also defines the limits beyond which she is not willing to challenge domestic ideology and the idea of women's separate sphere. To put it more generously, Holley draws on the principles of equality over those of liberty, both of which are essential to the ideology of domesticity but that are in an uneasy tension. In stressing equality, Holley insists on reciprocal responsibilities, on acknowledged interdependencies that circumscribe individual freedom. But in no way is she willing to surrender the idea that a just political system depends on the affectional bonds of heterosexual monogamous love.

Though many writers used comedy to draw lines against alternative visions of family-based and therefore sexually based politics, some few writers turned the tables, investigating sexual alternatives through the language of domesticity. Melville, for instance, plays fast and loose with sexual domesticity in the chapter "A Squeeze of the Hand" in *Moby Dick*. The beatific vision he describes of earthly happiness is of conventional domesticity:

> Would that I could keep squeezing that sperm for ever! For now, since by many prolonged, repeated experiences, I have perceived that in all cases man must eventually lower, or at least shift, his conceit of attainable felicity; not placing it anywhere in the intellect or the fancy; but in the wife, the heart, the bed, the table, the saddle, the fire-side, the country; now that I have perceived all this, I am ready to squeeze case [that is, the globules of oil that come from the sperm whale's head and that, in their resemblance to sperm, gave the whale its name] eternally. In thoughts of the visions of the night, I saw long rows of angels in paradise, each with his hands in a jar of spermaceti. (416)

Punning on the meaning of the word *case* in "in all cases" and in "to squeeze case," he tells us that sexual desire is the *ultima thule* of human happiness, and that it is best expressed in the home, where the ostensibly female heart supplants the ostensibly male intellect. Surrendering to the allure of domesticity leads to heaven, a heaven of eternal rapture, of perpetual sexual ecstasy.

But of course, the entire vision is a deferral from images of masturbation and of homosexuality, of squeezing sperm, and of squeezing the hands of other men squeezing sperm, culminating in an apostrophe: "Oh! my dear fellow beings, why should we longer cherish any social ascerbities or know the slightest ill-humor or envy! Come; let us squeeze hands all round; nay, let us all squeeze ourselves into each other; let us squeeze ourselves universally into the very milk and sperm of kindness" (416). In squeezing sperm, the narrator tells us he loses his goals, in this case Ahab's mad oath. Nineteenth-century moralists, concerned about masturbation, often decried it precisely because "self-abuse" supposedly robbed men of the drive to achieve their goals.[9] Melville, of course, inverts the formula, suggesting that masculine goals, usually self-destructive, should be checked, as domesticity was supposed to do. The homosexual elements of the scene, too, would disturb nineteenth-century moralists, in part because as Melville describes it, homosexual love strips men of their individuality,

individuality necessary to economic competition and to the pursuit of hetero-sexual love. Melville agrees, but argues that such a loss is preferable to the com-petitive and destructive alternative of excessive individuality. Again, conven-tional domesticity was, by providing a haven of communal interest, also supposed to check individualistic excess. Thus does Melville elide the differ-ences between homosexual and heterosexual love in order to assert the emo-tional validity of the unconventional.

Anyone who was both an idealistic believer in domestic ideology and a real-istic observer of that ideology as it was put into practice would have had good reason for confusion and frustration, which translates for those who ken the language of laughter into good reasons for comedy, as the preceding examples suggest. Indeed, the following study of various authors as they ventured into domestic comedy shows the extent to which men and women, sharing commit-ments to the paradoxical values of individual freedom and familial constraints, could blame one another for the constraints, humiliations, and disappoint-ments of domesticity, the degree to which they found common ground in their complaints, and most importantly, the degree to which they could find psychi-cally safe or dangerous alternatives to such a constraining ideology.

The key here is that while the humorous vision is a psychological response to stress, comic forms are a kind of language, with culturally formulated con-straints and openings, that enabled purveyors of humor to articulate that re-sponse. Through comic tropes and constructions, they were able to shape their vision of society and to see culture in ways that other modes of social construc-tion deny. In order to see how comedians were both enabled and disabled by their mode of writing, it is important first to see, historically, how that mode of discourse was defined.

## III. "The Follies of Love Are Remedial"

Given that the dominant intellectual approach to literature now is to see most of the world as a vast cultural construct, it is not difficult to dissect cultural or-ganizations as bound to time and place. But laughter is an expression of emo-tion, and it is much more difficult to see emotions themselves as being the product of culture. Of course, the biological bases of emotions are not the prod-ucts of culture, but the work of Susanne Langer, particularly in "The Cultural Importance of Art," would suggest that cultures have such powerful effects in providing the channels through which emotions are expressed as to make the biological basis of emotion only about half the picture. Langer argues that while emotions may be latent, they are so crude and ineffable as to require cul-tural expression through the language and symbols of art. If she is right, then even something as protean and difficult to control as humor is nonetheless channeled through cultural forms, and thus must be studied at least in part through an understanding of how a particular culture tries to explain and thus control it.

We have some formidable barriers in the way of understanding nineteenth-century conceptions of humor. Given today's dominance of models of power relations, and given that laughter still seems relegated to the realm of the psychic rather than the social, it is not surprising that Freud's theory of the joke (or as he called it "*Witz*") colors most of our expositions of comedy. Indeed, we now tend to use the words *comedy* and *humor* interchangeably, without any sense that in writing about "*Witz*" Freud was sealing off one psychic phenomenon from another that also expresses itself through comedy. In a very important essay quite distinct from his book on jokes, he writes of humor as having a very different psychodynamic, one in which the superego, rather than being a source of repression from which the ego and id must escape in aggressive laughter, actually solaces the ego through gentle, supportive laughter. Rather than aggressive, humor is, according to Freud, the tool by which healthy minds reconcile conflicting psychic impulses.

While he theorized it in ways that were a bit unusual for his day, Freud was not alone in drawing a distinction between humor and other sources of comedy, such as satire, wit, and irony. And while not all literary artists accepted these distinctions, all were constrained by them, as a look at Melville's ironic play with them in *The Confidence-Man* attests. Melville's Confidence Man as philanthropist (chap. 24) ironically attacks irony, and in so doing shows Melville's awareness of the conventional linkage of irony and satire: "'Ah, now,' deprecating with his pipe, 'irony is so unjust; never could abide irony; something Satanic about irony. God defend me from irony, and Satire, his bosom friend'" (986). In this case, the reader is probably supposed to reject the Confidence Man's statement, though when later the Con Man speaks of humor, the reader finds it more difficult to read the irony. Perhaps our Con Man speaks truth to trap the other con man:

> Humor is, in fact, so blessed a thing, that even in the least virtuous product of the human mind, if there can be found but nine good jokes, some philosophers are clement enough to affirm that those nine good jokes should redeem all the wicked thoughts, though plenty as the populace of Sodom. At any rate, this same humor has something, there is no telling what, of beneficence in it, it is such a catholicon and charm—nearly all men agreeing in relishing it, though they may agree in little else—and in its way it undeniably does such a deal of familiar good in the world, that no wonder it is almost a proverb, that a man of humor, a man capable of a good loud laugh—seem how he may in other things—can hardly be a heartless scamp. (1015)

Who can read the multiple ironies of this passage and its context?[10] Suffice it to say that in having the Confidence Man parrot popular ideas about irony, satire, and humor, Melville shows himself aware of the conventional distinctions, though the degree to which he resists them is virtually impossible to say.

These conventional distinctions, developed under the same philosophical tradition that spawned the ideology of domesticity, generated a significant challenge to Hobbes's theory that all comedy is rooted in aggression.[11] Again I turn to

Francis Hutcheson, who, trying to defend any natural human characteristic from moral obloquy, argued that Hobbes's superiority theory really did not account for laughter; instead, "That then which seems generally the cause of laughter is the bringing together of images which have contrary additional ideas, as well as some resemblance in the principal idea" ("Reflections on Laughter" 32). He agreed that wit—which manifested itself in satire and which used biting irony—could be used as a social weapon, but believed that more likely it was used as a social palliative:

> The implanting then a sense of the ridiculous, in our nature, was giving us an avenue to pleasure, and an easy remedy for discontent and sorrow. Again, laughter, like other associations, is very contagious: our whole frame is so sociable, that one merry countenance may diffuse cheerfulness to many; nor are they all fools who are apt to laugh before they know the jest. . . . We are disposed by laughter to a good opinion of the person who raises it. . . . Laughter is none of the smallest bonds to common friendships. (35–36)

By 1725, when Hutcheson began publishing his series of essays on laughter, commentators were beginning to talk of an innate capacity, a sensibility, what was soon to be called the sense of humor.[12] As the product of a fundamental sensibility that allowed the possessor to perceive and enjoy incongruity, and as a sensibility that was predicated on social sympathies, laughter came to be seen as amiable rather than aggressive. Indeed, the essence of the sense of humor as described by Hutcheson and others was to take pleasure in difference, and rather than estranging people, such pleasure bound them in friendship, or at least tolerance, which is the minimum precondition for the developing ideology of liberal individualism.

The very term *sense of humor* arose as a way of embracing those peculiar people who were said to be, in their eccentricity, "humorous," that is to say, of unbalanced humors and therefore abnormal or difficult.[13] By coopting the term, turning "humors" into a benefit rather than a detriment, and by postulating an innate sense that is able to perceive "humor"—that is, the discrepancy between an ideal and an individual declension from that ideal—as something pleasurable, Enlightenment thinkers turned accepted definitions of laughter from being necessarily a way to coerce conformity into a capacity to rejoice in nonconformity. In order to do so, they stressed the social nature of humor, describing it as a primary human bond.

Such theories as Hutcheson's were dominant from the late eighteenth century through the middle of the nineteenth. They legitimized humor in genteel eyes and made it, among other things, socially acceptable for women to write humor. I know it is now accepted that the patriarchy denied women the sense of humor, as Walker's book makes clear, but she quotes only a few oddball clergymen to make her point. True, early in the nineteenth century, when America was still trying to shed Calvinism, women and men alike were told that laughter was next to sinfulness, but by 1860, when women had equal access both to mass-market literary production and to the organs of high culture such as the

*Atlantic Monthly*, women writers were no strangers to humor. Obviously, the women whose works I treat in this study—Stowe, Freeman, Fern, and Holley—wove humor into their works to a substantial degree, but the list of women writers who used humor to one degree or another in their works could be extended substantially.

And the male writers whom the twentieth century has canonized recognized the humor of the major women writers who were their contemporaries. Howells, for instance, spoke of Freeman's subtle humor, but he spoke of its subtlety as stemming not from the putative delicacy of a woman's sensibility but rather from the New England tradition of dry drollery. In Twain's case, he acknowledged the humor of Harriet Beecher Stowe by invoking the name of one of Stowe's comic creations in order to characterize one of his own, "Jack Halliday, . . . the loafing, good-natured, no-account, irreverent fisherman, hunter, boy's friend, stray-dogs' friend, typical 'Sam Lawson' of the town" in "The Man That Corrupted Hadleyburg." What more thorough acknowledgment of the widespread recognition of Stowe's humor than in Twain's allusion to it in characterizing the main laugher of his story?

Humor, as opposed to wit or satire, was given an honored place in the sentimentalist's view of the *human*, rather than male, mind first because the exercise of any sensibility, including the sense of humor, was held to be ennobling and second, at the very least, because humor was perceived as a health-giving tonic to balance life's serious pursuits. In this latter capacity, it was seen as a legitimate release from the demands of decorum, but only under highly controlled circumstances.

Perhaps the best place to see this dynamic of controlled release both advocated and played out is in the works of Stowe, who, though always a serious moralist, never fails to interlard her stories with comic vignettes and characters. Indeed, developing an etiquette of humor so as simultaneously to redeem comedy from the charge of being socially disruptive and to hold the disruptive potentials, which she does acknowledge in many of her works, in check is one of the primary purposes in Stowe's companion books, *Oldtown Folks* and *Oldtown Fireside Stories*. Early in *Oldtown Folks* we are introduced to the Harvard wit, Bill Badger, whose caustic jests are simultaneously encouraged and constrained by one of the targets of his jests, Miss Mehitable Rossiter:

> "I always indulge myself in thinking I am welcome," she said. "And now pray how is our young scholar, Master William Badger? What news do you bring us from old Harvard?"
>
> "Almost anything you want to hear, Miss Mehitable. You know that I am your most devoted slave."
>
> "Not so sure of that, sir," she said, with a whimsical twinkle of her eye. "Don't you know that your sex are always treacherous? How do I know that you don't serve up old Miss Rossiter when you give representations of the Oldtown curiosities there at Cambridge? We are a set here that might make a boy's fortune in that line,—now are n't we?"

"How do you know that I do serve up Oldtown curiosities?" said Bill, somewhat confused, and blushing to the roots of his hair.

"How do I know? Can the Ethiopian change his skin, or the leopard his spots? and can you help being a mimic, as you were born, always were and always will be?"

"Oh, but I'm sure, Miss Mehitable, Bill never would,—he has too much respect," said Aunt Keziah and Aunt Lois, simultaneously again.

"Perhaps not; but if he wants to, he's welcome. What are queer old women for, if young folks may not have a good laugh out of them now and then? If it's only a friendly laugh, it's just as good as crying, and better too. I'd like to be made to laugh at myself. I think generally we take ourselves altogether too seriously." (1: 80–81)

Miss Mehitable clearly demonstrates her superior insight to the crowd at large, and is in a position to use laughter as a social corrective against Bill. Instead of humiliating him, though, she turns humor on herself, showing Bill both that he takes himself too seriously in showing off his prowess as a wit, and giving him a model of humor that is inclusive rather than abusive. She suggests the socially ameliorative power of laughter in the analogy to tears, suggesting that we laugh at others when feeling our own pain. What better way, she suggests, to take us out of our own feelings of inadequacy than to acknowledge their unimportance from a view larger than that of our own narrow pride, or better, to see their social value. Clearly, in not taking herself too seriously, she has established a place for herself within the Fireside circle, and not merely as a clown, but as an authority. All of this in spite of, or perhaps because of, her striking individuality, both as a physical being and as a character. The narrator's description makes Rossiter appear to be a cartoonish grotesque, a mere caricature of a human being, but one who has "a style of ugliness that was neither repulsive nor vulgar. Personal uncomeliness has its differing characters, and there are some very homely women who have a style that amounts to something like beauty. . . . And people liked her so much that they came to like the singularities which individualized her from other human beings" (78).

In Stowe's use of caricature, then, we see the humorist's attempt to claim for stereotyping a moral value. In exaggerating types as clownish, as externally different from an ideal or a norm, the humorist begins down the track of aggressive scapegoating. But by turning the emotional valence at the end from insisting on conformity to appreciating difference, the moral purpose of the stereotype is to find common fundamental ground behind the superficial, laughable differences. The laughter begins as ostracism, but in the way the humorist manages it, it can, at least in theory, end as a gesture of inclusion.

Worth noting, here, is that Rossiter herself turns her own wit into humor, and in so doing controls Bill's wit. Partly she insists on intention, that in not taking ourselves too seriously we give ourselves freedom to face life's difficulties. Partly, too, she stresses occasion, that what would be untenable in one context is tolerable, indeed beneficial, in another. Among young men at college, "racier" humor is, according to this grand dame of humor, allowable. By implication, in mixed audiences, or in serious places, any source of laughter would not be. Controls of humor, then, usually tended to reinforce the sexual double standard. Women were allowed to write humor, but it was not supposed to be satiric or "racy." But as long as humor works off of incongruity, irony is always latent in it. Thus, this double standard allowed much real satire to masquerade as humor. As long as it posed as diversion for certain audiences in certain hours, even something scurrilous and subversive—for example, George Washington Harris's Sut Lovingood yarns, which are set up as hunting tales—are deemed acceptable, as long as they are superficially distinct from political or social satire. In this capacity as relief from seriousness, humor often worked its way into serious works, breaking down eighteenth-century ideas of artistic and moral unity, in effect opening narrative to a plethora of voices, points of view, and emotional tones, perhaps even, as Bakhtin would have it, "carnivalizing" narrative.

Almost all nineteenth-century humorists and commentators on humor agreed with the eighteenth-century definition of comedy as the child of incongruities perceived by an innate sense of humor and contingent of the association of ideas. Not all, however, agreed about the social value of humor. Indeed, in America, with residual Puritanism frowning at almost any pleasure, humor was seen as distinctly subliterary until after the Civil War. More importantly, irony, and all of the aggression that it entails, was latent in incongruity, as at least Schopenhauer and Kierkegaard pointed out. While neither was well-known or influential in nineteenth-century America, the prevailing ideas made their conceptions at least latent and accessible to those practicing humorists who, empirically, pushed their medium up to and beyond its defined limits.

Schopenhauer's ideas, in fact, were picked up by George Santayana, Constance Rourke, and Walter Blair, the three American literary critics who have dominated academic discussions of American humor. According to Schopenhauer, comedy arises in perceiving an incongruity between perception and conception. Thus, the point of a humorist is to attack some idea by pointing out its inappropriateness to reality. From an empirical point of view, in the incongruity between ideas of grandeur and the reality of baseness, the butt of the joke will not be the base, but will be the inappropriate idealism that struggles in vain against the facts of this world. According to Blair, that is precisely what American humor, especially the humor of the frontier, does. In rejecting grandiose claims by the standard of "horse sense," American humorists helped American writers to reject the false culture of European gentility in favor of a home-grown American pragmatism. Thus, Schopenhauer's theory shows the subversive potentials even in humor, that no matter how genteel strictures were used to circumscribe the range and power of comedy by calling it humor, humor has the power to invert the constraints, to become wide-ranging and powerful by challenging the legitimacy of those very constraints.

Even less influential in his own day than Schopenhauer, Kierkegaard nonetheless articulates many of the difficulties presented by an amiable humor based on incongruity. Kierkegaard sees that incongruity may be the basis of comedy, but that there is nothing intrinsically amiable about it. Indeed, insofar as incongruity always entails the potential of irony, it entails the most powerfully egotistical of potentials. In his *Concept of Irony*, Kierkegaard characterizes irony as a dialectic of abstractions, rather than a dialectic between the abstract and the concrete. Thus, he sees the ironist in a position to destroy belief by consuming any abstraction in another, finer abstraction. Irony becomes "infinite absolute negativity" with an "infinite elasticity" that allows it to assault any knowledge and to consume it. Analyzing the concept by speaking of Socrates as its most profound practitioner, he declares "[t]he Socratic [i.e., the ironic] standpoint as one of complete isolation" (174). To the non-ironist, even to the disciple of Socrates, "the significance of his immersion in himself remains always inexplicable . . . , since the subtleties that attempt to reveal something about it bear no relation to it" (175). Indeed, the ironist is profoundly individualistic, the ultimate egotist, even by contrast to the sophist whose egotism expresses itself by the aggressive attempt to grapple with ideas.

> The Sophist is ever in feverish activity, ever grasping for something that lies in front of him; the ironist, on the other hand, directs this back into himself at every moment, and such an act with its consequent backward current is a determination of personality. The sophism is therefore a ministering element in irony; and whether the ironist uses the sophism to emancipate himself or to wrest something from another, he nevertheless assimilates both moments into consciousness, i.e. he enjoys. Enjoyment is therefore a determination of personality, even though an ironist's enjoyment is the most abstract of all, the most vacuous, the mere contour, the weakest intimation of that enjoyment possessing absolute content, i.e. happiness. (176)

Kierkegaard sees the ironist as possessing a consciously pleasurable life, one rich in individuality and possessed by the choice to annihilate all he comes into contact with. But this existence through negation entails a monumental price—enjoyment at the cost of happiness, power and independence at the cost of connection with others and faith in meaning.

The humorist, according to Kierkegaard, comes out on the other side of irony, capable of seeing, in incongruity, the absurdity of all knowledge, the self-fulfilling nature of any belief that is predicated on first principles merely willed rather than preexisting. But while the ironist finds enjoyment in reducing faith to nonsense, the humorist wills faith by passing through laughter: "Humor is the last stage of existential inwardness before faith" (*Concluding Unscientific Postscript* 259). While this is far more sophisticated philosophically than the systems of Hutcheson, and has far greater implications psychically, the moral implications are the same. Moral integrity, faith, happiness: all, says Kierkegaard, are contingent on surrendering irony to humor.[14] In developing incongruities, every humorist plays at some point with the line between doubt and faith, with the danger of surrendering to irony, or with the need to marshal irony as a defense of the self against untenable social pressures. As I discussed above, the family is one of those places where social pressures toward conformity are highly visible and powerful. The domestic humorist, then, is in a peculiar position to use the acceptable realm of laughter to chart a way to manage or reject these pressures. This is the drama that will be played out in many different ways throughout the rest of the book.

Kierkegaard is much more supportive of the distinction between wit and humor than is Schopenhauer, though he sees the competition between wit and humor as an existential choice between faith and nihilism rather than as a structurally defined distinction. Both philosophers, though, merely foreshadowed the impending disruption of the commonplace acceptance of amiable humor. Late in the century, Hutchesonian humor of "good will" was under pressure, culminating in Freud's "scientific" psychology of comedic aggression and in Bergson's antiscientific theory of comedic aggression. While incongruity persisted as the primary theoretical cause of laughter, most thinkers after Darwin returned to describing aggression as the theoretical motive of laughter. Many of America's most provocative humorists were writing at this time, when they were able to take advantage, after the Civil War, of the triumph of genteel morality along with its approval of humor at the same time they were able to push the boundaries of that definition. Writers like Twain and Freeman end up playing a dialectic between faith and doubt that comes to be a dialectic between optimism and pessimism.

Late-nineteenth-century pessimism about laughter, and about human nature more generally, has carried into twentieth-century comedic theory, as we can see in the recent discussions of the degree to which comedies are "subversive" or whether they merely "reinscribe" the "hegemonic" terms of "dominant ideology." But comedy, as influenced in practice at any given time by the prevailing theory, is too protean to be fully constrained. It always entails leverage against the weight of convention; it always entails at least a peep into an altered view of apparent realities. Thus it gives us a way to understand more about how people in the nineteenth century—or perhaps in any century—adjusted to dominant ideology. In seeing humor adapt, extend, challenge, modify and, in short, humanize the dominant nineteenth-century ideology of domesticity, we may find a reciprocal leverage to extend an understanding of humor itself. While such an effort to solve a problem for two variables may not be scientific, it is perhaps appropriate to humor in that it will simplify by complicating. May the spirit of comedy not be violated in the process.

TWO

# Home in a Rage

## I. Washington Irving: Laughing All the Way to the Bank

I begin with a writer whose importance to the tradition of comic literature that I am addressing cannot be overstated but whose status as an important American writer has been on the wane for the last several scholarly generations.[1] Washington Irving has been more or less moved to the edge of his canonical pedestal because he is too sentimental for twentieth-century tastes, yet that is precisely why he is of such great importance to the tradition of domestic humor. With *The Sketch Book*, Irving virtually singlehandedly imported humor into American literature. There had been much literary comedy before, even much written by Irving himself. But American comedy before *The Sketch Book* was witty, satirical, usually overtly political. Think of Benjamin Franklin's "Dogood Papers," or of Hugh Henry Brackenridge's *Modern Chivalry*, or Tabitha Tenney's *Female Quixotism*, or William Byrd's "History of the Dividing Line" and "Secret History of the Line." Each of these has a definite satirical bent, and in each case the reader can discern a strong, clear authorial point of view, usually carried by a positive narrator.[2]

*The Sketch Book*, though, is different, as Irving himself tells us as he gives notice to the death of Diedrich Knickerbocker in the introductory note to "Rip Van Winkle."

> The following Tale was found among the papers of the late Diedrich Knicker-bocker, an old gentleman of New York, who was very curious in the Dutch history of the province and the manners of the descendants from its primitive settlers. His historical researches, however, did not lie so much among books as among men, for the former are lamentably scanty on his favorite topics, whereas he found the old burghers, and still more their wives, rich in that legendary lore so invaluable to true history. . . . There have been various opinions as to the literary character of his work, and, to tell the truth, it is not a whit better than it should be. Its chief merit is its scrupulous accuracy, which indeed was a little questioned on its first appearance. . . . The old gentleman died shortly after the publication of his work, and now that he is dead and gone, it cannot do much harm to his memory to say that his time might have been much better employed in weightier labors. He, however, was apt to ride his hobby his own way; and though it did now and then kick up the dust a little in the eyes of his neighbors and grieve the spirit of some friends, for whom he felt the truest deference and affection, yet his errors and follies are remembered 'more in sorrow than in anger,' and it begins to be suspected that he never intended to injure or offend. (37–38)

Knickerbocker was Irving's front man for his social satire, and when he stopped writing for more than a half dozen years after the death of his fiancée, Matilda Hoffman, Irving did rather kill Knickerbocker off. But on reviving his memory in *The Sketch Book* in order to insulate his new narrator, Geoffrey Crayon, gent., from the most satirical pieces in the volume, he reforms Knickerbocker's character. Yes, Knickerbocker was apt to stir up the dust—that is, to make angry the targets of his satires—and yes, such scandal-mongering was a pain to Knickerbocker's friends. Nonetheless, we are told, implausibly, that the old Dutchman meant no harm, that he was in fact just an amiable humorist.

By implication, the two tales most likely to be read as satires in *The Sketch Book* are reduced to humor, and the book as a whole, we find at the very outset, is the product of a humorist. Indeed, it is in the narrator's introduction of himself that we see him presenting himself as an amiable oddball whose opinions are worthy of our notice only as they amuse us, not as they instruct us. His travels, he tells us, have taken him into the Europe of "storied and poetical association" where he "longed to wander over the scenes of renowned achievement—to tread, as it were, in the footsteps of antiquity, to loiter about the ruined castle, to meditate on the falling tower, to escape, in short, from the commonplace realities of the present and lose myself among the shadowy grandeurs of the past" (14). His meditations, then, which could be educational in their play with the associations of history, are intended merely as escape, as is his comedy, which could be instructional were it to be construed as satire. Indeed, if his sense of morality were as inaccurate as his sense of history, both his observations and wit would serve more harm than good if taken seriously. This is a portrait of the artist as a capricious man:

> I cannot say that I have studied them with the eye of a philosopher, but rather with the sauntering gaze with which humble lovers of the picturesque stroll from the window of one print shop to another, caught sometimes by the delineations of beauty, sometimes by the distortions of caricature, and sometimes by the loveliness of landscape. . . . When, however, I look over the hints and memorandums I have taken down . . . my heart almost fails me at finding how my idle humor has led me aside from the great objects studied by every regular traveler who would make a book. (15)

Notice, then, that this is to be the record of a sentimental journey, a journey that exercises not the memory or the intellect, but the emotions. It is to run the gamut from picturesque, to sublime, to ridiculous, merely for the sake of exercising taste. And the objects of taste are to be the subject of the narrator's humor—his "humor" then is our guide.

The parallels between Irving's *Sketch Book* narrator and Addison and Steele's description of "the Spectator" and his club in the first two numbers of the *Spectator* are striking. Both Crayon and the Spectator describe themselves as "humorists" whose humor is to observe rather than participate in life. The structure of such a pose is perfectly apt to journalism or to a book of sketches, making the ultimate commercial value of the pose the fact that it enables the journalist to cross the line from journalism to writing books with ease. Most American literary comedians, both satirists and humorists, wrote first and foremost for journals, only turning their journalism to books when popularity and volume of newspaper correspondence warranted the shift. Consider, for just a few examples, Sara Willis Parton's *Fern Leaves from Fanny's Port Folio* and its sequels, Frances Miriam Whitcher's *The Widow Bedott Papers*, Charles Farrar Browne's *Artemus Ward: His Book*, and Samuel Clemens's *Innocents Abroad*.

Another important point of similarity between Addison and Steele's Spectator and Irving's Crayon is the narrative persona as humorist, as a person whose peculiarities are both endearing and slightly off-putting. As oddballs, they are not direct mouthpieces for their authors, and as readers we are warned not to put ourselves exactly in the narrator's shoes. The distance this narrative stance grants the writer is part of the way that wit is softened into humor, and with the full blossoming of the idea of amiable humor over the course of the eighteenth century, Irving's stance is much more crucial as a way of containing wit than it ever was for Addison or Steele.

This need to soften the punch accounts for the most marked difference between Irving's model and his use of that model. The Spectator is a deadpan humorist, sober as a judge. But he is a judge, a judge of human behavior, and as such his stance is one of positive knowledge, backed by a class status of gentlemanly dignity and cultivated taste. Irving's Crayon is, by contrast, remarkably humble. No matter how close to the bone Irving's humor may at times cut, it is always softened not only by the polished and low-key diction of his storyteller, but by the storyteller's self-abnegation throughout. This pose of gentlemanly or ladylike humility, even in the face of aggressive self-assertion, is one of the hallmarks of American domestic humor. In Irving's case, his narrator claims that his humility is partly because he is a "degenerate" American humbled by the superior Europeans; in Caroline Kirkland's case, her narrator, Mrs. Mary Clavers, simply ascribes her narrative "failures" to her feminine propensity to ramble, though her tales are never rambling—every digression serves a pungent and precise narrative purpose. Sara Willis Parton's mock humility at the beginning of *Fern Leaves,* too, partakes of this spirit, and even Clemens, whose marked lack of humility in *Innocents Abroad* earned him the opprobrium of the genteel audiences who had grown used to the humble humorist, began Mark Twain's career as a modest, bumbling gentleman straight man to the raucous counterpoint of the low-class Mr. Brown. With few exceptions, like those of Frances Whitcher or of Charles Farrar Browne, nineteenth-century humorists insulated their comic tales of the "lower-classes" from "lower-class" voices, mediating differences through the voice of a genteel humorist.[3] It took the better part of the century for humorists to break down the barrier of the gentleperson narrator.

The rambunctious and disruptive potentials of comedy are partly contained, too, by the series of sketches. Insofar as sketches were to run the gamut of emotions, laughter is always balanced by so-called "higher" emotions. Laughter is put in its place, as it were, mainly as temporary relief from seriousness. For example, in *The Sketch Book,* the sentimental tale "The Wife" needs "Rip Van Winkle" for comic relief. Relief, though, was not the only justification for humor. By the early nineteenth century, aesthetic theorists held that any exercise of taste was ennobling, even, within limits, the exercise of the sense of humor. Thus, genteel humorists, as opposed to political satirists and those wits of the southwestern tradition, almost always set up constant counterpoints between humorous sketches and others. Notice that in Irving's book, few sketches mix emotions—most observe the unities in order to purify and intensify the emotional experience. Rather like a body builder doing specific exercises for specific muscles, the sentimentalist wrote specific sketches to exercise specific emotions. Even Clemens, who often broke down those barriers by quick juxtapositions of the sublime and the ridiculous, followed these proprieties as a matter of course. In his lectures, as he wrote his wife, Livy, he tried to develop a "narrative plank, with square holes in it, six inches apart, all the length of it & then in my mental shop I ought to have plugs (half marked 'serious' and the other marked 'humorous') to select from and jam into these holes according to the temper of the audience" (qtd. in Henry Nash Smith 35).

As I discussed in the last chapter, the political impetus behind the theory and practice of amiable humor was generally liberal, yet built into the standards of propriety by which sentimentalists judged the appropriateness of emotions is an antidemocratic elitism. The very need for the gentleperson narrator to gush with the appropriate sentiments, and the usual characterization of comic characters as lower-class, parallels very neatly the much older forms of satiric wit, forms used so often by the southwestern "humorists" of American literature, who usually framed their sketches of country bumpkins worthy of scorn with the travel narratives of gentlemen whose business or pleasure takes them temporarily out of the sphere of urbane company. In the case of sentimental humor, however, the framing and the way the tale is told are supposed to level the lower classes up. Indeed, countless sentimental sketches attest to the "good hearts" of members of the lower classes, or the moral worthiness of certain poverty-stricken individuals. Usually, in keeping with the proprieties of domestic ideology, sentimental sketches discover this goodness in observing the exercise of some domestic function. Nonetheless, the distinction between wit and humor that the humorist tries to make is apt to blur very quickly when the humorist's class instincts are riled. This is clearly the case in one of Irving's most famous tales, "The Legend of Sleepy Hollow."

Following the volume's last tale of British life, "The Angler," "The Legend of Sleepy Hollow" is the narrator's return to America, and the contrast between the two stories does not redound to the credit of Crayon's homeland. In "The Angler," Irving's narrator exercises his literary sensibilities in a sentimental contemplation of Izaak Walton's *The Compleat Angler* only to find in America that the "termagant" rivers do not allow such peaceful sport. But in Britain, he meets one of those poor people who overpopulate sentimental sketches, the poor man contented with his lot. The angler has translated his sport into an adequate profession, one that gives him pleasure as well as a living at the hands of the gentlemen sportsmen who employ him. Irving closes "this rambling sketch in the words of honest Izaak Walton, by craving the blessing of St Peter's master upon my reader, 'and upon all that are true lovers of virtue, and dare trust in his Providence; and be quiet; and go a angling'" (328). The juxtapositions, here, suggest that it is a Christian virtue to be content with one's lot, to stay still as much as possible, and to trust to Providence and one's social superiors to make one's lot in life a pleasant one.

The bucolic homily is clearly all the more meaningful to Irving when set in contrast to his tale of America. The turbulent Yankee spirit, embodied in Ichabod Crane, mouths the pieties of Providence in a puritanical way, but is unable to trust to that Providence at all. Ichabod, the college-bred young scarecrow from Connecticut, invades Sleepy Hollow with his impatience. He is always hungry, unable to live on the land; he only imagines himself living off of it, literally, by turning it into cash and moving on:

> As the enraptured Ichabod fancied all this, and as he rolled his great green eyes over the fat meadow lands, the rich fields of wheat, of rye, of buckwheat, and Indian corn, and the orchards burthened with ruddy fruit, which surrounded the warm tenement of Van Tassel, his heart yearned after the damsel who was to inherit these domains, and his imagination expanded with the idea how they might be readily turned into cash, and the money invested in immense tracts of wild land, and shingle palaces in the wilderness. (339)

Irving loathes the commercial and progressive spirit; as he put it in one of his notebooks of the period, "Commerce is a game where the merchant is one party & ruin the other" (qtd. in Williams, *Life of Washington Irving* 1: 166), though whose ruin is left remarkably ambiguous. In creating the caricature of Crane, he demonstrates his anxiety about the Puritan way of capitalism, but the humor crosses the line between amiably and indulgently enjoying Ichabod's peculiarities and outright scorn of his pretensions.[4] Not willing to put his objections to mobility on other grounds, such as stewardship, community, or continuity, Irving uses the shorthand of class to impugn American "progressivism."[5]

Thus, in spite of his use of a form that tends toward democracy, in spite of his effort to kill off his old satirical persona, Irving still has that satiric edge, the edge of the social conservative up in arms over progressive change. While his sentimentalism may have moved him to the edge of his canonical pedestal, his conservatism has been the reason that he has been given a giant push by critics, particularly by feminists who see him as a worthy target because he is so rigorously misogynistic.[6] Poor Irving, assailed for being too sentimental by critics who held sentimentalism in contempt because it was "too feminine" (whatever that means), only to be assailed all the more vigorously for being complicit with those men who so energetically attacked him. As someone who has worked hard to uncover the intellectual underpinnings of sentimentalism, I do not hold Irving culpable for his sentimentality, but as a feminist, I find his misogyny inexcusable. As a critic of humor, though, I think that much feminist criticism of Irving, best exemplified by Judith Fetterley's analysis in *The Resisting Reader*, misses the mark in ways that must be confronted if we are to make sense of humor at all. According to Fetterley:

> [T]he basic fantasy "Rip Van Winkle" embodies is that of being able to sleep long enough to avoid at once the American Revolution and the wife. The story imagines and enacts a successful evasion of civilization and of the imperatives of adulthood. Rip sleeps through those years when one is expected to be politically, personally, and sexually mature and thus moves from the boyhood of youth to the boyhood of an old age that promises to go on forever. In addition, he accomplishes something else: access to life in an all-male world, a world without women, the ideal American territory. (6)

Rip seeks, as Fetterley points out, to avoid the strive-and-succeed ethos of the new America, to avoid the "massive suppressions required by [Benjamin] Franklin's code of success" (2).

Rip, or should I say Irving, since Fetterley draws little distinction between the two, seeks, too, to avoid sexual maturity, to avoid the responsibilities entailed by sexual adulthood. Thus, Irving's innovation on the old folk motif of sleeping through adulthood in an effort to avoid sexual maturity is to correlate revolutionary America's ethos of progress with an ethos of sexual responsibility and to embody them in the villain, Dame Van Winkle:

> Irving's tale is distinguished from its source by his elaboration of the psychology behind the experience of protracted sleep, and this elaboration is in turn distinguished by women's involvement in it. What drives Rip away from the village and up into the mountains and what makes him a likely partaker of the sleep-in-

ducing liquor is his wife; all the ills from which Rip seeks escape are symbolically located in the person of the offending Dame Van Winkle. Thus, an essential part of the Americanness of Irving's story is the creation of woman as villain: as obstacle to the achievement of the dream of pleasure; as mouthpiece for the values of work, responsibility, adulthood—the imperatives of Benjamin Franklin. Significantly, Irving's tale connects the image of woman with the birth of America as a nation and with the theme of growing up. (3)

This is a particularly strong line of criticism, articulated by many critics, among them Philip Young and Leslie Fiedler.

Indeed, Irving does draw parallels between governmental authority and "petticoat government" in ways that clearly identify constraint with the rule of woman in the house. If it is true that "power is the issue in the politics of literature, as it is in the politics of anything else" (xiii), then the embodiment of evil in woman is an assertion of the legitimacy of masculine power over women.[7] So far, I have no objection to Fetterley's reading of "Rip," but the mechanism of power that she insists on is the mechanism of identification. She insists that readers are forced by the "impalpable" "design" (xi) of the story to identify with Rip and thus to share his sense of woman as superego, woman as the bar to happiness. Thus, says Fetterley, by resisting identification with Rip, the reader can resist the tale's misogyny and in the process resist the power of patriarchy.

While her understanding of Irving's attack on women is apt, I think Fetterley misses the political and psychological ramifications of this attack. Her entire line of argument turns on two large and finally untenable assumptions: first, that we readers are intended to identify with Rip and with Irving, and second, that Irving's misogyny is a simple product of an unbroken chain of unmitigated male cultural power. I suspect that, on the contrary, Irving's misogyny is a consequence of a perceived breakdown of male power, of the social turbulence of liberalism that had already in the late eighteenth century begun the long process of enfranchising women. As Jenifer Banks puts it:

> Theoretically, the republic depended on the virtue, intelligence, and responsibility of all of its citizens. Theoretically, this was a step toward greater equality as the model republican woman became a figure of competence and independence, of self-confidence and rationality. Irving seemed threatened by this movement toward women's independence and equality and the changes in the status quo that this philosophy implied. (258).

Banks's iterated "theoretically" implies how vexed and drawn-out the change was in our culture, but the fact of the change, no matter how partial or slow, must be taken into account if we are to understand the reactions of nineteenth-century writers to that culture. As for the former assumption, that the reader is supposed to identify with Rip, that is easy to test through a simple thought experiment: to read, for the sake of argument, the story from what Fetterley assumes to be the standard Rip/Irving/male point of view.

❈   ❈

Fetterley has good reason to assume that readers are supposed to identify with Irving and Rip, inasmuch as many critics who preceded her do, too.[8] In the spirit of this entire enterprise, I will begin my fantasy reading of Rip's "serious" plight with a reading from the once popular song, "It Takes Time," which takes Rip seriously only by inverting the meaning of Rip's flight from romance. In the version I know, Louis Armstrong, warning impatient romantic youth that "it takes time" to win true love, reminds us that "Rome wasn't built in a day, they say,/ not to mention pyramids and sphinx;/ It took old Rip Van Winkle twenty years/ to squeeze the livin' daylights out of forty winks." Here is Rip as role model, the sage we are to follow in our romantic quests, that is, if we take the comic reference seriously, which is difficult to do.

If nothing else, though, the song does reveal the crux of the story, the problem of time, of making it work for you. What troubles Rip is that he is patient in a world of bustle, that he wishes for a stable world even as the pace of "progress," that is mobility and change, increases all around him. The very beginning of the story speaks of journeys of discovery, and the discoverer who journeys to the Catskills finds them a "dismembered branch of the great Appalachian family" (38). Are they, too, migrants, obsessed with time as money, with progress, with motion, with bustle? Perhaps so; they *are* emblems of change rather than of stability, for they respond to every measure of time: "Every change of season, every change of weather, indeed, every hour of the day produces some change in the magical hues and shapes of these mountains." The story's narrator, whose very first line asks for authoritative confirmation of his tale from those busy travelers who have "made a voyage up the Hudson," insists in setting his story that this will be a story of change, of the marks of time.

What sets Rip apart from his own time and place is that he wishes no part of this progress of events. He lives in the past, literally, by living in "a village of great antiquity, having been founded by some of the Dutch colonists in the early times of the province," but he has cut himself off from the progressive tenor of that colonizing past, preferring to remain inactive in one place, "in one of these very houses (which, to tell the precise truth, was sadly time-worn and weather-beaten)." Already, then, before the Revolution, Rip stands out as a passive resistor to the American spirit of progress. Yet his resistance is so passive as to be almost nonexistent. Patience and tractability mark his character so much that he is dominated by anyone with a progressive spirit.

The primary symbol of this spirit is his wife, who not only is full of domestic bustle in keeping the interior of her house in order but also, in a timely fashion, reminds Rip of the temporal consequences of his stasis: "Morning, noon, and night, her tongue was incessantly going, and everything he said or did was sure to produce a torrent of household eloquence" (40). The everything he did was, of course, nothing: "Rip had but one way of replying to all lectures of the kind, and that, by frequent use, had grown into a habit. He shrugged his shoulders, shook his head, cast up his eyes, but said nothing" (40–41). He has a similar response when faced by the ghosts of Hudson and his men, the tutelary spirits of both this colony of people who broke from the great family of Europe and of the changeable mountains, also wayward children of a great family. Rip does what they tell him in silence. He passively waits upon them, not participating in their serious pleasure (the sexual implications of which are duly, and I think correctly, noted by both Fetterley and William P. Dawson among others) until he surreptitiously and without invitation drinks a liquor that puts him to sleep for the bulk of his adult life. Progress, activity, determination, sexuality, responsibility: the draught of life, which keeps the spirits of Hudson and his men active long after their merely physical deaths, merely puts Rip to sleep.

On his return to the now United States, Rip is more out of time than ever. Everything is changed. The villagers he meets he doesn't recognize; "the very village was altered; it was larger and more populous. . . . Strange names were over the doors—strange faces at the windows—everything was strange" (47). His own house, that symbol of the past, is in ruins. When he goes to the village center, he finds "[t]he very character of the people seemed changed. There was a busy, bustling disputatious tone about it, instead of the accustomed phlegm and tranquility" (48). Accused of being a traitor, he is in some physical danger, but his real woe is that his "heart died away at hearing of these sad changes in his home and friends, and finding himself thus alone in the world." In trying to look at the tale with sympathy for Rip, one must feel mournful about loss, and angry about the pace of change.[9]

If we are, in imagination, to seek a congruent sympathy for Irving as well as for Rip, we must realize that the changes of the Revolution were paralleled by the changes in family structure that I sketched in the last chapter. The missing assumptions in Fetterley's analysis are those pertaining to the marked shift in American family structure that was taking place even as Irving was writing. Fetterley insists that patriarchy is patriarchy, and that there is no shift from Calvinist theocracy to liberal, sentimental domestic ideology. The shift, as I suggested in the last chapter, was monumentally vexed both because it entailed change and because the changes it entailed were in so many ways paradoxical.

For Irving, the shift was particularly difficult. On the one hand, as the pampered youngest son of a mercantile family, he was encouraged in his literary aspirations by an indulgent, affectional family—precisely the kind of literary and artistic development encouraged by sentimental ideals of child rearing but discouraged by the older patriarchalism. On the other, he was raised as a political and social conservative, and when he found himself unwilling to join one of the conventional "professions,"—as a kind of wit he felt himself to be above such drudgery—he began his writing career as a satirist. The fractures in his own life between artist and conservative, between leisured gentleman and an individual who was required to earn his own bread, seemed to be held together by the support of his brothers and parents and by the prospect of a love match. With the sudden death of his fiancée, the prospects of his own domestic happiness were blighted and his interest in writing, too, seemed to collapse. He turned to his family for support for the next several years, ultimately turning to his brothers' merchant business, only to find himself tangled in the quick collapse of the very business that was to support him. The bankruptcy of his family's business drove him back into literature as a profession, but rather than write the satires of his past, he turned to writing sentimental sketches.

This is perhaps the greatest irony of all, one that may even move us from imaginary identification to, if we put stock in dead people, a hint of real sympathy. First the death of his fiancée fractured the illusion of haven in the family. Fear of sexuality made more sense in the nineteenth century than it does now for the simple reason that the high mortality rate made attachment risky, yet sentimental ideology made it essential. No longer by the turn of the nineteenth century was it commonplace not to name a child until it proved that it was likely to survive; no longer was it considered not only acceptable but a duty to remarry soon after the death of a spouse. The promise of the sentimental family was that emotional attachments were of primary value—the disappointment of mortality was in direct relationship to the importance of the promise. The death of Irving's fiancée obviously damaged his sense of creativity as it damaged his potential for adult procreativity, but the role of child in his parents' family proved to be no better haven. The economic difficulties of his family's business forced him abroad to act as agent, and the ensuing failure of the family's business threw him onto his own resources in a foreign land, not only not supported by, but not in proximity to most of his family. As Williams puts it in his biography of Irving:

> To understand his state of mind at this critical moment [in 1818 with the imminent bankruptcy of his brothers' business], we must realize that his adversities, beginning in 1809, were cumulative. He had lost during this period, before his real adjustment to life, his sister, his father, his mother, and his betrothed, and, so he now feared, that protection of the brothers upon which he had always relied. Lacking seventeen days, the death of his mother occurred just eight years after the bereavement from which he had not yet recovered. At the age of thirty-four, then, he had experienced two great sorrows, and, as he thought at the time, shame. (1: 152)

In the face of such failures of domesticity to provide its promised haven, how was Irving to write effective sentimental sketches that uphold the very beliefs that had so disappointed him?

The answer lies less in Irving's grim determination to become a professional writer than in the galvanic moment that released his creativity. According to Williams, the two years that Irving spent overseeing the demise of his invalid brother Peter's business in Liverpool were two years of despondency. He worked tirelessly to ward off Peter's inevitable bankruptcy, even sinking his own small capital into the effort. But his real hope lay in his determination to be a professional writer, a determination he pursued in his notebooks in his steady, pained, and labored efforts to write various essays and sketches. But in

1818, at the Birmingham home of his brother-in-law and sister, Irving's despondency broke in an evening of reminiscence:

> On an evening in June Irving found himself laughing with his brother-in-law at long-forgotten days in Sleepy Hollow. He fled to his room, but in a different mood; his heart was light: "thoughts came with a rush, faster than he could write them—all the faster, seemingly, for being fettered so long by the ice of his long mental despondency." Until midnight and through the small hours he wrote. At morning the June sun shown through the shutters, revealing him still bent over his table. The Van Warts at breakfast looked up to see him enter, radiant, the fresh manuscript in his hand. "He said it had all come back to him; Sleepy Hollow had awakened him from his long dull, desponding slumber; and then he read the first chapters of "'Rip Van Winkle.'" (1: 168–69)

The source of Irving's artistic creativity, then, is nostalgia, the indulgence of which is a primary feature of sentimental literature, in part because, according to the psychology of associations on which sentimentalism depended, the hold of parental influence over character is contingent on fond memories of childhood. Another of the paradoxes of sentimental domesticity, then, is that progressivism is contingent on nostalgia, and that commercially viable products, such as salable literature, required the manufacture of novel bits of nostalgia.

In the context of these paradoxes, it is possible to read "Rip Van Winkle" less for its "tone . . . of reconciliation and incorporation" than for the "fantasy tinged with terror, [the] dreamwork with hints of nightmare" (Fetterley 8). Irving's tale is about the failures of home precisely because it ties domestic happiness, play, and imaginative creativity to commercial competition. This, indeed, is the social background to Dame Van Winkle's power in the story. She voices the economic imperative of *her* family. Yet to Rip, the possibility of happiness in work can only be located in a nostalgic vision of communal effort. For an adult, the happiness of the home circle is not so easy to develop, especially given that the idea of haven implies that the outside world is antagonistic, and indeed by capitalistic standards it is. This is what Rip rejects, the isolation of himself in competitive adulthood. Rip works for everyone but himself, and in so doing secures companionship but pays the price of his own impoverishment. He seems to desire a larger sense of community, a sense of identity in group that domestic ideology disavows in insisting on the development of individuality constrained only by the bonds of the immediate family. Insofar as Rip is a manifestation of the past, of the Dutch, that is to say European, mentality, he represents a mode of social organization that is not centered in the home of a single married couple.

Perhaps this explains Irving's persistent interest in European, especially British, customs and history. His *Sketch Book* makes much more of England than it does of America, and Geoffrey Crayon's tour, he insists, will not be of the monuments of history, but rather of picturesque byways and such signs of decay as the British Museum or the graves of poets in Westminster Abbey. In later works, such as his Bracebridge Hall sketches, he turned to the English manor to articulate a nostalgia for an economic organization that is not predicated on the individual's success. Sentimentalizing feudalism, Irving's Brace-bridge Hall stories insist on family in the old sense of the word, meaning all who live in one manor regardless of kinship. Irving glorifies feudal connections, rooted in relationships that are not extinguishable by the deaths of individu-als—there is always a lord of the manor, even if individual lords may die. Thus, by Irving's misty rendition, the very existence of the manor is an economic anchor; right relations among the members of this kind of family give each member economic security without excessive labor. Clearly this conservative fantasy is rooted in a sense of powerlessness in the face of the economic uncer-tainties of capitalism.

Given this context, the reconciliation that Fetterley sees as securing the po-litical power of Rip is in fact a forced and unconvincing reconciliation. Rip's redemption is *deus ex machina,* but in a way that does not give one a secure sense of the value of Rip's approach. In fact, the ironic assertion of the veracity of Rip's tale even in the face of the fact that Rip "was observed, at first, to vary on some points every time he told it, which was, doubtless, owing to his having so recently awakened" (53) suggests that Rip simply "lighted out for the territo-ries" until it was safe to come back. Rip has paid an extremely high price for his avoidance of personal responsibility—he has surrendered years of companion-ship and the stability in community that he preferred in the first place. On his return, Rip is first accused of being a traitor, and is only allowed an honored place by virtue of his fantastic story. America does not offer a haven, suggests Irving, unless it is finally built on fiction, on lies—as Irving himself was trying to craft security out of his own kind of lying. In identifying with Rip, then, the reader sees not a ringing endorsement of male power, but a lament that eco-nomic and social circumstances rob men of power. They become pawns not only of mortality, but of economic and political forces that are capricious and uncontrollable. The easy scapegoat is the wife, who, by convention, was to in-spire masculine endeavor, but by Irving's fear of failure, merely goaded men to an impossible task. Irving aligns himself against capitalism, against the new power structure, and inasmuch as his objections are based on a conservative economic and social model, he aligns capitalism with female power and attacks the former through the latter. So at the end of our imaginary identification with Rip, we find that Fetterley is right that Irving's fiction tries to blame women for the woes of the world, but we also find that rather than forcing us to celebrate masculine power, it begs us to lament weakness and insecurity in the face of the powers of capitalism and of mortality.

❋    ❋

If laughter arises from perceiving incongruity, then the incongruities between such divergent readings of the political design of Irving's tale could very well make literary criticism the target of laughter. And indeed, maybe it should be when it takes humor so seriously. After all, Irving began his second writing ca-reer not in gloom but in laughter; laughter in reminiscing over his childhood enabled Irving to remove himself from the weight of his own circumstances.

He created a character who embodied his own fears, exaggerated that character, and then partially denied his own *identification* with Rip. This is why I disagree with Fetterley's reading of "Rip" and with the counterreading that comes from my little thought experiment. Fetterley's argument about the pernicious impact of canonical literature on female readers assumes that all literature forces the reader to identify with the characters being depicted. "In such fictions the female reader is co-opted into participation in an experience from which she is explicitly excluded; she is asked to identify with a selfhood that defines itself in opposition to her; she is required to identify against herself" (xii).

> To be excluded from a literature that claims to define one's identity is to experience a peculiar form of powerlessness—not simply the powerlessness which derives from not seeing one's experience articulated, clarified, and legitimized in art, but more significantly the powerlessness which results from the endless division of self against self, the consequence of the invocation to identify as male while being reminded that to be male—to be universal, to be American—is to be *not female*. . . . Powerlessness is the subject and powerlessness the experience, and the design insists that Rip Van Winkle/Frederic Henry/Nick Carraway/Stephen Rojack speak for us all. (xiii)

The complaint only has value if we are indeed intended to identify with the character, in this case, of Rip Van Winkle.

But Rip is not presented as a character with whom we are to identify. He is lazy, slovenly, cowardly, stupid, ugly, childish—in short, an object of derision. Any of these traits could be presented in a favorable light, especially if we were given some sense of an interiority to latch on to. Yet the narrators, Crayon and Knickerbocker, keep us at arm's length all the while. We are not given enough of the inside of Rip to be able to *identify*, that is to say, to imaginatively make the limits of our own identities coterminous with those of Rip. We can understand his motives, but we are not invited to become Rip. But even as we laugh in derisive superiority to Rip, we are also invited to be sympathetic to some degree. We are given cues to see some of those traits we hold in contempt as traits to be desired. He gets away with laziness and remains a child in the positive sense that he is able to play and be imaginative.

Here is the incongruity that sparks laughter, and it is the laughter of humor rather than of satire precisely because it is a laughter that holds both our desire and our revulsion in suspense. In doing so, the laughter allows for at least some degree of reconciliation in the reader of conflicting elements of the reader's self. Simple identification, as Fetterley suggests, is coercive in that it insists that a reader become an integrated monolithic self. But the natural state of the psyche, fragmented and substantially inchoate, cannot identify fully with a character in fiction without repressing incompatible elements of itself.[10] That is Fetterley's point, in that any woman who is forced to identify against herself is done psychic harm. Indeed, any simple one-to-one identification with a character requires not only internal repression, but projected aggression at "alien" others, others that symbolize the internal repressed. Such is the laughter of scorn. But amiable humor, such as Irving attempts to create in us as we gaze on Rip, holds identification in suspense between the poles of acceptance and rejection. To identify fully with Rip and against his wife is to develop a moping sense of injury, much as I suggested in the thought experiment above. To reject any identification with Rip is to scorn his position, to engage in derisive anger, often tinged with rage as in the case of Fetterley's beautifully composed, caustic attack on Irving and "Rip" *and* as in the case of Dawson's reading of "Rip" as satire. But to laugh without scorn at Rip is a way of acknowledging internal inconsistencies and tensions.

In Irving's case, he seems to have found, at least provisionally, a way to balance his attraction to sentiment and domesticity against his disappointments. On its own terms, then, "Rip" was reconciling Irving's "feminine" side of himself, the artistic side, the side that would create literature, with the "masculine" side of himself, the side that would turn literature into a profession when hitherto it had been held to be an avocation of either gentlemen or, increasingly, of gentrified "ladies" whose job in "sketching" was to beautify and ennoble the households in which they were becoming economically irrelevant. In "Rip Van Winkle," Irving scorns that femininity, yet also acknowledges its value to him, not as a gentleman dabbler in the arts, but as a professional writer who merely hides behind the persona of Geoffrey Crayon, gent.

Specifically, in "Rip Van Winkle," as Fetterley points out, "Rip rejects the conventional image of masculinity and the behavior traditionally expected of an adult male and identifies himself with characteristics and behaviors assumed to be feminine and assigned to women" (5). Among these are passivity, meekness, compliance, and a proclivity to gossip. This latter is perhaps the most important; Rip is an inveterate teller of tales, the truth of which has little to do with the pleasure he and his audiences take in them. His play with the neighborhood children is marked by his tendency to tell them "long stories of ghosts, witches, and Indians" (39). His "junto" of equally idle men spend their days "talking listlessly over village gossip or telling endless sleepy stories about nothing" (41). When finally enshrined in the village after the death of his wife, he is appreciated as "a chronicle of the old time 'before the war,'" and "he used to tell his story to every stranger that arrived at Mr. Doolittle's hotel" (53). As I've already mentioned, it is this tale that enables him to overcome the charge that he has betrayed his people. Yet the narrative structure of the piece suggests that Rip *has* betrayed his people, not only in that he has not inherited the "martial character of his ancestors" (39) or because he has spawned a son who will be no better than himself, but because he is, like his chronicler, Diedrich Knickerbocker, idle. Geoffrey Crayon, a character who is in no position to pass such judgment, has already commented on Knickerbocker's worthlessness on the same grounds that Dame Van Winkle condemned Rip's: "his time might have been much better employed in weightier labors" (35). Telling stories is not worth the time of a man who should be engaged in the weighty labor of making a living.

Here, then, is Irving's newest incarnation, Geoffrey Crayon, gent., whose leisured idleness takes him into odd corners of Europe so that he can sketch for our pleasure, commenting on writing itself as something lightweight. Yet he also defends Knickerbocker for having intended no harm. Crayon is telling us that the intention is all, and as Rip never intends to offend, and so earns the appreciative ear of most of the women in his village, so Irving is telling his readers not to judge Crayon, and ultimately himself, as the child of a martial race, but instead as a gentle soul. He asks his readers to read the book as a piece of sentiment. In that way, in begging his readers to indulge him, he turns an idle pastime to serious business. He is beholden to the sentimental distinctions of appropriateness—appropriateness of jests, of sentiments, of gendered behavior—to make his living, but he has to play both sides of the fence to do it. That incongruity is the source of the rage he directs at women, and it is also the source of the laugh he directs at himself, the laugh that lasted him all the way to the bank.

## II.  Fanny Fern: "It's a Way I Have When I Can't Find a Razor Handy to Cut My Throat"

Irving was alone neither in his rage of disappointment at the promises of sentimental domesticity nor in his ability to use sentimental fiction to transmute that rage to money. Sara Willis Parton, under the pen name Fanny Fern, frequently transmuted her pain into comedy. As she wrote to a reader who praised her humor, "You labor under the hallucination that I felt *merry* when I wrote all that nonsense! *Not a bit of it;* it's a way I have when I can't find a razor handy to cut my throat."[11] Apparently her sublimation of pain had market value. She became the most highly paid journalist of her day, commanding in 1855 the unheard-of price of one hundred dollars per column for the *New York Ledger*. In her 1857 volume of collected journalism, *Fresh Leaves*, she wrote in the preface that she was including "'The hundred-dollar-a-column story,' respecting the remuneration of which, skeptical paragraphists have afforded me so much amusement. (N. B.—My banker and I can afford to laugh!)" (v). Fanny Fern is another sentimental humorist laughing through tears all the way to the bank.

It is important to stress that Parton wrote through the conventions of sentimental sketches, and that her stories designed to evoke tears, what we now call "sentimental," are the measuring stick by which one must judge her comic output. According to her biographer, Joyce W. Warren, the tear-jerkers were merely a smoke screen for the satirist, who, in a very practical sense, attacked the bastions of masculine privilege in a patriarchal world. Granting that Warren is merely over-reacting to the characterization of Fanny Fern as "the grandmother of all sob sisters" by the likes of Fred Lewis Pattee, it is important to note how often Fanny Fern did strike the lachrymose chord. Notice, for instance, that her first several hundred-dollar columns were a serial story, titled "Fanny Ford," that jerks many more tears than it elicits laughs or even smiles.

Basically, "Fanny Ford" is the story of the marriage of Fanny Ford to Percy Lee. The tale begins with Percy falling in love with Fanny's mother, Mary Ford, only to have the marriage prevented by the arrest and conviction of Percy for embezzlement. Percy was susceptible to crime, especially as, living in fashionable New York and running with a rather dissolute crowd, he had not yet allowed himself to be morally redeemed by the piety of his innocent bride-to-be. Mary was the only child of a rich tailor, a man whose penurious and unscrupulous business machinations enabled him to rise from a working-class background to wealth and position. His daughter, though, seems to have held onto the superior virtue of her family's earlier self-reliant republicanism. A paragon of not only beauty but fidelity, she, at the word of her lover's fall into crime, falls into a trance. Her father, in grief over his daughter's grief, which he blames in part on his own social climbing, quickly loses control of his financial empire, curses god, and—experiences a sentimental change of heart the day before he dies. His wife, fearing for her daughter's future, marries her off to a dissolute former companion of Percy Lee. The heroine, still in a trance, bears a daughter, Fanny, before dying in childbirth; the child's father quickly thereafter marries a dancer-prostitute and renounces Fanny. After sequestering his daughter and mother-in-law in the garret of his mansion for some years, he finally dies of dissipation.

Grandmother and Fanny flee to the country, eking out a bare existence, where they meet with a poor peddlar, the recently released but unrecognized convict, Percy Lee. He, on seeing the daughter of his dead fiancée and after the fortuitous death of the grandmother, declares himself to be Fanny's uncle. He becomes her legal guardian, boarding her with a kind old woman and then at a school while he, traveling the while, works diligently but honestly to amass enough money to support a family. He then returns to Fanny after several years apart, and marries her. His former jailer tries to interrupt the wedding, but gets in a fight with a policeman at the church door and is shot dead. The end.

Lachrymose and melodramatic, this tale is nothing if not sentimental. If such is the fare Parton served in her first installments of the grand one-hundred-dollar column, it seems reasonable to call her a sentimentalist in both the current sense of the word—that is, as a writer of tearjerkers—and in the broader old sense of the word.[12]

This story is far from Parton's best, and as a modern reader I share Warren's feeling that Parton writes best when she writes comedy, especially sharply ironic satire that lays open to critical scrutiny the pretenses of sentimental domesticity, especially when it was used to deny women freedom and equality. Nonetheless, this story, like the bulk of her tales of pathos, is an index to Parton's moral values, the ones she developed in ways more interesting to us in her comic sketches. The tale is replete with Parton's favorite homilies. She attacks capitalists who amass money by exploiting their workers; she attacks Calvinists who are more concerned with outward forms of humility—and humiliation—than with Christian charity; she attacks educators who treat children as miniature adults to be forced into conformity. She encourages strive-and-succeed business ethics for men. She rejects as a scandalous barbarism any forced marriage for the sake of money; the only true marriage, she insists, is one based on mutual love. She insists that feminine purity and piety are powerful incentives toward the spiritual redemption of worldly men, as long as those men are capable of true love. In short, she endorses almost all of the commonplaces of sentimental domesticity and sentimental religion as alternatives to Calvinist patriarchalism.

This story, though, is different from Parton's usual newspaper columns in that it is both long and is held together by a plot. She worked mostly with the sketch, and even the long tale moves more as a string of sketches, each with its own moral force, than as a narrative. Consider, for instance, chapter 8, which has an interpolated conversation between two farmers, who advance the plot not at all; they do nothing more than provide an incorrect explanation of Mr. Ford's death. As far as they are concerned, retirement killed a man who spent his life working. Since we know he dies of a broken heart, their speculations do not serve our understanding of the story at all. The interpolated conversation really serves no other purpose than to show different ideals of child rearing, with Calvinist farmer Pike failing to discipline his boys no matter how much he wields the birch rod, and farmer Rice explaining that the more one checks children, the more likely they are to go wrong:

> Scolding never does any good no how—the boy is good enough by natur'—good as you was, I dare say, when you was his age. I wouldn't give a cent for a boy that hain't no friskiness about him, no sperrit like; but you see you don't know how to manage him. You are allers scolding, just as you say. . . . I tell you, Pike, it is enough to discourage any lad, such a constant growling and pecking; now I want my boys to love me when they grow up. I don't want them glad to see the old man's back turned. I don't want them happier any where than at their own home. That's the way drunkards and profligates are made—that's the way the village tavern thrives. I tell you, Pike, if you lace up natur too tight, she'll bust out somewhere. Better draw it mild. (*Fresh Leaves* 149)

Parton's anti-Calvinistic moralizing is more the point than is the plot, but the tone in this part of the narrative is comic. What is unusual about her long narrative, then, is that she does not maintain a consistent tone in it.

Typically, Parton's sketches work very hard to create a single mood for the entire piece. The exceptions are the several sketches that are made of two opposing subsketches, such as "Look on This Picture, and Then on That" (*Ruth* 250; see also *Fresh Leaves* 16), in which she sketches two households, one in which the paterfamilias is a forbidding tyrant, the other in which he is a loving companion to his wife and playmate to his children. Again, Parton's situation in the vanguard of sentimental domesticity as a progressive alternative to rigid partriarchalism is obvious; what needs commentary is the way in which she creates each sketch to be a perfect emblem in order to encourage the reader to feel pure dread over the first sketch, and pure joy over the second. Like Irving, Parton strives for emotional clarity in each sketch. To do so she creates a very flexible persona in Fanny Fern, one whose characteristics change in order to serve the emotional needs of the sketch she presents. For instance, in one sketch of advice to young women Fern talks of her husband "Mr. Fern" (February 14, 1852; qtd. in *Ruth* 225), yet in another advice column declares "Now *I* intend to be an 'old maid'" (June 12, 1852; qtd. in *Ruth* 230).

Similarly, in some of her columns she declares her antipathy to all men, calling them liars and hypocrites, as, for instance, in "Fern View of Napoleon as a Husband," where she attacks Napoleon's hypocrisy in his treatment of Josephine with the dismissive "How very like a man!" (*Fresh Leaves* 74). Yet in other sketches she declares her love of men, sometimes of their gallantry, sometimes of their capacities for love and constancy, and sometimes for their secondary sexual characteristics, as in the two adjacent sketches in *Fresh Leaves*, "The Confession Box" and "A Word to Parents and Teachers." In the former she confesses, "If all the men in New York had as handsome a beard as the editor of the _____, I would not object to see them h—air 'em" (265); the scandal of the pun to a nineteenth century audience, suggesting that Fern would be willing to join a harem for a good beard, shows how far she was willing to stretch her persona's character when her jokes required it.[13] Similarly, in the second sketch, which primarily tells teachers and parents not to torture children with too much schooling at an early age, she uses sexual innuendo to suggest that she lost her math anxiety when she reached puberty: "The multiplication table was the rock on which I was scholastically wrecked; my total inability to ascertain 'if John had ten apples, and Thomas took away three, how many John would have left,' having often caused me to wish that all the Johns in creation were—well, never mind that, now. I have learned to like Johns since!" (166). *The Oxford English Dictionary* assures us that *john* as a slang term for the client of a prostitute did not come into use in print in the United States until 1911; trusting the accuracy of the *O.E.D.*, we can assume Fern is using the word in two of its other slang forms: one, as a synonym for "man," "guy," "fellow," and two, through her quick juxtaposition of "John" with "Thomas," as a synonym for "penis."

For a final example of Fern's tendency to voice opposing opinions, consider her inconsistent opinions of marriage and child rearing. She usually voices her commonplace adoration of children, both in their beauty, as in "Best Things" when she says, "For statuary, fill my house with children, rosy, dimpled, laughing children" (*Fern Leaves, Second Series* 162) and because they are supposedly angels on earth, as she says in "Glances at Philadelphia": "Blessed childhood—thy shortest life, though but a span, hath yet its mission. The tiniest babe never laid its velvet cheek on the sod till it had delivered its Maker's message—heeded not then, perhaps—but coming to the wakeful ear in the silent night, long after the little preacher was in the dust. Blessed childhood!" (238–39). Not surprisingly, in the same sketch she says of breast feeding: "Beautiful as bountiful provision of Nature! which, if there was no other proof of God, would suffice for me" (236). Yet, much of her satiric output is directed against husbands and against the tyrannies of household management. Sometimes she even goes so far as to include children in her denunciations of domesticity, as in "Sunshine and Young Mothers." Responding to the commonplace that "every woman was made for a mother, consequently, babies are as necessary to their 'peace of mind' as health," Fern adopts the voice of an "old maid" to attack a bromide she so often endorses:

> NOW I WON'T STAND THAT! I'm an old maid myself; and I'm neither melancholy nor indigestible! My "PIECE of mind" I'm going to give you, (in a minute!) and I never want to *touch* a baby except with a *pair of tongs!* "Young mothers and sunshine!" Worn to fiddling strings before they are twenty-five! When an old lover turns up he thinks he sees his grandmother, instead of the dear little Mary who used to make him feel as if he should crawl out of the toes of his boots! Yes my mind is *quite* made up about *matrimony;* but as to the *"babies,"* (sometimes I think, and then again I don't know!) but on *the whole I believe* I consider 'em a d————ecided humbug! (*Ruth* 231; see also *Fern Leaves, Second Series* 144)

The parenthetical hesitation notwithstanding, Fern makes her thoughts unequivocal in this piece by flirting with the word "damned." Still, in the same book in which she anthologized "Sunshine and Young Mothers," she included an attack on suffragettes by assuming the propriety of women's role as nursemaid to children and husband: "Wives rant of their 'Woman's Rights' in public; husbands eat bad dinners and tend crying babies at home." ("Hour-Glass Thoughts," *Fern Leaves, Second Series* 124).[14]

The examples I have cited so far should show that Parton's persona as readily acts the clown as it does the chorus of a tragedy, as readily the iconoclast as the censor, often on the same subject. Her repertoire of topics, while large, is not so large that she doesn't recycle them—many times—but she rarely repeats them in the same mood. Indeed, to sentimentalist Fern, mood, as the manifestation of subjectivity, is an essential part of truth.[15] She virtually brags in her preface to her first book, *Fern Leaves from Fanny's Port Folio,* that her very inconsistencies will, when read sympathetically, yield a deeply human connection: "Some of the articles are sad, some are gay; each is independent of all the others, and the work is consequently disconnected and fragmentary; but, if the reader will imagine me peeping over his shoulder, quite happy should he pay me the impromptu compliment of a smile or a tear, it is possible we may come to a good understanding by the time the book shall have been perused" (vi). If she is to tell the truth about, say, married life, she is going to have to tell about all of the moods it brings, from euphoria to depression and everything in between. She does this, but in pieces, with each sketch standing distinct from all others in its emotional clarity.[16] Frequently, when her persona cannot compass a point of view or a feeling, she extends her emotional range by speaking not through her pseudonym, but through the voice of another character.

Even though her moods shift radically from sketch to sketch, and the conclusions she draws about the married state appear to vary as much, the straight pieces in Parton's oeuvre reflect with mirrorlike fidelity the system of values she holds in her satires. While her moods shift from piece to piece, the ideals by which she judges and feels about human behavior for the most part do not—

at least not while she sticks in the sermonistic mode with which nineteenth-century writers and readers felt most comfortable.[17] She was quick to turn from direct exhortation to satire, with the primary differences being of tone and stance as she uses sarcastic irony in her satires to invert the values she promulgates straight in other places. For example, compare the sermon "Something to Come Home To" (*Ruth* 330) to the satire "The Tear of a Wife" (236):

> *Something to come home to!* That is what saves a man. Somebody there to grieve if he is not true to himself. Somebody there to be sorry if he is troubled or sick. Somebody there, with fingers like sunbeams, gliding and brightening whatever they touch; and all for him. I look at the business men of New York, at nightfall, coming swarming "up town" from their stores and counting-rooms; and when I see them, as I often do, stop and buy one of those tiny bouquets as they go, I smile to myself; for although it is a little attention toward a wife, I know how happy that rose with its two geranium leaves, and its sprig of mignonette will make her. He thought of *her* coming home! Foolish, do you call it? Such folly makes all the difference between stepping off, scarcely conscious of the cares a woman carries, or staggering wearily along till she faints disheartened under their burthen. *Something to go home to!* That man felt it, and by ever so slight a token wished to recognize it. God bless him, I say, and all like him, who do not take home-comforts as stereotyped matters of course, and God bless the family estate; I can't see that anything better has been devised by the wiseacres who have experimented on the Almighty's plans. (331)

In talking of "stereotyped matters," Fern is among the early users of a term for a technique of replicating a form of set type as a metaphor to suggest uniformity. In this, she is suggesting that the essence of domestic bliss is mutual appreciation of individual effort. Her apostrophe to God's sanction of such an organization of home is in keeping with liberal Christian stress on religious nurture of individual souls in the one social institution capable of addressing individual needs.

None of these values is any different in "The Tear of a Wife," her satiric attack on those marriages in which men did "take home comforts as stereotyped matters of course:"

> "The tear of a loving girl is like a dew-drop on a rose; but on
> the cheek of a wife, is a drop of poison to her husband."

> It is "an ill wind that blows *nobody* any good. Papas will be happy to hear that twenty-five dollar pocket handkerchiefs can be dispensed with *now* in the bridal *trousseau*. Their "occupation's gone"! Matrimonial tears "are poison." There is no knowing what you will do, girls, with that escape-valve shut off; but that is no more to the point, than—whether you have anything to smile at or not; one thing is settled—*you mustn't cry!* Never mind back aches, and side aches, and head aches, and dropsical complaints, and smoky chimneys, and old coats, and young babies! *Smile! It flatters your husband.* He wants to be *considered* the source of your happiness, whether he was baptized *Nero* or *Moses!* Your mind *never* being supposed to be occupied with any other subject than himself, of course a tear is a tacit reproach. Besides, you miserable little whimperer, what have you to cry for?

A-i-n-t y-o-u m-a-r-r-i-e-d? Isn't that the *summum bonum*—the height of feminine ambition? You *can't* get beyond *that!* It's the *jumping-off place!* You've
arriv!—got to the end of your journey! Stage puts up *there!* You've nothing to do
but retire on your laurels, and spend the rest of your life endeavoring to be thankful that you are Mrs. John Smith! *"Smile!" you simpleton! (Ruth* 236)

Nothing in this piece necessarily attacks marriage as an institution. While it
can be read as such, in light of the other sketch, it seems more likely that what
Fanny Fern attacks is the way some men took for granted the subordination of
women in the domestic sphere. The piece suggests that reciprocity is the fundamental value on which marriage should be based; without it, individualism
taints the relationship, with women marrying for the status and men taking advantage of women's economic need.

The ironical "Tear of a Wife" makes its point through sarcasm laid on with a
trowel. Irony unchecked may be nihilistic, but, as much as some of her recent
commentators might wish it to be so, irony in Parton's hands does not spin into
pure iconoclasm.[18] She holds it in check by the positive values invoked by the
very emotional fervor that calls forth the sarcasm. Nothing subtle about her
irony; nothing radically dangerous in it either. What checks it is her total commitment to sympathy as the touchstone of moral rectitude. In a large number
of her pieces she explicitly sets forth sympathy as her moral standard, and her
fear that sympathy is too weak to bridge the gaps between rich and poor, men
and women, is the source of her anger in sketch after sketch. As she put it most
clearly in "What Shall We Do?" she holds selfish contentment in contempt if it
interferes with the power of an active heart to sympathize with the oppressed
and unfortunate even if that heart is incapable of doing anything to mitigate
suffering. Having first described her own inability to ignore the trouble of others because she is "so constituted that injustice and wrong to others rouses [her]
as if it were done to [her]self," she attacks men who can remain indifferent to
the world "if *their selfish present* be undisturbed. Well, rather than be *that* torpid
thing, and *it a man*, I would rather be a woman tied hand and foot, bankrupt in
chances, and worry over what I am powerless to help. At least I can stand at my
post, like a good soldier, because it *is* my post; meantime—I had rather be taken
off that by a chance shot, than rust in a corner with ossification of the heart"
(*Ruth* 336–37). By this standard, Parton insists that men, too, must learn to
cultivate their hearts, to become women's equals in moral sensitivity if they are
to live with any moral purposes. It is by this standard that she judges a certain
class of men who die of hardened hearts and in the process kill the women they
abuse by failing to love. Any man incapable of sympathizing with a woman's
humanity deserves, in Parton's view, the pure, uncomplicated scorn of "The
Tear of a Wife."

Yet sermon and satire were not Parton's only modes, and her pseud-onym,
which gave her flexibility in developing moods, also gave her the flexibility to
use humor to examine ideas she couldn't in less flexible modes. Humor is, to
Fanny Fern, a saving attack on seriousness, a defense against outrage and sensitivity. I already cited at the beginning of this section Fern's remark that she

uses laughter to ward off suicide. Discounting the statement for her characteristic hyperbole, the remark tells us that laughter was nonetheless her antidote to excessive sensibility, either in sympathy or in feeling one's own pain.

In treating sympathy, Fern gives advice to wives that they should not in all cases indulge by sympathizing with their husbands' bad moods. In "Don't Disturb Him," anthologized in *Fern Leaves, Second Series* as "Sober Husbands" (192–93), she argues that vigorous teasing is the way to restore a husband's good mood and, in the process, his health.

> I wouldn't stop [teasing him] for the Great Mogul, till I had shortened his long face to my liking. Certainly, he'd "get vexed;" there shouldn't be any fun in teasing him if he didn't'; and that would give his melancholy blood a good, healthful start; and his eyes would snap and sparkle, and he'd say, "Fanny WILL you be quiet or not?" and I should laugh, and pull his whiskers, and say decidedly, *"Not!"* and then should tell him he hadn't the slightest idea how handsome he looked when he was vexed, and then he would pretend not to hear the compliment— but would pull up his dickey, and take a sly peep in the glass (for all that!) and then he'd begin to grow amiable, and get off his stilts, and be just as agreeable all the rest of the evening *as if he wasn't my husband;* and all because I didn't follow that stupid bit of advice "to let him alone." (*Ruth* 251)

Implicitly, Parton tells us that the vitality of marriage, the possibility of keeping it from descending into a relation of bored complacency, depends on keeping a playful tension alive. Too close a sympathy between man and woman depresses both into the conventional boredom of the "stereotyped" acceptance of one another not as individuals but as furniture. Laughter is vital; sympathy runs the risk of being morbid.

More dangerous, according to Parton, than taking the glooms of others too seriously is to take one's own self too seriously. In "Fanny Ford," one of the comic asides occurs when Fanny Ford's boarding-school roommate teases her about the possibility of marriage. Ford takes the prospect quite seriously, and this encourages the roommate to make fun of marriage itself by describing it as a battle for dominance between men and women:

> Fanny laughed—"I suppose you think to wind *your* husband round your little finger, like a skein of silk."
> "With Cupid's help," replied Kate, with mock humility.
> "Of course, *you* will be quite perfect;—never, for instance, appear before your husband in curl papers or slip-shod?" asked Fanny; "never make him eat bad pies or puddings?"
> "That depends," answered Kate, "if he is tractable—not; if not—why not?"
> "You will wink at his cigars?"
> "He might do worse."
> "You will patronize his moustache?"
> "If he will my snuff-box," said Kate, laughing. "Heigho—I feel just like a cat in want of a mouse to torment. I wish I knew a victim worthy to exercise my talents upon."
> "*Talons,* you mean," retorted Fanny—"I pity him. . . . Kate, why do you al-

ways choose to wear a mask?" asked Fanny; "why do you take so much pains to make a censorious world believe you the very *opposite* of what you are?"

"Because paste passes as current as diamond; because I value the world's opinion not one straw; because if you own a heart, it is best to hide it, unless you want it trampled on." (*Fresh Leaves* 199–200)

Here Parton argues for the value of laughter as defense against a cruel world, but implicitly, the defense is also internal; laughter prevents Kate—or Parton—from feeling the motions of her own heart with too great a sensitivity.

In "The Advantages of a House in a Fashionable Square" (*Fern Leaves, Second Series*), a story of a family of social climbers who are painfully rejected by the snobs whom they have been courting, laughter does better than insulate the sufferers from their own pain; it enables them to see that they had misplaced their desires on a false goal. The story begins with a happy family in modest circumstances happily living within its quickly growing means, when the "lady" of the house falls under the sway of a "fashionable woman," Mrs. John Hunter, who denigrates everything modest and middle-class about their existence. Happiness is blighted as the family tries to live up to new standards. When they assemble all of the trappings of wealth and are still rejected by old money, they renounce their social climbing and move to the country, where they "have once more recovered their equanimity, and can afford to laugh when 'St. John's Square' and Mrs. Hunter are mentioned" (58). Parton shows healing and laughter as reciprocal, and best indulged by those who are without pretensions. To Parton, then, laughter of high spirits, not of satiric scorn, is a saving grace. Not only does it restore health to the depressed and protect the sensitive from heartache, it restores perspective and thereby enables good-hearted people to navigate the moral dangers of a complex world. In this she seems to subscribe to the sentimentalist's vision of humor.

Such humor is not found in the bulk of Fanny Fern's output; far more common is the satiric note. Some few of the humorous pieces are character sketches designed to extend, through indulgent laughter, our appreciation to characters not usually in the range of our affection. For instance "Aunt Hepsy," in *Fern Leaves, Second Series*, is a sketch of an old woman shopkeeper who, despite her age, poverty, and widowhood, is a universal favorite. The piece ends with her marriage to a rich old man to the spiteful envy of a neighboring "old maid" who wonders, "How do you suppose she did it?" The answer to the "enigma" of "how universally popular was Aunt Hepsy" is that Hepsy is courteous and tactful to all and spreads her sunny disposition on anyone, from the urchins who buy penny candy in her shop to the rich old gentleman who "Ventured into Aunt Hepsy's shop one day, to buy a watch-ribbon." The tale expounds no explicit moral, but makes clear the values of a democratic politeness and good humor not only to advance one's shopkeeping, but to advance one's human relations.

Other humorous sketches serve to teach readers how to feel about certain difficult situations, such as, in "Our First Nurse," the birth of one's first child. This sketch tells of the tyrannies exercised over the first-person narrator and her husband when they finish the "furnish[ing]" (*Fresh Leaves* 47) of their house with their first baby. While they are immune to the lure of luxuries and so can live in republican modesty, they assume they must have a nurse.

> We had, to be sure, a vague idea that we must have one, and *as* vague an idea of what a nurse was. We thought her a good kind of creature who understood baby-dom, and never interfered with any little family arrangements.
>
> Not a bit of it!
>
> The very first thing she did was to make preparation to sleep in my room, and send Charley off into a desolate spare chamber. Charley! *my* Charley! whose shaving operations I had watched with the intensest interest; mixing up little foam seas of "lather" for him, handing him little square bits of paper to wipe his razor upon, and applying nice bits of courtplaster, when he accidentally cut his chin while we were laughing. . . . well, any one, unless a bachelor or old maid, who reads this, can see that it was perfectly ridiculous. (47–48)

Ridiculous or not, the nurse has her way, supplanting the husband and infantilizing the wife, insisting that the new mother is weaker after bearing a child than she in fact is. The narrator tells, in humorous fashion, of her conspiracy with her husband to undermine the nurse's authority, and when the nurse accuses them of being children (one assumes because they like to laugh) "that was the last drop in our cup. Charley paid her, and I was so glad when she went that I laughed till I cried" (51).

To this point, the tale argues that each nuclear family must learn to be self-reliant if it wishes to secure its own happiness. But the consequence of self-reliance can be exhaustion in carrying the burden of a household alone, and it can be fear of ignorance when cut off from the knowledge of both an extended family and of specialist servants. At this juncture, Parton uses humor to suggest that difficulties can be sources of pleasure when viewed humorously:

> We both drew a long breath and sat down and looked at the new baby—*our* baby; and Charley asked me about its little sleeping habits, and I told him, with a shake of the head, that I could not speak definitely on that point; and then we discussed, in a whisper, the respective merits of cribs and cradles, and the propriety of teaching it, at an early period, that impressive line of Mrs. Hemans:
>
> "Night is the time for sleep;"
>
> and then Charley got up, and exchanged his musical boots for a noiseless pair of slippers, and changed the position of the shovel, tongs, and poker, and oiled the creaking hinge of the closet door, and laid a chair over the squeaking board in the floor, that he might not tread on it, and with one eye on the baby, gently shaded the lamp; and then he looked at me, and gave a little sort of congratulatory nod, and then he drew off his vest and hung it over a chair, and then—out rattled a perfect tempest of half dollars, quarters, shillings, and sixpences, on the hearth! Of course, the baby woke (frightened out of a year's growth), and screamed until it was black in the face. In vain its poor, inexperienced papa kissed it, scratching its little velvet face with his rough whiskers the while! In vain we both walked the floor with it. The fire went out, the lamp went; and just at daybreak it came to us like a revelation, the sarcastic tone of that hateful old nurse, as she said, "Good-by; I hope you'll get along *comfortably* with the dear baby!"

And so we did. Do you suppose one night's watching was going to quench our love, either for the baby, or for each other? No—nor a thousand like it! for, as Dr Watts, or Saxe, hath it, "It was one of the kind that was not born to die." (51–52)

The last "it" in the last paragraph has an ambiguous antecedent, but the best is "love." Parton says that love is not born to die over household tribulations. The possessive pronouns about owning husband and baby make it clear that she sees the possession of the proper emotional bias of love tempered by humor to be the root of domestic bliss.

These two examples show that Parton used humor not only to embrace "humorous" characters, but also to develop a perceptual flexibility, a way of transmuting potentially disturbing situations into sources of pleasure. This flexibility is the source of perhaps her most interesting kinds of sketches, the sketches of fantasy selves that allow her to escape from her anger, that allow her to explore human possibilities that the culture's ideology may predict but not allow.

Specifically, in spite of Parton's apparent acceptance of the culture's extreme postulate of significant physical, mental, and moral difference between men and women, Fanny Fern uses humor to explore both the meaning of sexual and gender difference and the possibilities of radical equality in her fantasies of cross-dressing. The cross-dressing sketches at times come out of her anger over injustice, as in the case of the companion pieces Warren anthologizes in *Ruth Hall and Other Writings*, "A Law More Nice Than Just" and "A Law More Nice Than Just, Number II" (299–304). In these, Fern begins with a political pretext of attacking the injustice of municipal laws that bar women from wearing pants. But in these two pieces she quickly drops the political cause in favor of a report of her fantasies of and experiments in wearing men's garb. In other cases, such as "Summer Travel" (*Fresh Leaves* 56–58), the fantasy is contingent on the inconveniences of women's clothing and roles, but is not sparked by outrage over injustice. In both cases, she plays with definitions of masculine and feminine to imagine what is essential and what merely costumary.

In "A Law More Nice Than Just," Fern's experience of cross-dressing is depicted as essentially comic in order to free it from the danger of trying to transgress laws or "fundamental" sex roles. In the process she insists on the differences in male and female shape and on "feminine" facility with pins and needles as a way of assuring her readers that she is not trying to homogenize the sexes:

One evening, after a long rainy day of scribbling, when my nerves were in double-twisted knots, and I felt as if myriads of little ants were leisurely travelling over me, and all for want of the walk which is my daily salvation, I stood at the window, looking at the slanting, persistent rain, and took my resolve: "*I'll do it,*" said I, audibly, planting my slipper upon the carpet. "Do what?" asked Mr. Fern, looking up from a big book. "Put on a suit of your clothes and take a tramp with you," was the answer. "You dare not," was the rejoinder; "you are a little coward, only saucy on paper." It was the work of a moment, with such a challenge, to fly up stairs and overhaul my philosopher's wardrobe. Of course we had fun. Tailors must be a stingy set, I remarked, to be so sparing of their cloth, as I struggled into a pair of their handiwork, undeterred by the vociferous laughter of the wretch who had solemnly vowed to "cherish me" through all my tribulations. "Upon my word, everything seems to be narrow where it ought to be broad, and the waist of this coat might be made from a hogshead; and, ugh! this shirt collar is cutting my ears off, and you have not a decent cravat in the whole lot, and your vests are frights, and what am I to do with my hair?" Still no reply from Mr. Fern, who lay on the floor, faintly ejaculating, between his fits of laughter, "Oh, my! by Jove!—oh! by Jupiter!" Was that to hinder me? Of course not. Strings and pins, women's never-failing resort, soon brought broadcloth and kerseymere to terms. (*Ruth* 300–301)

All of these assurances and her husband's raucous laughter to assure us that such an experiment is merely in jest notwithstanding, the change in costume is only the outward sign of Fanny Fern's willing adoption of masculine competitiveness: she rises to the bait of a dare, just like a schoolboy. The piece ends with her assertion that her experiment is going to end in a determined effort to learn to dress and walk like a man so that she can walk when and where she will—in order to preserve her health. That minor caveat does not really stand in the way of the expansive sense of freedom that she projects in this fantasy of gender neutrality. She makes it clear that no essential difference between men and women impedes her freedom.

What is important to notice about this fantasy is that Fern couches it, as she so often couches her calls to reform of gender relations, in the terms of equality under God: "I've as good a right to preserve the healthy body God gave me, as if I were not a woman" (302). As much, then, as she is willing to push the boundaries of social behavior in the name of equality, she only does so under the sanction of "God's" nature. This intellectual framework explains not only Parton's willingness to push the limits, but her inability to use humor to push them very far. Her very next column for the *New York Ledger* shows her recoiling in fright from the sexual implications of her own fantasy. Her next Fanny Fern column begins, "After all, having tried it I affirm, that nothing reconciles a woman quicker to her femininity, than an experiment in male apparel" (302). She says she misses the little politenesses that women receive from men, but the real fear is not that she will lose her femininity so much as that she will come to find women sexually attractive:

To have to jump on the cars when in motion, and scramble yourself on to the platform as best you may without a helping hand; to be nudged roughly in the ribs by the conductor with, "your fare, sir?" to have your pretty little toes trod on, and no healing "beg your pardon," applied to the smart; to have all those nice-looking men who used to make you such crushing bows, and give you such insinuating smiles, pass you without the slightest interest in your coat tails, and perhaps push you against the wall or into the gutter, with a word tabooed by the clergy. In fine, to dispense with all those delicious little politenesses, (for men are great bears to each other,) to which one has been accustomed, and yet feel no inclination to take advantage of one's corduroys and secure an equivalent by making interest with the "fair sex," stale to you as a thrice-told tale. Isn't *that* a situation? . . . Take it all and all, though, I thank the gods I am a woman. I had rather be loved than make love; though I could beat the makers of it out and out, if I did not think it my duty to refrain out of regard to their feelings, and the final disappointment of the deluded women! But—oh, dear, I want to do such a quantity of "improper" things, that there is not the slightest real harm in doing. (302–3)

I cut the quotation here to insist on the peculiar juxtaposition of the last two sentences. In the original, there is a paragraph break between them, as she goes on to talk of the harmlessly improper things as "I want the free use of my ankles, for this summer at least, to take a journey." Innocuous enough, but the quick juxtaposition with the fantasy of her sexual attractiveness to women makes a different point entirely. She seems to be saying, even as she disavows it, that she finds both men and women attractive, that making love is pleasurable to contemplate for the active challenge. She says she is passively "feminine" at the very moment she makes clear her desire for the freedom men have to be active and aggressive.

Perhaps this is most true of her writing when she is being most conventionally sexist in her attacks on women. In sketch after sketch, she describes women as catty, as competitive with one another, as incapable of friendship or compassion for one another if they share the same station and aspirations. Nowhere is this more shocking to the late-twentieth-century reader than in her hypocritical denunciation of female physicians in the sketch "Lady Doctors":

And so the female doctors are prospering and getting practice. I am sure I am heartily glad of it, for several reasons; one of which is, that it is an honest and honorable deliverance from the everlasting, non-remunerating, consumptive-provoking, monotonous needle. Another is, that it is a more excellent way of support, than by the mercenary and un-retraceable road, through the church-door to the altar, into which so many non-reliant women are driven. Having said this I feel at liberty to remark that we all have our little fancies, and one of mine is, that a hat is a pleasanter object of contemplation in a sick-room than a bonnet. I think, too, that my wrist reposes more comfortably in a big hand than a little one, and if my mouth is to be inspected, I prefer submitting it to a beard than to a flounce. Still, this may be a narrow prejudice—I dare say it is—but like most of my prejudices, I am afraid no amount of fire will burn it out of me.

A female doctor! Great Esculapius! Before swallowing her pills (of which she would be the first), I should want to make sure that I had never come between her and a lover, or a new bonnet, or been the innocent recipient of a gracious smile from her husband. If I desired her undivided attention to my case, I should first remove the looking-glass, and if a consultation seemed advisable, I should wish to arm myself with a gridiron, or a darning-needle, or some other appropriate weapon, before expressing such a wish. If my female doctor recommended a blister on my head, I should strongly doubt its necessity if my hair happened to be handsome, also the expediency of a scar-defacing plaster for my neck, if it happened to be plump and white. Still, these may be little prejudices; very like they are; but this I will say, before the breath is taken out of me by any female doctor, that while I am in my sense I will never exchange my gentlemanly, soft-voiced, soft-stepping, experienced, intelligent, handsome doctor, for all the female M.D.'s who ever carved up dead bodies or live characters—or tore each other's caps. (*Fresh Leaves* 111–12)

Once again, the impediment to Fern's ability to imagine full equality seems to be her fear of homosexuality. She prefers a male doctor because she finds a man handling her body to be preferable to a woman doing the same. The subtext of the piece, though, entails a striking role reversal. In this sketch, men are the soft, gentle, nurturing sex and women the aggressive, competitive, literally cut-throat one. Even in her comic insistence on sexual difference, then, Fern's humor suggests constantly that the fundamental equality of the sexes is much more extensive than was ever dreamed of in domestic philosophy. And the best way to uncover this equality is through humor rather than satire.

Humor to Parton, then, as it was to Irving, is an alternative to rage as an appropriate response not only to the constraints of domestic ideology, but also to her own ambivalent acceptance of those constraints. Granted, the endings of Fern's sketches tend to be more definite than Irving's, probably because Fern was more comfortable with her role as prophet, more comfortable with the satirist's desire for closure and absolute knowledge. As a progressive, she found her anger to be creative and galvanic, as it was not to the conservative Irving, and I suspect she had less self-doubt in her role as social critic. Nonetheless, Fanny Fern's *humor*, like Geoffrey Crayon's, creates a balance between statement and suggestion, between emphasis and implication, between reality and possibility that, if her growing popularity can be trusted, gives her work a vitality that has long outlived the causes for which she crusaded. Can we say the same of Irving? Perhaps not, though he continues to be read and admired even as his popularity wanes. In any case their use of humor shows deep cultural and psychological connections between two writers whose overt messages could not have been much more different.

# THREE

# Tending the Home Fires

*L*aughter is often the expression of joy that comes from compensation for some pain. So-called subversive satire yields a fairly simple compensation that comes from the liberation of anger, though as I suggested in the last chapter, nothing in such satire is fundamentally opposed to the status quo so much as it expresses a desire to change the flow of power within the status quo. That is to say, satire, as long as its irony is held in check by the satirist's commitment to a clear set of moral values, is the fantasy of a simple inversion of perceived power structures rather than a fundamental refiguring of the idea of power. Humor as a mode of compensation is more complicated, in that it opens conceptions of power and order to imaginative reconsideration. The pleasure such openness entails is often mitigated by the fear of openness and the danger of doubt that it also entails. But as a compensation, humor is much healthier than satire because it makes possible a flexible psychic alternative to repression and aggression, as I suggested was true for both Irving and Parton.

The two authors I discuss in this chapter, Harriet Beecher Stowe and Herman Melville, express their attraction to humor precisely because they see it as such an alternative. But the two have very different hopes for the power of humor—to Stowe it is a technique of management, to Melville it is one of understanding. As an ardent partisan of the ideology of domesticity, Stowe tries very much to use the socially sanctioned mode of humor as a safety valve that releases the anger that domestic ideology generates. She is confident that the tropes of humor are strong enough to enable it to vent steam without blowing the lid off. In particular, she is anxious about the repression entailed in domesticity's treatment of sexuality, and seeks a way to domesticate without destroying procreativity.

But just because humor can be an alternative to anger as a way of facing repression, it is not therefore any less volatile than anger. It has expansive potentials in its capacity to disrupt frames of reference, to reveal the artificial basis of ideology. Such seems to be Melville's attraction to domestic humor in the first place. Uncommitted to the ideology of domesticity, he is more interested in examining the paradoxes without endorsing their cause, and without any commitment to the sexual repression of middle-class mores, he uses humor incisively to cut to the heart of domesticity, that is, to sexual desire and sexual politics in the family. What the consequences of humorous investigation might be to domestic ideology seems less important to him than the exposure of knowledge itself, and the knowledge he uses humor to expose is the knowledge that much of what we hold as self-evident truth is merely projected desire. Such knowledge may be a tremendous threat to domesticity, but the lack of such knowledge, Melville suggests, is just as dangerous. Juxtaposed, the domestic humor of these two authors suggests much about the power of humor as a social and psychological tool, and shows something of the dangers its practitioners must try to manage and to exploit.

## I.  Harriet Beecher Stowe: "They . . . Must Be Allowed Their Laugh and Their Joke"

According to Charles H. Foster, "[i]n *Oldtown Folks* Harriet [Beecher Stowe] was surpassing herself in almost every respect and writing one of the unquestionable, but still generally unacknowledged, masterpieces of New England, indeed of American, literature" (176). I wouldn't go that far, but I would say that, had she vigorously edited the novel, Stowe would have written a book to rival *Uncle Tom's Cabin*. Flawed as it is by numbing repetition and Stowe's refusal to trust the power of fiction to convey a message when three or four sermons could do the trick, *Oldtown Folks* nonetheless has some shining features. The two most relevant to this study are the way Stowe manipulates a conventional seduction plot into an extensive and thoughtful examination of the spiritual possibilities of domesticity and the way she articulates and uses a theory of humor. This latter bore fruit not only in the sketches of comic relief that balance the serious chapters in the book, but also in Sam Lawson. A character who not only threatened to take over *Oldtown Folks* with his lazy, rambling tales and inclination to gossip, Lawson also became the internal narrator for a long series of local color sketches—many published in the *Atlantic Monthly* and all collected in a book, *Sam Lawson's Oldtown Fireside Tales*—that is one of the more important examples of postbellum American literary humor.

Of course, humor is not new to Stowe's work in these postbellum publications. Even *Uncle Tom's Cabin*, known most for its power to move people to tears, is filled with comic vignettes and humorous characters, though since so many of these are built on pernicious racial stereotypes, few now evoke the laughs they once did. Few readers today will laugh at, say, Topsy's antics, or Sam's deliberate obstruction of Haley's pursuit of Eliza, or—or any number of other comic scenes that balance the serious ones. Perhaps one sequence, though, still has the power to evoke a laugh, and that is Cassy's "haunting" of Legree's house. In creating a mock gothic tale that works as a successful bid for freedom, Stowe at least in this scene is in tune with today's language of acceptable comedy.

Still, her mixture of comic and pathetic, her use of gothic horror as a potential base for humor, and her use of a series of balanced sketches to structure the novel all show her continuities with eighteenth- and early-nineteenth-century narrative models. Given that her father allowed her to read no novels but those of Scott, that her education consisted of stylistic training through the *Lectures on Rhetoric* of Hugh Blair, the aesthetic theory of Archibald Alison, and the models of Joseph Addison, Richard Steele, and Oliver Goldsmith, and given that she began her writing with a series of New England sketches, it is not surprising that much of her work has an eighteenth-century feel to it. The interesting thing about *Sam Lawson's Oldtown Fireside Tales*, especially in the context of *Oldtown Folks*, is how clearly one can see that Stowe deploys eighteenth-century structures in order to contain without repressing what she sees as the most dangerous element of domesticity: sexual passion. But while she marshals the conventions of humor to control passion, the comedy itself keeps asking Stowe whether it is indeed possible to contain without repressing.[1]

But before I can analyze Stowe's use of humor in both the novel and the companion sketches, I will need to give a description of the novel and its relation to the tales in *Oldtown Fireside Stories*, as neither book is particularly well known over a century after they were first published and popular. *Oldtown Folks* is perhaps one of the most ambitious of American novels, combining a comedy of manners, three seduction plots, historical romance, local color realism, gothic romance, and spiritual allegory. The narrative is a first-person reminiscence told by Horace Holyoke, who lives with his mother, his Aunt Lois, and his grandparents in their large Oldtown homestead. Horace has a spiritual affinity with his dead father's intellectual inclinations, inclinations held in contempt by the workaholic Lois, who despises not only her sister's dreamy romanticism and her choice of husband, but Horace's spiritual yearnings, dreamy love of idle wandering in nature, and ghostly visions. The grandparents stand between as both orthodox Calvinists and compassionate human beings. Much of the novel is the comedy of manners that takes place in conversations around the kitchen fireplace when various neighbors come to gossip. The neighbor who appears most often is town ne'er-do-well Sam Lawson, who comes by on one pretext or another to mooch cider and vittles and pay for them in story telling. Much of the subject matter of the story telling concerns religious doc- trine, faith itself, questions of social class and democratization after the Revolu- tionary War, incidents of the war, and concerns about the work ethic and its re- lation to a spirit-killing greed.[2] These conversations, while tangential to the main seduction and marriage plots, grow disproportionately important within the book and beyond it, spawning the entire series of Lawson tales, all but one of which share this domestic setting and these themes.

The main action of the story begins with the introduction of two orphans, Tina and Harry, into the Oldtown community. Their mother, seduced into a phony marriage by a British officer and then abandoned when her "husband" returned to Britain after the Revolutionary War, struggles against poverty and despair until she dies, leaving her children at the farmhouse of "Crab Smith," a heartless Yankee taskmaster who claims Harry as his virtual slave and ships Tina off to his sister, Asphyxia Smith. The orphans show their characteris- tics—Harry a spiritual endurance, Tina a rebellious wit—before being rescued by the good-hearted denizens of Oldtown. Harry is invited to live with Horace and his family; Tina is sent to live with Mehitable Rossiter, a stately old woman whose spiritual and intellectual gloom is redeemed by the joyous good humor Tina brings to her household.

The action of the book drives toward good-hearted and spritely but frivolous Tina's seduction by and marriage to a bloated aristocrat whose dissipa- tion and disputation finally ruin him—he is killed in a duel—freeing the chas- tened Tina to marry the spiritually serious Horace. Simultaneously, it finds for Harry a suitable spouse in Esther Avery, the daughter of Horace's and Harry's schoolteacher. But along the way we learn much about Stowe's sense of the proper balance between comedy and seriousness, between this-worldliness and other-worldliness, between liberty and "license," between love and passion. The glue that holds all of these ostensible opposites in what Stowe believes to be the proper balance is the discipline of domesticity, which demands balances in order to be successfully a haven from worldliness on the path to salvation.

To Stowe, domesticity was a spiritual discipline far more benign, healthy, and practical than the rigid Calvinism of Jonathan Edwards and of her father. Edwards's rigor was, according to Stowe, a spiritual because psychic disaster. Edwards may have been "The greatest man, since Augustine, that Christianity has turned out. But when a great man, instead of making himself a great ladder for feeble folks to climb on, strikes away the ladder and bids them come to where he stands at a step, his greatness and goodness both may prove unfortu- nate for those who come after him" (2: 5). The disaster is particularly great for spiritual women who are unable to reconcile their intuitions of divine love with the strictures of systematic philosophy, as Stowe makes clear repeatedly in the detailed life histories, complete with extensive exegesis on the dangers of Calvinism, of numerous female characters in both Oldtown books. As in the case of Esther Avery,

[o]ne of those intense, silent, repressed women that have been a frequent out-
growth of New England society. . . . With many New England women at this
particular period, when life was so retired and so cut off from outward sources of
excitement, *thinking* grew to be a disease. The great subject of thought was, of
course, theology; and woman's nature has never been consulted in theology.
Theological systems . . . have had their origin, as in St. Augustine, with men
who were utterly ignorant of moral and intellectual companionship with woman,
looking on her only in her animal nature as a temptation and a snare. Consequently, when, as in this period of New England, the theology of Augustine
began to be freely discussed by every individual in society, it was the women who
found it hardest to tolerate or to assimilate it, and many a delicate and sensitive
nature was utterly wrecked in the struggle. (2: 54–55)[3]

Accordingly, Stowe sees the domestic circle as the place where men and
women, in moral and intellectual contact, grow out of systematic thinking and
into a bond of love, a redemptive and ultimately spiritual bond untainted by
the "temptation" of "animal nature." This is the place where the soul can exercise religion's "active and preceptive form,—what we may call its business
character,—rather than . . . its sentimental and devotional one" (2: 228). As
Stowe develops her system of religion, these two sides are in relation to one another as the rungs on the ladder that Edwards refuses to grant to the average
person. Through the divine business of worldly work the soul has the opportunity to refine itself, to make it ready for the "devotional aspect" of faith.

Indeed, the *Fireside* tale "The Minister's Housekeeper" is the comic fictional
presentation of this serious side of *Oldtown Folks*. In "The Minister's Housekeeper," young Huldy, who has, we are told, no designs on the minister because
she is too innocent of sexual passion or of worldly greed to consider such a
thing, nonetheless is a marvel at organizing the minister's affairs. While she
works hard, her very presence seems to whistle, as she moves with a natural energy and joy, much as a bird. As she touches the minister's life with her vitality
and with beauty, so does he find his sermons themselves softening from Calvinist rigor. Domestic love leads to spiritual regeneration, and, in spite of the jealousies of rival parishioners who would like to marry the newly widowed minister, Huldy ends up as his wife.

Huldy's own beauty in part, but more importantly, the spiritual zest with
which she faces the business of making life as beautiful as possible, is the tangible sign of a spiritual force at work in the business of daily life. As Stowe put it
in the earlier *The Minister's Wooing*:

There is a ladder to heaven, whose base God has placed in human affections, tender instincts, symbolic feelings, sacraments of love, through which the soul rises
higher and higher, refining as she goes, till she outgrows the human, and changes
as she rises, into the image of the divine. At the very top of this ladder, at the
threshold of paradise, blazes dazzling and crystalline that celestial grade where the
soul knows self no more, having learned, through a long experience of devotion,
how blest it is to lose herself in that eternal Love and Beauty of which all earthly
fairness and grandeur are but the dim type, the distant shadow. (579–80)

To Stowe, the home and its daily rituals of domesticity, then, are human ladders to heaven, the way by which the soul is, step by step, purified of egotism. But the soul's purification entails, ironically, a renunciation of the very worldly beauties that engender it in the first place. Stowe sees life as a struggle toward renunciation first of self-love through worldly love, then of worldly love through love of the divine.[4]

Not surprisingly, then, in her fiction, Stowe turns the elements of households into symbols of spiritual progress. For instance, she sees grandmothers as the most likely to have succeeded in this spiritual quest in that their hearts have been tempered by the duties of maternal care and the likely losses and disappointments contingent on maternity (*Oldtown Folks* 368). Insofar as grandmothers symbolize to her the spiritual ideal, she calls her saints and heroes, such as Cotton Mather, grandmothers.[5] For another example, houses themselves come to represent the success or failure of the discipline of domesticity. Indeed, Stowe even goes so far as to suggest that houses that have witnessed the failure of domesticity as spiritual discipline will be haunted by spirits seeking after death to guide the living back into conformity with a spiritual ideal.

All of this, of course, sounds little like the subject of comedy, and the tenor of the novel is indeed quite serious in its spiritual investigations. But Stowe also uses these themes as the subject of comedy, as at novel's end we learn that Crab Smith's wife, whom Crab hounded out of her life, now haunts him. When Lawson retails the story to the narrator, he sets up as comic the contrast between the woman's meekness, habitual to her in her efforts to follow the spiritual discipline of domesticity, and her husband's fear of her ghost. Says Lawson, "I told Sol 'bout it, last town-meetin' day, an' Sol, I thought he'd ha' split his sides. Sol said he did n't know's the old woman had so much sperit" (*Oldtown Folks* 2: 245). Partly, here, the comedy comes from the simple contrast between the serious business of spiritual progress and the mundane affairs of home life. For those who can see this comedy, this occasional mirth is a catharsis that makes it possible to face the serious business. Indeed, it is the power of mirth to remove from consciousness the serious implications of mundane matters that makes life possible: "Man was mercifully made with the power of ignoring what he believes. It is all that makes existence in a life like this tolerable. And our ministers, conscious of doing the very best they can to keep the world straight, must be allowed their laugh and joke, sin and Satan to the contrary notwithstanding" (2: 74).

Thus does Stowe see laughter as part of a psychic and spiritual economy that makes it possible for human beings to use the world as a ladder to heaven. Without balance, without relief from seriousness, life's troubles would kill, rather than discipline, souls, as happens in the case of the borderline comic character Asphyxia Smith, the "working machine" (2: 246). In contrast to Tina, she seems comic, until the conflict between the two of them threatens to murder Tina's soul as well as brutalize her body. But keeping her in humorous perspective, Sam Lawson, Asphyxia's alter ego, in describing Asphyxia's life articulates Stowe's philosophy of balance, of work relieved by wholesome play:

"Wal, mis' Badger," said Sam, . . . "I hes to recreate, else I gets quite wore out.
Why, lordy massy, even a saw-mill hes ter stop sometimes ter be greased. 'T ain't
everybody thet's like Sphyxy Smith, but she grits and screeches all the time, jest
'cause she keeps to work without bein' iled. Why, she could work on, day 'n'
night, these twenty years, 'n' never feel it. But, lordy massy, I gets so 'xhausted,
an' hes such a sinking 't my stomach, 'n' then I goes out 'n' kind o' *Injuning*'
'round, an' git flag-root 'n' sarsafrass 'n' sich fur Hepsy to brew up a beer. I ain't a-
wastin' my time ef I be enjoyin' myself. I say it's a part o' what we's made for." (2:
172–73)

The irony here is that while Sam articulates a need for balance within the individual, he himself lacks it entirely, being completely shiftless. What he provides, both to the story and to the community, is balance not within himself,
but between himself and others: "Every New England village, if you only think
of it, must have its do-nothing as regularly as it has its school-house or meet-
ing-house. Nature is always wide-awake in the matter of compensation. Work,
thrift, and industry are such an incessant steam-power in Yankee life, that society would burn itself out with intense friction were there not interposed here
and there the lubricating power of a decided do-nothing" (1: 32). To me, the
greatest surprise in finding Stowe not only developing a comic character but
giving him a book of his own was the degree to which she clearly relishes this
man who seems to violate the essence of domesticity as spiritual discipline. He
is a gossip who cannot keep food on the table for his own children, driving his
wife into shrewish rages. Like Rip Van Winkle, he drives his wife to her death
through his passive resistance to strive-and-succeed ethics.

But as I became familiar with Stowe's use of humor, I began to understand
her attraction to his psychic type. For one thing, even in physical adulthood,
he is a psychic child, and, as I will discuss below, Stowe's sense of the spiritual
value of childhood is central to her visions of both spiritual progress ("Suffer
the little children . . .") and of comedy. For another, this decided do-nothing
is, like all of the characters in both of these books, a radical individualist, but
unlike many of the individualities who are "sharp-cut" (1: 294) in their peculiarities, his is an individuality, a "humor," that would be poetical and harmless
if it only were given a sphere in which it could operate. His failure is the society's failure, in that it is inadequately tolerant of individuality.

For Stowe, the problem of refining the self into losing a sense of self is made
all the harder by her sense that individuals must find their own ways to heaven,
in keeping with their own natural and cultivated peculiarities but without violating the needs for a community of interest and Christian love. Characters
such as Asphyxia Smith show the danger of peculiarity without self-consciousness. Given the pressures they put on other individualities, they make laughter
into a necessary psychic vent, a release of repressed hostility that Stowe perceives as necessary:

As the reader may have observed, we were a sharp-cut and peculiar set in our
house, and sometimes, when the varied scenes of family life below stairs had
amused Harry more than common, he would, after we had got into our chamber

by ourselves, break into a sudden flow of mimicry,—imitating now Aunt Lois's sharp, incisive movements and decided tones, or flying about like my venerated grandmother in her most confused and hurried moments, or presenting a perfect image of Uncle Fliakim's [distortion of Eliakim to make him seem like a blue-bottle fly, always buzzing around] frisky gyrations, till he would set me into roars of laughter; when he would turn gravely round and ask what I was laughing at. He never mentioned a name, or made remarks about the persons indicated,—the sole reflection on them was the absurd truthfulness of his imitation; and when I would call out the name he would look at me with eyes brimful of mischief, but in utter silence. (1: 294–95)

The prose ignores the fact that these "sharp-cut" peculiarities usually infringed on the children's freedoms, if not on their backsides with birch rods, and to find these "varied scenes" to be "amusing," Harry has an attribute that saves both himself and his companion from taking to heart the pressures of the house.

Still, as a believer in humor, Stowe saw laughter as having a potentially much greater power. In a land of individualists, social frictions can be magnified—indeed, given that she writes of the postrevolutionary period and has Tories and Rebels vehemently argue their positions throughout the book and that she writes immediately after the Civil War, the problem of social compatibility in a democratic land was high on Stowe's list of concerns. To her, laughter worked as a social lubricant when, rather than being spiteful and closeted, it was good-natured and sociable, as in the case of the rural ministers' meeting:

Mingling very little with the world, each one a sort of autocrat in his way, in his own district, these men developed many originalities and peculiarities of character, which the simple state of society then allowed full scope. They were humorists,—like the mossy old apple-trees which each of them had in his orchard, bending this way and turning that, and throwing out their limbs with quaint twists and jerks, yet none the less acceptable, so long as the fruit they bore was sound and wholesome. . . . They seemed to have such a hearty joy in their meeting, and to deliver themselves up to mirth and good-fellowship with such a free and hearty abandon, and the jokes and stories which they brought with them were chorused by such roars of merriment, as made us think a minister's meeting the most joyous thing on earth. (2: 72–73)

The key to "wholesomeness" in Stowe's eyes was the use of humor rather than of wit, of using laughter not to scorn others, but to enable tolerance of others. In this form, laughter, as it is the lubricant to the soul in the body, is the lubricant between the individuals who make up the world. It is the balance to the moralistic intransigence bred by politics, race, social class, economics, and, especially, religion.

Stowe goes so far as to suggest that effervescent laughter is a conduit of love. For example, in Tina, the child who is able to bring together Tory and Rebel, rich and poor, old and young, Calvinist and Arminian, Stowe suggests that gaiety is perhaps the most powerful of attractions to love and affection:

Not a visage in Oldtown was so set in grimness of care, that it did not relax its lines when it saw Tina coming down the street; for Tina could mimic and sing and dance, and fling back joke for joke in a perfect meteoric shower. So long as she entertained, she was perfectly indifferent who the party was. She would display her accomplishments to a set of strolling Indians, or for Sam Lawson and Jake Marshall, as readily as for any one else. She would run up and catch the minister by the elbow as he solemnly and decorously moved down street, and his face always broke into a laugh at the sight of her.

The minister's lady, and Aunt Lois, and Miss Deborah Kittery, while they used to mourn in secret places over her want of decorum in thus displaying her talents before the lower classes, would afterward laugh till the tears rolled down their cheeks and their ancient whalebone stays creaked, when she would do the same thing over in a select circle for them. (2: 9)

This passage, while relishing the redemptive power of laughter, is not without a mitigating sense of danger. Tina disrupts the ceremoniousness of order, and in so doing threatens it.

Many of the stories show that danger, as for example, the *Fireside* story "The Parson's Horserace," in which Parson Williams, whose love of spirited horses accidentally involves him in a horse race, nearly loses his authority over his parish because he becomes the butt of repeated waggish jokes that suggest that he is either a hypocrite or unable even to control a horse, no less his parish. The idea of a spiritual minister not in control of the flesh, albeit horseflesh, is almost more than the minister's dignity can bear. His very anger becomes a new source of comedy for those around him, and, if time didn't allow the laughter to die down, the minister would have been laughed out of his place.

As for Tina herself, we are told that she needs to learn the distinction between appropriate and inappropriate laughter or run the risk of becoming shallow and merely flirtatious. Laughter in this negative sense is a power to do ill, to damage community by exalting some over others. In distinguishing wit from humor Stowe puts herself firmly into the camp of amiable humorists who try to bridle the dangerous powers of laughter without cutting off humor simply by differentiating between them on the basis of intention: humor is indulgent and self-abnegating, while wit is self-exalting. The trick for Stowe is to create comic tales that suppress egotistical pleasure while heightening a sense of communion in laughter.

The content of most of the comic scenes in *Oldtown Folks* and of the tales in *Oldtown Fireside Stories* certainly does nothing to control their aggressive, egotistical potentials. Indeed, the content is extraordinarily conventional and often would seem perfectly designed to encourage laughter at another's expense. From the simple slapstick of a dog in a church and a bull running wild inside a house, to jealousies in courtship, to seasickness, to the pretentious being brought down a peg, to the unsophisticated mocked for social climbing or for being themselves, to cross-dressing—these comic situations could easily play toward aggression. But in framing the stories twice, with the inside narrator Sam Lawson careful not to offend the delicate ears of his child listeners or the moral sensibilities of his female listeners, and with the outside narrator, genteel Horace Holyoke, distancing the reader from the stories not only through his own refinement but through the gentle glow of nostalgia, none of the stories carries any overt sting. In typical humorous form, then, aggression is removed by distancing the action of a tale from any immediate stake. By making the reader disinterested, the tales run the risk of making the reader uninterested, but never of being selfishly vested in them. But if this distance is not enough, the explicit commentary in the tales, even when it is critical of human behavior or motivation, is usually couched in very subtle and gentle ways. Usually, both Holyoke and Lawson put the most generous spin on the motives of almost any character's actions, and the few who do come in for reproof usually do so for their treachery (as in the case of the British sailor who, in cross-dressing, attempts to capture an American ship through subterfuge when unable to do so through force) or for their selfishness and inability to trust their neighbors.

The double framing, besides controlling diction and the moral, further distances the reader from direct identification with any of the comic characters in part because both narrators choose to distort the objects of representation into caricatures. Holyoke begins the game by turning Lawson into a caricature, and then Lawson himself embellishes on the characters he describes until the objects of our attention appear cartoonish. Of course, most of them are also stereotypical: the otherworldly minister who doesn't know that a Tom turkey will never hatch a clutch of eggs; the prying widowed parishioner who wants to marry the minister; the no-count low-class white trash who would rather search for treasure than work for his wife's living; the termagant wife who has more brains than her shiftless husband; the Indian woman with magical powers; the skinflint father who, it turns out, deeply loves the daughter he has berated for many years. While none of these stereotypical characters is intrinsically lovable, Stowe usually structures the stories so that the main characters reveal that they have "hearts of gold," as for instance in "Mis' Elderkin's Pitcher," in which a loyal but headstrong daughter, when finally free of her father's tyrannies, discovers that he has left her a legacy that will free her from the need to work for the rest of her life. Their battles are described in a way that is only partly comic, but the resolution away from her hatred of her father "domesticates" the wildness of her passion. Both characters show the better for the turn at the end; both caricatures end up like stuffed animals for children: they may represent lions and tigers and bears, but they are really soft pillows.

To Stowe, this softening of passion is one of the primary values of humor insofar as she is deathly afraid of passion, especially sexual passion, yet is equally afraid of repression. In her fear of passion, Stowe is quite typical of her day, seeing the redemptive power of womanhood in its power to engage a self-abnegating love that is not tainted by the selfishness of desire. Consider her reaction to a letter from her husband in which he admits that passion interferes with his spiritual progress: "I try to be spiritually minded, and find in myself a most exquisite relish, and deadly longing for all kinds of sensual gratification." Harriet replied, "What terrible temptations lie in the way of your sex—till now I never before realized it—for tho I did love you with an almost *insane* love before I married you I never knew yet or felt the pulsation which showed me that I could be tempted in that way . . . for I loved you as I now love God . . . and as I have no passion—I have no jealousy. . . . If your sex would guard the outworks of *thought*, you would never fall" (qtd. in Goshgarian 53–54). G. M. Goshgarian has done an excellent job of examining the contradictions of the concept of the "passionless female" in the "cult of true womanhood," so I needn't go into an extensive treatment of them here. Suffice it to say that many humorists exploited some of the contradictions for laughs, as I will point out later in this chapter and in chapters to follow. What is to the point here is that Stowe engages love, or what she repeatedly calls "affection" in *Oldtown Folks*, without passion, yet she knows that the two are closely related. "Affection," necessary to salvation, runs the risk of sparking sexual passion.

To guard the "outworks of thought" entails massive repression, usually through hard work ("Idle hands are the devil's playthings," and all of that), yet we see in so many of Stowe's characters, both comic and serious, that such repression in work leads to the death of affection and thus of the possibility of salvation. Neither Asphyxia Smith nor Aunt Lois has any softness, precisely because in repressing sexuality through hard work, each represses her "motherly loving kindness," too. How then, to guard the outworks of thought without repression? For women, the love of children, says Stowe, holds the key. The "old maid" Mehitable Rossiter comes to life and to religious faith when given the chance to raise Tina, to love her for her gaiety. But Tina's power of affection has the opposite effect on men—it elicits lust. The close proximity between affection and passion is, to Stowe, analogous to the similar proximity between humor and wit: humor and affection are not self-seeking whereas wit and passion are.

And this, finally, explains Stowe's attraction to Sam Lawson. Standing as the opposite of Aunt Lois, Lawson, seeking only idleness and to spread gossip, has a childlike innocence. Like Lois, he is devoid of sexual thoughts, but unlike Lois, he is so not because he represses them. He is presexual in mind, in spite of the fact that he is married and has children. He prefers, like Rip Van Winkle, to reject the responsibilities of adulthood by retreating into the shelter of boyhood, partly by serving as older companion to boys, generation after generation. And to some extent he is passionless because feminized. He is loved in the community because he entertains children, cares for sick neighbors, watches coffins, collects herbs—in fact fills many of the traditional functions of women without having to bear children. To Stowe, Lawson is the personification of humor—gentle, innocent, childlike. His retrospective longing, like Holyoke's, is for a presexual time, and the longing of nostalgia, insofar as it contemplates completed action, is passive, antithetical to appetite.

Stowe seems able to deal with sexuality neither in the serious side of her spiritual discipline nor in the comic side. Her vision of domesticity, predicated on motherhood, is strangely contingent on sexual intercourse yet lacking it. Not only is sex implicit but denied in the role of motherhood, it is the crux of the plot in *Oldtown Folks*, though never treated comically in its own right. Indeed, the wit of the seducer, Ellery Davenport, is part of his danger. His wit, in discovering incongruity, encourages skepticism and thus transmutes Tina's gaiety into a battle of wits. In so doing, his wit robs her of her childlike humor, her use of her sense of incongruity to relieve seriousness without damaging anyone's faith in the rightness of loving relations. Before Davenport's wit corrodes her energy, her humor does not violate bonds in egotism, nor faith in rationalism. It is pure play. Davenport's desire for sex, like his manipulation of wit, is too selfish to be safe. Sex, according to Stowe, needs to happen only when controlled in domesticity, which she essentially defines as the liberation of childish gaiety. Stowe sees the liberation of the—dare I say it?—"inner child" as the way to constrain sex without repressing it, to make it part of selfless renunciation rather than selfish gratification.

Such at least was her theory. However, humor as Stowe constructs it is too weak to bear the weight she gives it to carry. Love, in adult eyes, leads to sex. Stowe tries to etherialize love, to make it nonsexual, but by looking at it through nostalgia, by trying to make it the realm of the prepubescent child, she inadvertently opens childhood itself to sexuality, often homosexual, often incestuous. Consider, for instance, Horace's explanation of why he liked Harry, who, in his saccharine goodness, in his affinities to Henry Fielding's Blitul or Mark Twain's Sid Sawyer, should have been a target of contempt of the much more fractious and clumsy Horace. But instead, Horace tells us, Harry seduced everyone to his good graces:

> For Harry I felt a sort of rudimentary, poetical tenderness, like the love of man for woman. I admired his clear blue eyes, his curling golden hair, his fair, pure complexion, his refined and quiet habits, and a sort of unconsciousness of self that there was about him. His simplicity of nature was incorruptible; he seemed always to speak, without disguise, exactly what he thought, without the least apparent consideration of anything but its truth; and this gave him a strange air of innocency. A sort of quaint humor always bubbling up in little quiet looks and ways, and in harmless practical jokes, gave me a constant sense of amusement in his society. (1: 294)

Humor and innocency and the facts that Horace is both male and, at this point in the narrative, a prepubescent boy are all supposed to mitigate the sexual overtones of the first sentence. And Harry's beauty, in the preadolescent femalelike neuter of boyhood, is supposed to be an image of the divine that compels everyone to admire his fundamental truthfulness and innocency. Yet that first line won't go away; Horace's love for Harry is "like the love of man for woman," and while Stowe may say that "in time, it is the motherly feeling with which [a wife] regards her husband" (2: 239), she never suggests that the feeling with which a man regards a woman lacks sexual passion. Then, too, while Horace's love of Harry raises the prospect of homosexuality, that line about maternal love raises the specter of incest in marriage—even in Stowe's description of child-love, she implies the presence of incestuous feelings as well. Consider the fact that the two boys live in the same house as brothers and that Tina, Harry's sister, whom Horace loves as a sister, ultimately becomes, with Harry's encouragement, Horace's wife. It would be difficult to imagine Stowe conceiving a more incestuous nexus of relationships.

It might seem unfair to put such a post-Freudian spin on these pre-Freudian texts, but Stowe herself was not unaware of the sexual attractiveness of children. Indeed, in *Oldtown Folks*, she has Tina fondled by her teacher, leered at by a preacher, and even the stern and upright brother of Mehitable Rossiter falls for Tina's charms. While Stowe has Tina disgusted by such attentions, to suggest her innocence and purity, the power of sexual attraction drives the plot of the novel. Stowe puts lust into the center of the plot; her efforts to draw a line against lust by having us see it through the haze of "[a] sort of quaint humor" that is the province of innocent childhood simply cannot prevent the reader from seeing the logic of the narrative itself.

Stowe's theory of humor indeed led her into many convolutions, some of which her humor tries to mask, others of which become sources of unintentional comedy, as in the "The Widow's Bandbox" from *Oldtown Fireside Stories*. Framed as a cautionary tale to tell the boys of the dangers, for men as well as for women, of heterosexual passion, read against itself it seems to say that it is better to have sexual experience and to know what you are getting into than to remain innocent. The framed narrative of an incident in the American Revolution is about the attempts made by two British officers to take the United States' sloop *Brilliant* by subterfuge. While the sloop is lying in harbor at the remote Maine town of Camden, a "widow" approaches the ship, demands a private audience with the captain, and throws herself on his mercy: "'O cap'n' said she, 'I'm the most unfortunate woman. I'm all alone in the world,' says she, 'and I don't know what'll become of me ef you don't keep me,' says she" (2: 299).

Captain Tucker may have been easily taken in by her because, "like the generality o' cap'ns [h]e was up to 'bout everything that any *man* could do, but it was pretty easy for a woman to come it over him. Ye see, cap'ns they don't see women as men do ashore. They don't have enough of 'em to get tired on 'em; and every woman's an angel to a sea-cap'n" (2: 299). While the captain, a married man, does not immediately *act* on such an obviously sexual offer, it is clear that he is carried away by lust, and so accedes to the request of the "widow" that he carry her and her luggage, ostensibly her husband's corpse, to Boston. Already alerted to the probability of deceit by the reference to the ease with which sea captains can be taken in by women, the reader is not surprised to find that a sailor, Tom Toothacre, has his doubts. When watching the "widow" flirting, he keeps his head about him, refusing to share his shipmates' lust: "'Wal, what do you think?' says Ben. Tom gin a h'ist to his trousers," making sure he keeps his pants on, both literally and figuratively, and replies. "'My thoughts is my own,' says he; 'and I calculate to keep 'em to myself,' says he. And then he jest walked to the side of the vessel, and watched the woman a-gettin' ashore. There was a queer kind o' look in Tom's eye" (2: 301). The word "queer," here, means merely "different"; Tom's difference from the others is to have no passion. In Stowe's terms, passionlessness is as good for men as for women, as in this case it enables Tom to perceive that "she" is in fact a man masquerading. "'Ef that 'ere ain't a British naval officer, I lose my bet. I've been used to the ways on 'em, and I knows their build and their step.'"

Tom, because he refuses to be duped by lust, whether mitigated by refined gallantry, as in the case of the captain and his officers, or not, as in the case of most of the common sailors, saves the day, leading his shipmates to capture the cross-dressing officer and his confederate, concealed in the bandbox. After the story gets out, the captain spends the rest of his days living down the jealousy of his wife, but Sam exonerates him because "[f]olks'll have to answer for wus things at the last day than tryin' to do a kindness to a poor widder, now, I tell you. It's better to be took in doin' a good thing, than never to try to do good" (2: 307). Sam's homily, like his editing of sailor language, tries to put a kind spin on the tale, but given the opening frame, in which Sam complains that women, through Eve, brought the curse of work into the world and that they shouldn't hector men if the work therefore is never adequately done, Sam's generous closing bromide rings false. Indeed, what seems more true is that the entire story is misogynistic. It is the feminine British officer who is deceitful; his evil is equated to his effeminacy. If the American officers had known women better, they would not have been deceived by a show of tears, which is convincing substantially because it is so effectively feminine. Tom perceives the essential masculinity of even the, implicitly, very effeminate British officer.

More to the point, by the double consciousness essential to perceiving the incongruities that make comedy, one must see that the American officers are attracted to a man, to an effeminate man. I doubt Stowe was fully conscious of the fact that she imputes to the captain and other officers of the American ship homosexual tendencies, but I suspect that she had the lower-class sailor rather than the officers see essential differences because, not being gentrified, he implicitly understands sexual passion—homo- as well as heterosexual—more than could the refined and thus repressed officers. In the coded language of the tale, Tom may not have been feminized by gentility, but he may have been sodomized by the Brits: he "knows their build" well enough to perceive it through a disguise. Indeed, once one begins to see the latent and homosexual text in the story, it's hard to believe that the "passionless" Stowe wrote it.

Yet another reason that her comedy fails to fulfill its humorous task of controlling the disruptive tendencies of comedy while allowing the release of repression it also entails, is that Stowe does not consistently work comedy either to create or to collapse distinctions between people. Consciously, since her humor is meant to bridge gaps, it is contingent on a myth of fundamental difference that she consciously tries to maintain. She needs to show that the differences between men and women are so absolute as to be undisguisable by those who are sensitive enough to the differences to be able to know them. She explicitly tells us that the officers are taken in by the disguise out of pity, a pity that gets in the way of perception. Is pity not, in Stowe's binary construction of gender, a feminine trait?

Usually, cross-dressing in comedy brings to consciousness the artificiality of sex-role differences at the same time as it heightens consciousness of biological differences. Often such comedy turns on threatened exposure of genitalia to suggest that the really fundamental difference is sexual, but that socially there is no difference between men and women. Stowe refuses to give us this usual comedy—the officer only feels "foolish in his petticoats" *after* he is "found out." Stowe downplays physical differences between the sexes in order to accentuate an intangible and intuitively known and thus spiritual difference. In keeping with the grand themes of both Oldtown books, she insists on such extrarational understanding as the only knowledge, and in this case, the only possible knowledge is of fundamental difference. Yet, in the sexual binaries of domestic ideology, is an effeminate man, then, not really a woman? How can Stowe have an ideology based on fundamental difference, when her tales show so easily that the traits she portrays as fundamental are so easily shared? In "The Widow's Bandbox," cross-dressing does suggest an equivalence between men and women, at least in most particulars. While the telos of "The Widow's Bandbox" is from similarity to difference, often in her comic stories Stowe is unsuccessful at controlling the final vision so clearly. Or perhaps, rather, at some different level of consciousness she rebels against her own findings of difference.

In any event, numerous stories collapse the distinctions between men and women, often by reversing gender roles, but more often by confusing them, especially when dealing with ministers. By their very role as otherworldly, they were perceived in the popular culture as being effeminate.[6] Stowe plays the stereotype both ways. For one, in "The Minister's Housekeeper," the minister is completely incompetent to run his farm (even though Stowe earlier let us know that real ministers were usually farmers, usually quite practical). She picks up the stereotype of the incompetent man and the stereotype of the otherworldly, scholarly minister. But when he finally is made aware of the gossip in the community, he asserts his masculine power by choosing Huldy for his bride and silencing the gossips by "giving them something to talk about." He shows a shrewd awareness of psychology and the capacity to marshal his authority and his wit to defend his position from calumny and to secure the object of his sexual and spiritual appetite. His masculinity is confirmed at tale's end without impugning for a moment his spirituality. Thus, Stowe's story serves to destroy the definitions of womanhood as spiritual in contrast to masculinity's earthliness. Similarly, the tale "Laughing Out in Meeting," of a minister who is accused of being not spiritual enough because he has a masculine hilarity, the denouement of the story suggests just the opposite, that hilarity and spirituality are completely compatible; the binary opposition between masculine and feminine traits is collapsed and in the process the essence of Stowe's domestic agenda is compromised. Rather than feminizing men into passionless do-nothings such as Sam Lawson, many of her tales masculinize spirit, much to the confusion of her ideological purity.

But perhaps that is the most valuable function humor served for Stowe. In the late 1860s she was, as Joan Hedrick tells us, sorting through the implications of her growingly assertive feminism. She was reading more about female suffrage and finding herself attracted to the cause, even to the point of seeing women in marriage as in comparable servitude to the recently freed slaves. As Hedrick makes clear, Stowe never fully worked through the paradoxes and difficulties of her Victorian ideal of woman as angel in the house and her idea of marriage as sexual slavery, but clearly, when writing all of the Oldtown stories, Stowe was examining the plight of women in marriage, and all the while she had in mind the tale of Lady Byron's broken marriage. Stowe was an early partisan of the idea that Byron had not only violated the sanctity of his marriage vows through adulterous liaisons, but had done so incestuously by carrying on an affair with his half-sister. Stowe had this story directly from Byron's wife, whom she met in England in 1856. At the time, she counseled Lady Byron to keep the charge to herself to avoid scandal, but by 1867 when she began work on the Oldtown stories, she was sharing her belief with friends in private correspondence (Hedrick 356). By the time Oldtown Folks appeared in 1869, Stowe was beginning to sell her Sam Lawson tales while she began to write "The True Story of Lady Byron's Life" (Hedrick 347, 462 n. 83, 354–76). The temporal conjunction seems much more than accidental, especially as the Oldtown works address some of the same thematic material. It seems likely that Stowe's use of humor to address sexual passion, including incestuous desire, enabled her to address the subject much more directly.

So while Stowe justified humor as a strategy of containment, she used it at some level as a technique of exploration and expression. In considering humor a strategy of containment, she made it psychologically safe to examine desire, especially the dangers to women of being objects of desire. Did she also at some level explore the possibility of female desire? Perhaps in the virtual androgyny of her narrator, Horace Holyoke, Stowe was able to explore that which she said did not exist.

In any event, Stowe was politic in discussing sexual exploitation and the sexual double standard through the veil of domestic humor. When she published on the same topic quite directly and seriously in her Atlantic Monthly article "The True Story of Lady Byron's Life" (September 1869) and in Lady Byron Vindicated (1870), she nearly destroyed her career, and almost took the Atlantic down with her. Sexuality was not, in postbellum America, a topic for serious public discussion. The surprise is only that Stowe took the risk, something she probably could not have done without having first explored the subject through humor.


## II.  Herman Melville: "A Little Out of My Mind"

In his comic stories of home and hearth of the mid-1850s, Melville shares some of Stowe's grand concerns (expressed as much in her antebellum writings as in her postbellum humor), like the relationship of pleasure to spirituality and of the danger of the work ethic and greed to sensibility. Unlike Stowe, Melville never surrendered to the myth of home as spiritual discipline, so he uses humor not in an attempt to contain passion or to solidify differences between people, but instead to examine the very idea of difference, to see what the internal dynamics of the family are and why they lead people into insisting on conflicts between one another.[7] Indeed, his domestic comedies show him more willing to indulge the spirit of amiable humor than is Stowe. The eighteenth- and nineteenth-century conception of humor requires fairly solid categories of difference, signalled by stereotypical caricatures that are nonthreatening and thus lovable. But Melville, before he turned fully sour and became nihilistic in his irony, trusted humor as a tool of reconciliation further than did most of his peers.[8] He trusted humor not to make otherness safe, but to show that oppositions are internal as well as external, and that projecting them into monolithic categories is the way of madness. In embracing internal contradictions, he is able to explore the consequences of domesticity without recoiling in simplistic antagonisms.[9]

Perhaps this is best seen in his domestic tale of antagonism, "I and My Chimney," the action of which revolves around the narrator's battle with wife and daughters over remodeling the house by first removing the large central chimney and fireplaces. One way to look at the piece is to see in it Melville's simple resistance to feminine power in having his narrator refuse to compromise with his wife about the shape of their living quarters. Support for this reading of the piece as antifeminist can be found in his use of the stereotypical termagant wife who runs roughshod over her husband, unsettling his rational life with her obsessive concern with fashion. Yet while his tone is sweetly reasonable, the narrator is hardly a paragon of rationality, as readers can plainly see by tale's end. He, too, is madly, though comically, obsessed, locked in a conflict that defines his being as much as it defines his wife's. The two end the tale locked in an obsessive struggle that obliterates for them all other concerns. If the narrator, then, is not reliable, insofar as he becomes merely his wife's opposite, we need to interpret the story with some sense of what the narrator is not saying but what Melville is.[10]

The story begins with the narrator "expatiat[ing]" about himself, but more about his chimney, with which he seems to feel a profound metaphysical kinship. One conceit by which the narrator describes his connection with his chimney is by referring to the hearth as the center of domestic affections, and that the house with central chimney, with all flues "being grouped together in one federal stock" creates "proper fraternal feeling." Or at least the narrator implies such when he describes the opposite kinds of houses. For those in which

> the hall is in the middle[,] the fire-places usually are on opposite sides; so that while one member of the household is warming himself at a fire built into a recess of the north wall, say another member, the former's own brother, perhaps, may be holding his feet to blaze before a hearth in the south wall—the two thus sitting back to back. Is this well? . . . has it not a sort of sulky appearance? But very probably this style of chimney building originated with some architect afflicted with a quarrelsome family. (353)

While implying that his house breeds fraternal feeling, he has no brother sharing the warmth. He does, though, have a wife, as opposite in character as in
sex, and their family, too, is quarrelsome. The central chimney does not make
for familial bliss in this house, and by metaphorical extension, in any other. But
if the hearth warms not the home, then what has gone wrong with domesticity?

The narrator first intimates that the conflict is a product of commerce and
the competitive ethos. Describing city houses with their separate flues as being
the product of egotism and selfishness (353), the narrator explains that "stylish" men compete to erect the tallest houses on expensive city lots. They may
relish the competition, but the narrator warns that such houses, their walls
honeycombed with separate flues, are "treacherously hollow, and, in consequence, more or less weak" (354). The narrator himself spurns such stylishness.
His broad house is on poor land, where the soil is so poor that even "our rye
comes up, here and there a spear, sole and single like a church-spire. It doesn't
care to crowd itself where it knows there is such a deal of room. The world is
wide, the world is all before us, says the rye" (355). Ironic that in modish cities
of competitive individualists, individuals miss their chance for the isolation
and individuality of the impoverished country. The narrator relishes the isolation because he rejects progressivism. Or is it because he prefers the archaic fra-
ternity of a central fireplace?

> From this habitual precedence of my chimney over me, some even think that I
> have got into a sad rearward way altogether; in short, from standing behind my
> old-fashioned chimney so much, I have got to be quite behind the age, too, as
> well as running behind-hand in everything else. But to tell the truth, I never was
> a very forward old fellow, nor what my farming neighbors call a forehanded one.
> Indeed, those rumors about my behindhandedness are so far correct, that I have
> an odd sauntering way with me sometimes of going about with my hands behind
> my back. (353)

Growing old and crabbed, with "sciatica," a euphemism for pain in the ass,
with which he is "sometimes as crippled up as any old apple tree" (360), the
narrator relishes settling, along with his "old chimney, which settles more and
more every day" (352).

But while he and his chimney both show signs of age, the chimney is, as a
piece of property, not allowed to settle without a fight. When the top is damaged by unwise renovations of the roof, the damage is the target of satiric gibes
by his neighbors and his wife, all of whom wish to see a world in good repair.
While the narrator finds the ruin to be "picturesque," the mortgage holder finds
it to be risky to his interest in the property and demands that it be fixed. "All
the world over, the picturesque yields to the pocketesque. The mortgagor cared
not, but the mortgagee did" (357). Here, the narrator finds that the mercantile
and competitive world invades even his retreat of country poverty and isolation, refusing to let him settle, to contemplate his own mortality by contemplating the decay of his chimney, the pains in his body, and the "ashes not unwelcome at my feet, and ashes not unwelcome all but in my mouth, and who

am thus in a comfortable sort of not unwelcome, though, indeed, ashy enough way, reminded of the ultimate exhaustion even of the most fiery life" (361).

His wife, on the other hand, "is a natural projector. The maxim, 'Whatever is is right,' is not hers. Her maxim is, Whatever is, is wrong; and what is more, must be altered; and what is still more, must be altered right away. Dreadful maxim for the wife of a dozy old dreamer like me" (360). In strictly economic terms, she represents the forward-looking enterprising spirit. She, like her city counterparts, wants to build a stylish house, one with a central hallway suitable for dances and socializing, rather than paying homage, like her husband, to the retrograde style of a house in which the chimney "has the centre of the house to himself, leaving but the odd holes and corners to me" (353) and to his wife and daughters. No wonder that wife and daughters plot incessantly to tear out the old chimney and all of its central fireplaces in order to make their house not only stylish, but convenient.

All of this is certainly true to the story, but the manifold puns make it clear that Melville intends the chimney to represent the narrator's phallus, and that his wife, by declaring that "[w]hatever is must be altered," is speaking in part of altering her husband. Considering that male passion is to so many promoters of domestic ideology is the serpent in the house of God's discipline, it comes as no surprise that Melville would talk of domestic remodeling as an effort to castrate men. As Goshgarian points out, domestic ideologists feared male passion precisely because overindulgence in orgasm was supposed to deplete men of their vitality. In particular, masturbation was supposed to make them mad. While Melville's narrator, walking with hands behind his back, is not publicly an onanist, he is caught once in the private vice of "digging round the foundation" of his chimney, but in the process, he challenges the bromide that sex is antithetical to spirit. Indeed, in sexual drives, handled alone but implicitly in sexual relations as well, the narrator suggests a primal spirituality, one attuned not only to heaven, not only to the Apollonian principles of rationality and light, but also one attuned to earthy generation, to human origins in some darkness that joins with God's logos:

> Very often I go down into my cellar, and attentively survey that vast square of masonry. I stand long, and ponder over, and wonder at it. It has a druidical look, away down in the umbrageous cellar there, whose numerous vaulted passages and far glens of gloom, resemble the dark, damp depths of primeval woods. So strongly did this conceit steal over me, so deeply was I penetrated with wonder at the chimney, that one day—when I was a little out of my mind, I now think— getting a spade from the garden, I set to work, digging round the foundation, especially at the corners thereof, obscurely prompted by dreams of striking upon some old, earthen-worn memorial of that by-gone day when, into all this gloom, the light of heaven entered, as the masons laid the foundation-stones, peradventure sweltering under an August sun, or pelted by a March storm. (357)

Interrupted by a neighbor, and made jest of for trying to "loosen[ ] the soil to make it grow," the narrator in rage refuses to allow the neighbor to "be personal" (358), intimating the absolute connection between chimney as phallus and the man's fundamental identity as a mortal man.[11]

Indeed, the narrator's Christian awareness of his mortality, especially as signaled by the debilitated condition of his chimney,[12] is perhaps his one virtue in contrast to the energy of his "enterprising" wife, who "never thinks of her end. Her youthful incredulity, as to the plain theory, and still plainer fact of death, hardly seems Christian" (361). Endorsing the narrator at this point, Melville suggests, then, that all of the wife's progressiveness, all of her industry, all of her refusal to appreciate sex, are part of a refusal to accept mortality. Insofar as she—along with her allies the architect, the mortgage holder, and the still youthful daughters—represents the capitalistic, competitive culture, Melville seems to be suggesting that the entire culture is afraid of sexuality because sexuality, the urge to procreate, implies mortality. Like Stowe's working machine Asphyxia Smith, the narrator's wife works to avoid reality: "while spicily impatient of present and past, like a glass of ginger-beer she overflows with her schemes; and, with like energy as she puts down her foot, puts down her preserves and her pickles, and lives with them in a continual future; or ever full of expectations both from time and space, is ever restless for newspapers, and ravenous for letters" (361). In rejecting such an energetic repression of feelings, especially those that lead to an understanding of mortality, Melville shares with Stowe a contempt for strive-and-succeed ethics.

But in the ways they treat sexual passion there is a marked difference indeed. To Melville, sexual passion in itself is not deforming. Only when denied does it become a spiritually debilitating force. The narrator clearly grows slowly mad in his defense of his chimney, becoming, by book's end, a recluse in his effort to hold his property. As his uncle lost the house by not having any children, symbolically by spending his days accumulating wealth at the expense of procreation, so the narrator perversely finds himself trying to defend his property *against* his wife and children themselves. There seems to be a parallel disruption in masculine generation, that as uncle cannot pass his power to nephew, so father cannot pass his power to his daughters without his wife's sanction. Male and female become opposites, with the women trying to protect their mortality from the onslaught of male drive, declining though it may be. The narrator's passion, which seemed contented to die out in glowing embers and ash, is rekindled, but not as a generative power, merely as antagonism, as boorish self-defensiveness.

While the women seem to have male passion on the run here, effectively caging it in the cellar of the house, refusing to let it go abroad for fear of being emasculated, they, too, are caged by their own passionate attack on masculine passion. What Melville sees that Stowe will not is that in suppressing masculine passion, women become obsessed with it, passionate in their denial of it. Passion, says Stowe, inhibits spiritual understanding. Yes, says Melville, but no less so than does a passionate rejection of physical love itself. Thwarted passion becomes monstrous to both men and women because it denies them access to fundamental truths of human existence—that life ends for the individual, but that in sexual love is a regenerative power that is not merely of the body, but that has extensive metaphysical or psychic implications. Lose that knowledge, says Melville, and lose one's spirit.

Not surprisingly, then, Melville's humor often insists on looking at the fact that Stowe's humor denies—sex is at the center of domesticity. If domesticity is a spiritual discipline, then sex is its essence; if earthly affections are the ladder to heaven, then sex must be the most important rung. At least that is one of the comic implications of Melville's story "Cock-a-Doodle-Doo! or, The Crowing of the Noble Cock Beneventano." Melville insists on this unconventional conjunction of sex and sacrament by building the story around an overloaded symbol, that of a rooster, or, as Melville always calls it in the story, a cock. The very pun on *cock* insists on the sexual side of the symbol, with the cock standing not only for the phallus but also for vitality and good fortune—according to Scottish folklore, "a stone from the cock's stomach was supposed to inspire the one who swallowed it with strength and courage" (239)—and also for exaggerated "masculinity." Attributes of "cockiness," such as lust, pugnacity, vanity, and arrogance are the very traits that, in domestic ideology, made men necessary to run the world's affairs but too worldly to have strong spiritual affinities. In these senses, Melville plays on cockiness as the antithesis of spirit and even of civilization.

Nonetheless, the cock also has strong spiritual significance in Christian symbology. In the simple syncretism of religious iconography, Christianity borrowed the cock from sun-worshipping religions as the harbinger of morning and turned it into the harbinger of the resurrection of the son. Further, a cock, according to the New Testament, crowed to announce that Peter had fulfilled Christ's prophecy in denying Christ (Matt. 26:34, 74–75). Consequently, the cock is one of Christ's messengers, as well as St. Peter's personal symbol, whose task it is to remind Christians not to deny their lord. Thus it serves as a symbol of the resurrection not only because it announces the rise of the sun but also because its crow marked a necessary step in the humiliation of Christ prior to his death and resurrection. The cock's crow, then, more broadly came to symbolize the end of the sway of darkness and evil and the beginning of the reign of goodness. At its crow each morning, it is widely held, evil spirits, including the devil, must vanish. Types of Gabriel, cocks will mark the coming of the Judgment Day when they crow for the last time.

It is this complex symbolic background that Melville uses to explore the relationship of sexuality to spirituality and finally to challenge the very concept of a divinity beyond the self. The story begins in the spring, with the natural world showing hints of new life to come amid the rubbish of the dead winter, all of which the narrator makes explicitly metaphorical of his understanding of life and of God: "All round me were tokens of a divided empire. The old grass and the new grass were striving together. In the low wet swales the verdure peeped out in vivid green. . . . The woods were strewn with dry dead boughs, snapped off by the riotous winds of March, while the young trees skirting the woods were just beginning to show the first yellowish tinge of the nascent spray" (268–69). A kind of progenitor of T. S. Eliot, the narrator accentuates the death, reveling in his perception that April is the cruelest month. The narrator gives us his mood in full, but with a retrospective humor, marked by puns, by alliteration, by a contrast between the narrator's mood and the slim grounds he has for the mood, and particularly by the progression through which he goes from large political and social and religious concerns to his own desperate need for money. We cannot take his generalizations seriously in this context; rather, by contrast to our superior understanding of the neutrality of that divided empire to the narrator's own piddling concerns, his bleakness becomes our joy.

Or at least it does as soon as we see our narrator rally. On hearing a cock crow, his mood instantly changes, and all he perceived before as the signs of death's triumph over the divided empire, he now sees as signs of the beauty of enduring vitality. From that instant, the narrator goes on a Rabelaisian search for the cock. The search is marked by a euphoria as extreme and desperate as the opening despair. The phallic references, of course, suggest that his desire is sexual and hypermasculine—it is a kind of madness that leads him to beat a dun, add another mortgage to his farm, feed himself heartily on beefsteak and stout (sexual implications deliberate), to cast aside grief, and even to challenge death itself to meet him. "I thought over my debts and other troubles, and over the unlucky risings of the poor oppressed *peoples* abroad, and over the railroad and steamboat accidents, and over even the loss of my dear friend, with a calm, good-natured rapture of defiance. I felt as though I could meet Death, and invite him to dinner, and toast the Catacombs with him, in pure overflow of self-reliance and a sense of universal security" (274). The oxymoron of a "calm . . . rapture" describes aptly the absurdity of the narrator's overreaction to spring fever, though the religious framework of his response to the divided empire, his willingness to meet death, and the term "rapture" itself all keep the double sense that this may be a religious ecstasy lurking as a possible interpretation.

The parody reference to William Wordsworth's "Resolution and Independence," in which the poet describes despondency lifting in a vision of divine transcendence, only heightens the confusion over which meaning to ascribe to the narrator's new euphoria. Does Melville mock the transcendental urge by calling it merely sexual passion or does he endorse it by suggesting the transcendental power of sexual passion? Surely the narrator at first is not attuned to spiritual possibilities in the rooster's crow. His early concerns are all financial, and he has a profound sense of emasculation in poverty. Consequently, he seeks the rooster among the rich estates to his east, imagining that none but a rich man could have such power. He knows of worldly riches to the east, but misses the Christian implications: God, incarnated as a poor man, also came from the east.

When the narrator finds the rooster's owner, Merrymusk, a poor man who maintains his family by working as a sawyer, his perspective begins to shift. He sees a family wasting away under the influence of terminal disease, yet each member is inspired "with a wild and spiritual delight" (285) over the rooster's crowing. He is unable, in the language of economic power, to convince Merrymusk to part with the bird. Impoverished in money, Merrymusk is rich in manhood, owning his emblem of energy and being rich enough to share its voice with all the land. *"Poor* man like *me?* Why call *me* poor? Don't the cock *I* own glorify this otherwise inglorious, lean, lantern-jawed land? Didn't my cock encourage you? And I give you all this glorification away gratis. I am a great philanthropist" (286). Merrymusk insists on the "glorification," on the spiritual richness he has cultivated in raising his cock.

Later, when the narrator visits the Merrymusk shanty only to see the deaths of each and every Merrymusk, he sees these deaths in explicitly religious terms. He sees Merrymusk, "The strong soul in the feeble body," die in a convulsive assertion of "wild ecstasy of triumph over ill," a triumph marked by the crowing of the cock. The narrator is "terrified with exceeding wonder" at the cock who "hung from the shanty roof as erewhile the trophied flags from the dome of St. Paul's." His terror is much like that of the shepherds terrified by the angels who announced Christ's coming, but Merrymusk's wife has no such terror. "She fell back, without a sigh, and through long-loving sympathy, was dead" (287). Here the domestic ideal of love leading lovers to heaven is marked by the cock's trumpet blast of exaltation. Next, the cock crows for the children, who are transfigured by the sound:

> The pallor of the children was changed to radiance. Their faces shone celestially through grime and dirt. They seemed children of emperors and kings, disguised. The cock sprang upon their bed, shook himself, and crowed, and crowed again, and still and still again. He seemed bent upon crowing the souls of the children out of their wasted bodies. He seemed bent upon rejoining instanter this whole family in the upper air. The children seemed to second his endeavors. Far, deep intense longing for release transfigured them into spirits before my eyes. I saw angels where they lay.
> They were dead. (287–88)

Even though the single-sentence second paragraph insists on a physical fact of death in contrast to the seeming spiritual transfiguration, the narrator is by this time completely caught up in the spiritual reading of the cock's meaning. To him, the children become angels, carriers of God's message that death will be overcome in Christ. He buries the entire family under a tombstone, which he has inscribed with a quotation from the Bible: "O death, where is thy sting? / O grave, where is thy victory?" (288). He is convinced of the truth of Christian resurrection.

Melville, on the other hand, is not. The Christian implications suggest that the cock may indeed be a harbinger of a glorious resurrection for the narrator, but the fact that it is a cock, a symbol of the sexual impulse, that brings this message of triumph undercuts the plausibility of this reconciliation. All of the efforts to spiritualize these rather brutal deaths notwithstanding, the persistent sexual connotations of "cock" cannot be eradicated. It is hard to take seriously the idea that the entire family is transfigured by the ejaculations of a cock. And while the narrator should take Christian virtues to heart by this etherial message, what he does instead is persist in his cockiness: "[N]ever since then have I felt the doleful dumps, but under all circumstances crow late and early with a continual crow. COCK-A-DOODLE-DOO!—OO!—OO!—OO!" (288). A conversion that is merely one of mood seems hardly to endorse a spiritual reading of the entire tale.[13]

It is useful to consider this tale as analogous to "The Doubloon" from *Moby Dick*. In both cases, we are presented with a symbol that is unreadable because too readable. What we end up understanding, therefore, is a reflection of the mind of the reader rather than any stable external or transcendental meaning. We have already seen in the way the narrator's reading of the landscape itself shifts with his mood, that his interpretations are merely projections of his anxieties and desires. Which is not to say that because meaning is subjective there is no external reality. Realities exist, as the reality of the world as an empire divided between death and life exists quite clearly. The narrator, though, does not wish to see these realities, to look squarely at the equivalence, the balance between vitality and mortality. So he shifts the meaning of the cock's crow, of the essence of the life force, from a worldly and thus mortal one to a spiritual one. His sense of apotheosis arises from his view of a loving family, as impoverished as it may be, leading one another to bliss through their shared revelry in that spirit of vitality. Embracing domestic ideology, the narrator etherializes the impulse, denies sexuality by giving it an otherworldly meaning. Still, Christian renunciation aside, his life is governed by that final living crow of defiance, not of transcendence. The meanings he grants to his own sexual urges, we thus see, are really his way of defeating his own fear of mortality. He has seen that the procreative urge has done no more in reality than give life to a family only to have it die. In worldly terms, sex and procreation do not guarantee life. Etherealize the impulse, make it an emblem of divine love rather than of worldly desire, and the fear of death evaporates. What this story finally tells us, then, is that the quest for spiritual transcendence is a mark of the seeker's fear of death, and, consequently, of the life that makes death inevitable. To Melville, the symbols of religion are marks of the psyche rather than the other way around, and the true mark of faith in life is to read those religious symbols aright in order to understand one's own inner life and relation to other lives.

In "The Apple-Tree Table; or, Original Spiritual Manifestations," Melville creates for us an opportunity to read the psychic realities behind many spiritual journeys, including those of Thoreau, of the Fox sisters and other spiritualists, and most importantly, of those who see the home as the spiritual center of each person's life. And once again, at the center of his investigation is his sense that sexual feelings are usually articulated indirectly, often through the language of spirituality, and most explicitly through the rapidly spreading belief in "spiritualism," the belief that one could communicate with the dead through spiritually sensitive mediums.

By the mid-1850s when Melville wrote this story, the Fox sisters, the virtual founders of spiritualism—or at least, those opportunists who tapped the latent religious enthusiasm of the emotional and religious playground of upstate New York in such a way as to turn spiritual belief into active and widespread solicitation of the dead—had developed a new cult predicated on their abilities to communicate with "spirits" by having the spirits knock on tables and walls in response to questions. The sisters began their game when they were in their early teens, playing on their mother's gullibility, and ultimately on the gullibility of literally thousands of believers, many, like Horace Greeley, of respectable standing.

Such patronage notwithstanding, and while the details of the hoax were not revealed until the late 1880s, the whole movement had an aura of disrespectability around it, partially because of the low social standing of the Fox sisters themselves—their family was quite poor, dependent on a moody and irascible "reformed" alcoholic father for a living—and partially because the very idea of communicating with spirits had a vague aura of license, especially sexual license, that was very disturbing to many critics. If I may be permitted a bit of an anachronism to show the pitch to which such resistance came, Thomas DeWitt Talmage's 1888 "Sermon on Spiritualism" makes the point with the proper degree of hysteria:

> I indict Spiritualism also because it is a social and marital curse. The worst deeds of licentiousness and the worst orgies of obscenity have been enacted under its patronage. The story is too vile for me to tell. I will not pollute my tongue nor your ears with the recital. Sometimes the civil law has been invoked to stop the outrage. Families innumerable have been broken up by it. It has pushed off hundreds of young women into a life of profligacy. It talks about 'elective affinities,' and 'affinital relations,' and 'spiritual matches,' and adopts the whole vocabulary of free loveism. In one of its public journals it declares 'marriage is the monster curse of civilization.' It is a source of debauchery and intemperance. If Spiritualism could have its full swing, it would turn this world into a pandemonium of carnality. It is an unclean, adulterous, damnable religion, and the sooner it drops into the hell from which it rose, the better both for earth and heaven. For the sake of man's honor and woman's purity, I say let the last vestige of it perish forever. (Jackson 202)

Of course, Talmage's frenzy is substantially inspired by the Claflin family's uses of spiritualism, in particular, Victoria Claflin Woodhull's combined message of feminism, free love, and spiritualism. But the suggestion of some kind of sexual violation inherent in spiritual and metapsychological phenomena dates to well before the Civil War, as can be seen in Nathaniel Hawthorne's *The Blithedale Romance*.

This is but one part of the religious and intellectual context that Melville manipulates in his story. The other is the less literal spiritualism of transcendentalists, in particular of Henry David Thoreau. In the penultimate paragraph of *Walden*, Thoreau retails the story of a

> strong and beautiful bug which came out of the dry leaf of an old table of apple-tree wood, which had stood in a farmer's kitchen for sixty years, first in Connecticut, and afterward in Massachusetts,—from an egg deposited in the living tree many years earlier still, as appeared by counting the annual layers beyond it; which was heard gnawing out for several weeks, hatched perchance by the heat of an urn. Who does not feel his faith in a resurrection and immortality strengthened by hearing of this? Who knows what beautiful and winged life, whose egg has been

buried for ages under many concentric layers of woodenness in the dead dry life of society, deposited at first in the alburnum of the green and living tree, which has been gradually converted into the semblance of its well-seasoned tomb,—heard perchance gnawing out now for years by the astonished family of man, as they sat round the festive board,—may unexpectedly come forth from amidst society's most trivial and handselled furniture, to enjoy its perfect summer life at last! (222–23)

The entire plot of Melville's story follows the line of this story, though the narrator tells us for certain nothing more than it is indeed a bug that comes out of the table, not a spirit at all.

That does not mean for certain, though, that a spiritual reading is not appropriate. The climactic dialogue between the professor of natural history and the narrator's daughter at the end of the tale shows the girl's move from being a literal believer in spirits to a more literary believer, reading the world for the signs of spiritual growth rather than seeing direct contact between them:

"Why, now, she did not *really* associate this purely natural phenomenon with any crude, spiritual hypothesis, did she?" observed the learned professor, with a slight sneer.

"Say what you will," said Julia, holding up, in the covered tumbler, the glorious, lustrous, flashing live opal, "say what you will, if this beauteous creature be not a spirit, it yet teaches a spiritual lesson. For if, after one hundred and fifty years' entombment, a mere insect come forth at last into light, itself an effulgence, shall there be no glorified resurrection for the spirit of man? Spirits! spirits!" she exclaimed with rapture, "I still believe in spirits, only now I believe in them with delight, when before I but thought of them with terror." (397)

At first, then, spirits to the girl were merely the signs of mortality, horrible premonitions calling her to her own ultimate demise. But familiarity, and beauty brought to light, enable her to cast a different interpretation on her own fear, transmuting it from a thing of darkness to an emblem of light.

Still, while the story does parallel Thoreau's, some significant changes radically alter the meaning of the parallel. First, soon after the bug emerges, and sooner after Julia's enraptured interpretation of the bug's meaning, the bug simply dies. Second, the "astonished family of man" is made a particular family of a particular man, and the story's meaning, as such, becomes less a parable for all time, than a study of a single time and place. Third, the table whence the bug comes has a history of its own meanings that shift according to the ideas, values, and especially moods of its beholders. The overdetermination of meaning once again doubles back on the readers, including not only those of us reading the story from the outside, but also each of the characters inside the story, who in reading the various symbols of nature and religion reveal themselves and the dynamic of the family as a whole.

The stage for this revelation is set in a family of four—the narrator, his wife, and two daughters—who occupy an old house, the locked attic of which is reputed to be haunted. Neither husband nor wife believes in spirits, and the narrator even goes so far as to say that his disbelief helped him buy the house, for its reputation lowered its price. The tale begins with the narrator's first glimpse of the old table in a corner of the attic, and his description of the "necromantic little old table," with its "three crooked legs, terminating in three cloven feet," suggests that the basic antagonism in the story will be brought about by that primal antagonist, Satan, through the agency of the "satanic-looking little old table" (378) and the narrator who "resolved to surround this sad little hermit of a table, so long banished from genial neighborhood, with all the kindly influence of warm urns, warm fires, and warm hearts; little dreaming what all this warm nursing would hatch" (380–81). He takes this decision after first exploring the attic, surrounded by emblems of light and darkness, of death and resurrection, of Faust and Mephistopheles in opposition to Jacob's ladder to heaven. The table itself, at first showing only "one hoofed foot, like that of the Evil One," is the object he implicitly wishes to redeem through the ministrations of domesticity.

All of this would suggest the stereotypical opposition between man and wife, with the man, Satan's agent, bearing his cloven hoof into the family. Yet the narrator's wife is not the embodiment of spirituality. As is so often the case in domestic comedy, the wife defies her culturally assigned role, being a "female Democritus" (394), running her life by principles of rationality. The opposite of her rationality is her daughters' complete irrationality. "Superstitiously grieved at my violating the forbidden solitude above, [Julia] associated in her mind the cloven-footed table with the reputed goblin there. She besought me to give up the idea of domesticating the table. Nor did her sister fail to add her entreaties. Between my girls there was a constitutional sympathy" (381). Their mother sees it as her "maternal duty" (381) to destroy the girls' superstitions. She is one who doesn't "believe in spirits, especially at break-fast time" (385). Neither does she believe in using spirits of the alcoholic kind, and the only way in which the narrator and his wife seem conventionally opposite is in their disagreement over his weekly punch.

His weekly punch and his introduction of the table into the family mark the narrator's position as middleman, if not medium, in the story. When bringing the table down from the attic, he sparks his daughter's hysteria:

> As for my daughter Julia, she never got over the strange emotions upon first accidentally encountering the table. Unfortunately, it was just as I was in the act of bringing it down from the garret. Holding it by the slab, I was carrying it before me, one cobwebbed hoof thrust out, which weird object, at a turn of the stairs, suddenly touched my girl, as she was ascending; whereupon, turning, and seeing no living creature—for I was quite hidden behind my shield—seeing nothing, indeed, but the apparition of the Evil One's foot, as it seemed, she cried out, and there is no knowing what might have followed, had I not immediately spoken. (381)

At first unmoved by her fears of the cloven foot, emblem of the devil's lechery, he is impervious to the implications of that fear—his daughters are on the verge of adolescence and as such are filled with the terrors of dawning adulthood.

Blind to the kind of fear his daughters' reaction suggests, he simply agrees with his wife that the girls will have to habituate themselves to the table:

> By degrees, the girls, at breakfast and tea, were induced to sit down with us at the table. Continual proximity was not without its effect. By and by, they would sit pretty tranquilly, though Julia, as much as possible, avoided glancing at the hoofed feet, and, when at this I smiled, she would look at me seriously—as much as to say, Ah, papa, you, too, may yet do the same. She prophesied that, in connection with the table, something strange would yet happen. But I would only smile the more, while my wife indignantly chided. (381–82)

The narrator's indulgent smile marks his difference from his wife. Having no fear in his own marriage of that emblem of lust, and having a wife as comfortable with their relation as is he, all is in order. But as he gets pulled into his daughter's fear of sexuality, he vacillates himself, perhaps because of his very closeness to his daughters. After all, it is he who plays comforter to their fears. While his wife chides, he smiles, and later, when the fear of spirits augments, it is the father who recognizes the depth of their terror, even as he denies it as a way to soothe it:

> My daughters looking pale, I insisted upon taking them out for a walk that morning, when the following conversation ensued:
> "My worst presentiments about that table are being verified, papa," said Julia; "not for nothing was that intimation of the cloven foot on my shoulder."
> Nonsense, said I. "Let us go into Mrs. Brown's, and have an ice-cream." (392)

One senses that, while he may not protest too much, he protests too emphatically. He wants to leave the house as much as do they because he vacillates between their fear and his wife's calm.

Indeed, it is while reading the ghost stories in Cotton Mather's *Magnalia Christi Americana*, which he also rescued from the attic when he found the table, that he begins to fear spirits himself. Captured by the old Calvinist's belief in a world in which the devil and his powers are allowed sway over the fundamentally depraved impulses of corrupt human beings, the narrator falls "under a sort of fascination. Somehow, too, certain reasonable opinions of mine seemed not so reasonable as before" (382). When fully captured by his own terror, he hears the ticking of the first of two bugs trying to get out of the apple-tree table. Under the spell of Mather, the narrator fears the sound of life crawling to light. And the next day when his daughters hear the same ticking, like that of a death-watch, they too respond in terror. Father and daughters are bound in a communion of fear, while the mother tries valiantly to use her old strategy of familiarization in the face of this new terror. The daughters immediately conclude that the sound is caused by spirits, and the narrator finds himself wondering if they speak true: "All that day, while abroad, I thought of the mysterious table. Could Cotton Mather speak true? Were there spirits? And would spirits haunt a tea-table? Would the Evil One dare show his cloven hoof in the bosom of an innocent family? I shuddered when I thought that I myself, against the solemn warnings of my daughters, had willfully introduced the cloven hoof there. Yea, three cloven feet" (387). Does the guilt in these speculations suggest a latent incestuous desire? Or does the narrator want nothing more than to keep his daughters presexual? After all, it is not he who tells his daughters to behave like rational beings; it is not he who is "pained by such childish conduct" (391).

Nor is it he who insists that his daughters stay awake with the entire family to watch the second bug crawl forth from its apple-tree womb. "My wife . . . insisted that both Julia and Anna should be of the party, in order that the evidence of their senses should disabuse their minds of all nursery nonsense" (394). In watching the hatching of the second bug, the wife's wisdom is proven, though not quite as she herself would have imagined it. The bug is so beautiful that "Julia and Anna could not have stood more charmed. . . . To them, bug had been a word synonymous with hideousness. But this was a seraphical bug; or, rather, all it had of the bug was the B, for it was beautiful as a butterfly. . . . Julia and Anna gazed and gazed. They were no more alarmed. They were delighted" (395). The wife had expected mere commonplace sensual perception to have brought the girls down to earth, but the very beauty of the bug enables them to maintain their belief in the heavenly meaning of the "resurrection" of the bug from the table. As I noted above, Julia's ground of belief shifts from the literal to the figurative, suggesting a dilation of intellectual powers, a maturation commensurate with sexual enlightenment. This beauty is part of the cycle of birth and death.

The bug dies quickly thereafter, suggesting in Melville's usual antitranscendental way that to call such human interpretations proofs of divinity is going too far. What he insists, rather, is that how we believe in spirit marks how willing we are to see the realities of our situations. To ignore knowledge, especially the knowledge that sexual relations lie at the center of the family, leads a family into gothic horror, horror that impedes growth and happiness. To view life from a humorous perspective, on the other hand, yields the knowledge that prevents such debilitating ignorance.

# FOUR

# Home, Sweat Home

The previous chapter suggested how difficult it is to constrain humor, to fence in its potential to see the world in unorthodox ways. The cases of Mark Twain and Marietta Holley suggest that for humor to work its magic, it is equally necessary to fence out of humor's realm competing serious constructions of reality. Seriousness can be seen as the repression and suppression of individual freedom required both by physical and social exigencies. It can also be seen as the realm that protects individuality from some of the most vigorous consequences of reality. This paradox is particularly interesting in the face of domesticity, both because humor was considered a relief from dangerous levels of seriousness in the philosophy that sanctioned domesticity, and because many of the ideologues of domesticity, when describing home as a haven, implied that home was a place of, if not idleness, at least of relaxation. In a sense, then, the ideology of domesticity made home the proper place for humor.

But comedians of domesticity rarely forget that chores are as much a part of domesticity as home itself, and, in many comic sketches, work is a metaphor for constraint. As usually played out—in Stowe's sketches, in some of Fanny Fern's sketches, or most aptly in the whitewashing sequence in Twain's *The Adventures of Tom Sawyer*—, domestic humor attacks work as a constraint that speaks metaphorically of the psychic repression that domesticity entails and that humor transcends. But humor needs certain kinds of restraint in order to flourish. It needs to be fenced off from seriousness, to have certain ugly realities whitewashed, in order to give it the room it needs to play out its possibilities. In the case of Tom Sawyer, Twain reveals this when, in the opening of *Adventures of Huckleberry Finn,* he has Tom argue that resistance to authority is a game that requires social respectability in the first place: Huck can't join Tom's band of robbers unless he stays with the widow to become civilized. Can humor both require and transcend limits? And what level of limitation facilitates humor without killing it? These are not simple problems for the humorist, because the duties of "work" can be either the death of humorous freedom, the subject of humor itself, or the insulation from seriousness that humor needs in the first place. So humorous "attacks" on domestic work are often not so much pleas for full freedom as they are play with freedom in the safe realm of domesticity, where doubt can flourish when surrounded by certainty. It is the child playing at being many different kinds of adult while protected by real adults.

I want, in this chapter, to support this point by showing two humorists who, when leaving the safe ground of doubt within domestic ideology, killed their senses of humor in an overly rigid definition of moral duty. In the "works" of both Holley and Twain, the moral duties of domesticity finally assume more importance than the imaginative safety that domesticity temporarily provided them. Ironically, both finally fail as humorists—that is to say that their satire overwhelms their humor—because both accepted the idea of female moral superiority within the realm of domesticity, though the mechanism by which that idea led to the failure of humor worked in opposite ways in the lives of these two authors.[1] I will begin with Twain, whose humorous resistance to female moral authority allowed him the luxury of humor, but whose sense of moral inadequacy coupled with an overwhelming sense of duty eventually led him into an aggressive, cynical, and nihilistic satire.

## I.  Mark Twain: "I Couldn't Do Nothing but Sweat and Sweat, and Feel All Cramped Up"

Much like Herman Melville himself, Mark Twain could well have taken Melville's advice about using humor to open to consciousness the inconsistencies of family life in order to prevent those inconsistencies from driving him mad. Twain may have had the century's most acute mind for discovering incongruities and paradoxes, but as a moralist, he did not trust his comic perception. He often wanted to reduce every paradox to a single correct answer, and he spent much of his considerable intellectual energy fighting the paradoxes that the rest of his energy was devoted to finding and exploring. Naturally, then, his desire for moral absolutism caused him great distress when he confronted any intellectual, political, or social subject, most especially when he confronted his paradoxical feelings about family and about himself as a member of families.

Consider the paradoxical development of family relations in his master-piece, *Adventures of Huckleberry Finn*. Granted, it has long been held as a mark of faith that, whether his ideas were good or not, Twain clearly demonstrated that the family was a trap, that "sivilization" was to be avoided at all costs, even if it meant "light[ing] out for the Territory ahead of the rest" (362). While many critics have held this gesture of defiance to be the mark of Twain's satiric insight into the corruption of American culture, other critics have taken him to task for preaching cowardly flight when loving commitment to community is the only morally sound answer to the problems of family and community life. Wendell Berry, for instance, in his essay "Writer and Region," says:

> The book ends with Huck's determination to "light out for the territory" to es-cape being adopted and "sivilized" by Tom's Aunt Sally. And here, I think, we are left face-to-face with a flaw in Mark Twain's character that is also a flaw in our national character, a flaw in our history, and a flaw in much of our literature. As I have said, Huck's point about Miss Watson is well taken and well made. There is an extremity, an enclosure, of conventional piety and propriety that needs to be escaped, and a part of the business of young people is to escape it. But this point, having been made once, does not need to be made again. In the last sentence, Huck is made to suggest a virtual identity between Miss Watson and Aunt Sally. But the two women are not at all alike. Aunt Sally is a sweet, motherly, entirely affectionate woman, from whom there is little need to escape because she has no aptitude for confinement. The only time she succeeds in confining Huck, she does so by *trusting* him. And so when the book says "Aunt Sally she's going to adopt me and sivilize me and I can't stand it. I been there before," one can only conclude that it is not Huck talking about Aunt Sally, but Mark Twain talking, still, about the oppressive female piety of Miss Watson. Something is badly awry here. At the end of this great book we are asked to believe—or to believe that Huck believes—that there are no choices between the "Civilization" represented by pious slave owners like Miss Watson or lethal "gentlemen" like Colonel Sher-burn and lighting out for the Territory. This hopeless polarity marks the exit of Mark Twain's highest imagination from his work. (75)

Berry goes on to say that Twain's failure, and the failure of our culture, is to equate boyhood with freedom and power to the neglect of family and commu-nity, the tragic acceptance of which marks the "meaning, and the liberation, of growing up" (76).

While I find such criticism apt, I think Samuel Clemens would have been astounded at it. He was a committed family man, one who bought the idea of a woman's moral superiority to, and thus legitimate social control of, men. When in his early years he argued, in his Mark Twain persona, against suffrage for women, he did so because politics would "sully" women:

> That must be a benefit beyond the power of figures to estimate, which can make us consent to take the High Priestess we reverence at the sacred fireside and send her forth to electioneer for votes among a mangy mob who are unworthy to touch the hem of her garment. . . . There is something revolting in the thought. It would shock me inexpressibly for an angel to come down from above and ask me

to take a drink with him (though I should doubtless consent); but it would shock me still more to see one of our blessed earthly angels peddling election tickets among a mob of shabby scoundrels she never saw before. ("Female Suffrage" 220–21)

When in later years he supported women's suffrage, he argued, much as do many nowadays who believe that if women held public office the country would not be in such dire condition, that women's moral superiority would elevate the tone of political discussion and the caliber of political action. In his speech "Votes for Women," he said with only light irony:

> Referring to woman's sphere in life, I'll say that woman is always right. For twenty-five years I've been a woman's rights man. I have always believed, long before my mother died, that, with her gray hairs and admirable intellect, perhaps she knew as much as I did. Perhaps she knew as much about voting as I.
>
> I should like to see the time come when women shall help make the laws. I should like to see that whip-lash, the ballot, in the hands of women. As for this city's [New York City's] government, I don't want to say much, except that it is a shame—a shame; but if I should live twenty-five years longer—and there is no reason why I shouldn't—I think I'll see women handle the ballot. If women had the ballot to-day, the state of things in this town would not exist. (*Speeches* 103)

Mark Twain opposed to women? Doubtful of the legitimacy of their moral authority? Wanting to escape the civilizing influence of domesticity? He'd have said, "Nonsense."

It is vaguely possible that the opinions of Berry and others have been influenced by the twentieth-century tradition of criticism, the tradition that has canonized Twain for his antisentimental, antigenteel vernacular satire. For the better part of a century, now, he has been touted as the great and successful enemy of sentimental conventionality, and *Huckleberry Finn* has received extravagant praise as the groundbreaking book of a new, vigorous, masculine American literature, one true to America's virile language and its preference for the realities of nature over the artificialities of a feminized culture. It has long been an article of faith that Twain revealed to other writers the potentials of American language and the American situation. I probably don't need to cite Hemingway's famous report that all of American literature begins with *Huckleberry Finn*, nor do I need to quote T. S. Eliot at length to remind you that he praised Huck for preferring the great brown god of the Mississippi to the fatuousness of conventional American culture. Writers better known for their literary criticism have pushed similar readings of Twain. For instance, George Santayana, the critic who coined the derisive term "genteel tradition" to disparage sentimental culture and the women who he said promoted it, praised Twain's humor for exposing this stuffy tradition's inappropriateness to the vigorous realities of American life. H. L. Mencken called Twain the best American writer for much the same reason. In fact, Twain was "rescued" from his enormous popularity and installed in the canon of America's "great" writers precisely because he seemed, in his humor, to take on the genteel tradition.

The work of such writers and critics of the first third of the century did much to establish the mid-century direction of Twain criticism, culminating in H. N. Smith's brilliant and extremely influential *Mark Twain: The Development of a Writer*, and taking some interesting detours along the way in such pieces as Leslie Fiedler's "'Come Back to the Raf' Ag'in Huck, Honey,'" in which Fiedler suggests that going to river on a raft with men is Twain's image for latent homosexuality in American culture. But all such criticism is contingent on a debatable combination of ideas including, most importantly, that Twain was unambiguously and unabashedly antisentimental. There is some truth to this idea, but a partial truth elevated to the status of a full explanation leads more to obscurity than to clarity.

There is much truth in the claim that Twain deliberately attacked sentimental gentility, especially in the 1880s when he wrote and published *Huckleberry Finn* and *A Connecticut Yankee in King Arthur's Court*. At that time he was studying moral philosophy and had turned against the sentimental tradition— which he had wholeheartedly endorsed when he cowrote *The Gilded Age*—for deceitfully arguing that morality is based in altruism. He instead opted for a materialistic monism with a utilitarian bent, cribbed primarily from Herbert Spencer but influenced also by Spencer's American popularizers, John Fiske and William Graham Sumner. Under their direction he came to believe that all people were primarily selfish, so that sentimental altruism was merely a hypocritical front to hide an underlying disregard for the welfare of others.[2]

But to say that this is all that Twain's literature entails suppresses the fact that Twain didn't really like his utilitarianism or the monistic realism on which it was based. His favorite book on moral philosophy, W. E. H. Lecky's *History of European Morals*, was unabashedly sentimental, and even though Twain disagreed with its conclusions, he didn't want to. As he put it in a one of his marginal notations in his copy of Lecky's *History*, "It is so noble and beautiful a book, that I don't want it to have even trivial faults" (qtd. in Blair *Mark Twain* 131). Of course, for it not to be true is more than a trivial fault, but for all that Twain thought he was attacking Lecky's ideas, his desire for sentimentalism to be the best and truest moral philosophy shows up as a constant subtext in *Huckleberry Finn*. Indeed, that subtext provides the morality that most readers respond to even though they can pretend that they prefer the cynicism of the antisentimental satire.

I have addressed these points at length in *Sentimental Twain*, and they are too large to prove here, but I need to cite some suggestive examples that show a more complicated response to the interrelated ideas of morality and femininity and family than most critics usually give the book credit for. Let me begin at the beginning and call attention to .the radical differences between the two women who most critics tend to lump together as a single manifestation of feminized "sivilization": the Widow Douglas and Miss Watson.

One should look first at the conventional representations of them as physical and social beings. The widow, as we are forced to recall from *The Adventures of Tom Sawyer*, is wealthy and handsome, childless by virtue of her widowhood, but matronly in appearance and behavior. Her sister, "a tolerable thin old maid with goggles on," lacks a home of her own and is brought to her sister's household out of charity, one assumes. In her scrawny ugliness and her spinsterhood, she looks the part of her sterile rigidity. Here, though we now blanch at the sexism of the stereotypes, Twain is simply using a fifty-year-old set of American literary conventions, established by such sentimental classics as Catherine Sedgewick's *A New England Tale* and any number of Harriet Beecher Stowe's novels. Writers like Stowe and Sedgewick developed such images in their political battle against Calvinism. They tended to show women oppressed by Calvinist asceticism as being withered and rigid, dried up by the antisentimental religion of their fathers. On the other hand, they tended to show women who had embraced a liberal, humanitarian, sentimental Christianity that allows them much greater moral and political scope as being rich, full, matronly. Such descriptions were used conventionally to argue for the superior morality of sentimental Christianity and for the superior power and happiness of women who embraced it.

Primed by such stereotypical images, a nineteenth-century reader would have seen that Twain's book endorses sentimental Christianity over Calvinism. Miss Watson is a biblical literalist who, after telling Huck to pray in the closet to get what he wants, exhorts him with visions of hellfire and damnation and a rather boring version of John Bunyan's heaven. When Huck tries out her literal interpretation of the Bible and finds it wanting, he turns to the widow for clarification:

> I went and told the widow about it, and she said the thing a body could get by praying for it was 'spiritual gifts.' This was too many for me, but she told me what she meant—I must help other people, and do everything I could for other people, and look out for them all the time, and never think about myself. This was including Miss Watson, as I took it. I went out in the woods and turned it over in my mind a long time, but I couldn't see no advantage about it—except for the other people—so at last I reckoned I wouldn't worry about it any more, but just let it go. (13–14)

This passage would seem to support Twain's idea that self-interest is what really motivates people, but in fact, Huck endorses the widow's point of view in many ways. In the book's opening paragraph, Huck tells us that the widow doesn't lie, so that we expect her opinion to carry some weight with him. Clearly it does, as we see her vision of heaven makes Huck's "mouth water" (14). Given the power she has over Huck, in spite of his early resolution, he does not just "let it go"; instead, he keeps trying her morality until he gets it right, as I'll explore briefly below.

Many critics make much of Huck's resistance to the widow's civilization, but they fail to note that Huck begins to get used to the widow's ways and finds that he likes them as time passes. In fact, he would not have left, he would have had no adventures, if Twain hadn't had his father violently appropriate him from respectability. Twain's vision of Huck's growing acceptance and joy in a loving household is far from condemning the sentimental ideal of family. Similarly, when Huck finds a comrade at the Grangerfords, he settles in without so much as a murmur against ways he would once have called "raspy." He likes the Grangerfords, even though their household is more rigidly organized than the widow's and is more colored by Calvinist patriarchalism. His appreciation has less to do with order or doctrine than with the pleasures of comradeship.

Huck explicitly confronts the Grangerfords' moral doctrines twice. He listens on a Sunday to the family converse about the sermon, "all about brotherly love, and such-like tiresomeness; but everybody said it was a good sermon, and they all talked it over going home, and had such a powerful lot to say about faith, and good works, and free grace, and preforeordestination, and I don't know what all, that it did seem to me to be one of the roughest Sundays I had run across yet" (147). Huck clearly cannot yet distinguish between the two major conflicting versions of Christianity operative in America in the nineteenth century, but equally clearly, Twain expected his readers to see that the Grangerfords are picking up the disagreement between the widow and her sister. They argue over points of doctrine, particularly over the relative efficacy of grace and good works to earn salvation.

They do not, however, argue over the importance of brotherly love, as their entire code is built on the idea of brotherly love in fairly literal terms. They are a clan, and their feud is based on the love of, if not their brothers and cousins, at least the honor of their brothers and cousins. As Calvinists living in a community made up of two extended families essentially at war for dominance of the area, they represent the antithesis of sentimental liberalism, with its exaltation of the nuclear family in free and peaceful trade, competition without violence (as it was envisioned in the late eighteenth and early nineteenth centuries), and families based on love rather than honor. When Harney Sheperdson and Sophia Grangerford elope, their success in building a modern family sparks the cataclysmic end of the archaic model of family life. Twain would say that he was supporting the ideal of a truly loving family, though, significantly, the birth of that new family is in an act not only of generational defiance, but of "heading off for the territories." The essential paradox of sentimental liberalism is foreshadowed here, with Huck watching those who want to escape the burdens of the past, of family and history, running away. How different is it for one to escape than for two?

Until the feud destroys the Grangerfords, running away is the last thing on Huck's mind. While he doesn't understand the theological arguments that the family members are as enthusiastic about as they are about their feud, Huck exposes his true sympathies in his reading of the Grangerfords' copy of a Calvinist classic, "'Pilgrim's Progress,' about a man that left his family it didn't say why. I read considerable in it now and then. The statements was interesting, but tough" (137). Interesting because mystifying; tough because both difficult to understand and difficult to live. Huck, who only leaves homes when violence forces him to, cannot understand why a man would leave a family without good reason. The abstract reasons of puritan piety, which in *The Innocents Abroad* Twain condemned as being selfish in its interest in the individual's salvation, are completely alien to Huck's natural affinity for human beings. As Twain put it elsewhere in the 1880s, "[t]o become a right Christian, one must hate his brother, his sister, his wife, etc. The laws of God and nature being stronger than those of men, this one must always remain a dead-letter" ("Three Statements" 58). The "interesting but tough" statements of Calvinism certainly never overcome the laws of Huck's nature. Indeed, gregariousness was one of the primary motives to human altruism according to sentimentalists, and when Twain has Huck cry over Buck's death, we are treated to a manifestation of the most real and powerful gregarious sympathy.

Huck over time finds that his gregarious impulse leads him to violate his own perceived self-interest in order to help others. Take, for instance, his actions when he watches the King and the Duke con the Wilks girls. As the girls, whose very sentimentality exposes them to the frauds in the first place, begin to make Huck "feel at home," Huck grows angry and ashamed at his involvement in the con. His conscience first assails him when Mary Jane Wilks accuses her sister of hurting Huck by calling attention to his lies:

> "What is it you won't believe, Joe?" Says Mary Jane, stepping in, with Susan behind her. "It ain't right nor kind for you to talk so to him, and him a stranger and so far from his people. How would you like to be treated so?" . . .
>
> Says I to myself, This is a girl that I'm letting that old reptile rob her of her money!
>
> Then Susan she waltzed in; and if you'll believe me, she did give Hare-Lip hark from the tomb!
>
> Says I to myself, And this is another one that I'm letting him rob her of her money! . . .
>
> "All right then," says the . . . girls, "you just ask his pardon."
>
> She done it, too. And she done it beautiful. She done it so beautiful it was good to hear; and I wished I could tell her a thousand lies, so she could do it again.
>
> I says to myself, This is another one that I'm letting him rob her of her money. And when she got through, they all jest laid theirselves out to make me feel at home and know I was amongst friends. I felt so ornery and low down and mean, that I says to myself, My mind's made up; I'll hive that money for them or bust. (224–25)

And he does, too, at great personal risk to himself, a risk that readers tend to discount because of the situation comedy involved. Still, Huck has made a moral turn here. Listening to Mary Jane echo the widow's morality, and watching that morality in action, and feeling the benefits of it himself, he is converted to sentimental altruism.

This conversion is the prelude for the scene that most readers feel to be the moral center of the book, when Huck decides to go to hell if necessary to free Jim. Again, critics like to point out that Huck mimics the lingo of the corrupt slaveholding culture in his belief that the right thing would be to return Jim to Miss Watson. But what such critics tend to miss is that Huck's counterresponse, the one he thinks will damn him, is actually a rendition of the widow Douglas's sentimental morality. After he writes the letter that makes him feel "[g]ood and all washed clean of sin for the first time," Huck chooses to think rather than pray:

> I . . . set there thinking; thinking how good it was all this happened so, and how near I come to being lost and going to hell. And went on thinking. And got to thinking over our trip down the river; and I see Jim before me, all the time, in the day, and in the night-time, sometimes moonlight, sometimes storms, and we a floating along, talking, and singing, and laughing. But somehow I couldn't seem to strike no places to harden me against him, but only the other kind. I'd see him standing my watch on top of his'n, stead of calling me—so I could go on sleeping; and see how glad he was when I come back out of the fog; and when I come to him again in the swamp, up there where the feud was; and such-like times; and would always call me honey, and pet me, and do everything he could think of for me, and how good he always was; and at last I struck the time I saved him by telling the men we had small-pox aboard, and he was so grateful, and said I was the best friend old Jim ever had in the world, and the only one he's got now; and then I happened to look around, and see that paper. (270)

In spite of beginning with his sense of hell learned from Miss Watson, Huck shifts to memory of good deeds, of Jim's sacrifices for Huck's sake. As the widow would have people do good for others, so Jim has done for Huck, and these deeds soften him toward Jim. The sentimentalists would argue that the association of pleasure with good deeds ameliorates selfishness and brings human beings into the circle of sympathy. Clearly, that is what Jim's behavior toward Huck has done. Finally, Huck recalls his own good turn for Jim, and he recognizes the pleasure and the bond that comes from self-sacrifice. That is when he chooses to tear up the paper and "go to hell." Obviously, while Miss Watson's terminology is more vivid to Huck and so he sees his actions as tantamount to damnation, he acts according to those sentimental precepts of the widow's that he had promised to "let go." He did about as good a job of letting them go as he did of going to hell.

Of course, the "evasion" chapters immediately ironize this moral resolution, so it is wrong to say that Twain intended finally to endorse sentimental ethics. But then, in using scenes from *Huckleberry Finn* in his around-the-world lecture tour a decade later, he chose the "small pox and the raft" scene—the moral prelude in parallel to the climactic "go to hell scene"—as the one to illustrate his proposition that "a sound heart" is better than a "deformed conscience." The terminology at least suggests that Twain found the allure of the sentimental moral position, and the fact that he chose a scene of sentimental moral "crisis" for his lecture suggests that he did not find the ironic ending of *Huckleberry Finn* to be a satisfying last word.

Over the next hundred years of interpretation, few advocates of the book have denied, evasion chapters notwithstanding, that Huck's battle with his conscience is the moral center of the book. Clearly it is based on sentimental ethics, and its development depends on many conventions of sentimental fiction. Acknowledging the sentimentality of this crucial scene, then, raises the important question of why critics have been so imperceptive for so long about what *Huckleberry Finn* fully entails. Why have we not only suppressed so much sentimental literature from the canon altogether, but why have we also refused to see that it is a central feature of one of the books on which the canon is built? The answer lies partly in the history of Twain's installation in the canon. Men like Mencken and Santayana and Hemingway all felt marginal in American culture and found a scapegoat in the women they blamed for the culture's putative decay. Their attitudes have had a persistent power that still influences the canonized interpretations of "classic" American literature.

Partly, this persistent power lies in the dominance of a Freudian understanding of the relations between the sexes. Clearly, the symbolic rendition of sentimental moral philosophy into literature ascribed ideals of altruism and compassion to women, and in so doing established a simple moral battle between masculinity and femininity. Freud's model of psychic development enabled critics to see the sexual repression such a binary construction enabled. It should not surprise, then, that male artists and intellectuals of the first part of the century, many of whom were inspired by Freud and exalted "masculine independence" as freedom from the repressive constraints of civilization, would turn on this simple binary construction. Similarly, we, too, spend most of our intellectual energies in rejecting this binary, but we have added to our understanding of the psychosexual repression an understanding of the political oppression such a binary construction generates. This is all to the good in that it helps us deconstruct the constraining images of women that Twain relies on to convey his ideas. But it does not explain why either Twain or his culture would have engaged in the elaborate pretense of ascribing moral power to women when in fact political power remained in the hands of men. I think Twain's career can cast important light on that problem.

To see how Twain's career can yield such insight, it is worth returning to Wendell Berry's analysis first. He says that Twain's failure is that he refuses to see in the community the cathartic potentials of tragedy.

> What is wanting, apparently, is the tragic imagination that, through communal form or ceremony, permits great loss to be recognized, suffered, and borne, and that makes possible some sort of consolation and renewal. . . . Without that return we may know innocence and horror and grief, but not tragedy and joy, not consolation or forgiveness or redemption. There is grief and horror in Mark Twain's life and work, but not the tragic imagination or the imagined tragedy that finally delivers from grief and horror. He seems instead to have gone deeper and deeper into grief and horror as his losses accumulated, and deeper into outrage as he continued to meditate on the injustices and cruelties of history. (78)

I would say that humor, too, can serve the cathartic purpose of tragedy, but Berry's point is nonetheless well taken. The tragic imagination looks at the imperfections of life—especially the realities of pain and mortality—and affirms the value of an imperfect world. Twain had great difficulty in affirming the value of imperfection, and part of the reason for that was his acceptance of the moral superiority of women.

He accepted as true the binary constructions of sentimental dualism, that philosophical effort to link both spirit and matter, to make conceptually accessible both the possibility of human improvement and spiritual immortality as being compatible with earthly error and the flesh's corruptibility. The idea of corruptibility helps us to see into the psychology behind this philosophical effort, because *corruption* implies both the simple natural process of decay and the moral revulsion that assumes human responsibility for that decay—"In Adam's fall/We sinned all." The sentimental vision tried to move away from such rigidly perfectionist moralism to a gentler idea of gradual improvement through how we live our lives, but no sooner did sentimentalists divide the spiritual and earthly proclivities between men and women than they allowed a wedge of the older moral rigidity back into the picture. Twain was plagued by this binary. As a man, he was ostensibly out of touch with moral perfection, yet, being ostensibly estranged from it, he both aspired to it as an ideal and turned from it in revulsion as an unattainable and therefore cruelly false hope.

Significantly, the ideal of moral perfection is usually one of negation, that is, of the negation of sin rather than of the promotion of good. At least that is how Twain's moral imagination seems to have tended. As a satirist, he was inclined to castigate human beings for folly, and to do so by reference to a moral ideal. The problem for him in part was that, as a man ostensibly estranged from that ideal, negation was dangerous. Notice that in *Huckleberry Finn*, whenever men try to operate from their standards of idealism, they do so, or at least wish to do so, violently. The new judge may be the significant exception as he tries to reform pap by domesticating him. In his home, in the presence of his wife, he manages to convince pap to take the pledge, to discover his humanity as a middle step from being an animal, a "hog," to becoming a spiritual heir to the kingdom of heaven. Pap, as a fallen man, merely cons the judge, selling the clothing that the judge has given to pap as a sign of pap's reformation and as a token of pap's new belonging to the community and using the proceeds of the sale to buy alcohol. The drunken pap returns to the judge's home to domesticate his drunkenness. When the judge surveys the ruin of his domicile the next day, he spurns the feminine approach of moral suasion and suggests instead that pap can be reformed only by shotgun. Half a novel later, Sherburn reforms a drunk with a gun, and, after he murders the drunken Boggs, the town decides to avenge the loss of the fallen man with the death of the reformer. Sherburn then reforms the crowd with a shotgun. Not restrained by feminine gentleness, Sherburn turns idealism into violence.

In his next novel, *A Connecticut Yankee in King Arthur's Court*, Twain has hardworking Hank Morgan show even more graphically the consequences of masculine idealism. Morgan, a bachelor cut off from his own community, seeks power for the ostensible good of the people. He intends to take the British out of the Dark Ages into the light of progress, into the light of the morally reformed, hardworking nineteenth century. He does fall under the influence of a woman, Sandy, but he subjects himself to her not because he believes in the legitimacy of her influence, but rather because the court has pushed him into a quest and he would at this point rather rule through influence and persuasion than through power. Yet during their journey, his experiences convince him that the "feminine" approach to reform through influence will not work: "[A]ll gentle cant and philosophizing to the contrary notwithstanding, no people in the world ever did achieve their freedom by goody-goody talk and moral suasion: it being immutable law that all revolutions that will succeed must *begin* in blood, whatever may answer afterward. If history teaches anything, it teaches that" (183). Later in the book, Morgan's idealism grows so absolute, his morality so completely intolerant of human error that he suggests that it would be best to hang all of humanity rather than to allow piecemeal cruelty to persist in perpetuity.

Morgan's connection with Sandy offers no palliative to his moral absolutism. Under the guidance of a woman, Morgan feels no moral constraint. Indeed, Sandy's is not a voice of moral constraint, but is rather the voice of liberated curiosity and imagination. Morgan takes the role of moralist in this journey, patronizing Sandy's intelligence and finally falling in love with the woman he thinks he is merely protecting. Morgan waxes sentimental briefly, turning his attention from affairs of state to the state of his family. However, after he is forced abroad with Sandy and baby to restore the baby's health, he returns, alone, to face down the culture that he holds in moral contempt. The consequence is disastrous. Morgan engages in genocide in order to cleanse the nation, and his efficiency at killing finally redounds to his disadvantage when the plague the "corrupting" bodies breed kills off his moral elite of innocent boys. The moral capacity to say no to vice, when in the hands of men powerful enough and unsympathetic enough to act on their moral rigidity, is ultimately nihilistic in Twain's imagination. It is the Calvinist's God, full of wrath and judgment, but without pity for the frailties of human beings. Certainly Twain's own satiric bent pushed his imagination endlessly toward nihilism, and some of his bitterest and most nihilistic pieces, "The Chronicle of Young Satan," for example, turn to a Calvinist God in bitter contempt. The angel Satan, in "Chronicle," is willing to destroy human beings without compunction, and in standing in for God with the name of the devil, he exemplifies Twain's sense that moral absolutism in the hands of masculine power is fundamentally evil. No wonder he preferred to surrender moral legitimacy to women, to the half of humanity he considered kind enough to exercise the moral veto power by voice alone rather than through physical violence.

When Twain does put moral idealism in the hands of women, he is able to surrender his own moral rigidity. In the case of the biblical literalist Miss Watson, Twain is able to project and condemn the very absolutism that he carried within himself, and he is able to laugh at, rather than condemn and destroy, the "evils" of his male character Huckleberry Finn. Of course, in a lazy boy, the evil that Twain feels is the essence of masculinity is still weak enough to be harmless, and something weak is worthy of the indulgent laugh of humor. But Twain still needs to exculpate such a boy in the context of women. Better, Twain finds it possible to find moral goodness in such a boy when gentler women are willing to accept him in spite of his own poor self-conception. The Widow Douglas, Mary Jane Wilks, Sophia Grangerford—all of these women are motivated by love and compassion, and each of them moves Huck away from reciprocating the violence of men into a more compassionate moral stance. In this dialectic with gentle and moral women, Huck becomes a source of humor rather than an object of ridicule. Readers are thus so inclined to identify with Huck that many forget that Huck does not speak for Twain, that Twain intends always to keep an ironic distance between himself and his creation.

Without that distance, the satire fails. But perhaps that is just as well, because by the book's end, when satiric irony squeezes out the possibility of humorous tolerance, Huck loses moral stature. He begins to look like what he always proclaimed himself to be: a no-good, low-down, ornery rapscallion. The evasion chapters leave most readers angry at Huck for failing to live up to his moral growth. But perhaps we should really be angry at Mark Twain for surrendering his own compassion for the neglected boy, for surrendering his own willingness to see, through women's eyes, the possibility that even fallen men have moral capabilities that are redemptive. Just before Twain has Hank Morgan proclaim the need for violent revolution, he says of the people of feudal Briton, "Their very imagination was dead. When you can say that of a man, he has struck bottom, I reckon; there is no lower deep for him" (182). Through Morgan's words, Twain passed sentence on himself, for while he could easily imagine ideal goodness, he failed, finally, to imagine the tolerance that makes it possible for human beings to struggle meaningfully toward such an ideal. In a perpetual sweat of indignation, he almost forgot how to laugh.

## II. Marietta Holley: "That Sweat Was the Best Thing They Could Have Done. It Kinder Opened the Pours, and Took My Mind Offen My Troubles."

Marietta Holley was known in the popular press as the "Female Mark Twain" (Winter 1) with good reason. Besides being very popular comic writers, both Clemens and Holley began their book-publishing careers through the distinctly low-class American Publishing Company, whose subscription books had the wide and lucrative sales that the higher caste trade publishers only rarely attained.[3] So while financially successful, both were denied by their mode of publication the literary status to which they aspired. Furthermore, as writers of vernacular humor, they compounded their status problem by writing in a mode that was not taken too seriously as an art by America's self-proclaimed arbiters of taste. Neither Twain nor Holley wrote genteel humor strictly in the sentimental tradition; Holley, in particular, kept most of her books in the first-person narrative voice of the vernacular character, "Josiah Allen's Wife," that is, Samantha Allen.

The two shared traits more significant than their mode of publication. Thematically, both Clemens and Holley used the tension between hard work and the desire for leisure as a running gag that drove many of their works. Granted, while Clemens's narrative voice, Mark Twain, is the voice of chronic laziness and Holley's Samantha Allen is just the opposite, both exploit the tension between desire and work to create humor. For both, the tension between work and play is metaphorical for the tension between necessity and freedom. And in the case of each, this tension embraced the tension between the pleasures of humor and the duty of satire. While satire has its own satisfactions, it makes a hash out of humor, and, again like Clemens, Holley struggled, both within individual books and over the course of her career, with the conflicting pulls of satire and humor. As it did to Clemens, the duty of satire, inasmuch as it was reinforced by gender roles, gradually pulled Holley out of her humor and turned her into a monistic, preachy, self-righteous satirist—the very kind of person she loved to make fun of in her earlier books.

In making fun of self-righteous characters in her early books, Holley makes them fun. Indeed, her most brilliant humorous insight was to build into the structure of her mouthpiece, the first-person narrator Samantha Allen, self-deflating self-complacencies that enable the reader to see her sincerity as both the source of her truths and the vehicle of a falsifying narrowness. Samantha commits numerous solecisms that open her sayings to humorous ambiguity, as for instance when, asserting her moral steadfastness, she says that her "principles are foundered on a rock." Given her propensity for mixing metaphors and for using the metaphor of the ship as soul, any principles "foundered" inspire little confidence. Another of her favorite solecisms, "pillow" for "pillar" calls to mind one of Twain's earliest windbags, the Oracle from *The Innocents Abroad*, who spoke of the "pillows" rather than the pillars of Hercules. No character with such a derivation is supposed to inspire in the reader an absolute faith in her rightness, though her righteousness is transparent.

This righteousness is the structural joke that holds the episodes together in Holley's second book, *Josiah Allen's Wife as a P.A. and P.I.: Samantha at the Centennial*. "P.I." stands for *private* investigator, the title she is given by the sexist "Jonesville Creation Searchin' Society" because, as a woman, she is not allowed to share in their public and official mission to the Centennial Exhibition in Philadelphia. But when given this oxymoronically public title by the society, she speaks out "in a noble voice." "[A]nd says I: 'No! I will not go as a P.I., I will go as a P.A.;' and I continued in still firmer axents, 'I am not one of the whifflin' ones of earth, my mind is firm and stabled, and my principles are high and foundered on a rock; if I go at all I shall go as a Josiah Allen's wife, P.A., which means Promiscuous Advisor, in the cause of Right'" (140–41). In arrogating to herself the grand title of "Promiscuous Advisor, in the cause of Right," she makes official her multivolume cause to correct the sins of the world—to martyr herself, as she constantly puts it, in the cause of right.

Samantha often does speak in the cause of Holley's opinions of right, promoting not only women's suffrage and economic independence, but also temperance, children's rights, "and etcetery," as she would put it. But Holley compromises the intensity of Samantha's crusade by having her sometimes crusade inappropriately. Throughout her visit to the Centennial, for example, Samantha accosts strangers and gives them a piece of her mind. Time and again, she gets the point wrong, and when her auditors turn beet red with suppressed laughter, she assumes that they have been affected as she intends by her speeches. For instance, when Samantha overhears a conversation that she believes impugns the moral integrity of the religious martyr John Rogers, her spiritual hero, she breaks indignantly into the conversation and "advises":

> I was settin' down in the centre of the room on as soft a lounge as I ever sot on, a lookin' at the perfectly gorgeous display of silks and velvets a displayin' themselves to me, when a good lookin' feller and girl come in, and sot down by me, and they was a talkin' over the things they had seen, and I a mindin' my own business, when the young feller spoke up, and says he to the girl:
> "Have you seen John Rogers goin' to the Parson to git married?"
> "No," says she.
> "Well, says he, "You ort to."
> I turned right round and give that young feller a look witherin' enough to wither him, and says I: "That is a pretty story to tell to wimmen, that you have seen John Rogers goin' to the Parson to git married."
> "I did see it," says he, jest as brazen as a brass candlestick.
> Says I firmly, "You didn't."
> Says he, "I did."
> Says I with dignity, "Don't you tell me that again, or I'll know the reason why. You never see John Rogers a goin' to git married. John was burned up years ago; and if he wan't, do you think he was a man to go and try to git married again when he had a wife and nine childern, and one at the breast? Never! John Rogers'es morals was sound; I guess it will take more than you to break 'em down at this late day."
> The young feller's face looked awful red and he glanced up at the young woman and tried to turn it off in a laugh and says he:
> "This is John Rogers Jr., old John Rogers'es boy."
> "Why how you talk! says I in agitated tones:
> "Which one is it; is it the one at the Breast?"
> "No!" says he. "It is the seventh boy, named after his father. . . . You'd love to see his 'Goin' to the Parson,' it is a beautiful statute." (427–28)

This is one of the rare instances in which the target of her moralizing responds by twitting Samantha. Often, they simply walk away in confusion or politeness.

Throughout *Josiah Allen's Wife* Samantha seems goaded into "advising" by a powerful moral sentiment, though Holley has Samantha intrude her ignorance even into matters of simple facts, such as confusing "Brussels" and "bristles" when looking at Brussels lace, calling the Centennial the "Sentinal" and arguing with her husband about the proper name when he calls it the "Sentimental," or confusing "stationery" and "stationary":

> I found many handsome things there [in Portugal's display]; splendid paper of all sorts, writin' paper, and elegant bound books, and some printin' on satin, invita-

tions to bull fights, and other choice amusements. I told Josiah I should think they would have to be printed on satin to git anybody started to 'em. And jest as I was sayin' this, a good-lookin' woman says to me: "Splendid stationery, isn't it?"

I see she had made a blunder and it was my duty to set her right, so says I to her: "I don't know as it is any more stationary than paper and books commonly is; they are always stationary unless you move 'em round."

She looked at me sort o' wonderin' and then laughed but kep' her head up as high as ever. It beats all what mistakes some folks will make and not act mortified a mite; but if I should make such blunders I should feel cheap as dirt. (449)

Samantha never learns, but as readers, we do. At the least we learn how narrow Samantha is in her ignorance. In a larger sense we learn the importance of a catholic perspective.

Of course, in creating a self-defeating mouthpiece, Holley makes it difficult to carry her points. When she shifts to satire, the whole fabric of her argument tends to collapse in a vortex of irony. But at her best, Holley holds irony in check by making most of her main characters sympathetic in their intentions. Their weaknesses are functions of their circumstances; what we find finally noble or ignoble in various characters is how they respond to their own shortcomings. Samantha becomes an effective spokesperson precisely because she struggles to see the value of a broad perspective in promoting progress.

As Holley has Samantha say early in *Josiah Allen's Wife* in describing a conservative member of her community:

Elder Easy is a first-rate man, and a good provider, but awful conservative. He believes in doin' jest as his 4 fathers did every time round. If anybody should offer to let him look at the other side of the moon, he would say gently but sweetly; "No, I thank you, my 4 fathers never see it, and so I would rather be excused from beholdin' it if you please." He is polite as a basket of chips, and well meanin'; I haint a doubt of it in my own mind. But he and Samantha Allen, late Smith, differs; that female loves to look on every side of a heavenly idee. I respect my 4 fathers, I think a sight of the old men. They did a good work in cuttin' down stumps and so 4th. But cities stand now where they had loggin' bees. Times change, and we change with 'em. They had to rastle with stumps and brushheaps, it was their duty; they did it, and conquered. And it is for us now, who dwell on the smooth places they cleared for us, to rastle with principle and idees. Have loggin' bees to pile up old rusty brushwood of unjust laws and customs, and set fire to 'em and burn 'em up root and branch, and plant in their ashes the seeds of truth and right, that shall yet wave in a golden harvest, under happier skies than ourn. (75–76)

This is the characteristic Samantha; she has her own strong opinions, but she refuses to judge those, including herself, who do not live up to this vision of progress. As such, she argues for the value of a humorous approach to life's complexities, an approach that acknowledges the mixed nature of human works, that progress only comes through a gradual revelation of the right in the face of entrenched wrong.

Nowhere in Holley's works is this made more effectively manifest than to-

ward the end of *Josiah Allen's Wife*. Samantha meets an acquaintance from her
first book, a "female lecturer" who wants to change the world through violent
protest. She sees hypocrisy and makes a single truth out of it: "What do you
think of men meetin' here to celebrate National Independance and the right of
self-government when they hold half of their own race in political bondage?"
(525). Samantha's mild response, "I think it is a mean trick in 'em . . . as
mean as pusly [parsley], and meaner" (525–26), merely inspires the lecturer to
vent her monistic hatred:

> "Oh!" says she, turnin' her nose in the direction of the Main Buildin' [of the ex-
> hibition] and shakin' her brown lisle thread fist at it, "How I despise men! Oh,
> how sick I be of 'em!" And she went on for a long length of time, a callin' 'em
> every name I ever heerd men called by, and lots I never heerd on, from brutal
> whelps, and roarin' tyrants, down to lyin' sneekin' snipes; and for every new and
> awful name she'd give 'em, I'd think to myself: why my Josiah is a man, and Fa-
> ther Smith was a man, and lots of other relatives, and 4 fathers on my father's
> side. And so says I:
>
> "Sister, what is the use of your runnin' men so?" says I, mildly, "It is only a
> tirin' yourself; you never will catch 'em, and put the halter of truth onto 'em,
> while you are runnin' 'em so fearfully; it makes 'em skittish and baulky." Says I,
> "Men are handy in a number of ways, and for all you seem to despise 'em so, you
> would be glad to holler to some man if your horse should run away, or your
> house git a fire, or the ship go to sinkin', or anything." (526–27)

Here Samantha refuses to get caught up in her own belief in her own moral superiority. While on the one hand she considers men to be horses, mere work animals, she also accords them sympathy as human beings, seeing in them her own
relations and the man she has married. Even her metaphor of men as horses is, in
Samantha's worldview, not so negative, for she values work above words, and
while her own hypocrisy is to talk incessantly and bombastically, she usually does
so *after* she has finished her own work or while she knits or sews.[4]

To Samantha, dignity and progress are found in labor. Hence, her answer to
the lecturer's diatribe against men is to point out the artifacts of material
progress on display at the exhibition:

> "Look there," says I, pintin' my finger eloquently towards the main Halls: Ma-
> chinery, Agricultural—and so forth—see the works of that sect you are runnin' so
> fearfully; see their time-conquerin', labor savin' inventions, see—"
>
> "I won't see, says she, firmly, and bitterly. "I won't go near any of their old ma-
> chines. I'll stand by my sect, I'll stick to the Woman's Pavilion." (528)

But Samantha has been and is impressed; she sees in such signs of progress the
signs of genius and incipient goodness, the signs of struggle toward the right.

Because the tangible signs of human genius and virtue are to her nineteenth-century eyes such compelling arguments of progress, Samantha sees
woman's labor as the key to women's progress. She sees that the signs of female genius on display in the Woman's Pavilion are tangible arguments
against the commonplaces of woman's weakness. But she insists that militant

direct action is bootless: "Here she hollered right out interruptin' me; says she: 'Less vote! less take a hammer and go at the men, and make them let us vote this minute'" (531). In "less" for "let's" Holley concisely makes the point that Samantha remakes several times over the next three pages; that a battle of conscience needs to be won patiently and nonviolently:

> Says I, "I'd love to convince men of the truth, but it hain't no use to take a hammer and try to knock unwelcome truths into anybody's head, male or female. The idee may be good, and the hammer may be a moral, well meanin' hammer; but you see the dander rises up in the head that is bein' hit, and makes a impenetrable wall, through which the idee can't go; that is a great philosophical fact, that can't be sailed round, or climbed over. . . . Nobody can git any water by breakin' up a chunk of ice with a axe; not a drop; you have got to thaw it out gradual; just like men's and wimmen's prejudices in the cause of Wimmen's Rights. Public sentiment is the warm fire that is a goin' to melt this cold hard ice of injustice that we are contendin' ag'inst; laws haint good for much if public opinion don't stand behind 'em pushin' 'em on to victory." (531)

Of course, a small piece of ice melts faster, but Samantha is determined to use "feminine suasion." Samantha's "mother" nature works slowly, whether melting ice or sprouting the seeds of truth. Any worker in the field of right has to work through the superior, feminine power of natural change.

Here, then, are some of the contradictions that lead Holley herself into the dangers of a monistic satire. Samantha's sermons are like that hammer, though they may not so much raise the dander as close the eyes of the reader. Inasmuch as Holley knows this, she makes it a point of the humor; twice in *Josiah Allen's Wife* Samantha's sermons actually put her listener to sleep. Holley insists that Samantha is right, but that she must work gradually to promote that right. Holley also insists that Samantha, in her own narrowness, is not fully right; that any advocate of progress must be willing to allow that her own work is only partial; that the truths of her day might become the errors the next generation must battle.

This puts Holley in something of a bind. Inasmuch as her goal is, as she puts it on the title page to her first book, to provide "a beacon light to guide women to life liberty and the pursuit of happiness," and it is simultaneously, as she put it on the title page to her second book, to provide "a bright and shining light, to pierce the fogs of error and injustice that surround society and Josiah, and to bring more clearly to view the path that leads straight on to virtue and happiness," Holley needs both to criticize and to provide constructive alternatives. But the criticism of satire, the criticism that masquerades as critical acumen, is a blurred sort of vision—it can destroy but cannot create. In having the men in the Creation Searchin' Society buy unneeded spectacles so that they can view the Centennial while upholding their "reputation" for intelligence, Holley metaphorically derides faulty vision.

But while she can depict the "creation searchers" haughtily criticizing paintings that, were they willing to see the world sympathetically, would move them, she cannot deny that cynicism works:

"How mad it makes me, Josiah Allen, to see anybody find fault and sneer at things they can't understand."

"Well," says Josiah mildly, "you know they have got a reputation to keep up, and they are bound to do it. Why, they say if anybody haint dressed up a mite, if you see 'em lookin' at handsome pictures, or statutes, or anything of that sort, with a cold and wooden look to their faces, and turning their noses up, and finding fault, you may know they are somebody. I suppose," says Josiah, "The 'Creation Searchers' can't be out-done in it; I s'pose they put on as hauty and superior-silly-ous looks as anybody ever did, that haint had no more practice than they have."

Josiah will make a slip sometimes, and says I, "[Y]ou mean super-silly, Josiah."

"Well, I knew there was a silly to it. They say," says Josiah, "that runnin' things down is always safe; *that* never hurts anybody's reputation. The pint is, they say, in not bein' pleased with anything, or if you be, to conceal it . . ."

Says I, "The pint is, some folks always did make natteral fools of themselves, and always will I s'pose."

"Well," says Josiah, "There must be *sunthin'* in it, Samantha, or there wouldn't be such a lot a gittin' up a reputation for wisdom in that way."

I couldn't deny it without lyin'. (482–83)

Fault-finding Samantha here is humorous in showing her hypocrisy in "correcting" Josiah while complaining about complainers. But the problem is a much larger one for Holley. How is she both to be creative and yet to clear moral stumps at the same time? More importantly, how is she to find the right to speak for the right? How does she know justice from injustice when she, too, lives in the fogs that surround society and Josiah?

In every one of her books, in spite of her awareness of the dangers of hypocritical self-righteousness, she slips into bombast when she is certain of the rightness of her crusades. Great expanses of even the early books are virtually unreadable, so heavy-handed are they in their didactic irony. Especially when dealing with the temperance crusade, Holley's moral modesty disappears. In a thirty page chapter (that feels like three hundred) of *Josiah Allen's Wife,* in which the Creation Searchin' Society debates temperance, Holley passively accepts the moral superiority of women and uses it as an argument for female political activism. While in creating Samantha, Holley seems to have been aware of her propensity for moral absolutism and self-righteousness, she occasionally loses sight of the dangers of it.

Still, even though she always puts contradiction under pressure to resolve itself into clear answers, Holley for the most part in the early books uses humor to sift through the fog, to find manifold truths in all of the contradictory evidence that her world gives her. Holley was never sure whether poetry was worthless twaddle or profound expression of the human soul; she could never really decide whether she believed in the dignity of work or believed that intellectual leisure was superior; she always held duty and pleasure in a compound tension with self-righteousness and open-mindedness; she wrote with obsessive fascination about adultery while promoting monogamy; with perplexity about the relative value of simplicity and sophistication—whether beauty of soul lay in natural behavior or cultivated manners and high education. Correlatively, she did not know whether all of the material progress that she hoped would usher in moral progress was really dangerous in its perfectionism. This list of Holley's ambivalences could be extended for many pages.

In her early works, Holley did not feel confident in her abilities to resolve these tensions, and so out of her humility came humor. At the center of all her humor and difficulty is her early insecurity about the moral value of domesticity. Holley herself, a poet and recluse in her early years in rural New York state, never married, yet extolled the virtues of domesticity. Her refusal to marry was in part a consequence of her belief in domesticity—she stayed at the homestead to live with her mother and sister after all of her brothers moved away. In many of the books, Holley makes humorous hay out of the tensions between domesticity and American mobility. What does it do to the family to have each generation become isolated from every other? How do home associations have any power when society is so mobile? And is mobility itself a source of shallowness and materialism, or is it intellectually broadening to those who would otherwise be isolated in small-town narrowness?

These questions were of extreme importance in Holley's own life—her reclusiveness did not end until, through the success of her writing, her fortune made it possible and her fame made it necessary for her to travel. She was virtually dragged out of her house on her first tour by an admirer who wanted her to speak to his female academy about temperance. Until her fifth novel, *Samantha at Saratoga*, Holley's books were all based on imaginary travels. Holley herself was an avid reader, but her propensity to live life vicariously is the antithesis of her character Samantha. In many ways, Holley was more like the hapless poet, Betsey Bobbet, a caricature so wonderfully drawn in *My Opinions and Betsey Bobbet's*, Holley's first book.

To see the richness and the humor of Holley's delineation of Betsey Bobbet, it is useful to look at the precursor of Betsey in the work of one of America's first female comic writers, Frances Miriam Whitcher. Whitcher, like Holley from upstate New York, made her fame by publishing a series of sketches in Joseph C. Neal's *Saturday Gazette* about the Widow Bedott, a social-climbing, garrulous small-town dweller who is on the make for a new husband. She masks her designs in part behind a facade of grief over the loss of her first husband, and even though she's an ignorant gossip, she aspires to gentility in writing what she calls poetry:

> Why—when he died, I took it so hard I went deranged, and took on so for a spell they was afraid they should have to send me to a Lunatic arsenal. But that's a painful subject, I won't dwell on't. I conclude as follows:
>
> > I'll never change my single lot—
> >     I think 't would be a sin—
> > The inconsolable widder o' Deacon Bedott,
> >     Don't intend to get married agin.

Excuse my cryin'—my feelins always overcomes me so when I say that poitry—
O-o-o-o-o-o! (31)

In spite of her genteel front, or rather because of it, Bedott fools nobody. It is
clear she was a domestic tyrant who bossed and talked her husband into his
grave. She is out to make an improving match the second time around, and
while she seeks status primarily, wealth is not far behind on her shopping list.
She finally snags a clergyman, to the amusement of her nephew, Jeff, who
mocks her every step of the way.

Whitcher does not introduce Jeff very quickly, but by the time she does, she
has already prepared us to share his point of view. After a brief humorous opening, the sketches quickly become brutally satiric. We never know for sure if the
widow is as addle-pated as she appears in the first sketch, but we do know for
sure that her poetry and mannerliness are all a front. She plays clinging vine
merely to secure a husband over whom she can lord it for life. She becomes de-
testable and a object of scorn quite quickly; the authorial point of view is one
of harsh judgment, not only at the false gentility of a woman writing poetry, but
over the moral worthlessness of a woman pursuing a man.

Holley takes essentially the same character, only making her a spinster instead of a widow, in Betsey Bobbet. But the degree of judgment is far from the
same. Granted, Holley has Samantha attack Betsey in no uncertain terms in
My Opinions and Betsey Bobbet's. Samantha complains that Betsey is too sentimental, among other things: "She is awful sentimental, I have seen a good
many that had it bad, but of all the sentimental creeters I ever did see Betsey
Bobbet is the sentimentalest, you couldn't squeeze a laugh out of her with a
cheeze press" (27). Yet the fact that Samantha almost never laughs undercuts
her authority in attacking Betsey for having no sense of humor.

Samantha reserves her most pungent attacks for Betsey's poetry, not only because it is poetry, but because she uses it as a romantic weapon:

> I can believe anything about Betsey Bobbet. She came in here one day last week,
> it was about ten o'clock in the mornin'. I had got my house slick as a pin, and my
> dinner under way, (I was goin' to have a biled dinner, and a cherry puddin' biled,
> with sweet sass to eat on it,) and I sot down to finish sewin' up the breadth of my
> new rag carpet. . . . The fire was sparklin' away, and the painted floor a shinin'
> and the dinner a bilin,' and I sot there sewin' jest as calm as a clock, not dreamin'
> of no trouble, when in came Betsey Bobbet.
>
> I met her with outward calm, and asked her to set down and lay off her things.
> She sot down, but she said she couldn't lay off her things. Says she, "I was comin'
> down past, and I thought I would call and let you see the last numbah of the
> Augah, there is a piece in it concernin' the tariff that stirs men's souls, I like it
> evah so much."
>
> She handed me the paper, folded so I couldn't see nothin' but a piece of poetry
> by Betsey Bobbet. I see what she wanted of me and so I dropped my breadths of
> carpetin' and took hold of it and began to read it.
>
> "Read it audible if you please," says she, "Especially the precious remahks

ovah it, it is such a feast for me to be sitting, and heah it reheahsed by a musical vorce.["]

Says I, "I spose I can rehearse it if it will do you any good," so I began as follers:

"It is seldem that we present to the readers of the Augur (the best paper for the fireside in Jonesville or the world) with a poem like the following. It may be by the assistance of the Augur (only twelve shillings a year in advance, wood and potatoes taken in exchange) the name of Betsey Bobbet will yet be carved on the lofty pinnacle of fame's towering pillow. We think however that she could study such writers as Sylvanus Cobb, and Tupper with profit both to herself and to them. EDITOR OF THE AUGUR."

Here Betsey interrupted me, "The deah editah of the Augah had no need to advise me to read Tuppah, for he is indeed my most favorite authar, you have devohed him haven't you Josiah Allen's Wife?"

"Devoured who?" says I, in a tone pretty near as cold as a cold icicle.

"Mahten, Fahyueah, Tuppah, that sweet authar," says she.

"No mom," says I shortly, "I hain't devoured Martin Farquar Tupper, nor no other man, I hain't a cannibal."

"Oh! you understand me not, I meant, devorhed his sweet, tender lines."

"I hain't devoured his tenderlines, nor nothin' relatin' to him," and I made a motion to lay the paper down, but Betsey urged me to go on, and so I read.

*Gushings of a Tendah Soul.*

Oh let who will,
Oh let who can,
Be tied onto
A horrid male man

Thus said I 'ere
My tendah heart was touched,
Thus said I 'ere
My tendah feelings gushed

But oh a change
Hath swept ore me
As billows sweep
The "deep blue sea."

A voice, a noble form,
One day I saw;
An arrow flew,
My heart is nearly raw.

His first pardner lies
Beneath the turf,
He is wandering now,
In sorrows briny surf.

Two twins, the little
Deah cherub creechahs,
Now wipe the teahs,
From off his classic feachahs

Oh sweet lot, worthy
Angel arisen,
To wipe the teahs,
From eyes like hisen

"What do you think of it?" says she as I finished readin'.

I looked at her most a minute with a majestic look. In spite of her false curls, and her new white ivory teeth, she is a humbly critter. I looked at her silently while she sot and twisted her long yellow bunnet strings, and then I spoke out,

"Hain't the Editor of the Augur a widower with a pair of twins?"

"Yes," says she with a happy look.

Then says I, "If the man hain't a fool, he'll think you are one."

"Oh!" says she, and she dropped her bunnet strings, and clasped her long bony hands together in her brown cotton gloves, "Oh, we ahdent soles of genious, have feelin's, you cold, practical natures know nuthing of, and if they did not gush out in poetry we should expiah. You may as well try to tie up the gushing catarack of Niagarah with a piece of welting cord, as to tie up the feelings of an ahdent sole."

"Ardent soul!" says I coldly. "Which makes the most noise, Betsey Bobbet, a three inch brook or a ten footer? which is the tearer? which is the roarer? deep wateis iun stillest. I have no faith in feelin's that stalk round in public in mournin' weeds. I have no faith in such mourners" says I. (32–36)

They talk back and forth about the value of poetry, until Betsey proclaims:

"The Editah of this paper is a kindred soul, he appreciates me, he undahstands me, and will not our names in the pages of this very papah go down to posterety togathah?"

Then says I, drove out of all patience with her, "I wish you was there now, both of you, I wish," says I, lookin fixedly on her, "I wish you was both of you in posterity now." (37)

A more decided judgment not only of Betsey Bobbet's poetry, but poetry itself could not be had. Yet in spite of her uncharacteristic wish for someone else's harm, Samantha finds herself yolked to Betsey throughout the book, as they keep each other company on their respective quests—Samantha to see Horace Greeley to convince him to work for women's suffrage, Betsey to catch a husband by badgering him with poetry.

The link of the two is in part the patently political one of Betsey proving Samantha's point that the ideology of domestic "spears" makes it necessary for women to sell their souls for marriage, any marriage. Give women an independent ability to earn an income, and Betsey Bobbet (and for that matter, the Widow Bedott) would not exist. Holley shifts the moral blame from individual behavior to cultural necessity. Part of Samantha's characterization as a working dynamo on a farm is a reminder that women in rural life have an economic utility unknown to upper-class women in genteel urban life. Republican simplicity, suggests Holley, has a benefit that is being lost in urbanization.

Less obvious but equally important, Samantha and Betsey are linked in their profound similarity as characters. Samantha, in My Opinions, tells us that she was resolved to live an unmarried life before widower Josiah courted her. Her appearance and character, at once homely and independent, make her the stereotypical old maid (except that she is fat rather than thin). Is the accident of her mysterious marriage the only thing that differentiates her from Betsey? Not entirely, in that her practicality is of a completely different kind than Betsey's. Her practical approach to making a livelihood is to earn her living; Betsey's is to find a husband. But this history masks a similarity in approach to life; both are obsessed with their own crusades, out to make converts of men. At one point in the story, the two come across Ulysses S. Grant, and Betsey almost kills him with one of her interminable and awful verses; Samantha rescues him, but one book later, in *Josiah Allen's Wife*, she presumes on her act of mercy to badger him with one of her interminable lectures.

In a way, then, Samantha and Betsey are two of a kind; both are "humorists" riding their respective hobbyhorses. That their hobbyhorses are opposites makes them useful foils for one another, and their combination makes it clear that neither is completely in the right about things, though clearly Holley has a closer sympathy to Samantha than to Betsey. But not when it comes to poetry, for Holley makes it clear that Samantha is not a worthy judge. Uneducated and ignorant, Samantha is an easy target for her Jeff, that is, her stepson Thomas Jefferson Allen, who teases *her* about *her* ignorance much as Jeff Maguire teases his Aunt Priscilla (Silly) Bedott. Samantha is easily fooled by Thomas Jefferson's parodies of her pretensions to philosophy, as when he explains the preferability of the term "lyceum" to her term, "Debatin' school."

> And Thomas Jefferson labored with me, and jest as his way is, he went down into the reason and philosophy of things, knowin' well what a case his mother is for divin' deep into reasons and first causes. That boy is dretful deep; he is comin' up awful well. . . . Says Thomas J. to me, says he, "I haint a word to say ag'inst your callin' it Debatin' school, only I know you are so kinder scientific and philosophical, that I hate to see you usin' a word that haint got science to back it up. Now this word Lyceum," says he, "is derived from the dead languages, and from them that is most dead. It is from the Greek and Injun; a kind of a half-breed. Ly, is from the Greek, and signifies and means a big story, or, in other words, a falsehood; and ce-um is from the Injun; and it all means, 'see 'em lie.'" (*Josiah Allen's Wife* 23)

That Samantha could be so easily fooled is a sign of her ignorance, an ignorance that extends to prosody; neither she nor her husband even knows what an epic poem is. When they hear a bad one, Samantha calls it an "epock" poem, Josiah an "epicac" poem. While in this case it is, Holley does not endorse the blanket condemnation of "impractical" poetry implicit in Samantha's and Josiah's remarks.

Holley's judgment about Bobbet's poetry is the same as Samantha's but her judgment of the poetic impulse is just the opposite. Holley herself wanted to be a poet first and foremost, even though her poetry is a just a degree or two less bad than Betsey's. It is derivative romanticism, heavily influenced by Tennyson and by Victorian medievalism. What's more, some of it expresses sentiments dangerously like those of Betsey, namely that women are weak, unworthy of love, and needing to be captured and dominated by men. Bear with me while I cite two examples:

*A Woman's Heart*

My heart sings like a bird to-night
That flies to its nest in the soft twilight,
      And sings in its brooding bliss;
Ah! I so low, and he so high,
What could he find to love? I cry,
      Did ever love stoop so low as this?

As a miser jealously counts his gold,
I sit and dream of my wealth untold,
      From the curious world apart;
Too sacred my joy for another eye,
I treasure it tenderly, silently,
      And hide it away in my heart.

Dearer to me than the costliest crown
That ever on queenly forehead shone
      Is the kiss he left on my brow;
Would I change his smile for a royal gem?
His love for a monarch's diadem?
      Change it? Ah, no, ah, no!

My heart sings like a bird tonight
That flies away to its nest of light
      To brood o'er its living bliss;
Ah! I so low, and he so high,
What could he find to love? I cry,
      Did ever love stoop so low as this?
                    (*Poems* 204–5)[5]

*Home*

A spirit is out to-night!
      His steeds are the winds; oh, list,
How he madly sweeps o'er the clouds,
      And scatters the driving mist.

We will let the curtains fall
      Between us and the storm;
Wheel the sofa up to the hearth,
      Where the fire is glowing warm.

Little student, leave your book,
      And come and sit by my side;
If you dote on Tennyson so,
      I'll be jealous of him my bride.

There, now I can call you my own!
    Let me push back the curls from your brow,
And look in your dark eyes and see
    What my bird is thinking of now.

Is she thinking of some high perch
    Of freedom, and lofty flight?
You smile; oh, little wild bird,
    You are hopelessly bound to-night!

You are bound with a golden ring,
    And your captor, like some grim knight,
Will lock you up in deepest cell
    Of his heart, and hide you from sight.

Sweetheart, sweetheart, do you hear far away
    The mournful voice of the sea?
It is telling me of the time
    When I thought you were lost to me.

Nay, love, do not look so sad;
    It is over, the doubt and the pain;
Hark! sweet, to the song of the fire,
    And the whisper of the rain.

(139–40)

Holley herself at least suspected that her poetry was drivel, as is suggested by her apology in the preface to her book of poems:

> All through my busy years of prose writing I have occasionally jotted down idle thoughts in rhyme. Imagining ideal scenes, ideal characters, and then, as is the way, I suppose, with more ambitious poets, trying to put myself inside the personalities I have invoked, trying to feel as they would be likely to, speak the words I fancied they would say.
>
> The many faults of my verses I can see only too well; their merits, if they have any, I leave with the public—which has always been so kind to me—to discover.
>
> And half-hopefully, half-fearfully, I send the little craft on the wide sea strewn with so many wrecks. But thinking it must be safe from adverse winds because it carries so low a sail, and will cruise along so close to the shore and not try to sail out in the deep waters.
>
> And so I bid the dear little wanderer (dear to me), God-speed and *bon voyage*.
>
> Marietta Holley.<br>New York, June, 1887.

The weird thing is that, while Holley signs her own name to this disclaimer, she published the book under the authorship of Samantha Allen. Of course, Samantha would never write poetry, no less try to publish it, so it is clear that by 1887 when Holley published her *Poems*, she was letting the mask slip, or perhaps she was no longer seeing Samantha as a mask at all.

    This is a crucial point in Holley's career, because it shows Holley moving beyond the self-denigration that paradoxically enabled her to publish in the first place. Apparently, this reclusive poet who wished to write of ideal characters and scenes, all products of her imagination, denigrated herself when she created an ideal of pragmatism in Samantha, but in denigrating herself, Holley was also able to liberate herself from her own serious self-constraints. By turning to humor to look at an extreme of pragmatism and an extreme of romanticism, Holley gives free rein to both. And the other extremist characters, too, are free to spout their peculiarities.

In other words, in the first two books Holley subdivides the facets of her own self into various monistic characters—the practical, heavyweight (over two hundred pounds) Samantha, her lightweight dreamer of a husband, the romantic "humbly" Betsey Bobbet. The fun is not in the victory of one over another, but in the play between them, that all of them go to make up this mysterious world. In particular, these odd characters address Holley's greatest puzzle, the mystery of love. Samantha constantly asks why she fell in love with Josiah, comically suggesting both that her love is ludicrous because she would have been better on her own, and that it is wonderful because worldly love, as a type of the divine, is infinitely expansive and creative. This mysterious ambiguity is what holds not only Samantha and Josiah together, but holds the books in humorous tension.

The fact, though, that Holley did publish the poems, especially under the name of Samantha, marked not only a growth in her self-confidence, but the beginning of the end of her ability to hold on to humor.[6] As her public gave her confidence, she tried to reconcile her own internal differences in one character—that of Samantha. Samantha becomes more genteel; she and Josiah become rich retirees, always on the go. Gradually, over the course of the books, as Holley is brought into a circle of reformers and is encouraged to become a spokesperson, she makes Samantha speak more elegantly, with less comic ambiguity. While many of her "tics" remain, such as using "forward" for "forehead," the general timbre of the language is greatly elevated. Consider, for instance, this passage about child rearing in *Samantha on Children's Rights*: "Now, a father and mother are to their children the controlling power, the visible Deity of their lives. They stand in the High Place in their souls. Let 'em tremble and quail if they don't hold that high place reverently, thoughtfully, prayerfully. The making or the marring of a life, an endless, immortal life, is in their hands, let 'em tremble at the thought" (9). The suspended predication of "The making or the marring . . . is in their hands" suggests premeditation, as does the incremental change in the iterated use of "let 'em tremble." In the earlier books, the mark of Samantha's prose was its chatty, unpremeditated nature. Iteration was common, but always appeared to be unconscious or was let down with a bump with such closing remarks as "as I said before." The old Samantha is a gossip on paper; the new is a *writer*.

Holley's illustrators, as she left the American Publishing Company for various trade houses, register this change in Samantha's characterization, as can be seen from illustrations of Samantha from *My Opinions and Betsey Bobbet's* (1872) and *Samantha on Children's Rights* (1909). In the latter (fig. 4.1), Samantha, merely visiting a neighbor, is more elegantly and fashionably dressed, quite sympathetic and gentle appearing. She is thinner than the child-beating neighbor, who "weighin' from two to three hundred pounds, wuz standin' over that little mite of humanity" (157). In the former (fig. 4.2), Samantha is grotesque; she is the weighty one, the one who even dressing for a rare photograph looks dowdy and mean. While we know her to have sympathies, we also know her as one who has a Yankee control over her emotions. This is the same woman who, when in *Josiah Allen's Wife* she is travel-

SHE WUZ WHIPPIN' LITTLE KATE, HER FACE ALL SWELLED UP WITH WHAT
SHE CALLED RELIGIOUS PRINCIPLE.

FIGURE 4.1                                                    *Page* 157.

FIGURE 4.2

ing, to the Philadelphia "Sentinal" to use Samantha the crusader's typical military language—loses one lens out of her spectacles and so sees the world, at least until Josiah fixes her glasses, through one-sided vision. In the later books, Samantha maintains her narrow vision, but Holley, who once made even Samantha's narrowness a theme of her books, seems to lose sight of it herself.

As Samantha becomes more clearly *the* mouthpiece for her creator, Josiah loses stature, becoming both sillier and meaner. In *Samantha among the Brethren* (1890), there are moments when Samantha's love for Josiah is clear, but for the most part, the two are at war, substantially because he is a pure reactionary on women's rights. He shows little of his earlier flexibility or pride in Samantha, and no longer, as in the first two books, is he ever right in their marital turf squabbles.

Even in the first two books, though Holley was careful to show that women could be just as silly as men, just as morally unsound as men, and just as lazy as men, Samantha always used examples of male cupidity, stupidity, and stubbornness to make her universal points about human nature. As long as Holley maintained distance from Samantha, as long as she made it possible for us to read Samantha's own hypocrisies, then her larger point about the commonality of human struggles toward improvement remained accessible. It seems that by the time Holley finished her third Samantha and Josiah book, *My Wayward Pardner; or, My Trials with Josiah, America, The Widow Bump, and Etcetery* (1880), she was already beginning to believe in the moral superiority of women. From there, no matter how skeptical she may have been of domesticity, with its rigid, arbitrary definitions of male and female attributes and "spheres," Holley fell for the biggest essentialist distinction of them all. When she did, she continued to write satire, but duty had conquered pleasure and humor was squeezed out by Samantha's weighty didacticism.

# FIVE

# Madness Runs in Families

In the preceding chapters I have tried to show not only that humor is used to articulate certain attitudes about domesticity, but also that it served as a way to explore new possibilities within and without the range of ideas that conform to the ideology. I have also tried to suggest that humor's range and powers are finally limited by a need for conceptual security, by the final inability of comedians to deal fully with the chaos that their own practice makes available to them. What I hope to have shown thus far with respect to humor is that it is both an opening into new psychic and social territory, but that it paradoxically needs the old as a safe ground in the first place. It is a paradox of structure and freedom being mutually interdependent and opposite, much as the American ideology that required domesticity as an intermediate ideology puts freedom and equality into a paradoxical tension. It is also a paradox of inside and outside not only being interdependent by the binary construction that defines each only in terms of the other, but also of requiring a mutual communication, a knowledge of what the other entails in order to maintain the dialectical opposition of each to the other. The freedoms of humor at the expense of domesticity require full knowledge and ultimately the acceptance of the constraints of it as well.

The humor of Mary Wilkins Freeman and of George Washington Harris arises from these metaparadoxes themselves as much as from the subject matter of domesticity at the heart of all the other humor I have discussed so far. Both Freeman and Harris push the limits of humor, in the generic terms postulated in the nineteenth century, and the limits of comedy in any terms by making the dialectic between the possibilities and costs of humor along with the analogous possibilities and costs of domesticity the focal points of humor itself. They push the limits of laughter to the edge of a very uncomfortable madness, a madness in Harris's hands of complete chaos, a madness in Freeman's hands of obsessive order. In so doing, they raise the stakes, suggesting the prices to be paid for either freedom or order, and, in bringing to consciousness the fabric of comedy that usually remains unconscious, their humor becomes extraordinarily demanding, with the payoff in pleasure being all the more intense for those few readers who find it possible to laugh.

## I. George Washington Harris: Howl in the Family

George Washington Harris's one collection of comic tales, *Sut Lovingood. Yarns Spun by a Natural Born Durn'd Fool*, pushes quite to the edge of the possibilities of humor as defined in the nineteenth century. Sut is the incarnation of egotism, of riotous anarchy. He is a slapstick version of Kierkegaard's idea of irony as egotism exerting itself through negation. Whereas Kierkegaard's ironist, Socrates, negates through the power of ideas alone, Sut is more blunt, though in his own way no less clever; he has a fundamental perception for the physical action that will demolish order and restore chaos. *Sut Lovingood's Yarns*, then, seem less suited to a book on amiable humor than to a study of aggressive satire. Yet these tales serve my purpose for several reasons.

First, Harris, who had worked substantially as a political hack and proslavery satirist during his antebellum career, compiled those of his Sut sketches without overt political purpose into a book in his desperate postbellum attempt to make money. In so doing, he deliberately disclaimed satiric intention, choosing to float the book as humor.[1] On the title page, after all, Harris uses as his first epigraph to the book the lines, "A little nonsense, now and then, / Is relished by the wisest men." It is worth looking at his claim to see if humor can indeed stretch so far without falling completely into satire. Second, many of the tales deal with the subjects of family and sexuality in ways that test the limits of domestic ideology, especially as domestic ideology was infused with Victorian prudery. Finally, the tales reveal much about the power of the vision of domestic partnership, as even Sut Lovingood, the ultimate debunker of ideals of almost every stripe, the man with the perfect nose for hypocrisy and for the potential selfishness of sentimentalism, is by the end of the book substantially domesticated, not by marriage of his own or by his parents' family, but by viewing an ideal domestic partnership.

As for the first point, the book is not self-evidently "humorous" as distinguished from derisive, ironic, satiric. "Humor" in nineteenth-century terms may indulge individualities, peculiarities, "humors," but it is always justified as serving morality in spite of its liberal tolerance of difference. Harris tells us, in the elaborate punning on "yarns" on the title page, that these yarns may not be so narrowly moral as they should be: they are, after all "warped," as we are told in the ungrammatical "warped and wove for public wear." No doubt most of the moralists whose humor I treat in this book would spurn Sut's sexual appetite, his vengefulness, his especially low estimates of the clergy, the law, the rich, and teetotalers, and his low estimate of human nature in general.[2] While Stowe could suggest that horseflesh was a lure to make people fall to their baser sides, she rarely, as Harris often did, described human beings *as* horseflesh (or fowl, or bull, or dog, etc.); and what other humorist would show a world populated by people conspicuously less intelligent than a man who describes himself as a "nat'ral born durn'd fool"? If Sut's nature is so debased, and his nature is superior to all around him, then his tales seem to be telling us that Enlightenment liberalism lies about the benignity and dignity of human nature. All of this is true to the tales and explains why Edmund Wilson could say that the Sut stories are the most morally repulsive works of real literary quality written in America.

Inasmuch as Harris was in many ways a political conservative, his satires argued that human beings are essentially incapable of self-government. He fought for the slave system and the aristocracy of the educated and ostensibly superior because, in his virulent racism and classism, he held them to be worth fighting for.[3] In creating Sut, Harris was, I believe, trying to promote this agenda, and indeed, in framing his Sut stories with the educated "George" as the reporter who gives us these tales of human depravity, Harris signals that we are to read the stories as satires. Or at least, that is the impression one gets by reading the yarns as freestanding stories, as most of us have in the anthologies that have preserved "Parson Bullen's Lizards" and "Mrs. Yardley's Quilting." In "Parson Bullen's Lizards" in particular, the reader is invited by the frame narrator to mock the hicks who populated the hill country. Even the parson is illiterate and requires the use of a merely semiliterate notary, as we discover upon reading in the opening lines of the tale the solecism-riddled reward poster that begins, "AIT ($8) DULLARS REW-ARD. 'TENSHUN BELEVERS AND KONSTABLES! KETCH 'IM! KETCH 'IM!" George is supercilious in his amusement. He tells us that he "found written copies of the above highly intelligible and vindictive proclamation stuck up on every blacksmith shop, doggery, and store door, in the frog Mountain Range. Its blood-thirsty spirit, its style, and above all, its chirography, interested me to the extent of taking one down from a tree for preservation" (48–49). When later he sees Sut and reads his copy of the poster to the illiterate troublemaker, he lies to Sut, "for the sake of a joke," about how widely known are Sut's escapades. George lends the impression that he is in control, that he taunts Sut into revealing an embarrassing story for the sake of his and our pleasure, a pleasure constituted of derisive laughter.

As I discussed in chapter 2, the use of a frame narrator is a mark of many kinds of comedy, as much of derisive comedy and pure satire as of humor. A humorous frame, however, usually works differently from a satiric frame. A humorist, like a satirist, usually uses a frame narrator to separate the reader from the inside narrator of a comic tale but never allows that separation to be simple or complete. The outside narrator often tells readers that, in spite of differences between reader and inside narrator, readers should have sympathy with the inside narrator; they should try to overcome difference even as they laugh at it. Less directly, humorous framed stories often have the frame narrator surrender control over the story so that the inside narrator establishes an emotional connection with the reader directly. Derisive comedians do not intentionally surrender control over what they frame; instead they tell us that we should merely laugh at the framed subjects. Humorists do not allow us to have such pure responses, and they often structurally complicate our responses by surrendering control to the subjects of their narratives.

In the larger context of Harris's book, we can see that Harris gives Sut at least as much control over the narratives as he gives to George. For one, the opening story of the book is dominated by Sut as storyteller. He cashes in on his ugliness and orneriness to exaggerate his formidability, even creating a lineage for himself as the child of an unmitigated "durn'd fool" of a man whose character is "unmollified." Under this character he is both able to subdue through superior wit all those who would travesty him, and to enchant the rest with his ability to spin a yarn. He lets no one but himself insult him, and in thus making himself the butt of all jokes, he simultaneously acts as object of derision and as the superior being who calls to our attention that which we hold in derision. We are thus beholden to him for our pleasure twice over, and thus end up in his power.

George himself, though he tries to create the illusion of his own control in his opening comments in occasional stories, shows himself to be a worthless storyteller and under the thumb of Sut in the tale "Eaves-Dropping a Lodge of Freemasons." George's inferiority as a raconteur is made all the more obvious by his effort and failure to stand as Sut's equal. The tale begins with George playing coy in order to force Sut and the rest of his hearers to demand the tale of why "Lum Jones hid out from the masons?" Says Sut, "Now durn your little sancterfied face, yu knows mity well why he hid out. Yu an' Lum were the fellers what *did hit*, an' this crowd orter make yu tell ur treat. I think yu orter du bof" (114). "The crowd" thus egged on, insists, and George tries to tell the story, but makes a stilted botch of it, taking a genteel eternity merely setting the scene: "Those who remember Knoxville thirty-five years ago, must still almost see 'the old stone Courthouse,' with its steep gable front to the street; its disproportionately small brick chimney, roosting on the roof at the rear; its well-whittled door-jambs, its dusty windows, its gloomy walls and ghostly echoes . . ." (114). Sut grows contemptuous, cuts George off, and takes over:

> "Oh, komplikated durnashun! That haint hit," said Sut. "Yu's drunk, ur yure sham'd to tell hit, an' so yu tries to put us all asleep wif a mess ove durn'd nonsince, 'bout echo's, and grapes, an' warnit trees; oh, yu be durn'd! Boys, jis' gin me a hoult ove that are willer baskit, wif a cob in hits mouf, an' that ar tin cup, an'

arter I'se spunged my froat, I'll talk hit all off in English, an' yu jis' watch an' see ef I say 'echo,' ur 'grapes,' ur 'graveyard' onst." (115–16)

The battle between the two narrators unhinges the reader's clear sense of superiority. In identifying with the literate and genteel narrator, the reader finds that the humor doubles back, scoffing at the shortcomings of overrefinement as well as at the crudities of the underrefined.

Given that the reader is left unsure of what attitude to take toward Sut, the moral position of satire also grows blurred by the deliberate ambiguity of humor. For some readers, like Edmund Wilson, this vortex of confused identification invites revulsion. Like straight satire, these stories enable us to view the sordid side of humanity, but unlike satire, they do not give us a safe vantage point from which to view it. Satire protects its audience from the very vices they wish subconsciously to indulge. With the Sut stories, any appreciation of Sut's anarchy forces the reader to recognize the great pleasure that such anarchy, *at least in prospect,* entails. For those willing to acknowledge the attractiveness of Sut, though, the humor that first reveals the reader's own hypocrisy in enjoying vice ultimately endorses morality more securely, more absolutely, than any narrowly censored, fully correct comedy possibly could. While Sut follows no rules, he does seem often to follow a kind of fundamental morality, insisting on fair play and honesty each time he tells of chastising characters by exposing their hypocrisies.[4] Sut's brutal honesty, while lacking tact, reveals truths about power and exploitation and about fundamental human drives, and it is the truth that sets Sut, and by extension his readers, free.

This is particularly true of "Parson Bullen's Lizards," subtitled in the book's table of contents, "(Retribution)". Sut has reason to seek retribution against Bullen since Bullen, catching Sut and his paramour, Sal, in the bushes, beats Sut until he compels Sut to subject himself to exhortation at the next camp meeting: "I *hed* to promise the ole tub ove soapgreas tu com and hev myself convarted, jis' to keep him frum killing me" (51). Sut doesn't honor the promise to convert because he recognizes the hypocrisy behind it, that Bullen is playing for power and prestige rather than for Christianity, as is made clear in part by the reactions of the believers at the meeting who, upon seeing Sut on the mourner's bench, where he "kivvered es much over my straitch'd face es I could wif my han's tu prove I wer in yearnis," let out sighs of relief and exaltation: "I hearn a sorter thankful kine ove buzzin all over the congregashun" (52). If Bullen can gather a hard nut like Sut, then he demonstrates his superior spirituality, which converts into social prestige, and perhaps cash.[5] Sut sees Bullen's overreaching as an opportunity rather than as a constraint: "An' es I know'd hit wudn't interfare wif the relashun I bore tu the still housis roun' thar, I didn't keer a durn. I jis' wanted to get *ni* ole Bullin, onst, onsuspected, an' this wer the bes' way tu do hit" (51).

Clearly Sut is out to avenge himself on Bullen, but his emotional intensity has less to do with the pain Bullen inflicted on his body than the pain inflected on his pride and, especially, on his woman. Not surprisingly, the ostensibly selfish Sut does not wish to have his lover see him beaten: "My poor innersent frien' wer dun gone an' I wer glad ove hit, fur I tho't he ment tu kill me rite whar I lay, an' I didn't want her to see me die" (50). Surprisingly, though, he saves his real anger for Bullen's willingness to compromise the young woman's reputation by spreading the story, both to the public at large, and, especially, to the young woman's parents. The parents, demonstrating their piety by boarding the preacher, hear of their daughter's sexual encounter with Sut from the guest who has been fed by the daughter's cooking, and that is what really irritates Sut:

> That night, a neighbor gal got a all fired, overhandid stroppin frum her mama, wif a stirrup leather, an' old Passun Bullin, hed et supper thar, an' what's wus nur all, that poor innersent, skeer'd gal hed dun her levil bes' a cookin hit fur 'im. She begged him, a trimblin, an' a-cryin not tu tell on her. He et her cookin' he promised her he'd keep dark—an' then went strait an' tole her mam. Warnt that rale low down, wolf mean? The durnd infunel, hiperkritical, pot-bellied, scaley-hided, whisky-wastin, stinkin ole groun'hog. He'd a heap better a stole sum *man's* hoss; I'd a tho't more ove 'im. But I paid him plum up fur hit, an' I means to keep a payin him, ontil one ur nurther ove our toca pints up tu the roots ove the grass. (51)

Sut is crudely chivalric in defending his lady's reputation, which he implies Bullen has stolen, a crime worse than stealing a "*man's*" horse. Sut's sense of honor here is surprisingly conventional: he sees his lover not as a mere object of desire, but as a "frien'" and worthy of his protection. His machismo does not extend to the prurience of telling his exploits at the expense of his "frien's" reputation. In fact, in his refusal to give her name to George, he suggests that George, like Bullen and the others, is more interested in sex as a topic of conversation than as an action engaged in by lovers, and that prurience is the kind of hypocrisy that Sut is most concerned to fight against. He becomes something of a crusader for "innersense" in sexuality, suggesting that the ban on sex is what sullies the minds of the prudish. He seeks, as the tale's subtitle tells us, "retribution," rather than mere revenge; he is an agent of a higher morality even as he is motivated by his own personal sense of outrage.

It is a commonplace of American comedy that camp meetings are really covers for sexuality; so commonplace, in fact, that in *Oldtown Folks*, Stowe responds at one point to the charge by inverting it. She says that as divine love begins to flow at revivals, it is no surprise that such love extends outward into human relations. Harris will have none of such justifications. He instead suggests that "hardshell" Calvinism has a prurient and hypocritical interest in prudery. By forcing sexuality into its own approved channels, fundamentalist religion allows the power of this primal force to flow into its own hands. In forcing Bullen to expose himself at a camp meeting, Sut exposes the hypocrisy not only of Bullen himself, but of the camp meeting generally. After Bullen sheds his clothes to rid himself of the "hell-sarpent" lizards, the female part of the congregation—at least those who are not already occupied with their own "sweethearts" (57)—pruriently watch the naked Bullen sprint for the woods:

> Ole Barbelly Bullin, es they calls 'im now, never preached ontil yesterday, an' he hadn't the fust durn'd 'oman to hear 'im, *they hev seed too much ove 'im.* Passuns ginerly hev a pow'ful strong holt on wimen; but, hoss, I tell yu thar ain't meny ove em kin run start nakid over an' thru a crowd of over three hundred wimen an' not injure thar karacter *sum.* Enyhow, hits a kind ove show they'd ruther see one at a time, an' pick the passun at that. (58–59)

Sut exposes elemental hypocrisies, here of Parson Bullen and of the congregation generally, but his self-deprecation and absolute honesty about his own motives keep him from being hypocritical. He is absolutely true to impulse and to emotion, and to a large extent that is admirable.

It is hard to imagine Harris actually endorsing sentimentalism, but in having Sut pursue his own brand of morality in response to his primal feelings, Harris is not as far from Harriet Beecher Stowe as he would have liked to believe. In one story, "Rare Ripe Garden-Seed," Harris follows the typical formula of sentimental liberal Christianity in its battle against Calvinism. Harris has Sut feel the saving power of sympathy, especially sympathy for widows and the poor:

> Sheriffs am orful 'spectabil peopil; everybody looks up tu em. I never adzacly seed the 'spectabil part mysef. I'se too fear'd ove em, I reckon, tu 'zamin fur hit much. One thing I knows, no country atwix yere an' Tophit kin ever 'lect me tu sell out widders' plunder, ur poor men's co'n, an' the tho'ts ove hit gins me a good feelin; hit sorter flashes thru my heart when I thinks ove hit. I axed a passun onst, whan hit cud be, an' he pernounced hit tu be *onregnerit pride,* what I orter squelch in prayer, an' in tendin chuch on colleckshun days. I wer in hopes hit mout be 'ligion, ur sence, a-soakin intu me; hit feels good, enyhow, an' I don't keer ef every suckit rider outen jail knows hit. (229)

Of course, Sut's next line is one of thankfulness for the discomforts a sheriff often experiences, so the extent of his sympathy does not reach as far as Stowe's, but then perhaps it is merely that he articulates his anger at the hypocrites with less gentility. Harris's Sheriff John Doltin is not significantly worse than Stowe's Simon Legree, and in reacting to the evils of these characters, readers are encouraged to feel glee over the discomforts of villains. Unlike Stowe and most other sentimentalists, though, Harris does not always hide the pleasure of watching others' discomforts behind a moral mask. As he has Sut put it in the preamble to "Contempt of Court—Almost," a part of "human nater the yeath over" is that "ef anything happens to sum feller, I don't keer ef he's yure bes' frien, an' I don't keer how sorry yu is fur him, thar's a streak ove satisfackshun 'bout like a sowin thread a-runnin all thru yer sorrer. Yu may be shamed ove hit, but durn me ef hit ain't thar" (245).

Harris is quite honest about this human glee in malevolence. To a large extent, Sut's passions are patently not admirable, and the fact that his impulses, and those of his neighbors, so often are destructive without being motivated by an elemental sense of justice shows Harris's willingness to test the limits of sentimentalism. Consider, for instance, in "Mrs. Yardley's Quilting" that Sut, by setting in motion the destruction of both Mrs. Yardley's quilts and her authority over her quilting bee, is probably seeking revenge for the Yardleys' punishing Sal after Bullen squealed on her (Estes 59). But when Sut actually strikes the horse on the rump in order to make the horse serve as the agent of destruction, Sut takes a perverse thrill out of sympathy with pain:

> I jis' tore off a palin frum the fence, an' tuck hit in bof hans, an' arter raisin hit 'way up yander, I fotch hit down, es hard es I cud, flatside to'ards the groun, an' hit acksidentally happen'd tu hit Wall-eye, 'bout nine inches ahead ove the root ove his tail. Hit landed so hard that hit made my hans tingle, an' then busted into splinters. The first thing I did, wer tu feel ove mysef, on the same spot whar hit hed hit the hoss. I cudent help duin hit tu save my life, an' I swar I felt sum ove Wall-eye's sensashun, jis' es plain. (143)

Sut has had plenty of experience with "sensashun," so he knows that the power of sympathy will give him enough understanding of the sensation so that he can feel, too, his own power in inflicting pain. According to sentimentalists, the power of sympathy is supposed to prevent sadism; Harris suggests that it is merely a spur to it.

In the context of relations between men and women, the power of sexual sensations is to Harris, as to his contemporaries, of great concern. Rejecting the idea of a hierarchy of sentiments themselves, Harris does nonetheless argue for a proper use of feeling. In rejecting the typical hierarchy, he refuses to set the powerful emotions of lust out of the bounds of acceptable sentiments. When Sut is not motivated by his thirst for liquor, his desire to tell a good story, a "skeer," revenge, or pride, he is motivated by lust. His encomium on sex in "Mrs. Yardley's Quilting" is perhaps the most complete statement of his belief in the value of lust, and the two trios of stories about marriage— "Blown Up with Soda," "Sicily Burns's Wedding," and "Old Man Burns's Bull Ride"; and "Rare Ripe Garden-Seed," "Contempt of Court—Almost," and "Trapping a Sheriff"—put Sut's theories into a practice that shows Harris's opinions on the legitimate role of lust in love and marriage.

Virtually every nineteenth-century American advocate of domestic ideology acknowledged masculine appetite, but Harris may be the one nineteenth-century American author who, with barely any mollifying indirection, insists that women, too, have strong appetites for drink and sex. As he put it in "Mrs. Yardley's Quilting":

> [Mrs. Yardley] hed narrated hit thru the neighborhood that nex Saterday she'd gin a quiltin—three quilts an' one cumfurt tu tie. "Goblers, fiddils, gals, an' whisky," wer the words she sent tu the menfolk, an' more techin ur wakenin words never drap't ofen a 'oman's tongue. She sed tu the gals, "Sweet toddy, huggin, dancin, an' huggers in 'bundance." Them words struck the gals rite in the pit ove the stumick, an' spread a ticklin sensashun bof ways, ontil they scratched thar heads wif one han, an' thar heels wif tuther. (138)

Harris seems to be here a harbinger of the twentieth-century sexual revolution in acknowledging the subjective side of woman's physicality.[6] It might be as accurate to see this as Harris's continuing contact with eighteenth-century ideas of appetite. According to Hutcheson and his contemporaries, the sexual passions were primary bonds intended by a benign Providence to mitigate human selfishness enough to enable the begetting and rearing of children. Sex to these commentators was moral in that it was necessary, and a mark of the wisdom and benignity of Providence to make necessity pleasurable. While Harris would not obviously have endorsed the benignity, he did seem to accept the social utility of the sex drive. In Sut's words, "Quiltin's, managed in a morril an' sensibil way, truly am good things—good fur free drinkin, good fur free eatin, good fur free huggin, good fur free dancin, good fur free fitin, an' goodest ove all fur poperlatin a country fas'" (139). In a larger historical perspective, there is nothing unusual in Harris's point of view. The odd ones were Harris's contemporaries who, in etherializing marriage as divine discipline, left out the rather secular side of eighteenth-century liberalism, and in so doing granted to women only the power to be objects of sexual desire.

In restoring to women their sexual subjectivity, Harris puts them in positions of power, power that stems directly from emotion. He does not, however, insist that such power is intrinsically benign. The point of the Sicily Burns stories is that emotion runs the gamut, and is as likely to be disruptive or abusive as benign. In Sicily Burns's case, she has enough knowledge of sexual passion to know how to use it to her advantage. She knows that her looks drive men wild, as Sut spells it out in pages of elaborate metaphors designed to suggest the power of sexual urges:

> Three ove her smiles when she wer a tryin ove herself, taken keerfully ten minutes apart, wud make the gran' captin ove a temprunce s'iety so durn'd drunk, he wudn't no his britches frum a par ove bellowses, ur a pledge frum a—a—warterpot. Oh! I be durned if hits eny use talkin, that ar gal cud make me murder ole Bishop Soul, hissef, ur kill mam, not tu speak ove dad, ef she jis' hinted she wanted such a thing dun. Sich an 'oman cud du more devilmint nur a loose stud hoss et a muster groun', if she only know'd what tools she totes, an' i'se sorter beginnin tu think she no's the use ove the las' durnd wun tu a dot. (76–77)

Sut's judgment of Sicily's knowledge comes from experience, experience that Sicily supplants emotions of love with those of power.[7]

The consequence is a joke of real cruelty. She leads Sut on, "jis' a scrimpshun, sorter like a keerful man salts uther pepil's cattil in the mountin, barly enuf tu bring em back tu the lick-log sum day—that's the way she salted me, an' I 'tended the lick-log es reg'lar es the old bell cow" (78–79). Sicily lures Sut with the promise of "a new sensashun" (80), which turns out to be the sensation of violent, uncontrollable vomiting from a large dose of soda she cons him into swallowing. Of course, the imagery of Sut gushing streams of white, frothing liquid suggests uncontrollable ejaculation, but the sensation is extremely uncomfortable to Sut regardless. He is clearly humiliated by the revelation that Sicily does not reciprocate tender feelings at all. Her pleasure in feelings comes instead from the feeling of superiority and power she is able to develop by humiliating her suitors. When Sut "stole a hang-dorg look back," he saw that "thar lay Sicily, flat over her back in the porch, clapin her hans, screamin wif laughin, her feet up in the air, a kickin em a-pas' each uther like she wer trying tu kick her slippers off." Sut's lust grows pathetic when he wishes he were not "Too bizzy tu look at em" (81). Adding insult to injury, Sicily calls out, "Hole hit down, Mister Lovingood! hole hit down! hits a cure fur puppy luv; hole hit *down!*" (82).

This last comment is what turns Sut against her for violating the appropriate use of sensation. In retrospect, he tells George that her parting words wer "Jis' the durndes' onreasonabil reques' ever an 'oman made ove man" but that it proved that she is "pow'ful on docterin" because "She cur'd my puppy-luv wif wun dost, durn her" (84). He begins to see that she uses her looks to gain status, first by humiliating the white-trash Sut, then by using them to attract a preacher for a spouse. Sut turns the tables on Sicily by disrupting her wedding feast by encouraging a bull, covered with swarms of angry bees, to waltz through the house where the wedding party is celebrating the day. Sut's commentary makes explicit the point of the revenge:

> Sicily, she squatted in the cold spring, up tu her years, an' turn'd a milk crock over her head, while she wer a drownin a mess ove bees onder her coats. I went tu her, an' sez I, "Yu hes got another new sensashun haint yu?" Sez she—
> "Shet yer mouth, yu cussed fool!"
> Sez I, "Pow'ful sarchin feelin bees gins a body, don't they?"
> "Oh, lordy, lordy, Sut, these yere 'bominabil insex is jis' burnin me up!"
> "Gin 'em a mess ove sody," sez I, "that'll cool 'em off, an' skeer the las' durn'd one ofen the place." (95)

In suggesting that soda will subdue the bees' ardor, Sut here compares himself to one of the "insex," suggesting that both his sexual madness and the final madness of revenge are natural, the simple results of Sicily playing with nature's ways.

Indeed, Sut himself seems less and less human and more like an embodiment of natural forces as the story unfolds. Sut begins his revenge with a mind to do something as sophomoric as shaving the tails of Sicily's horse and the horse of Clapshaw, her new husband. But instead, he notices that Sock, the Burns's domesticated bull, "hed jis' got back frum mill, an' wer turn'd intu the yard, saddil an' all, tu solace hissef a pickin grass." Sut sees this bridled brute "a nosin' roun, an cum up ontu a big baskit what hilt a little shattered co'n; he dipp'd in his head tu git hit, an' I slipp'ed up an' jerked the handil over his ho'ns" (90). That is the extent of Sut's action—everything else follows as a matter of course. A bridled bull put under further constraints backs up, violently, until he destroys beehives, house, feast and all. In destroying the beehives, Sock releases "insex." That Sut is immune to bee stings himself rather furthers the point that he is somehow representative of extrahuman powers, of an emotional intensity that is not under the control of human culture.[8]

Again as an agent of retribution rather than of mere revenge, Sut's ploy shows the ultimate failure of human behavior that violates a fundamental sexual morality. Sicily, in marrying for prestige, in manipulating the power of passion in her passion for power, prepares herself for an unfortunate marriage. Sut's angry "insex," natural agents of sexual power, sting the newly married couple into such a state of overall swelling that they cannot consummate their marriage. "Why, George, her an' him cudent sleep tugether fur ni ontu a week, on account ove the doins ove them ar hot-footed, 'vengeful, 'bominable littil insex. They never will gee tugether, got tu bad a start" (96–97). This is Harris's commentary on the use and abuse of sexual feelings to secure power rather than love. While his sexual explicitness and violence are far from standard in come-dies of domesticity, his message is really quite conventional.

This is equally true of the other series of stories about marriage, the ones having to do with curing Sheriff John Doltin of chasing married women. The series begins in "Rare Ripe Garden Seed" with the story of Wat Mastin discov-ering that his new wife has given birth to a child that he did not father. Fur-ther, he suspects that, while he was away in Atlanta working as a blacksmith for a steamboat manufacturer, his wife has been steadily seeing her lover, Sher-iff John Doltin. Sut, with his usual ubiquity, happens to be on hand conve-niently to intercept a love note from Doltin to Mary Mastin. Sut has been chased by the sheriff for some time, so he sees the note as his chance to force the sheriff to end his pursuit. More, as the avenging spirit of the area, he in-tends to *go halves wif Wat, fur I wer sorry fur him, he wer so infunely 'posed upon*" (242).

At this point, Sut expresses the opinion that women are fundamentally de-ceitful: "I went tu school tu Sicily Burns, tu larn 'oman tricks, an' I tuck a dirplomer, I did, an' now I'd jes' like tu see the pussonal feeters ove the she 'oman what cud stock rar ripe kerds on me, durn'd fool es I is" (242). "Rar ripe kerds" is a mixed metaphor rising from the story. "Rare ripe garden seed" is sup-posed to make things double in size and value in half the time they normally do, and was the lame excuse invented by Mary's mother to make Wat "own the child." "Kerds" are "cards." In other words, Sut gambles that his hand is so strong that he cannot be bluffed by any feminine subterfuge. The apparent misogyny of his opinion is made worse in the beginning of the next story by his Calvinist statement of the "onregnerit" (245) evil of all human beings at all times. Sut, at this point in the second story, seems to be on the way to the hard-shell Baptist position of misanthropy as well as misogyny, but the intensity of his statement is flat contradicted by his sympathy for Wat and, more broadly, the tender religious feeling of sympathy he expressed in the first of these tales for widows and poor folk unjustly served by sheriffs. Thus the first half of this sequence of three tales sets up a dialectic that the second half works out.

The battle is fought primarily on the grounds of domestic relations, with Sut's initial sentimentalism spawned by sympathy for women and his turn to Calvinism spawned by the disruption of marriage by two adulterers who take advantage of Wat Mastin's overpowering lust in the first place and then, in his sexual exhaustion, his willingness to leave home to work in heavy industry. The third story in the series, "Trapping a Sheriff" returns to sentimentality—modified by Harris's willingness to include the joy of revenge among legitimate sentiments—when Sut sees two cases of women following the model of domesticity. The first of these is the sheriff's wife, who without complaint suffers through her husband's infidelities, but pays the price in wasting away:

> Thar sot the sheriff's wife, in a rocking cheer. She were boney an' pale. . . . [T]here were a new moon ove indigo onder her eyes, away back intu them, fifty foot or so. I seed her tear wells; thar windlass wer broke, the buckits in staves, an' the waters all gone; an' away still furder back two lights shin'd, saft, like the stars above 'jis 'afore thar settin. . . . She wer a coughin wif her han' on her hart, like she hed no mor spittil nur she had tears, an' not much louder nor a crickit chirpin in a flute; yit in spite ove all this, a sweet smile kiver'd her feeters, like a patch ove winter sunshine on the slope ove a mountin, an' hit staid thar es steddy an' bright es the culler dus tu the rose. I 'speck that smile will go back up wif her when she starts home, whar hit mus' a-cum frum. She must onse been mons'us tempin tu men tu look at, an' now she's loved by the angils, fur the seal ove thar king is stamp'd in gold on her forrid. (257)

Some of the metaphors here are typical of Sut, but others are startlingly conventional. Sut finds her to have once been physically attractive, and the conjunction of her beauty with her heavenliness is completely typical of domestic ideology. Here Sut sees a woman worthy of seducing men to heaven, but she is betrayed by a thankless philanderer. The image converts Sut into believing in an afterlife that will repay present injustice with future justice: "As I look fus' at him, an' then at her, I'd swore tu a herearter. Yes, *two* herearters, by golly: one way up behint that ar black cloud wif the white bindin fur sich as her; the tuther herearter needs no wings nor laigs ither tu reach; when you soaks yersef in sin till yer gits heavy enuf, yu jes' draps in" (257–58). Thus this image of the sheriff's wife is the conventional one of woman as angel, betrayed by her brutal husband, but showing that there must be eternal justice after all.

The second image of domesticity furthers Sut's softening, this time to believe not so much in eternal rewards, but rather in the possibility of home as haven in an otherwise unfeeling world. He sees in Wirt Staples and his wife, Susan, a positive side of home life, one of absolute love and perfect compatibility. The male side of this perfect pair was introduced in "Contempt of Court—Almost," as a man of sufficient courage, dignity, strength, and presumption to stand up to the powers-that-be in favor of the dignity of his cousin Wat Mastin. Wirt himself is Sut's ideal man, not only for his character, but for his person:

> Tu look at him, yu cudn't think fur the life ove yu, that he hed over-bragged a single word. . . . The mussils on his arms moved about like rabbits onder the skin, an' ontu his hips an' thighs they play'd like the swell on the river, his skin wer clear red an' white, an' his eyes a deep, sparklin, wickid blue, while a smile fluttered like a hummin bird roun his mouf all the while. When the State-fair offers a premin fur *men* like thy now dus fur jackasses, I means tu enter Wirt Staples, an' I'll git hit, ef thar's five thousand entrys. (253)

Under the spell of such a man and under the spell of his sympathy for both Wat Mastin and for the sheriff's wife, Sut agrees to help Wat and Wirt break the sheriff of his habit of chasing women.

Given Sut's pleasure in chasing women himself, it is significant that his sympathy overwhelms his mischievousness. But when he sees Wirt and Susan Staples together, Sut falls under the spell of sanctified love. What first captivates Sut is that Susan joins in the planning:

> Wirt's wife did the planin, an ef she aint smart fur an 'oman, I aint a nat'ral born durned fool. She ain't one ove yure she-cat wimmin, allers spittin an' groanin, an' swellin thar tails 'bout thar vartu. She never talks a word about hit, no more nor if she didn't hev eny; an' she hes es true a heart es ever beat agin a shiff hem, ur a husban's shut. But she am full ove fun, an' I mout add as purty es a hen canary, an' I swar I don't b'l'eve the 'oman knows hit. She cum intu our boat jis' caze Wirt wer in hit, and she seed lots of fun a-plantin, an' she wanted to be at the reapin of the crap. (260)

Here is Sut's ideal, a woman who knows how to take pleasure without making a fuss about it. She lives for the living, loves for the loving, and is not concerned about how it will show. She is without hypocrisy. She has, in absolutely conventional terms, a "true heart."

Again, too, she has the capacity in her own beauty to exercise power over men, but in using that power unconsciously according to her heart, her love for her husband, and her love of fun, she makes her home a place of pleasure and comfort. Intriguingly, when Sut falls under the spell of such an ideal home, his usual directness about sexuality is buried under euphemism. Displacing sexual appetite with appetite for food, Sut delivers a long eulogium on the food Susan has prepared and served before finally waxing lyrical describing Susan herself:

> Es we sot down, the las' glimmers ove the sun crep thru the histed winder, an' flutter'd on the white tabilcloth an' play'ed a silver shine on her smoof black har, es she sot at the head ove the tabil, a-pourin out the coffee, wif her sleeves push'd tight back on her white roun' arm, her full throbbin neck wer bar to the swell ove her shoulders, an' the steam ove the coffee made a movin vail afore her face, es she slowly brush'ed hit away wif hur lef han', a-smilin an' a- flashin hur talkin eyes lovinly at her hansum husbun. I thot ef I wer a picter-maker, I cud jis' take that are supper an' that ar 'oman down on clean white paper, an' make more men hongry, an' hot tu marry, a-lookin at hit in one week, nor Whitfield convarted in his hole life; back-sliders, hippercrits, an' all, I don't keer a durn. (262)[9]

Sut acknowledges that after that day, "I gets dorg hongry every time I sees Wirt's wife, ur even her side-saddil, ur her frocks a-hangin on the closeline," but she seems to be a woman for whom, in spite of his hunger, he makes no "play." Instead, he works with her husband and her husband's cousin, to chastise those who would violate marriage by violating love. The series of three stories, then, even though it ends with violently humiliating the sheriff in retribution, ends by endorsing conventional domesticity, with Sut's anarchic nature substantially constrained by an ideal of domestic bliss.

Significantly, this couple's bliss creates a haven of individual freedom

against the demands of law and respectability. This may be one of the fundamental points of domestic ideology and inasmuch as Sut sees this ideal image
and finds his own egotism checked by it, it would seem to work in Harris's mind
at both furthering the positive side of individuality and constraining the negative. It is important, though, not to overemphasize the conventionality of the
Sut stories. True, the book does work to a climax of domestic harmony in the
penultimate story, "Trapping a Sheriff," but the denouement is a reaffirmation
that Sut is fundamentally different, fundamentally outside of such order. While
Harris may at least temporarily bridle and direct Sut's destructiveness in this vision of domestic harmony, Sut is still the child of the king of fools, and his
"famerly disposishun" toward anarchy shows finally where Harris's vision di-
verges from the commonplace vision of domestic order.[10] According to Harris,
anarchy, like madness, runs in families, indeed must run in families if families
are to persist from generation to generation.

Harris shows no anxiety about juxtaposing creativity, procreativity, and
death. In creating Sut, he created a trickster god, or at least a mythmaker who
makes himself the hero of his own hyperbolic tales. I have already noted that
Sut, as he describes himself, has supernatural powers—resisting bees, being virtually ubiquitous. He repeatedly says that he is not fully human, and any reader
must finally agree. Sut is elemental anarchy, and what he shows in his creativity
is that anarchy is a necessary precondition of fecundity of mind and body. Further, he shows the necessary link between mind and body and spirit—his essence
is to collapse the distinctions, to show that any effort to create a new order entails breaking down the old, that fecundity is predicated on mortality. Every
chance he gets, he kills the law and violates order, insisting that any system of organizing human relations is bound to become hypocritical the further it removes
itself from the emotional and physical wellsprings of behavior. Hypocrisy is a
killing kind of constraint. On the contrary, Sut's very being suggests that to stay
in touch with elemental powers is to liberate one from almost all constraints.

That Sut emphasizes the physicality of human behavior would seem at first
glance to suggest just the opposite, that elemental powers are the powers of
constraint. Sut sees human beings as controlled by animal needs to eat, drink,
and copulate. That those animal urges are the wellsprings of human behavior
Sut makes abundantly clear by reducing every escapade into a primal animal
behavior, usually of chasing or fleeing. Time and again, Sut strips people of
their clothing, has them pursue or flee or be run away with by horses and
bulls, frequently accompanied by bees or hornets, dogs and cats, and, in the
case of those who die in the process, ending up with buzzards or worms. These
tales require of the reader a vivid visual imagination; they are incomprehen-
sible to those who lack the ability to translate words into imaginary bodies
and to see the contortions of those bodies as meaningful. Meaningful is the
key. Sut's antics suggest that pretensions to human superiority to the animal
world merely mask realities and therefore make human beings all the more
susceptible to powers that they either do not understand or do not even recognize. Sut's power comes from his proximity to animal nature. Aware of
brute facts, he either directs nature's power to serve his own physical needs or

translates his knowledge into metaphors that make his world rich with creative meaning.

Much as he strips sheriffs and parsons of their clothing to expose their fundamental nature for his own benefit in their humiliation, Sut strips language of as much conventionality as he can in order to free it for his purposes. In some cases, this attack is the subject matter of his talk, the way he turns dialogue into monologue, as when he mocks the heroic effusions of Henry Wadsworth Longfellow's "Excelsior":

> "STOP that noise, Sut, I can't sleep."
>
> "Nize? Well, I be durn'd! Calls superfine singin ove a hart-breakin luv song, what's purtier by a gallun an' a 'alf, than thut cussed fool thing *yu* wer a-readin, jis arter supper 'bout the youf what toted a flag up a mountain by hissef ove a nite, wif "exelcider" writ ontu hit, nize! Why, I speck yu'd call the singin ove the cherrybeans, howlin. *Yu* be durn'd. . . . Now yu's a cussin at my luv song, I wants tu say a word about that "Excelcider" youf ove your'n, what sum Longfeller writ. *I* say, an I'll swar tu hit, that eny feller, I don't keer hu the devil he is, what starts up a mountin, kiver'd wif snow an' ise, arter sundown, wif nuffin but a flag, an' no whisky, arter a purty gal hed offer'd her bussum fur a pillar, in a rume wif a big hath, kiver'd wif hot coals, an' vittils, (here Sut rose to his tip-toes, and elevated his clenched fists high above his head,) am a dod durn'd, complikated, full-blooded, plum nat'ral born durn'd fool; he warn't smart enuf tu fine his mouf wifout a leadin string. (123–24)

This is typical of Sut's plain, antietherial debunking, stressing animal motives over any heroic ones, insisting that fancy meanings are empty of meaning.

More important, the entire book is an attack on linguistic convention. It fractures conventional language, turning even the most practiced of readers into beginners; in the face of Sut's idiosyncratic grammar and the orthography that represents it, words at first stand for little. They call attention to their artificiality as symbols. Only gradually, when the reader is weaned from conventional expectations, do the meanings begin to appear, as with Sut's solecism "Excelcider" for "Excelsior." While at first it seems nonsense or a mistake, eventually it reveals itself as a pun suggesting that Longfellow's youth is merely drunk on excellent cider. Once Sut's meanings appear, they often, especially when Sut invents metaphors, reveal themselves to be extraordinarily vivid, lucid with a freshness and vitality that depends on how thoroughly the stilted conventions have been turned out of the reader's mind. Harris's stories are primers in the power of language to capture thought and to make it vivid by making it personal.

The constraints of conventionality are the raw material of creativity only if we are willing to take risks, to distort, disrupt, disrobe, dismember what has gone before. Sut holds this creative destructiveness to be as true of family life as of language. This is the radical individuality of imagination run amok, but in its wake it leaves something new, a new generation of ideas and the capacity to appreciate again the elemental forces that old conventions had hidden. But ironically, what Harris does is to force us to play by his rules; if we are to surrender the security of our old conventions, we can only exchange them for his or for ones of our own. In some ways, what Harris does is parade in exhilaration in the ultimate isolation of radical individuality. If we follow his will, we will destroy his works with as much relish as Sut uses on Longfellow's "Excelsior."


## II. Mary Wilkins Freeman: Inherit the Will

Mary Wilkins Freeman's work, like George Washington Harris's, does not shy away from the close connections between death and creativity, and, like Harris's, it is obsessively concerned with individual freedom and the consequences to freedom of social and biological constraints. Unlike Harris's, Freeman's stories are not so sanguine (nor so sanguinary) about the possibilities of freedom. Her stories repeatedly confront choices between individual freedom and social connections, between justice and compatibility. She uses comedy less to resolve these tensions in favor of freedom than to face frankly the costs, both social and individual, of resolving these tensions in either direction. Showing that each of us has no choice but to make choices, Freeman's humor finally serves as compensation for those costs.

Before I can discuss how her humor works, though, I must first address the question of whether Freeman's works are humorous at all. Indeed, in the published criticism specifically devoted to Freeman, "The Sharp-Edged Humor of Mary Wilkins Freeman," a 1991 essay by Shirley Marchalonis, seems to be the only current work on Freeman's humor, and it, too, begins with an apologia: "To propose a humorous reading of Mary Wilkins Freeman's work certainly contradicts most published criticism. Yet her earliest important critic, William Dean Howells, and most contemporary reviewers, even as they gave her the 'local color realist' label that has so limited reading of her work, saw a mixture of 'humor and tenderness' or 'humor and pathos,' particularly in her stories" (222).[11] The few other critics who even in passing mention Freeman's humor do so from a distinctly serious point of view, namely, the view that Freeman was a realist and that reality is not funny. In particular, recent critics for the most part counter the old consensus—that Freeman was the master chronicler of decline who vividly described stunted lives—by insisting that Freeman was really chronicling the hidden strengths of women who, though boxed in by the patriarchy, were in fact irrepressible. Susan Toth's "A Defiant Light: A Positive View of Mary Wilkins Freeman," for example, extols the heroism of Freeman's characters, all but ignoring the humor even as she mentions it: "Freeman has turned it ['A Village Singer'] into a challenge to selfish community spirit, an individual's refusal to be denied humanity and justice, and a sometimes humorous, occasionally pathetic but never maudlin character study of a remarkable old woman" (126). Toth's faint sense of comedy is overwhelmed by her grand sense of heroism.

Excepting the article by Marchalonis, Toth's slight reference to Freeman's humor is about as good as it gets, for several reasons. First, early critics dismissed Freeman's feminism in "The Revolt of Mother" on the grounds that we are not to take any politics seriously in a comic tale (Edward Foster 92–93). Thus, the current generation of critics does not want to acknowledge Freeman's comic side for fear of reopening such a rich writer to the charge of triviality, especially when she works so well as a feminist writer. Second, current models of authorship often prevent critics from seeing that an author can create distance between herself and her characters. Such a commonplace of criticism should not need emphasis, but consider the model of reading and writing presented by Mary R. Reichardt in her recent book on Freeman, A *Web of Relationship: Women in the Short Stories of Mary Wilkins Freeman*.

In the introduction to her book, Reichardt quotes copiously from current theorists of writing by women:

> Judith Kegan Gardiner corroborates Gilbert and Gubar's findings, explaining in "On Female Identity and Writing by Women," "[A] female author is engaged in a process of testing and defining various aspects of identity chosen from many imaginative possibilities . . . the woman writer uses her text, particularly one centering on a female hero, as part of a continuing process involving her own self-definition and her emphatic identification with her character. . . . Thus the author may define herself through the text while creating her female hero." "The hero is her author's daughter," Gardiner posits; a woman writer forms a distinctive, nurturing-like relationship with her female characters. Moreover, she may seek through them vicarious fulfillment of those hopes and dreams left unrealized, perhaps, because of her decision to pursue an artist's career at the expense of a "normal" woman's life of marriage and child rearing. This closeness between author and character, Gardiner continues, "indicates an analogous relationship between woman reader and character," thus accounting for the "personal" closeness women often feel toward literature. (xvii–xviii)

It is impossible for Reichardt to see Freeman's comic distance from her characters if her model of authorship disallows it.[12]

But mostly, the realism label gets in the way of understanding the full reach of Freeman's work because the teleologies of our literary histories squeeze comedy out of aesthetic "progress." In periodizing the late nineteenth century as a moment of transition from local-color realism to naturalism, literary histories do not know what to do with humor, based as it is on extravagant fantasy, caricature, exaggeration, and absurd implausibilities.[13] Given that Freeman wrote local-color fiction, most critics insist on Freeman's realism, and in so doing they still see her according to that grand flow of realism that reached its crest in the early twentieth century. Seeing in Freeman a chronicle of New England's decline is to see in Freeman a necessary transitional step from the more "uplifting" and nostalgic local color of, say, Harriet Beecher Stowe's Oldtown stories to the bleaker naturalism of the turn of the century. Such a history, while true enough, enables us to miss another marked and parallel shift in literary styles, from the amiable humor of the late eighteenth and early nineteenth centuries to the modern sense of comedy as veiled aggression. Ignoring the fantasy of comedy for her putative realism, critics miss how thoroughly involved Freeman was in this latter aesthetic debate.

Freeman, as a writer of sketches and local-color tales, was able to take advantage as much of the old aesthetic of the sentimentalists as she was of the new, antiromantic realists. Though she tried to mask her affinities for sentimental fiction, her work nonetheless shows her use of many sentimental conventions, though she opportunistically mixed them up in developing extremes of pathos or of humor in many of her tales. As a sentimentalist, Freeman would of course write pathetic tales, and most of her output has at least some touch of pathos. As a sentimentalist, though, she had available to her the entire gamut of "sentiments," including humor, and she took advantage of her openings.

In this variety of moods in her tales and sketches, she is no different from Fanny Fern, or Harriet Beecher Stowe, or Washington Irving, or Mark Twain. Consider, for example, "A Village Singer." As Twain does throughout his work, Freeman sets up the comic punchline in this story as a contrast to some more genteel sentiment. The plot begins with a scene that could be developed for its comic potentials or its pathetic ones with Candace Whitcomb, the recently displaced singer of a New England village church, disrupting the premier solo of her young replacement, Alma Way.[11] Candace lives next door to the church, owns her own parlor organ, and is therefore in a perfect position to sabotage the church's musical offerings by playing her own organ and singing her own songs precisely when the new soprano begins her first work. The congregation is outraged, and the emotional tenor of the piece is carried at first by Wilson Ford, Whitcomb's nephew and Alma Way's fiancée, who threatens to "go in there and break that old organ up into kindling wood" (22) if Candace repeats her disruptive performance.

Of course, Candace does play again, and the confrontation between nephew and aunt is verbally violent, each paying a dear price for the satisfaction of anger. Wilson loses his inheritance and with it the possibility of being able to marry; Candace loses her last connection to the community in losing the love of her favored nephew. Here Freeman builds the pathos. In her cruel disappointment, Candace contracts a sudden illness, the external signs of a broken heart: "Nobody but herself thought until the very last that she would die; the doctor called her illness merely a light run of fever; she had her senses fully. But Candace gave up at the first. 'It's my last sickness,' she said. . . . She did not seem to suffer much physical pain; she only grew weaker and weaker, but she was distressed mentally" (33). Her distress is not only her sorrow at the cruel rejection she had experienced at the town's collective hand, but also her guilt at spurning the minister, her nephew, and her 'rival,' a woman who was entirely innocent in the exchange, never having connived for the job and only taking it after she had been assured that Candace had been decently and pleasantly dismissed with her concurrence that it was for the best.

In true sentimental fashion, the dying woman appears to experience a deathbed change of heart. She calls the minister to her and apologizes to him. She then calls both her nephew and his fiancée to her bedside for a touching, tearful farewell:

> Candace smiled. "Come in," she said feebly. And Alma and Wilson entered and stood beside the bed. Candace continued to look at them, the smile straining her lips.
>
> "Wilson!"
>
> "What is it, Aunt Candace?"
>
> "I ain't altered that—will. You an' Alma can—come here an'—live—when I'm—gone. Your mother won't mind livin' alone. Alma can have—all—my things."
>
> "Don't, Aunt Candace." Tears were running over Wilson's cheeks, and Alma's delicate face was all of a quiver. (35)

What more pathetic scene could we desire? The changing of the guard is sanctioned by the proud but dying woman, so feeble that she stammers in her speech, but determined to right the wrongs of her own stubbornness before she departs. She even goes so far as to surrender her things to the rival who has already captured her old job and the heart of her nephew.

The final touch of pathos comes when the repentant woman asks Alma to sing for her, but the last line violates the pathos in a wry reversal:

> "I thought—maybe—Alma'd be willin' to—sing for me," said Candace.
>
> "What do you want me to sing?" Alma asked, in a trembling voice.
>
> "'Jesus, lover of my soul.'"
>
> Alma, standing there beside Wilson, began to sing. At first she could hardly control her voice, then she sang sweetly and clearly.
>
> Candace lay and listened. Her face had a holy and radiant expression. When Alma stopped singing it did not disappear, but she looked up and spoke, and it was like a secondary glimpse of the old shape of a forest tree through the smoke and flame of the transfiguring fire the instant before it falls. "You flatted a little— on soul," said Candace. (35)

That last bit of dialogue in its absolute contrast in mood to the entire two pages preceding has a powerful comic impact, and it casts a different light on the story. Candace's stammering, once so like the minister's pathetic inarticulateness, now seems to be the consequence of rage choked into submission. Yes, Candace capitulates. Yes, the entire story takes place in the spring of the year, marking the rise of a new generation. Yes, Candace has made way for the change, but she does so finally with an ill grace that as much as asserts her ultimate superiority over her rival. Her rival will do no more than occupy her place, but Candace's spirit will linger as a judgment of how well, or poorly, that place is filled. Candace flattens Alma Way; that is, if the Spanish *alma* for "soul" means anything, Candace flattens the soul's way. What is it for the soul's way to be flat? Is it a smoothing of Candace's spirit's path or the humiliation of the next generation? Either way, the pathos is radically modified by comic triumph, in a willful assertion that defies the conventionality of the ending that we apparently were about to receive.

In the context of the last line, much of the rest of the story, too, appears anew through a comic tint. The stammering minister's confrontation with Candace, in which he, a professional orator who is unable to speak his mind, looks silly in contrast to Candace's inspired eloquence. A generous reading makes Candace and the town quite advanced in tolerance in appreciating a minister who stutters. But in light of the ending, it seems just as likely that Freeman wants us to laugh, or at least partly laugh, at the minister's infirmity. During this encounter, Candace recounts the story of her dismissal, a truly painful one in which the choir throws her a party, but Candace has not been told in advance that the party is to "celebrate" her retirement: at the party itself she learns that she has been fired. She turns the gift album she received as a memento into a footstool in a comic gesture of defiance that furthers the minister's bewilderment. Of course, this can be read as painful, as it indeed is to the characters involved, but the radical contrast between the styles of the two characters involved gives the reader the option to transmute the pain into comedy. But as comic as the contrast may be, the residue of pathos still carries weight. The ambiguity, here, is the ambiguity of humor rather than the clarity of satire.

That Freeman wrote humor is not unusual; most writers of her day included at least some comedy in their output. What marks Freeman's work, and Twain's as well, as different from the sentimental tradition from which it was derived is its mix of moods in a single story. According to sentimental aesthetics, variety in feelings is valuable, but the variety should be between rather than within stories in order to make sure that any one story creates any feeling at all and to attempt to make the feeling as intense as possible. Ideal purity of single emotions was the point of the sentimental sketch. Even Fanny Fern, who acknowledged that she often wrote comedy when she was feeling angry, usually wrote emotionally pure sketches. Freeman does not. Since her "humor and tenderness" or "humor and pathos" are mixed, it is easy for a reader to neglect one side of the mixture, especially when the readers are critics who are trying to prove the serious value of Freeman's work.

To neglect the balance, though, is to neglect a very important feature of Freeman's approach to life and literature. Granting that our knowledge of the details of her life is limited, especially compared to the unmanageable documentation of so many nineteenth-century lives, it is not easy to know much about the mind behind the stories except through the evidence of the stories themselves. We do, fortunately, have a substantial body of her letters, though, collected by Brent L. Kendrick in *The Infant Sphinx*. These show a playful personality, a mind that reveled in perceiving comedy in the tragic or pathetic. Consider, for instance, her letter of November 5, 1887, to her friend and editor, Mary Louise Booth:

> We have had a casualty in the neighborhood. A little pet dog belonging to one of the neighbors came home terribly scalded a week ago. Someone threw hot water on the poor little thing. I went in to see him the other day, and I never saw anything at once so pathetic and funny. There he lay all covered up with a sheet, with his ugly little black head on a pillow, and when I spoke to him, he winked in the most knowing and appealing manner. They sit up and watch with him nights, and feed him on *Mellin's Food*, and they have had two doctors. I prescribed wine, which they think has benefited him. I think of setting up for a dog-doctor. (*Infant Sphinx* 82)[15]

In this letter, she speaks about a situation that obviously means relatively little to her (though her letters reveal her to be a real lover of pet animals), but she takes the same tragicomic approach to a political cause that does matter to her. In her May 15, 1888, letter to Booth, she writes:

> Randolph is licensed to sell liquor now, and we are having *such* a time. Every night the streets are full of drunken men, and it does not seem safe for one to go out after dark. I lately joined the W.C.T.U. We have been having a deal of fun over it, for I do not in the least believe in it, and have broken the pledge since I took it. But it does make me feel as if something should be done, to see such a terrible state of things. I have been threatening to go down to the saloons myself and—pray them out. I suppose we shall have to endure it for a year. Randolph is a wretched little village in many respects, although I know I have a great lack of loyalty to speak so of my birthplace. (89)

The jaunty tone shows a comic distance that Freeman keeps even from subjects about which she cares, such as her own personal safety and the political steps she has taken to help secure that safety. While she obviously felt committed enough to the cause to join the Women's Christian Temperence Union, she also expresses the feeling that the W.C.T.U.'s extremism is comic itself, and she also feels that the prayerful approach to drunkenness, while the only one readily available to women, is more than a bit silly.

Such a double perspective, a willingness and ability to see simultaneously both the serious and comic sides of a situation, is a central feature of her literature, as she makes clear in many letters talking about her work. Notable is a February 19, 1890, letter to her friend Henry Shaw, who had apparently offered her some anecdotes for her to write up into stories. In her letter she thanks him profusely and, speaking of these anecdotes, says, "I shall be delighted to use the second, and also the third, which is so full of that pathetic humor which these narrow-lived country-women so often furnish" (102). She worked such "narrow-lived" characters, both male and female, into many of her stories, and tested the effect on her good friend and housemate, Mary Wales, as her 1886 letter to Booth shows:[16] "I have just finished a story, which I do not dare send as yet. It is so very tragic. Mary Wales who always giggles at my pathetic points, has just burst into a flood of tears much to my alarm. I thought she was laughing, and there she was crying. I may change it, and marry the man instead of killing him, but I fear it wont be as artistic" (68). Freeman apparently was concerned about writing stories that were unremittingly tragic. With Wales as her audience, she tested to see whether there was an admixture of comedy in her stories. When not, she did not "dare" to publish, preferring to consider revisions that would modify the tragic potentials.

Internal evidence in many of her stories bears out the evidence of these letters that Freeman wished to mix giggles with tears. At times she makes the mixture explicit, as in "A Modern Dragon," one of many of her stories about parental jealousy over children's loves. While the story is not among her most successful, it suits my purpose in that it states explicitly that Freeman sees both comedy and pathos in a tense situation. When Freeman describes a confrontation between two mothers, the one pleading for her daughter's worthiness while failing to understand the other's jealous attachment to her own son, Freeman tells us explicitly that the confrontation was "at once pitiful and comical" (75). In this instance, Freeman tries to force us to view the struggle from a comic distance in order to be able to understand it at the same time she invites us to sympathize with the characters' feelings so we can appreciate the power of irrational attachments.

In "A Conflict Ended," a story I find completely successful in its blend of "humor and tenderness," this mixture of comedy and pathos is one of the main points of the story, which suggests the importance of understanding the world through *all* of one's feelings in order to be flexible enough to grow and change. Typical of a Freeman story, it is a tale of two stubborn characters in conflict, each of which requires the other as a point of reference to establish individuality, each of which is willing to pay a price of isolation from the other in order to defend that individuality. From story to story, Freeman examines the costs of choosing to maintain the struggle or to surrender it. In this particular tale, the central conflict is maintained by the indomitable willfulness of Marcus Woodman and of Esther Barney, the one goaded into stubbornness out of his willingness to defy ridicule, the other by her willful refusal to tolerate anything that impinged on her "peculiar cast of mind, her feeling for the ludicrous so keen that it almost amounted to a special sense, and her sensitiveness to ridicule" (393).

Freeman sets the story against the backdrop of the town's religious schism, begun ten years before the action of the story when the Congregational church settled a new minister whose (one assumes) Arminianism chases a third of the congregation to the town's Baptist church. The story begins, then, against a backdrop of unregenerate wills refusing to treat the new minister or one another with Christian charity. In the eyes of Esther's young apprentice, Margy, the old conflict is silly through and through, and we are introduced to Esther through Margy's eyes, though Esther's emotional coldness stifles Margy's glee into embarrassed silence:

> One old lady, who had made herself prominent on the opposition, trotted by this morning with the identical wiry vehemence which she had manifested ten years ago. She wore a full black silk skirt, which she held up inanely in front, and allowed to trail in the dust in the rear.
>
> Some of the stanch Congregational people glanced at her amusedly. One fleshy, fair-faced girl in blue muslin said to her companion, with a laugh: "See that old lady trailing her best black silk by to the Baptist. Ain't it ridiculous how she keeps on showing out? I heard someone talking about it yesterday."
>
> "Yes."
>
> The girl colored up confusedly. "Oh dear!" she thought to herself. The lady with her had an unpleasant history connected with the old church quarrel. (382–83)

From virtually the beginning, as we meet the main characters, Freeman puts in motion the constellation of themes and images that drive the story to its conclusion. The image of the skirt, held proudly up in front but trailing in the dust behind suggests the absurdity of pride, that maintaining a false front serves merely to hide from one's self the futility and ridiculousness of pride itself. Then, too, we see the emotionally vibrant young Margy able to see what Esther cannot, that human behavior is both laughable and painful. In her quick sensibilities and sympathy, she turns an emotional about-face after Esther says but a single word, a word not in opposition to Margy's observation but in affirmation of it. Margy has both a sense of the absurd and a sense of compassion that makes her ability to laugh serve her larger humanity. At this point, the apprentice is in the shadow of her teacher, but the exchange between the two becomes reciprocal. The milliner merely teaches her apprentice how properly to make clothing—the external garb of pride; the apprentice teaches her mistress the power of emotion to cut through artificial rigidities.

The next scene, between Marcus Woodman and Esther Barney on the Congregational church steps—where Woodman has sat every Sunday for ten years, refusing to enter the new minister's church—shows the similarities and differences between the two willful protagonists. Esther offers Marcus a parasol to protect his bald head from the fierce sun. He refuses; she insists, but while neither budges, his passive negation is impervious to her offer: "There could be no contact even of antagonism between them. He sat there rigid, every line of his face stiffened into an icy obstinacy. She held out the parasol towards him like a weapon. Finally she let it drop at her side, her whole expression changed" (384). She then resorts to indirection, and finally Woodman asks for the parasol but only after the two acknowledge that they have a similar fear of looking foolish: Marcus says, "Of course you know I can't set out here holding a parasol; folks would laugh." As if folks hadn't been laughing at him for ten years! Esther replies, "I don't know but it would look kinder queer, come to think of it" (385). Neither wants to be foolish, but both *are* foolish in their obsessive concern for appearances of consistency.

Margy, on the other hand, is inconsistent in her determinations to defend her dignity because she is extremely determined to follow her love. When courted by the highly eligible George Elliot,[17] she "fell in love with him easily" only to be thwarted by Elliot's mother: "Poor Margy found that it was not so easy to thrust determined old age off the stage, even when young Love was flying about so fast on his butterfly wings that he seemed to multiply himself, and there was no room for anything else, because the air was so full of Loves. That old mother, with her trailing black skirt and her wiry obstinacy, trotted as unwaveringly through the sweet stir as a ghost through a door" (386). The rigid mother insists on living with her son, and Margy and George at first fall out over the prospect. But Margy, even in her grief able to see the absurdity of the situation, is able to surrender her pride to her passion. She wins her lover back, and even though her lover, in his male chauvinism, insists that "[i]t's a woman's place to give in" (392), Margy wins the point at issue when she learns that George's mother is not to live with them after all.

At this stage of the story, the difference between milliner and apprentice is

marked. While they have parallel impediments to the course of their love affairs, their responses couldn't be more different. In Margy's case, "There was a
whimsical element . . . which seemed to roll uppermost along with her grief"
(388). But to Esther, the absurdity of her disappointment is what solidifies her
determination not to give in:

> I tell you what 'tis, Margy Wilson, you've got one thing to be thankful for, and
> that is that there ain't anything ridickerlous about this affair of yourn. That
> makes it the hardest of anything, according to my mind—when you know that
> everybody's laughing and you can hardly help laughing yourself, though you feel
> 'most ready to die. . . .
>   "You turned him off because he went to sitting on the church steps?"
>   "Course I did. Do you s'pose I was going to marry a man who made a laughing-
> stock of himself that way? (388–89)

What Esther misses is that Marcus makes a laughing stock of himself for ten
years because he refuses to admit the wit of a joke directed at him in the first
place. When Woodman said that "if Mr. Morton was settled over that church,
he'd never go inside the door himself as long as he lived," a wag in the congregation challenged him to see the absurdity of his remark by singing out,
"'You'll have to set on the steps, then, Brother Woodman'" (389). Had he been
able to accept the joke—that is to say, had he been able to admit his error by
seeing the situation in another light, the drama would have ended right there
in a healing communal laugh. But Marcus shares Esther's stubborn horror of
laughter.

Following her apprentice's example of submission, Esther finally goes to
Marcus to patch up their quarrel. She agrees to marry him even if he continues
to stand outside of the church, that is to say, outside of grace and charity in submission to his own will. To her surprise, Marcus breaks down in sobs, which Esther, in her New England stoicism, close relative to stubborn pride, persists in
rejecting because it is "ridickerlous" (395); "I do hate to see you looking so
silly" (397). But she has learned her lesson; she learns to submit herself to the
silly in order to find her way into grace. When married, the couple approach
the church steps only to have Marcus, out of force of habit, decide to sit on the
church steps. Esther decides to sit with him, but he is unable to subject the
woman he loves to the same indignities he has suffered. He could deny the joke
in his own behavior, but in seeing it in someone else, he has no choice but to
acknowledge and thus transcend the absurdity of his behavior. When she tells
him of her determination to sit with her husband on their "wedding Sunday,"
"He stood for a moment staring into her face. He trembled so that the by-
standers noticed it. He actually leaned over towards his old seat as if wire ropes
were pulling him down upon it. Then he stood up straight, like a man, and
walked through the church door with his wife. "The people followed. Not one
of them even smiled. They had felt the pathos in the comedy" (398). This victory over laughter is the victory of humor over wit. Marcus, in finally refusing
to be a fool, though struggling, foolishly, to be a man, turns the eyes of the curi-

ous from mockery to appreciation. Not that the comedy disappears; it is only enriched by its capacity to reveal pathos. In the process of overcoming his folly by acknowledging it, he finds a new kind of pride and dignity: "The sitters in the pews watched Marcus wonderingly as he went up the aisle with Esther. He looked strange to them; he had almost the mien of a conqueror" (398). Christ-like, he gains the victory over his own living death, what he called "an awful life" (396), by finally subjugating his pride for the love of his wife.

So at one level this entire story is a plea for the value of humor as an emotional key to unlock inflexibility. Similarly, it is a plea for humor as an antidote to social Darwinism. Freeman here, by using the sentimental formula in favor of liberal Christianity, is fighting less against Calvinism per se than against the neo-Calvinism of the social Darwinists, who preached competitive conflict as the refining fire that saves the fittest and kills off the weak. Freeman, with her vague reference to a doctrinal battle within the church, reminds readers of the old, but more or less irrelevant battle between Calvinism and liberal, sentimental Christianity in order to set up the parallel between Calvinism and social Darwinism. She foregrounds the latter by insisting on conflict in the title and by establishing the characters as fundamentally combative. She ridicules this character in order to show the preferability of cooperation, though in treating the characters themselves with compassion, she even transmutes her ridicule to love. Here we see the formula of amiable humor working at its highest moral pitch and showing its profound advantage over homily in that it is moral without moralizing.

Freeman shows a similar resistance to naturalism, the artistic code of the social Darwinist times in which she wrote, in her comic defense of sentimental verse, "A Poetess." American humorists had long made fun of doggerel verse, as should be apparent from my discussion of Marietta Holley. Freeman may have been responding to this tradition in general, but I suspect she wrote this piece primarily in response to various attacks on the poetry of Julia Moore, who called herself "The Sweet Singer of Michigan" in the title to her first collection of verse, later retitled *The Sentimental Songbook* (1876). By any aesthetic standard, her verse is bad.[18] Even in her defense of sentimental poetry, Freeman does not defend the artistic quality of sentimental verse. Her poetess, Betsey Dole, lacks the capacity to write anything original: "Betsey in this room, bending over her portfolio, looked like the very genius of gentle, old-fashioned, sentimental poetry. It seemed as if one, given the premises of herself and the room, could easily deduce what she would write, and read without seeing those lines wherein flowers rhymed sweetly with vernal bowers, home with beyond the tomb, and heaven with even" (146–47).[19] Anne Romines would have us believe that the "It seemed" pushes criticism aside, implying that Dole's verse only seems trite (113). Such a qualification does not overcome the obvious criticisms of the rest of the passage, yet, without going to Romines's extreme, one must admit that the criticism here is very gentle in tone, nothing like that of the other critics of sentimental obituary poetry in general and of Julia Moore in particular.

Consider, for instance, the *Rochester Democrat*, which opined, on the publication of Moore's verse, "Shakespeare, could he read it, would be glad that he was dead. . . . If Julia A. Moore would kindly deign to shed some of her poetry on our humble grave, we should be but too glad to go out and shoot ourselves tomorrow" (Blair, "Moore" 106). Or consider the Worcester *Daily Press*, which editorialized, "The poet is one who reaches for the sympathy of humanity as a Rhode Islander reaches for a quahaug, clutches the soul as a garden rake clutches a hop vine, and hauls the reader into a closer sympathy than that which exists between a man and his undershirt" (Blair, "Introduction" 107). Most critics attacked Moore for her lack of sophistication, for as Mark Twain put it, "She has the touch that makes an intentionally humorous episode pathetic and an intentionally pathetic one funny" (110).

Twain, who had parodied obituary verse from the beginning of his writing career, turned cartwheels of satiric delight over Moore, though not merely for her artistic incompetence. His "Ode to Stephen Dowling Bots, Dec'd" in *Adventures of Huckleberry Finn* fries larger fish; it attacks some fundamental attitudes of sentimentalism expressed in such morbid poetry. Particularly, Twain attacked the obsession with death and self-sacrifice that was encouraged by sentimentalism and for that matter by the larger Christian tradition of meditating on one's own mortality. The sentimentalists had coopted the sterner Calvinist view of death with the idea that our confrontation with death was a learning experience designed to cultivate our sensibilities. In having sympathy with suffering we were to be in communion with our common mortality, and that communion would encourage true charity, the altruism that would lead to one's salvation. Thus it was an essentially nostalgic frame of mind, one interested in the melancholy of memory, interested more in feeling than in action. As I have explained in the last chapter and elsewhere,[20] Twain's attitudes toward sentimentalism were more complicated than critics have generally allowed, but from Freeman's point of view, Twain's attack on sentimental poetry was uniformly antisentimental. He refused in his parodies of obituary verse to see any emotional or social value in sympathetic indulgence, to see any value in contemplating death, but instead saw vitality in one's ability to run from a morbid culture.[21]

Freeman uses her mixture of pathos and humor to defend sentimentalism in "A Poetess". As usual, Freeman gives the reader virtually no cues about what tone the story will develop until after she sets the scene. When we are finally introduced to two of the three characters, it is in the context of Betsey, the poetess, not having grown food enough in her small garden to keep herself fed because she prefers to grow flowers. Her visitor, Mrs. Caxton, shown as a young woman full of irrepressible vitality, wearing a "gay cashmere-patterned calico dress with her mourning bonnet" (141), speaks the practical criticism that makes Betsey appear comic:

> "If I was in your place I shouldn't feel as if I'd got enough to boil a kettle for," said Mrs. Caxton, eyeing the beans. "I should 'most have thought when

you didn't have any more room for a garden than you've got that you'd planted more real beans and peas instead of so many flowerin' ones. I'd rather have a good mess of green peas boiled with a piece of salt pork than all the sweet-peas you could give me. I like flowers well enough, but I never set up for a butterfly, an' I want something else to live on." She looked at Betsey with pensive superiority. (143)

Like Twain's narrator in *Roughing It,* who says that "nothing improves scenery like ham and eggs," Freeman's Mrs. Caxton speaks from a strictly practical point of view.

In this context, the reader is shown the absurdity of the poetess herself: "Betsey was near-sighted; she had to bend low over the beans in order to string them. She was fifty years old, but she wore her streaky light hair in curls like a young girl. The curls hung over her faded cheeks and almost concealed them. Once in a while she flung them back with a childish gesture which sat strangely upon her". Completely frivolous in her choice to pursue beauty first and food second, Betsey looks absurd, as well as demure, and the criticism of Mrs. Caxton seems perfectly apt. The reader is encouraged to agree at this point that "folks that write poetry wouldn't have a single thing to eat growin' if they were left alone" (143). Later we learn that Betsey has brought her poverty on herself not only by growing flowers instead of food, but by having spent most of her patrimony on her father's funeral (151). We also see her avoiding food in favor of artistic production, but her starvation carries her to the point of unhealthy weakness, weakness that has made her susceptible to tuberculosis.[22]

But at the very moment when the reader is shown the absurdity of Betsey's behavior from the point of view of the practical Mrs. Caxton, the tone is immediately complicated by Caxton's sudden about-face into sentimental histrionics herself. "'And that brings to mind what I come for. I've been thinkin' about it ever since—our—little Willie—left us.' Mrs. Caxton's manner was suddenly full of shamefaced dramatic fervor, her eyes reddened with tears" (143). As suddenly, the tone of the piece changes, and the value of the ludicrous poetess shifts. Mrs. Caxton, mourning for the loss of her son, commissions from Betsey some obituary poetry. Caxton's grief is real, though not particularly tactful, when she complains that no one, least of all the childless, unmarried Betsey, can understand her grief and "[n]obody can do anything, and nothin' amounts to anything—poetry or anything else—when he's *gone.*" Still, in grief Caxton turns to sentimental homilies, such as how good a "sufferer" little Willie was (144), and she directs Betsey to make mention of many details about the child's life that will help her to memorialize him. The quotidian details, such as "how pleased he was with his little new suit" (144) seem hardly fitting for the profundity of the occasion, but that is precisely Freeman's point: grief knows no propriety, and the natural expression of grief serves important emotional purposes that cannot fairly be judged by normal standards.

It is Betsey's abnormality, one she chooses to follow with the passion of an artist, that makes her humble verse serve its purpose much better than anything the minister, an educated poet himself, can say to Caxton. The minister speaks the equally trite—or shall we call it time-honored because it has the grandiose dignity of church sanction?—consolation of God's divine plan, but Betsey does a better job of consoling Caxton because she uses sympathy to enter into her feelings. Indeed, her very modesty, the modesty that makes her believe that Caxton is right that a childless woman cannot understand, is the crux of her sympathetic power:

> "I s'pose I can't feel about it nor write about it anything the way I could if I'd had any children of my own an' lost 'em. I s'pose it *would* have come home to me different," Betsey murmured once, sniffing. A soft color flamed up under her curls at the thought. For a second the room seemed all aslant with white wings, and smiling with the faces of children that had never been. Betsey straightened herself as if she were trying to be dignified to her inner consciousness. "That's one trouble I've been clear of, anyhow," said she; "an' I guess I can enter into her feelin's considerable." (147)

The result of her passionate sympathy and total devotion to her art is that her product is appropriate to its audience and does more good than even Caxton thought possible. "'It's beautiful, beautiful,' she said, tearfully when she had finished. 'It's jest as comfortin' as it can be'" (150).

The comedy, then, is turned away from ridicule of Betsey's silliness, and instead becomes a way of enjoying the value of her peculiarity. The end of the story veers away from the comic by reproaching those who would scorn women who write for women and uneducated folk who write for the uneducated, by reproaching those who mistake conventions of propriety for the real emotional intention that makes art valuable. Similarly, Freeman chastises those who insist on conformity by reminding them that nonconformists serve valuable purposes. Not only is it the practical Caxton who makes sure that the impractical poetess doesn't starve physically (though she actually does a poor job of it), it is the impractical poetess who keeps the farm wife from starving emotionally. Freeman shows the absurdity of Betsey, but she also shows the absurdity of Caxton, whose mourning and vitality are an incongruous mix, whose grief seems so poorly exercised that it seems more fraudulent than real until Betsey's verse itself gives consolation that makes the grief seem natural and fitting and fully congruous.

※    ※

So much of the comedy in Freeman's stories depends, as does that in Harris's tales, on the ability of the reader to visualize characters and scenes, but whereas in Harris's case, visual imagination is a prerequisite for understanding the action of the tales themselves, in Freeman's case it is an essential to finding her balance in mood. So often, if one reads her tales for plot alone, one misses the comedy in the pathos. Time and again, the physical descriptions are the primary keys that these characters are exaggerations, caricatures, and are to be seen as emblematic and therefore not fully worthy of sympathy. They are to be seen as types, as projections of certain psychic attributes, and as such are to be analyzed as well as felt. This is certainly true in the case of "A Poetess," as the image Freeman creates of Betsey is so implausible as to be comic. It is equally true of the two main characters in "A Conflict Ended," with Marcus Woodman described as "a man of about fifty, who . . . had a singular face—a mild forehead, a gently curving mouth, and a terrible chin, with a look of strength in it that might have abashed mountains. He held his straw hat in his hand, and the sun was shining full on his bald head" (383). He looks like Half Dome in Yosemite and his looks stand for his character—rock stubborn, more rigid than the wood in his name. Freeman manages to blend images and ideas in ways that not only make the ideas concrete, but also make the formulations seem less serious and more playful than they would be if developed in less extreme fashion.

In perhaps no other story is this more the case than in Freeman's most analyzed story, "A New England Nun." Louisa's behavior, whether one calls it neurotic or not, is surely extreme, the extremity of comedy.[23] But the individual motions, when imagined carefully, most certainly speak to Louisa's psychic motivations. Consider the Chinese-box of aprons with which Louisa covers her genitals. Through the story, she dances a dance of a thousand veils, removing one apron after another only to reveal yet further protection below. Consider, too, her treatment of Caesar, the ferocious puppy declined into flaccid old age. Louisa has spent the dog's vitality by keeping him chained and feeding him a diet of corn cakes. By the plot of the story, the dog must be uncommonly old, at least fourteen years, yet, in spite of a diet that would kill an omnivorous human being, the carnivorous dog lives on. This is not intended to be realistic; the image of constrained animality maintaining a reputation for ferocity regardless of the truth is obviously a *comic* metaphor for repressed sexuality. Even the tale's setting contrasting the activities of the outside world with the controlled order of the inside suggests vividly that the tale will be about the efforts of sexuality to intrude on Louisa's celibacy, with even the sounds of the night intruding: "[T]he chorus of frogs floated in at the open window wonderfully loud and shrill, and once in a while a long sharp drone from a tree-toad pierced it" (3).

Freeman sets up the extremity of Louisa's resistance to sexuality as something comic, but she does not therefore set it up as something contemptible. Again, in the imagery of the sexually active world, one finds the reasons for Louisa's actions, reasons that have a force that is not to be dismissed by simplistic ridicule. The story opens in the late afternoon.

> [T]he light was waning. There was a difference in the look of the tree shadows out in the yard. Somewhere in the distance cows were lowing and a little bell was tinkling; now and then a farm-wagon tilted by, and the dust flew; some blue-shirted laborers with shovels over their shoulders plodded past; little swarms of flies were dancing up and down before the people's faces in the soft air. There seemed to be a gentle stir arising over everything for the mere sake of subsidence—a very premonition of rest and hush and night. (1)

A premonition of rest and hush and night, marked by shadows, waning light, and frenetic activity that does nothing more than stir up dust that will merely subside all hints at mortality. The sexual activity of the night, of the mating calls of frogs and toads, is a defense against mortality, but as such it is messy and fully implicated in mortality itself.

This is the "birthright" that Louisa surrenders at the end of the tale when she decides not to marry.[24] She remains inside, placid, counting her days toward the inevitable end, but an end drawn out by its resistance to any activity that would cut it short, such as death in childbirth, or merely death from the worry that active living often entails.

> Serenity and placid narrowness had become to her as the birthright itself. She gazed ahead through a long reach of future days strung together like pearls in a rosary, every one like the others, and all smooth and flawless and innocent, and her heart went up in thankfulness. Outside was the fervid summer afternoon; the air was filled with the sounds of the busy harvest of men and birds and bees; there were halloos, metallic clattering, sweet calls, and long hummings. Louisa sat, prayerfully numbering her days, like an uncloistered nun. (17)

Freeman's imagery shows that either Louisa's "narrowness" or participation in the active world entails a price. To describe the active world, Freeman creates an ambiguous image in which men are both harvesters and harvested, as are the "birds and bees" that euphemistically replace human sexuality as both agent of fecundity and of mortality. To describe the alternative, she shows an image of isolation with procreative impulses turned inward into a petty yet artistic control over inner space and consciousness.

Each choice of life has its own comic and serious implications; each has its value and its cost. That, as I suggested at the beginning of the chapter, is what Freeman's humor is all about—to give us the distance we need to see the variety of possible courses open to us, and to make us tolerant of the differences between people who have paid the personal prices that their choices entail. Differences between people, as Freeman's humor develops it, have value. Even if each difference entails a price of unbalanced or distorted perspective for the "humorist," the social price of ostracism is much greater and much crueler. Any derisive laughter at any of Freeman's characters carries with it a moral taint, making it difficult to laugh at all. But surely she wanted us to laugh in most cases. In story after story, she exaggerates every character, the individualists as well as the conformists. We are meant to laugh, but the laughter is meant to be embracing rather than estranging. At the very cusp of the twentieth century, in a day when the idea of amiable humor was being dismissed as false sentimentality that masked the true nature of comic aggression, Freeman's stories insist that sympathy and laughter are not incompatible, that on the contrary, they support one another admirably by enabling us to love and understand at the same time.

# SIX

# Humorneutics

The God laughed seven times: Ha-Ha-Ha-Ha-Ha-Ha-Ha.
God laughed, and from these seven laughs seven Gods
sprang up which embrace the whole universe; those were
the first Gods. . . . When God laughed . . . for the sev-
enth time, drawing breath and *while he was laughing he cried,
and thus the soul came into being.* And God said, "Thou shalt
move everything, and everything will be made happier
through you." When God said this everything was set in
motion and filled with breath.
　　　　—Egyptian creation myth, in Marie-Louise von Franz,
　　　　　　*Patterns of Creativity Mirrored in Creation Myths*

The practical sense of humor is that it transforms the effect
of error, the result of wrong, and reformulates pain as pleasure. . . . Each act of violence, each aggression, is embraced, beautifully misunderstood. The whole history of
grief is reduced to the size of a small black brick.
　　　　—Neil Schmitz, *Of Huck and Alice:
　　　　　　Humorous Writing in American Literature*

Laughter has a deep philosophical meaning, it is one of the
essential forms of the truth concerning the world as a
whole, concerning history and man; it is a peculiar point of
view relative to the world; the world is seen anew, no less
(and perhaps more) profoundly than when seen from the
serious standpoint.

　　　　　　　　　　—Mikhail Bakhtin,
　　　　　　　　　　*Rabelais and His World*

## I. Truth versus Laughter

From an ancient myth of the creative power of humor, to a contemporary Freudian critic who understands humor not as creativity in any absolute sense, but rather as misconstruction of the world, to Mikhail Bakhtin who suggests that in the Renaissance, humor was held to be an alternative point of view, a philosophical position of great profundity—these three epigraphs suggest something of the problem confronting a study of humor. In its very seriousness, a serious study of humor may limit rather than expand our understanding. Neil Schmitz is one of the most discerning commentators on American humor, and throughout this book I have been indebted to his insights, but framed by these two very different conceptions of humor, Schmitz's seems remarkably limited, remarkably stuck within the "serious standpoint" that of course sees any other standpoint as giving wrong answers to the puzzles of the world. Thus, I begin this chapter by referring to a nineteenth-century comic cautionary tale, John Phoenix's "A New System of English Grammar," one point of which is that it is absurdly easy to be seduced into believing ardently in absolute truth. I then apply the point of this story to two approaches to comedy before I ignore my own advice and present a total theory about the nature of comedy.

Phoenix's sketch, the entire text of which I include in an appendix, describes his putative frustration with the imprecision of the English language, concentrating on the lamentable fact that "the adjectives of the English language [a]re not sufficiently definite for the purposes of description. They have but three degrees of comparison—a very insufficient number, certainly, when we consider that they are to be applied to a thousand objects, which, though of the same general class or quality, differ from each other by a thousand different shades or degrees of the same peculiarity" (32). Phoenix then articulates in painstaking detail the inadequacy of the language and his arduous search for some language that would supply the defect. Serendipitously, he one day finds the object of his search in the nomenclature of a "scientist," that is, a visiting charlatan phrenologist (whom Phoenix, ardent believer in truth, trusts wholeheartedly). The phrenologist assesses Phoenix's traits on a scale of one to twelve. Phoenix, ignoring the assessment but enchanted by the method, makes his discovery.

> I saw at a flash how the English language was susceptible of improvement, and, fired with the glorious idea, I rushed from the room and the house; heedless of the Professor's request that I would buy more of his [Hair] Invigorator; heedless of his alarmed cry that I would pay for the bottle I'd got; heedless that I tripped on the last step of the Gyascutus House, and mashed there the precious fluid (the step has now a growth of four inches of hair on it, and the people use it as a door-mat); I rushed home, and never grew calm till with pen, ink and paper before me, I commenced the development of my system.
>
> This system—shall I say this great system—is exceedingly simple, and easily explained in a few words. In the first place, "*figures won't lie.*" Let us then represent by the number 100, the maximum, the *ne plus ultra* of every human

quality—grace, beauty, courage, strength, wisdom, learning—every thing. Let *perfection*, I say, be represented by 100, and an absolute minimum of all qualities by the number 1. Then by applying the numbers between, to the adjectives used in conversation, we shall be able to arrive at a very close approximation to the idea we wish to convey; in other words, we shall be enabled to speak the truth. Glorious, soul-inspiring idea! For instance, the most ordinary question asked of you is "How do you do?" To this, instead of replying, "Pretty well," "Very well," "Quite well," or the like absurdities—after running through your mind that *perfection* of health is 100, no health at all, 1—you say, with a graceful bow, "Thank you, I'm 52 to day;" or, feeling poorly, "I'm 13, I'm obliged to you," or "I'm 68," or "75," or 87 ½," as the case may be! Do you see how very close in this way you may approximate to the truth; and how clearly your questioner will understand what he so anxiously wishes to arrive at—your *exact* state of health?

Let this system be adopted into our elements of grammar, our conversation, our literature, and we become at once an exact, precise, mathematical, truth-telling people. It will apply to every thing but politics; there, truth being of no account, the system is useless. But in literature, how admirable! (37–39)

Then follows an example opening of a novel, which he can't complete because he has to defend himself against a lawsuit brought by the phrenologist for the theft of a bottle of hair invigorator. The piece ends with a postscript:

I regret to add that having just read this article to Mrs. Phoenix, and asked her opinion thereon, she replied that "if a first-rate magazine article were represented by 100, she should judge this to be about 13; or if the quintessence of stupidity were 100, she should take this to be in the neighborhood of 96." This, as a criticism is perhaps a little discouraging, but as an exemplification of the merits of my system it is exceedingly flattering. How could she, I should like to know, in ordinary language, have given so *exact* and truthful an idea—how expressed so forcibly her opinion (which, of course, differs from mine) on the subject? (41)

Phoenix's sketch stands as a prescient parody of late-twentieth-century techniques of assessment, from standardized tests, to judging athletic events, to public-opinion polling, to the more colorful, or should I say off-color, vocabulary by which many people evaluate the objects of their sexual appetites. More broadly, but more to my point, Phoenix's creator, George Derby, often wrote comic tales of earnest inventors who misapply the precision of Newtonian science to the world of the human mind. It is a danger I've been flirting with in my efforts to find a precise vocabulary to describe various nineteenth-century modes of comedy.

Much of what I have done so far in this book depends on an insistence that there is a difference between humor and other forms of comedy such as satire. I assume a cultural construction of comic modes, but that does not preclude deeper psychic constants, comic pleasure's biological substrate that is not culturally constructed at all. It is the interplay between this substrate and the cultural template, which attempts to constrain the comic impulse, that makes any study of comedy so difficult. Indeed, almost all theories of comedy take into account both the social and the individual nature of the comic response, yet while, as John Morreall points out, these theories can be loosely grouped into relief theories, aggression theories, or incongruity theories, differing emphases make the range of theories of the comic so wide as to be laughably inadequate as global explanations of the phenomenon. Many recent researchers, fearing the futility of any large-scale attempt to explain the comic, have turned instead to examining small aspects of it, from studies of heart rate and galvanic skin response (Langevin and Day) to the ethics of ethnic and sexual jokes (Boskin).

I do not intend here to take up another chapter's—or perhaps volume's—space detailing the range of theories or covering even a fraction of the research into laughter and comedy. Such surveys abound. For such a review from a "scientific" point of view, see Paul E. McGhee and Jeffrey H. Goldstein's first chapter in *The Psychology of Humor,* or for a less compact but more recent study that incorporates much medical and psychological research see Robin Andrew Haig's *The Anatomy of Humor: Biopsychosocial and Therapeutic Perspectives.* For a selection of excerpts from major theorists of the Western intellectual tradition, see John Morreall's *The Philosophy of Laughter and Humor.* For a breezy and dismissive survey, see Norman N. Holland's *Laughing: A Psychology of Humor.* Holland obviously enjoys the aggression of tearing apart everyone's theory but his own more than do I, but I will need to address two approaches to comedy that confront the interplay between the biological and the social aspects of comedy in order to expose the problems that I think a theory of humor needs to confront in order to be both descriptive and to give useful insights into the ethics of comedy. In doing so, though, I will surrender to the twentieth-century use of the terms in dropping the nineteenth-century distinctions between humor and other forms of comedy. Since such distinctions are no longer in use, my insistence on them will only confuse the issue as I switch from accounts of modern theories to my own analysis. From here on, with exceptions that should be clear from context, I use "humor" and "comedy" roughly synonymously.

The problems I want to confront are problems only because recent theorists of humor, with the possible exception of Bakhtin and not excepting myself, take comedy too seriously. They do not know how to understand pleasure. For Freud, still the most influential theorist of the psychology of comedy, humor was a problem precisely because he couldn't figure out how a healthy mind could have so much fun in self-deception countenanced by the superego. In his well-known treatment of jokes, Freud expressed the classic combination of aggression and relief theories of comedy, that jokes were the id and, to a lesser extent, the ego, venting the energy of repression in veiled hostility at either the superego or, in some cases, at external forces of oppression, such as bosses, the police, politicians, and so forth. But his less well known examination of humor removes aggression from the picture.

As with his theories of jokes and "the comic," Freud understands humor to be a "pleasure . . . from a saving in expenditure of affect" (111). In each case, the body summons energy to perform some task, but in the comic situation's deflection from the need to perform that task the body releases the energy in the form of laughter at the same time it feels pleasure in not having to do the work it anticipated. As opposed to joking, which consists of the saving of energy marshaled to repress sexual or hostile feelings, humor is the saving of emotional energy marshaled to confront suffering.

> Like wit and the comic, humor has in it a *liberating* element. But it has also something fine and elevating, which is lacking in the other two ways of deriving pleasure from intellectual activity. Obviously, what is fine about it is the triumph of narcissism, the ego's victorious assertion of its own invulnerability. It refuses to be hurt by the arrows of reality or to be compelled to suffer. It insists that it is impervious to wounds dealt by the outside world, in fact, that these are merely occasions for affording it pleasure. (113)

While this is often true, it is not so obvious as Freud makes it out to be. In fact, the perplexity with which he faces the how and why of what he terms so obvious shows that humor is not so simply determined as he would like it to be.

Freud finds it difficult to see why humor, which by its "repudiation of the possibility of suffering . . . takes its place in the great series of methods devised by the mind of man for evading the compulsion to suffer—a series which begins with neurosis and culminates in delusions, and includes intoxication, self-induced states of abstraction and ecstasy" (113), does not quit "the ground of mental sanity, as happens when other means to the same end are adopted" (113–14). He answers this question by assuming that "the humorous attitude . . . consists in the subject's removing the accent from his own ego and transferring it on to his superego. With the superego thus inflated, the ego can appear tiny and all its interests trivial, and with this fresh distribution of energy it may be an easy matter for it to suppress the potential reactions of the ego." In other words, the humorist "is treating himself like a child" (114). All well and good, but it raises another difficult question for Freud, whose prose reflects his astonishment when he tells us, "In many other respects we know that the super-ego is a stern task-master. It may be said that it accords ill with its character that it should wink at affording the ego a little gratification. . . . It is also true that, in bringing about the humorous attitude, the super-ego is in fact repudiating reality and serving an illusion. . . . [W]e have still very much to learn about the nature of that agency" (116). Yes, he does have much to learn about that agency, and about the nature of pleasure as well.

Freud's tripartite and hierarchical model of the mind does not really explain this pleasure, the pleasure so often compared to play in the annals of humor studies.[1] Most critics who follow in Freud's path simply choose to ignore the problem. Consider, for instance, Alan Dundes, who reduces all comic phenomena to jokes and joke cycles. These, he says, are serious business and are essentially aggressive. An old line, going back to Hobbes and his classical antecedents, but while it cannot be denied that much comedy is aggressive, much is not, as Freud well knew. At least two critics of American humor, James M. Cox and Neil Schmitz, have done an excellent job of addressing the distinction, and both look at humor, as did Freud, as an effort to sublimate pain in laughter. Schmitz in particular insists that human beings have a compulsion to suffer, and that humor denies that compulsion. It is a psychological escape valve.

Such a hypothesis is the necessary consequence of what Schmitz calls Freud's cartoon of the mind, with ego and id and superego in a dynamic battle of repression and desire. How appropriate for Schmitz to call it a cartoon, because it *is* a gross simplification and distortion of the mind's dynamic. Of course, the hydraulic model of energy build-up and dissipation on which Freud founded his theory has been long discredited, but the tripartite division itself should alert one to the absurdity of the model and the fatuousness of Freud's "problem" of humor. The stored memories of authority in each person's mind are much more complicated than the simple voice of the father as the voice of denial. Each parent is encoded as a variety of moods, actions, and stories, as well as admonitions. And often the parental voice *is* one of solace, which is the way Freud explains humor. But it is also, for most people, one of delight, of exhilaration, of play—of exemplifying the entire range of emotional possibility at work. The self is much more subdivided than into three, and insofar as each of us includes memories—linguistic and nonlinguistic—of parents and other authorities manifesting that diversity, then the "superego" itself is divided.

But this objection to Freud's model is really a minor quibble. What seems to me the ultimate inadequacy of Freud's interpretation of humor lies in his insistence that we are compelled to suffer. Freud's system of psychology, even though it changed over the course of his career, is based on a mechanical model of mind and, even as he increasingly renounced the neurological systems on which he originally based his theories, he never renounced the mechanical, Newtonian determinism of his scientific predisposition. Recognizing his deterministic bias, then, I wonder, when I see him insist that we are "compelled to suffer," about the agency behind that compulsion. Who or what compels us? What arrows of reality strike all of us? Truly all of us experience some degree of pain in life—some may be said truly to feel it most of the time. But to suffer is to give meaning to pain, to categorize it in abstract terms. Not every person is compelled to suffer; indeed as a compulsion, it finds its origins in the mind that makes life monistically meaningful in terms of suffering and describes "pleasure" as "repudiating reality and serving illusion." To call one emotional reaction to the world truth and the other illusion is a neurotic compulsion to find the world meaningful in one dimension only. Pleasure is as real as pain, and the humorist, even when using the abstract reality of pleasure's existence to compensate for immediate and actual pain, is not "repudiating reality" but instead insisting that meaning can be larger than the moment, that there is more than one meaning available to humanity. Humor in this sense is a defiant assertion of the contingent and plural nature of truth.

But to give Freud his due, he says that the compulsion to suffer is the knowledge of mortality, that our meaning-making is always constrained by the sense of our own ultimate deaths. Bakhtin speaks well to this concern in his treatment of folk humor when he speaks of the creativity of carnival as expressing profound ambivalence—it acknowledges the deaths of individuals, but because it links individuals into the whole of "the people," it asserts the eternal endurance of life in spite of the prospect of the individual's death. To Bakhtin, humor transcends mean egotism in social connection.

But in strictly individual terms, such transcendence *is* a lie. Without denying Bakhtin's idea that humor is transtemporal in its power to bond the individual to the life of the community, it is important to recognize the power of humor for the individual to see life not as an end but as a present. Laughter is a life fit, a manifestation of the feeling that life is worth having not in defensive terms alone, not merely as a defense against death, but also for its own sake. Insofar as laughter comes from the perception of incongruity, it is paralyzing; it prevents choices; it prevents purposive activity designed to get to the end of things. It suspends time; it insists on the richness of the present. Under the power of double vision, when knowing that truth and meaning are provisional and contingent, one sees that death is not the meaning of life, only the end. And that everything that happens between birth and death can be made meaningful, too. When purposive action is geared to warding off death, then death is the central category of experience that makes life meaningful, and one is swallowed in morbid monism. But laughter makes one feel that life is filled with possibilities.

For both these internal problems and for the fallaciousness of his brain physiology, I discard Freud's theories of comedy as legitimate global theories and instead look to recover his evidence and to see his theories as provisionally useful models in order to postulate a new hypothesis of comedy.[2] At least Freud, even as he dismisses pleasure from the realm of truth, seems to appreciate it. Many late-twentieth-century critics moralize against comedy with a residual puritanism suggestive of the old Christian belief that laughter, if not a sin in itself, at least leads to sin (Bakhtin 73; deSousa 227–28). Reformers usually lack a sense of humor, but in attacking comedy, many of these mistake the messenger for the message, as in the case of Joseph Boskin. In his "The Complicity of Humor: The Life and Death of Sambo," he blames racist jokes as the agency by which racism is perpetuated rather than seeing it as one of many vehicles through which racism is articulated. To the serious Boskin, comedy is dangerous because it derationalizes us and thus makes us susceptible to learning things we had better not, like pernicious stereotypes about racial minorities:

> The comic is invariably involved with repetitive play. After all, if humor possesses an ephemeral quality and its immediate expression is short-lived, then one of its protective qualities is repetition. Humor is conveyed from one generation to another, from one socio-economic group to others, by its unending reiteration. And repetition not only erodes reason but also leads to responses in which critical judgment can be seriously impaired. . . . Bergson explains this process further. Humor can circumvent reason, he implies, precisely because of its duplicating nature. Worse yet, the very replication upon which humor depends has the effect of creating an entity separate from its initial causes. (257)

Laughter, according to Boskin, suspends our perceptions of reality, leading to the creation of stereotypes, images divorced from any reality and untouchable by fact. Comic and audience, then, "are involved in a complicity of illusion, and in the case of a stereotype, of a specific kind of illusion. Furthermore, that illusion conveys a sense of reality and perpetuates the action" (260).

I'll address many of his assumptions—that comedy and play are equivalent, that comedy derationalizes, that words can connect absolutely with truth if only defined narrowly through the medium of logic—below. What concerns me here is that Boskin obviously does not trust emotion or human culture. He sees them as essentially deceptive. While in quoting Erving Goffman about the social construction of selfhood he acknowledges the contingent nature of cultural mores and the development of individuality within those mores, he still is devoted to a transcendent idea of truth. Any emotion, such as the pleasure that is concomitant with laughter, in derationalizing human beings lends power to social illusion and detracts from the transcendent value, both metaphysical and moral, of "truth" as derived from logic. Were John Phoenix's wife to reply to Boskin's desire to have logic supersede emotion, she would call it 96 futile because 99 wrong. Logic itself, like language, is a cultural artifact. Its use is motivated by emotional drives for consistency, determinacy, absolutism—by a profound fear of doubt. Boskin can mask it neatly in the garb of a moral humanism, but his desire for transcendent rationality puts him, strangely, in the same intellectual camp as Freud, willing to overlook his own obvious irrationality in service of his irrational desire to be reductively and deterministically rational.

This is perhaps most clearly seen in the way Boskin ignores not only the experience most people have of much comedy, but even the overarching points of some of the theories he quotes in bits and pieces. He distorts, for instance, Bergson's theory when he suggests that laughter, as a kind of social control, is a fundamentally conservative communication:

> One of humor's basic functions is as a form of social communication, serving both an individual and a group purpose although not necessarily at the same time or in an identical manner. As an essential form of social communication, humor is integrally connected to the cultural code of society. The code itself is a consequence of diverse yet criss-crossing forces. It devolves from historic patterns recognized and accepted by the populace, and it is buttressed by assumptions about time and space, the values implicitly understood by the majority, and a common consciousness regarding present forces. . . . [I]n *Laughter*, Henri Bergson's seminal analysis of the sociality of humor, the complicity of the process was also elaborated. "Our laughter is always the laughter of a group." (254)

He thus sees it as a kind of conspiratorial language, a language designed not so much to convey information as to prevent changes in the code as a whole. Insofar as comedy requires a knowledge of the cultural code, "[h]umor is vital as a means of creating and maintaining a state of internal equilibrium and stability. Emotions of anxiety and tension are often countered by the protective play of certain mechanisms, especially the act of 'humoristic displacement' as Freud termed it" (254). Notice that Boskin conflates Freud's terms to insist that humor functions with the same tendentious aggressiveness as do jokes. It is almost as if Boskin sees comedy as the language of social aggression against outsiders, as the fundamental psychic ploy to defend the cultural code from anything alien.

Why, then, is so much humor directed against the palpable absurdities of any cultural code? Language itself, the primary medium by which human beings construct culture, is one of the most fruitful of fields for comedy. Language, as one of the essential tools of cultural construction, is brought to bear to restrict comedy, to channel emotions of all kinds so as to support culture itself. Language itself, though, is one of the primary sources of humor precisely because it is so thoroughly artificial, and anything artificial, anything constructed, is always open to deconstruction through its internal inconsistencies. Anyone who follows absolutely without flexibility any cultural code prompts laughter, not so much by outsiders as by insiders. As Schopenhauer's theory puts it, the incongruity between life as abstracted and life as lived, or to put it in modern parlance, the cognitive dissonance between cultural mores and the realities of existence, can cause laughter. According to Schopenhauer, that is the point of laughter, to rescue us from the absurdities that our own minds are able to deceive us into believing. Incidentally, Bergson, too, found comedy a culture's method of retaining its flexibility. Laughter at the deviant who takes a culture's codes so seriously that he or she becomes a machine is the way the mass prevents itself from ossifying. These ideas are the ones that, since Walter Blair and Constance Rourke defined the field, have dominated criticism of American humor, specifically that American humorists were able to point out the inappropriateness of European philosophies to life in America.[3] While that is not true of all American humor, that it is true of so much American humor and that it was not the humor of the occasional iconoclast but the humor of broad sections of the literate public suggests that Boskin reads comedy too narrowly. Comedy is at least as likely to free a group up as to narrow it down, to break stereotypes as it is to reinforce them. The problem for a moral absolutist like Boskin is that comedy seems to be able to work both sides of the moral street.

Boskin's and Freud's fears of being deceived by the "lies" of laughter, or more to the point, their fears of being forced to see the limits of their own epistemologies, are analogous to the fears that cause many people's anger at puns.[4] According to those who are outraged at puns, or even those who merely stand superior to puns by judging them the lowest form of humor (and why should people with blunted senses of humor arrogate unto themselves the right to pass such judgment?), puns appear to violate order by violating meaning. Chaos reigns when one plays with words. Or does it? What does a child do to learn language but play with sounds and meaning, to discover the joy in finding meaning in the world, to find words to objectify subjective states, and in so doing make them usable beyond immediacy? What is real but inchoate becomes real and orderly, meaningful. The greatest pleasure is to stand on the border between reality and meaning, to feel the reciprocal interpenetration. To pun, to *play* on words, is to recover that original creativity in making words to match mental categories; to find not the destruction of reality, but the fecundity of it, the manifold meanings that a single, monolithic construction of reality disallows.[5] In acknowledging that a single sound can represent multiple meanings, one recovers primal connections between subjective and objective, between necessity and choice.

## II. Comic Arousal

Biologically, an awareness of choice and freedom may be the primal value of the comic feeling itself. The body and brain obviously undergo significant changes when a person laughs. Similarly, studies have shown significant physiological changes correlated with the feeling of "humor." These changes are concisely described as an increase in arousal, and they are, physiologically, quite similar in many ways to the responses the body has to other states of emotional arousal. Heart rate increases, epinephrine and nor-epinephrine levels rise, blood pressure rises (though it quickly drops off), galvanic skin response changes: in short, as Haig puts it, "[t]he changes in the autonomic nervous system during humor are similar to those occurring during states of aggression, fear or other states of heightened emotion" (34). How easy, then, to conclude that the humorous response is, indeed, the same as fear and aggression. But the parallels are not as important as the differences, as in the case of blood pressure quickly falling off after an initial rise (Haig x; Groves 51), signaling that humor has a calming effect. Other studies lend stronger evidence that humor is different from other forms of arousal in that it leads to a pleasure that is essentially calming. Not only does humor increase pain tolerance (Hudak; Cogan et al.), but its production of endorphins (Haig; Groves 51) seems to explain why humor can alleviate depression (Danzer, Dale, and Klions) and anxiety (Yovetich). Recent studies on how humor boosts the immune system, too, bear out the age-old adage that laughter is the best medicine, suggesting that the feeling of humor has profound benefits on health (Groves 51–52; Haig 5–7). These studies are the specific correlates to the sweeping claims made by Norman Cousins, in *Anatomy of an Illness as Perceived by the Patient,* on the role of attitude, especially of humor, on health. Humor, either as a mood generated in response to specific stimuli or as a larger personality trait, mitigates the harmful bodily effects of fear and aggression.

This recent research calls into doubt the extent of the applicability of traditional theories of humor as veiled aggression. As Daniel E. Berlyne, one of today's most provocative scholars of humor, puts it:

> What they [i.e., "advocates of the various classical and recent theories of humor"] have to say warrants the deepest respect and reflection. But, if our arguments so far have been too broad, their explanations are too narrow. Apart from insufficiencies

of definition with regard to the factors they invoke, these theorists show that their theories fit certain kinds of jokes, which they cite, quite admirably. They have, however, invariably failed to make sure that their theories can encompass all conceivable instances of humor. Furthermore, they usually fail to give us much inkling of why the mechanisms they describe should produce pleasure. (55)

That most theories of humor do not explain why and how the arousal of humor can be pleasurable is introspectively observable, too. In the cases of aggression and fear, as any student of an introductory psychology class can say, the body gears for the opposed physical responses known by the mnemonic rhyme "fight or flight." But humor is a state of arousal with no apparent telos. Correspondingly, it has no apparent location in the brain. True, if the comic feeling gives rise to laughter, the neural pathways giving rise to the motor responses involved are easily mapped, as Frederic R. Stearns points out. But the entirety of the brain can be involved in the comic mood; each time, of course, the limbic system, responsible for mood itself, is involved through its profound attachment to the "higher" parts of the cerebral cortex, but the perceptual lobes as well as the frontal, "intellectual" lobes can be involved. If something is funny enough, the energy of arousal may be dissipated in laughter, which is as invigorating to the body as any other strenuous exercise (Haig 34–35, 44–45). But psychically, comedy has no telos. It is the surrender of seriousness in a relish of the present moment. As such, it releases mind and body both from any purposive exercise, any directed movement or attention to accomplishing a goal.

In this suspension of seriousness, humor differs from its close relative, play, which is often performed with a vigor and intensity that is the opposite of the pleasurable feeling of humor. *Play* in a loose sense is pastime that is pleasurable, and in this sense humor can be considered a kind of play. But usually the word *play* is used with a direct object and that object is a *game*. In this sense, play's seriousness is that a game requires its participants willingly to embrace a set of rules that for the duration of the game define one's existence. It is a playing of roles in which the actors suspend their disbelief in their parts. As such, games usually have goals, as often defined by duration as by fulfilling a specific task. Humor, on the other hand, lacks the directed intensity of games precisely because it refuses to see the world, however temporarily, according to a single set of rules. Deprived of valid rules, the mind temporarily cannot act, cannot assume a single part and play it.

In its lack of telos humor differs, too, from its most closely related state of psychic arousal, curiosity. The truly curious person confronted with a puzzle or problem does not assume answers in advance because he or she is not playing a part in a closed system of a game, but even though the role of discoverer is open-ended and to a large degree undefined, it does have a directed purpose in trying to resolve the puzzle that prompts the curiosity in the first place. Cognitive theorists often equate curiosity and humor primarily because they both require the intellectual processing of a puzzle, the incongruity that sparks humor being of the same kind as that which sparks curiosity, only yielding a "pleasurable" resolution quite quickly. Such theories work with some humor, but do not explain why people like to tell jokes, sing comic songs, watch comic movies, and so on, repeatedly. If surprise and the goal of resolving the incongruity of that surprise were really essential to the comic mood, then a retold joke could never be funny. In that repetitive quality, humor more closely resembles play than it does curiosity.

Does humor, then, have no deeper intrinsic purpose, no structural purpose? Is it then merely a peculiar biological response that has been given meaning and purpose only in socially constructed contexts? I think not, but in order to explain my sense of why humor exists and how that biological existence is in turn manipulated by culture, I, like Freud before me, need a theory of how the mind works, how consciousness comes out of anatomy, in order to explain the relation of humor to consciousness. I need a theory that explains consciousness embodied. Many have been published in the last decade as neuroanatomy has made significant advances. The one that best answers the questions raised in this study is Gerald M. Edelman's theory of neuronal group selection, most recently articulated in its full physiological and philosophical context in *Bright Air, Brilliant Fire: On the Matter of the Mind.*

Edelman's theory of mind is materialistic, he believes that mind—that is, the sense we have of volitions and consciousness rather than the matter of brain cells themselves—is embodied. In saying this, though, he does not participate in the older Newtonian rationalism that reduces matter to mechanism, that sees the world as determined by simple and absolute relations between cause and effect. On the contrary, Edelman's high praise of William James as a founder of modern psychology and as a philosopher of great significance is a sure sign of his antideterministic, antireductionistic theory of mind: "As William James pointed out, mind is a process, not a stuff. Modern scientific study indicates that extraordinary processes can arise from matter; indeed, matter itself may be regarded as arising from processes of energy exchange. In modern science, matter has been reconceived in terms of processes; mind has not been reconceived as a special form of matter" (6–7). Avoiding mechanistic determinism, he also avoids genetic, environmental, or cultural determinism. Given that he calls his theory "neural Darwinism," his antideterministic bias may come as a surprise to cultural historians who know *social* Darwinism as a ruthless determinism. As a contemporary Darwinist, though, Edelman sees the essence of biological organizations of matter, including the processes of mind, not as a determined victory of the best heredity, but rather as the effectiveness of diversity in allowing for adaptation to a chaotic world.

As such, he is significantly not a genetic determinist, either. He insists that, especially in the formation of the neurological "hardwiring" of the brain, genetics provide merely a loose set of structural parameters while the precise connections made both in prenatal development and in the life-long process of restructuring that is the neurological basis of mind, cell processes working back and forth between environment, genes, and random motion are the flexible "determinants" of mental structures: "Genes specifying the shapes of proteins are not enough; individual *cells*, moving and dying in unpredictable ways, are the real driving forces" (60). "The genetic code does not provide a specific wiring diagram for this repertoire. Rather, it imposes a set of *constraints* on the selectional process. Even with such constraints, genetically identical individuals are unlikely to have identical wiring for selection is epigenetic" (83).[6] Thus mind is a process designed to maximize flexibility within important constraints.

Note, too, the analog between the cell as system, the connections of cells into larger systems and the idea of mind as process. While to understand mind we must understand the workings of its smallest components, mind as a whole is more than the sum of its parts. This, coupled with the fact of life-long restructuring of the connective structures between the smallest parts, that is, neurons and neuronal groups, suggests that the properties of mind, including memory and "knowledge" are always provisional and corrigible, completely contingent on the interactions between categories of perception and thought as developed over time and the demands of the present and the projected demands of the future.

The interactions between these three levels of mind—of perceptual categorization, of remembered categorization, and of projected categorizations of the future—are the large-scale features of the processes of consciousness. One can grasp the Darwinian basis of Edelman's theory—and this basis is ultimately important to humor—by looking first at the lowest of these. There is much evidence to show that certain areas of the cerebral cortex are genetically assigned to particular perceptual functions. There are general areas, for example, for sight and for speech. But Edelman points out that these areas, these "maps" of cortex that correspond to particular stimuli in the world, are not static throughout one's life. He sees each of these areas as being composed of neuronal groups that, highly interconnected with millions of other groups of neurons throughout the brain, grow stronger connections when stimulated, creating neural pathways that compete for dominance with other neural pathways. Through a process that Edelman calls "reentry," the "maps" of stimuli that these neuronal groups create signal one another to correlate information. What he calls reentry is the constant interaction between neuronal groups to create multiplex categorizations of reality. That is, repeated successful "reentry" strengthens the connections between groups, making for neural patterns that become categories of perception. The combined changes between entrant groups more or less converging on a similar problem of perception leads to the development of perceptual categories, without which all the hardwiring in the world will not lead to perception at all.

At its very root, then, perception is categorization specific to the mind of a single individual, though the relative consistency of the outside world enforces a high degree of similarity in categorization between individuals. Biological constraints limit what would otherwise be total mental freedom to construct a world according to the accidents of a mind's own development. But through a Darwinian selection of successful mappings, that is, ones that both have a high degree of correlation with parallel mappings and that lead to useful behavior, the brain is actually altered. The successful neural mappings, says Edelman, more or less crowd out the less successful ones, within the constraints of the outside world and within the constraints of basic "values" more absolutely programmed into the limbic system.

> According to the TNGS [Theory of Neuronal Group Selection], the driving forces of animal behavior are thus evolutionarily selected value patterns that help the brain and the body maintain the conditions necessary to continue life. These systems are called homeostats. It is the coupling of motion and sensory sampling resulting in behavior that changes the levels of homeostats. Aside from those occasional species-specific behavior patterns that have been selected for directly by evolution, however, most categorization leading to behavior that changes homeostatic levels occurs by a *somatic* selection of neuronal groups in each animal. Categorization is not the same as value, but rather occurs *on* value. It is an epigenetic developmental event, and no amount of value-based circuitry leads to its occurrence without experiential selection of neuronal groups. But it is also true that without prior value, somatic selectional systems will not converge into definite behaviors. (94)

> Neuronal groups that respond initially to a stimulus have, on the average, a higher likelihood of responding to a similar stimulus when it is subsequently presented, but that likelihood is modulated by value systems. (97)[7]

The crucial points here for my theory are the interactions, even at the lowest order of consciousness, between internally chosen categories of perception and the real world. The match is rarely perfect because the world is a diverse and changing place, and the mind's categories are never sufficient to embrace all of the world. The greater the flexibility of the mind to embrace significant features of the world, the more flexible the organism. The analog, then, between the selective competition between brain structures and the selective pressures on the individual with a mind may be similar with regard to their telos—selective advantage—but their other similarity, a tension between the values of diversity and consistency—makes a significant disjunction between perceptions and the real world an ongoing reality. William James was right: "the knower is not simply a mirror floating with no foothold anywhere, and passively reflecting an order that he comes upon and finds simply existing. The knower is an actor, and coefficient of the truth" ("Remarks" 23).

The basic process of neuronal group selection that Edelman identifies at the lowest level of awareness is repeated for the next two levels of consciousness, what he calls the "remembered present" and what is generally referred to as self-consciousness, or what he calls "consciousness of consciousness." In these two phenomena, the process of neuronal group selection is the same, but the groups that are selected are stimulated not by the outside world, but rather by the brain itself. If neuronal groups attached to organs of perception make neural mappings of the world, the next level of consciousness is a collection of mappings of mappings, what he calls a "bootstrapping" operation of developing a more complex consciousness of the present. That is, memories of earlier categorizations are compared by reentrant signaling much as correlated groups reentrally compare the results of immediate stimuli. The result is that new maps are immediately placed in the context of old ones so that new perceptions are immediately categorized by remembered knowledge; at the same time remembered categories are adjusted to absorb new information. Again, the tension between flexibility and consistency is the driving tension of this selection.

Consciousness of consciousness, then, is a further bootstrapping operation that develops symbolic meanings as mappings of mappings of mappings. This is the self-consciousness that allows us to imagine ourselves as actors in a postulated symbolic future, as an analog self, a mapped presence in time and space. Culturally derived symbolic language allows an explosion of mental power on the basis of this map of self, but language in Edelman's model develops as an accretion of metaphor developed through semantics rather than through syntax, as opposed to Noam Chomsky's idea of an innate syntax as the foundation of language. In other words, language itself is yet another system of categorization that arises out of the mind through its self-involved, recursive development of conceptual categories rather than as a simple reflection of transcendant order.

## III. The Mind's Jubilee

The relevance of all of this for a theory of humor is that if neural pathways are strengthened or weakened in competition with one another, then at a certain point, reentrant mappings notwithstanding, categorization of reality will become rigid and determining; successful categories grow so dominant as to seem extramental and transcendent. The mood of humor is, I hypothesize, a biological mechanism to resist such rigidity, such global and determined thinking. Specifically, the mood of humor makes neuronal groups susceptible to new mappings. By heightening arousal, a fancy word for openness to experience, without any telos to that arousal, the mind is open to new ways of conceptualizing what it has already conceptualized.

To relax earlier successful categories in order to allow the mind to respond to other possible categories is the value of humor. Since higher consciousness is a function of reentrant signaling between neuronal groups, it is a series of conceptual groupings that achieve a fairly high order of consonance with one another. In the process, discordant groupings are weakened, shut out of the dominant "picture" of reality. Humor opens the mind to discordant mappings. It is, in essence, the capacity to hold in mind conflicting conceptions without choosing between them. It requires simultaneous recognition of conflicting conceptions in a context in which only one should be allowed. To recognize incongruity is to return categories to an equal footing and to allow a new grouping of their component categories to manage cognitive dissonance.[8] Within the state of humor itself, that management is mainly tolerance, suspension of the need for resolution. What the mind does after the humorous mood allows for a leveling of hierarchies between categories moves, strictly speaking, beyond the realm of humor into the realm of seriousness. Satire, for instance, is the effort to reassert the primacy of a single interpretation on incongruity, an effort to reestablish hierarchy through the dismissal of one or more options. There may be pleasure in such a reestablishment of monolithic order, but, as I see it, such pleasure is no longer purely the pleasure of humor.

I came across an example of the root of satire—simple scorn—being used precisely in this way when I recently attended a matinee performance of *Oedipus the King*. Seated behind me was a class of high school students who resisted the high seriousness of the play with derisive laughter. Not that they weren't at times captivated by the play. A profound silence attended the play's more intense moments, but the students responded vigorously to any hint of incongruity, as when toward the play's end the chorus laments that no story could be more terrible than that of Oedipus, one of the students cracked, "that's for sure," and the class laughed. The outspoken student reoriented the focus from within the play to the play as a whole. Pity was no longer needed; humor suggested the possibility that Sophocles' vision of suffering at the hands of all-powerful gods might just be a bad story. But the students, in turning their glee at release from the seriousness of Sophocles' vision, turned back into their own juvenile (and I mean that with no contempt; if fifteen-year-olds can't be juvenile, what's the point of childhood and adolescence?) point of view. Humor freed them from the constraints of someone else's monism; scorn, that is, the limitation of the humorous response to its destructive side, returned them defensively to their own.

In either event, while tension was part of the spur to the humor these students first exercised and then turned to scorn, their pleasure was not necessarily a reaction to the release of tension. Indeed, the pleasure of humor is best understood not through the bladder theory of psychic processes—pleasure comes when the mind is emptied of its tensions—but through Edelman's theory of categorization on values. In the case of humor, the pleasure is perhaps best seen as a limbically structured orientation to reality that, when activated, is the value on which humorous perception is performed. It is the valuation of manifold possibility, of the suspension of activity in favor of multiple categorizations. The other values on which the mind categorizes tend to work toward specific goals, even, as in the case of curiosity, if that goal is to solve a puzzle, to end cognitive dissonance. Such values are oriented toward action; humor is a value oriented toward inaction, or rather toward the minimal action of appreciation itself.[9]

What's more, the full power of the alternative understandings that the humorous mood engenders does not even have to come fully to consciousness. Perhaps, even, it works best when consciousness, too, is suspended. Nothing kills a joke faster than explaining it, because explanations require the rational reaction to incongruity, which is one of serious puzzlement—if two things appear irreconcilable, then how can we confront the "problem" in order to reconcile them? Conscious reactions tend more toward frustration or curiosity. Humor, for most people, is most active when consciousness is minimized. Of course, if one comes to develop a socially sanctioned and conscious appreciation of humor, then conscious understanding can add additional sources of aesthetic appreciation without damaging the humorous response, but, if I can judge by how much my students resist analyzing humor, such a cultivated capacity both to be conscious of what humor tells us about our own minds and to remain appreciative of the humor itself does not come easily. Such an understanding forces a scholarly perspective, a perspective of skepticism that insists on human ignorance, on the provisionality of understanding, and on the sense that truths are negotiated through a difficult process of hypothesis and challenge. Humor may be a shortcut to such a point of view—without the work or the necessity of consciousness—but it seems to be usually temporary, not so much a full contradiction of as a suspense of the everyday sense of truth as absolute.[10]

I'm no neurologist so I speak from a very limited empirical base of my observations of my own responses and of those of other people, and I also speak from hearsay in correlating other theories. What seems common to most theories of humor is that there must be at least some destructive component to it; it must destroy, at least temporarily, a fixed monistic understanding in order to allow at least temporary perception of an alternative understanding. Consider, for instance, so-called sick joke cycles, for instance "dead baby jokes," or their turn-of-the-twentieth-century equivalents, the Little Willie rhymes, such as:

Willie found some dynamite,
Didn't understand it quite;
Experimenting never pays,
It rained Willie for several days.

"Willie, where's your sister Nell?"
"Mother, I threw her down the well."
"Willie, you provoke me with your ways,
Now the water will be muddy for several days."

Willie and the other brats
Ate a case of Rough on Rats.
Father said, when Mother cried,
"Don't you cry, they'll die outside."

From the back of Mother's mirror
Willie licked the paint all off,
Thinking in his childish error
It would cure the whooping cough.
At the funeral Willie's mother
Laughed to neighbor Mrs. Brown,
"'Twas a chilly day for Willie
When the mercury went down."

"Ha, Ha, Ha," said Willie's mother,
"Ho, Ho, Ho," said Mrs. Brown,
"'Twas a chilly day for Willie
When the mercury went down."[11]

These jokes engage a certain glee in imagining destruction, destruction of siblings and of pesky children in part, but more importantly, of central cultural beliefs and mores, as, in the case of these rhymes, the doctrines of childhood innocence and the compulsion to care for children. One finds distance from objects of love and affection; one finds freedom from repression of ideas that conflict with cultural and personal norms.

This destructive mechanism is probably limbic; it is probably an altered state of emotional involvement to create the necessary distance that enables disengagement from a preferred understanding. No surprise that some theorists therefore see humor as unemotional: the sense of detachment has parallels to rational analysis. Yet humor clearly is emotional; the feeling of pleasure is marked, but the degree of emotional attachment to the object under scrutiny is usually altered—not destroyed, for total destruction of one conception would prevent comic perception. Comic perception requires simultaneity of conception. It requires not total divorce of emotional attachments, but a leveling of emotional attachment. It is possible in comic perception simultaneously to identify with and suspend identification with the object of comic perception.

If I am correct, the element of destructiveness that so many commentators have marked as part of comedy is not intrinsically nihilistic, though comic multiple perspective, as in Melville's *The Confidence-Man*, can be pushed into the nihilism of irony. Comedy is not intrinsically nihilistic because it entails, in simultaneous perception and categorization of opposites, a creativity. That both creative and destructive aspects of comedy coexist does not mean, however, that in all manifestations of comic moods the two forces are balanced. On the contrary, the competition between moods, between limbically controlled values, is as much a part of the process of the humorous response as is the engagement of the comic response itself. Under other psychic pressures, comedy can be distorted to overemphasize the creative power, as in amiable humor, or the destructive power, as in biting raillery.

Even though social and individual circumstances can alter the balance of destructive and constructive elements within humor, the mood of humor broadly speaking recovers flexibility in the face of relentlessly serious single-minded constructions of meaning. It allows the mind a neutral space to reevaluate conflicting constructions of reality; it serves to make positive use of the internalized dissonance between conflicting conceptions of reality. The mind is multiple in its mappings of meaning, and larger visions of meaning are contingent on constant correlation of those maps, each of which has the potential of dissonance as well as consonance with all others. Humor allows new arrangements of old mappings of mappings. In acknowledging the complexity of this process we can explain the conflicting reports of comic engagement. What comedy yields is identification at distance—one must see connections that are not usually seen, but at the same time, there must be a distance in order to see more than one simultaneously. Remember that this all takes place in a competitive mental system, one that establishes hierarchies of meaning in the selective strengthening of certain mappings and certain reentrant pathways. Each mind highly values stability, but each mind still requires flexibility, which is damaged by the hierarchical, stable success of certain conceptualizations. Even though successful mental patterns may defend against incursions, comedy is the mind's jubilee—a return to neutrality in order to make rearrangements possible.

To put it another way, the pleasure of humor is a side of a homeostasis between choices and choosing that is the essence of freedom. To extrapolate from Edelman's theory of the mind, the stability of behavior that comes from the successful competition between neuronal groups is a kind of repression of alternatives by successful mappings. Each mental choice, when made, requires a repression of alternatives, or else the mind becomes paralyzed in recrimination. Choice can lead to action only if the alternatives originally present are repressed, leading to a sense of stability and, in the extreme, of necessity. But too much such repression leads to a dangerous rigidity. Humor is the balance to serious pursuit of a made choice. It instead suspends action and expands choices.

The conflict between moods of humor and moods of seriousness, between creative anarchy and restructuring and flexibility on the one hand and stability and consistency on the other are central problems each individual faces. Any choice entails repression because choice entails seeing alternatives and repressing some in pursuit of another. The alternative, to remain free to choose, is actually to destroy the freedom of action. It entails no repression, but it requires a stasis, a paralysis. In these terms, humor, then, is an expanded state of paralysis, of suspended choice. Both options and action are necessary components of freedom, of volition; the comic mood, if I am right, is the mood that expands the present to expand the range of choice. It makes it pleasurable to stay inactive in the present while remaining in a state of mental excitation. It provides the exhilaration of living momentarily without repression. But of course, the paralysis of inaction, of not following a single choice, is ultimately dangerous. Comedy, then, is inhibited by danger, by seriousness; the comic mood, if it can be developed at all under circumstances of seriousness, usually is warped into satire, scorn, or invective. Incongruity as a source of mind-opening is disallowed in an angry reaction designed to end the state of humorous withdrawal from purposive activity.

Perhaps the most extreme test, here, the test of gallows humor, can best make my point. Beyond doubt, impending and unavoidable death is dangerous, and equally beyond doubt, the mind can respond to such a prospect seriously. But if the threat is an inevitability, then serious action is futile. No serious, that is purposive, action will make any difference. The person who surrenders to this reality can fall back into the mood of humor, of acute perception of life in the moment, of the full reality of the situation, including not only the reality of impending death, and the reality of powerlessness in the face of it, but the reality of life in the moment and the connections of that life to a larger conception of life. The activity of choosing by necessity suspended, or at least made moot, toying with that knowledge becomes a potential source of acute pleasure. Make hope a real possibility, and humor dissolves into serious efforts to realize that hope.

Ordinary life, though, does not so obviously tell one when to suspend action in favor of humorous reassessment. Incongruity theories in the abstract try to explain the moment of humor as a collision of conceptions, as a paradoxical juxtaposition, as a temporary violation of expectation. In the structure of individual jokes, this is often the case. Humorous perception can, also, be a consequence of a developed personality type, or as a consequence of major disruptions of a person's worldview. As I describe it in chapter 2, Washington Irving's humor of *The Sketch Book* was both a consequence of his personal wittiness as developed in his early years and of incongruities forced on a him by large-scale life choices, or, rather, by inconsistencies in social ideologies that he felt fully when his efforts to live by those inconsistent ideals led him to feel a deep sense of failure. Irving's initial reactions to his losses were serious—his depression over love lost led him to hard work as an escape in action. When that failed, his depression returned, but he found his way out of it through humorous manipulation of the seriousness of his life. He escaped into the safety of completed action, of recollection, and in the imagined past found a safe ground on which to examine the paradoxes that had plagued him. The result was not merely a tool for managing disappointment, not merely compensation for loss, but also a source of renewed energy and creativity, a creativity that enabled Irving to resume a productive and directed life, even though it did not lead him to more than a spasmodic and periodic reexamination of the ideology that led him to crisis in the first place.

As I developed it in chapter 4, a tendency to entertain incongruity does not necessarily lead to a comfortable or creative humor. Socially prescribed models of appropriate behavior circumscribe the possibilities of humor, as I will discuss below, but personal circumstances and proclivities do as well. In the cases of Mark Twain and Marietta Holley, strong desires for certainty forced each to turn humorous perception in the direction of satire, of certainty. In Holley's case, the satire arose when she surrendered her doubts and became dogmatic in her assurance of moral superiority. Twain's case is, I believe, more typical in that his satiric closure of his humor arose from his sense of inferiority and inadequacy. Being a mere "phunny phellow," a toothless humorist in a culture that allowed humor as recreation but didn't respect it as a direct avenue to truths, Twain felt unappreciated and skeptical of his own worth. Yet when he ventured into serious satire, he found that he was often dismissed anyway, and the tension between his desired role of literary moralist and his socially required role as mere humorist led him to disgust and anger. As he put it in the posthumously published "A Cat-Tale" in a putative dialogue with his daughters, Susy says, "You must know a wonderful deal, Papa." To which he replies, "I have that reputation—in Europe" (131). The ironic scorn hinted at here is, I suspect part of the driving force behind the nihilistic satire of so much of the late Twain. The pessimism of his later phase is an authoritarian judgmentalism based not on confidence but on insecurity—his satire doth protest too much.

## IV. Ideology versus Humor

If the psychic work performed by humor is to break down mental rigidities, then the socially contagious nature of comedy would suggest that its social role might be the same, to break down social rigidities in the interests of social adaptability to changing circumstances. Indeed, every public speaker who tells a joke to "break the ice" knows at some level that social receptivity to an outsider is improved when the group is in a humorous mood. Such a belief in the *socially* ameliorative powers of humor fuels the activity in what William F. Fry calls the grass-roots, worldwide, transcultural "humor-use movement," which has established programs

> in a relatively large number and range of settings, including convalescent facilities, nursing homes, hospitals, outpatient treatment resources, public institutions, corporate and business entities, universities and other academic centers, military forces, governmental and community agencies—in other words, in almost any conceivable setting where groups of individuals are gathered for mutual interaction. . . . A particularly striking indication of the vitality of this movement has been the recent establishment in several places of exploration of the potentials of humor as a conflict resolution mechanism. ("Biology" 118)

Obviously I share much of Fry's optimism about the potentials of humor, but his panegyrics need to be qualified by significant caveats. Humor may always work as a "physiologic and psychologic protection . . . from the detrimental impacts of negative stress" (118), but its potential for social disruption limits its ultimate acceptability in social settings. Specifically, the larger the collectivity and the greater its need for social coherence, the more it is fundamentally at odds with humor, in much the same way that an authoritarian personality excludes or alters humor to defend a threatened sense of selfhood.

The analogy to selfhood is a tricky one in that no collectivity has the clear physical boundaries of a body, though the metaphor serves my purpose here precisely because this metaphor is so commonly a part of the ideology of culture itself. Countless human cultures have defined themselves in "racial" terms by ascribing to certain characteristics of bodies an essential character, and numerous political ideologues have defined the functioning of political structure by analogy to the body—the body politic. But it is important to keep in mind the metaphorical structure of political "bodies." It is a truism of modernity that "culture" is accidental, that those concepts cultures try to define as transcendentally true or natural are merely the central ideas that cultures most need to defend against skepticism or antagonism if they are to cohere at all.

On fundamental points, then, cultures need rigid structures, clearly defined mores, to give them enough consistency to cohere. When codified, or when held together by symbolic heads of polities, societies at core resist or constrain humor because they need to present an image of monolithic consistency and of comprehensive meaning. As a friend of mine put it when I was describing the function humor has of restoring to a person's mind a feeling that truth is plural, "in the Bible, Christ never laughs." Given the needs societies have to present an image of consistency, they tend to be intolerant of humor.

Complete intolerance of humor, though, is simply impossible. Though some societies can and do discourage individuals from developing senses of humor, humor is so fundamental a part of the human psyche that it is not fully repressible. For those individuals who do repress it, the consequence is often mental instability. For those who do not, humor becomes a potentially explosive outlet for revolutionary energies. Warped under the pressure of too much cultural suppression, the destructive side of humor reigns, either as simple displaced aggression or even as an adjunct to rioting. So rather than outlaw it altogether, most cultures develop forms and forums that allow humor a limited, safe time and place. In Navajo culture, for example, taboos restrict the telling of coyote tales to winter. Western cultures for the most part allow some sort of carnival, saturnalia, or jubilee that serves either to vent the revolutionary potential of comic perception or to channel it back into support for the culture itself.

This is where the analogy to the authoritarian personality is useful. Cultures tend to sanction satire as a public manifestation of comedy, channeling the destructive elements of comedy outward at an alien other. Cultural forms often distort the comic moods experienced by their members into acts of scapegoating. They do so substantially because public comedy usually entails some disruption of a culture's codes, and in such circumstances, those perceiving the incongruity often find that the pleasurable feeling of the comic mood is challenged by some other passion, some worry or concern that the center will not hold, that a culture's construction of reality is in danger.

Observation of incongruity in a culture's codes can elicit comedy, but the concomitant fear, augmented by the conservative power of society generally, tends to turn the destructive power of comedy outward, much as in my example of the high school students watching *Oedipus*. In distorting the liberating aspect of comedy, which entails a certain amount of destructive iconoclasm, under the pressure of fear, comedians can direct the destructive power outside of the culture to attack only alien ideas, thereby protecting the culture from the potential rearrangement that comic play could entail. Perhaps the most disturbing aspect of humor is that even in insisting, as it does, that the laugher should see more than one possibility in order to see comic incongruity and should therefore identify at a distance with the object of laughter, comic double vision can so quickly turn from latent connection to insistent alienation.

I speak of cultures here as if they are agents, though a more accurate model may be that cultures are forums in which individual agents negotiate present agency through traditional forms, negotiate present agency against traditional taboos, and negotiate individual consciousness with the desire for social belonging. These three axes map the dimensions of comic play. That the forms any individual uses are inherited gives the illusion of social agency larger than the individual, an illusion that substantially determines individual perception. Individual members of any given culture, in using the culturally sanctioned forms of comedy, end up supporting rather than challenging the culture that their comedy feeds on. In the complex interaction, then, between culturally traditional forms of expression and an artist's emotional connection to that tradition is born cultural control.

I can perhaps best make this connection between the personal and the social by referring to the illustrations in *A Connecticut Yankee in King Arthur's Court* as typical examples of satire. Dan Beard, the artist commissioned by Mark Twain to illustrate *Connecticut Yankee*, was not told to bring out the political messages in the book, but his sense of the American nationalism that Twain had invested into the book, along with his shared sense that the economic excesses of what Twain had earlier called "the Gilded Age" were poisoning American liberty and equality, led him to illustrate the book almost exclusively with political cartoons. While he held himself to be politically progressive, using his art to support what he held to be broadly democratic values, his use of satire tended to shut down the liberating element of comedy and to augment fear of change through fear of the alien.

Beard's illustrations are typical of political comedy in that, like so much political caricaturing, many of his drawings work by calling attention to the animal features of human existence and assigning them to the target of attack. He had cues from the book inasmuch as Twain's narrator calls people rabbits and mules, among other things, and describes medieval human beings—figurative representatives of superstition—in the constant company of animals such as rats and curs. One of the earliest illustrations in the book, the initial illustration for chapter 2, shows a drunken nobleman in the company of fighting dogs (fig. 6.1). The dog slipping under the man's bench is in such proximity as to look like an extension of the man himself, and the peculiar headgear the man sports gives his head a rather canine appearance. Thus does Beard deliberately blur the lines between man and beast.

Beard's illustrations were not always in close service of Twain's literal meaning. He picked up on the feeling behind the book and projected his own political imaginings on other parts of the text. For instance, in illustrating the section of *Connecticut Yankee* when Sandy assumes that a bunch of pigs are enchanted princesses, Beard took Queen Victoria as his model for the illustration "The Troublesomest Old Sow of the Lot" (fig. 6.2). To depict a queen as a sow is a remarkably effective cultural shorthand for absolute derision and to associate the monarch's wealth and power with obesity and animal gluttony.

In using the animal imagery of the pig, Beard's illustration is fairly easy to read. But often, the specific meanings of the symbols clash. Consider figure 6.3, for example, one of Beard's attacks on nobility. Beard illustrated Morgan's complaint that British serfs are meek as rabbits in the face of the arrogance of the nobility with a drawing of an animal fable. Beard picked up on the implication that rabbits are nature's idea of lunch in portraying the ravenous nobility as a lion with table service rendered by the clergy as fox. In American nineteenth-century political iconography, the lion represented Britain, and to "twist the lion's tail" was to invoke American nationalism via anti-British sentiment deeply rooted in the country's identity as an antimonarchical country. But the image had a second pool of meaning for Irish-American voters, whose hatred of the British arose from a different history. City politicians in particular refined the art of "twisting the lion's tail" as a way of securing Irish-American votes. Thus Beard's image of the rapacious lion taps two deep sources of American nationalism, one nativist and the other immigrant.

The nativist strain of nationalism is further refined and intensified in the image of the Roman Catholic clergy as the crafty, rapacious fox that merely serves temporal power rather than spiritual ends. This imagery taps into a Protestant antipathy to Roman Catholicism, with all of the latent anti-Irish, anti-immigrant sentiment that such bigotry also implies. As is frequently the case when political satire turns to iconography in service of the irrational, the meanings of the symbols become overdetermined. But the emotional reactions they elicit are much simpler and more congruent in their limitation of comedy to the destructive side of comic perception through the agency of fear. The internal fracture lines in American culture blur in the overdetermined meanings of these political images, and they have the potential of eliciting, in comic scapegoating, an illusion of cultural consensus.

In the process, open-mindedness and cultural flexibility get lost. Beard's ostensible political liberalism, then, is, like Twain's, haunted by an intense fear that the culture was under assault, and his satire works through images that combine both human and animal characteristics in order to assault the

FIGURE 6.1

FIGURE 6.2

"aliens" held, at some level, to be responsible. This is a very common motif in political comedy, with cartoons showing human beings as gorillas, pigs, rats, etc., usually to represent a nationality or race of people as only quasi-human. In turning human beings into animals, such images make it possible to treat the human "enemy" as subhuman. But the double vision of comedy insists on retaining an understanding that the enemy is simultaneously human and subhuman. If merely animal, it holds no threat. If completely human, it deserves compassion and pity. The double vision of comedy is used to establish identification in distance—the further use of derision to seal off the creative aspects of humor then forces the terror that incongruity can create onto that enemy. While Twain's and Beard's work may not have led to any real political persecution, that their imaginative exercise in *Connecticut Yankee* ends with slaughter suggests something of the psychodynamics as well as the politics involved.

This is the use of humor that so horrifies Boskin, but it is less an intrinsic part of the humorous response than it is a socially constructed manipulation of the destructive side of comedy in service of hatred. Still, even in its most socially warped form, the root of humor remains multiple vision. Remove the socially motivated compulsion to act on that vision, and it can create a broader sense of one's own connections not only with other human beings, but with the world as a whole. Inasmuch as societies as a whole cannot allow that flexible identification and maintain their integrity, it is no surprise that cultural patterns of comedy so often breed hatred. But in the privacy of each individual mind, at the profound level of understanding that Bakhtin describes, humor may serve as a leveling force and a force of creative potential, but only in the tranquility of inaction, only in the mental ground of safety where the mind is able to imagine futures that do not have to be. Such imaginative power is the lifeblood of freedom, of individual agency, of the possibility of being fully human.

## V.  The Manners of Comedy

I notice as I try to work through these ideas that as I generalize about societies in the abstract, my large scale generalizations about the cultural use of humor have a thin-blooded lifelessness consequent not only on the reduction neces-

"WHY THEY WERE NOTHING BUT RABBITS."

FIGURE 6.3

sary to make it apply to all cases, but also because it assumes that collectivities have agency. Only when the examples come down to particular agents working against a cultural field do these generalizations seem to work. What is necessary, then, to any discussion of the cultural work of and control of comedy, is to describe the context as fully and particularly as possible in order to see how individual comedians use comedy. I began this process in the first chapter in talking about the large-scale ideological background behind the moral aesthetics of humor as developed by such philosophers as Francis Hutcheson, and in subsequent chapters I have given some specific examples of humorists working under that umbrella tradition. What remains is to try to draw this material into a whole by giving some sense of the particularity of this tradition to the American scene over the course of the nineteenth century, while keeping in mind my theory of comedy.

I have already noted the large-scale distinction drawn in aesthetics between modes of comedy designated wit, sarcasm, and satire on one side and amiable humor on the other. These formal distinctions did not, as I have shown, hold as well as commentators hoped, though they did have significant impact on the range of possibilities available to comedians. What is distinctive about American culture of the nineteenth century, following cues from British aesthetics, was the widespread acceptance of amiable humor as a divinely sanctioned, positive attribute of human life. Virtually every moral philosopher or every popularization of moral philosophy published in America in the nineteenth century embraced "humor" as it attacked "satire" and "wit."[12]

Even the almost humorless Emerson wrote an essay entitled "The Comic," in which he praised comedy as a tool by which the philosopher may be put in touch with the eternal wholeness of things: "The best of all jokes is the sympathetic contemplation of things by the understanding from the philosopher's point of view" (159). Typically, Emerson transcendentalizes even the least transcendental of human characteristics, but his effort is not unusual for the nineteenth century, even though his sense of the divine is less Christian than that of most of his contemporaries. He sees comedy as a tool to higher understanding, and also as a temporary respite from the serious business of transcendental contemplation:

> A perception of the Comic seems to be a balance-wheel in our metaphysical structure. It appears to be an essential element in a fine character. Wherever the intellect is constructive, it will be found. We feel the absence of it as a defect in the noblest and most oracular soul. The perception of the Comic is a tie of sympathy with other men, a pledge of sanity, and a protection from those perverse tendencies and gloomy insanities in which fine intellects sometimes lose themselves. A rogue alive to the ludicrous is still convertible. If that sense is lost, his fellow men can do little for him. (161–62)

We see here the typical move of the post-Enlightenment religious apologist of humor in America; humor is not marginalized or excluded from the realm of divine attributes, but it is distinctly lower in the hierarchy of those attributes than other "fine" aspects of character. It mediates between the evil of the "rogue" and the divinity of the saint, calling the former to higher knowledge, and preventing the latter from the dangers of growing too high in seriousness.

In such an evaluation of humor, American culture manifested its dual and schizophrenic derivation from Protestant Christianity and from Enlightenment moralism. The traditional Roman Catholic way to deal with humor was to exclude it entirely from official discourse and then allow, through ritualized carnival that incorporated residual pagan rites, occasional departures from Christian stricture in temporary occupation of those cultural practices (and psychological needs) that were excluded by serious culture (Bakhtin).

What nineteenth-century America as a whole did not have as an outlet for comedy was any significant, widespread equivalent of carnival. American Christianity, true to its Puritan ascetic roots, had stripped the culture of worldly festivals—either pre-Lenten, the Christianized Saturnalia of Christmas, or the fertility festivals of May. Arguably, there were exceptions. Local variations of carnival existed in slaveholding states, as Frederick Douglass describes in My Bondage and My Freedom, as a way to channel the revolutionary energies of comic perception into a self-defeating excess. Agricultural life never fully dispensed with harvest festivals, such as corn-shucking bees.

Political life, too, was marked by a very turbulent, almost carnivalesque use of comedy in political campaigns, Fourth of July celebrations, and militia musters, but the record of this comedy shows it almost always to have been twisted into satire. It is easy to find examples of political satire that play on xenophobia and racism as well as on class stereotypes and misogyny. But as Bakhtin puts it, satire is the diminution of humor into mere rhetoric. In the early republic, rhetoric was exalted as the most important art of the citizen; a corresponding outpouring of satire was the natural result.

This helps explain the loss of humor in the works of both Mark Twain and Marietta Holley. As they aggressively sought to occupy the political ground, their comedy veered toward the cultural forms defined as appropriate to political discourse. The consequence was, unfortunately, a loss of the flexibility and optimism at the root of comic perception.

Of equal importance to this study, as satire was a popular mode of political expression, and politics were in the public, male sphere, satire was considered a masculine mode of comedy. Thus, many commentators, when confronting Fanny Fern's writing in newspapers, the forum of political and economic discourse, insisted that no woman could write with such satiric force and that Fanny Fern must therefore be the pen name of a man (Warren 101). Even at the end of the century, when the idea that woman's sphere could embrace politics had ceased to be a novelty, many reviewers assumed, before Holley revealed herself, that the pseudonym "Josiah Allen's Wife" masked a masculine writer (Winter 1).

Correlatively, satire as a form of comic aggression was on principle excluded from the domestic sphere. This is perhaps best seen in the etiquette books and in the moral philosophy texts of the nineteenth century, most of which sanction some form of comedy as appropriate to social, as opposed to political, activity, but only if it is of generous spirit, if it is "humor" rather than "wit." For instance, take the very popular *The Gentleman and Lady's Book of Politeness and Propriety of Deportment*, which, in its fourth American edition of 1837 advises "the Youth of Both Sexes" that:

> Society is not . . . an arena for the use of those perversely clever people, who think themselves furnished with a patent to insult with grace. Whatever may be the keenness of their sarcasms, the piquancy of their observation, or the smile which they excite in me, I do not on this account the less refuse to allow to those caustic spirits the name of polite persons, or of good *ton*; for, in politeness there must be good feeling. . . . One such picture, which, certainly is not highly colored, would render pleasantries always odious; but to indulge in pleasantry is not to resemble such mischievous persons, thank heaven! it is far otherwise; for mild, kind, and harmless pleasantry should be taken in good part even by those who are the subjects of it. (Celnart 121–22)

Notice that not only is the author sanguine about the distinction between good-humored and ill-humored pleasantry, she insists that well-bred gentlemen and ladies in private social circumstances should submit with good cheer to good-humored fun. Laughter in such circumstances is never given the free rein of carnival, but neither does it need to explode into excess when given a regular and consistent forum. Thus, the sanction of humor in the pages of even such august journals as the *Atlantic Monthly* should come as no surprise: humor may not have been held to have been the highest form of literature, but that it was *literature* was doubted by few.

The clear opposition that so many commentators postulated between good-humored and ill-humored pleasantry is, of course, not so easy to find in fact, as the difficulties Stowe experienced in her efforts to maintain a gentle tone throughout her comedy attest. Some moralists of the period therefore came close to denouncing comedy altogether, as did James Burgh in his 1846 *Rules for the Conduct of Life:*

> As nothing is more provoking to some tempers than raillery, a prudent person will not always be satirically witty where he can, but only where he may without offence. For he will consider that the finest stroke of raillery is but a witticism: and that there is hardly any person so mean, whose good will is not preferable to the pleasure of a horse laugh. If you should by raillery make another ridiculous, . . . remember that the judicious part of the company will not think the better of you for your having a knack at drollery or ribaldry. . . . In the case of one's being exposed to the mirth of a company for something said or done sillily, the most effectual way of turning the edge of their ridicule, is by joining the laugh against one's self, and exposing and aggravating his own folly; for this will show that he has the uncommon understanding to see his own fault. (22)

Burgh's anxiety about "raillery" is the most obvious part of this passage to the modern eye, but to his own peers, the distinction between humor and raillery would have been latent, in that humor can be created out of raillery by the butt of the humor acquiescing in a joke's insight while refusing to accept the mean-spiritedness of the attack. I cited in chapter 1 Stowe's development of such humor in *Oldtown Folks* through the character of Mehitable Rossiter.

But it is important to note that these attitudes that allowed humor did not have deep roots in American culture. The deep roots had been sunk by fundamentalist Protestantism, with its overwhelming emphasis on the literal and absolute truth of the Bible. Unfortunately for American humor, the Bible is not very forgiving of laughter. The Old Testament does give a bit of room to laughter. While it usually refers to laughter as nothing more than an outward sign of scorn, different parts of different books sometimes refer to laughter as a sign of joy, and Proverbs says that "a merry heart doeth good like a medicine" (17:22). Ecclesiastes sees laughter as a sign of folly, but also says that there is a season for laughter.

The New Testament, on the other hand, does not waffle at all about laughter. According to Luke, "Blessed are ye that weep now: for ye shall laugh" (6:21) in the kingdom of heaven, and those worldlings who take pleasure now had best take heed: "Woe unto you that laugh now! for ye shall mourn and weep" (6:25). St. Paul, in his letter to the Ephesians explains why:

> Be ye therefore followers of God, as dear children; and walk in love, as Christ also hath loved us, and hath given himself for us an offering and a sacrifice to God for a sweetsmelling savour.
>
> But fornication, and all uncleanness, or covetousness, let it not be once named among you, as becometh saints; neither filthiness, nor foolish talking, nor jesting, which are not convenient: but rather giving of thanks. For this ye know, that no whoremonger, nor unclean person, nor covetous man, who is an idolater, hath any inheritance in the kingdom of Christ and of God. Let no man deceive you with vain words: for because of these things cometh the wrath of God upon the children of disobedience. (5:1–6)

Paul sees the "inconvenience" and "deceitfulness" of "foolish talking," "vain words," and "jesting" as the equivalent of "fornication," "uncleaness," and "covetousness." The idea of harmless humor is absolutely alien to fundamentalist Christianity.

What's left to such Christians is to follow the Book of James's advice for how to renounce the world: "Be afflicted, and mourn, and weep: let your laughter be turned to mourning, and your joy to heaviness" (4:9). Spirited Christians doubtless found such advice difficult to follow, but for those who couldn't weep and mourn, James does give one out: "Is there any among you . . . merry? let him sing psalms" (5:13). These are the roots of American Protestant asceticism. The Protestantism that was powerful enough to exclude most kinds of ritual from church practice, that insisted that ascetic forms of devotion should govern worldly practice, and that held comedy in contempt did not surrender easily before what Henry F. May calls the Didactic Enlightenment. The enlighteners in America, then, needed to walk cautiously; they displaced fundamentalist rigor in part by coopting rather than directly challenging Christian piety.

Therefore, the modes of humor that cultural moderators sanctioned needed to dovetail with a modified Christianity. I could cite dozens of such commentators, but I'll restrict myself to two typical midcentury moralists, Louisa C.

Tuthill and Catherine Beecher, for exemplary pronouncements from a post-Enlightenment Christian perspective on the use of comedy. The first of these, from Tuthill's *The Young Lady's Home,* is the more anxious about the value of "amusement" and the more censorious about the dangers of "wit," which Tuthill discusses under the heading of sarcasm:

> It is dangerous to be severe upon the faults of our friends, even in jest. Like blows given by boxers, at first in sport, they often end in angry earnest. Lively *repartee* may sometimes be agreeable; when it delicately avoids personality, it may give brilliancy to conversation; but this can seldom be avoided. Defend us from the quips and quirks of a habitual punster, who snaps up your honest words, and turns them into traitors before your eyes.
>
> "To women, *wit* is a peculiarly perilous possession, which nothing short of the sober-mindedness of Christianity can keep in order . . . ." Woe to the woman who gains the reputation of wit. She is expected never to open her mouth to speak, without dropping pearls and diamonds; if her wit be not chastised into meek subordination, she is feared by one sex and hated by the other. Even although it be thus chastised, there are many who look upon it in its harmless playfulness as they would upon the gambols of an uncaged tigress. (169–70)

The energy with which she denies women the luxury and pleasure of wit almost suggests that, in spite of her use of a quotation from Scottish Enlightenment moralist Dugald Stewart as the epigraph for the entire book, she has not yet come out from under the Calvinist disdain for *any* pleasure as worldly and therefore sinful.

The end of her chapter on conversation, however, suggests where and thus how an American woman is to exercise her sense of humor:

> Madame de Stael was so fond of conversation, that it was misery for her to live out of Paris; for there only, in her estimation, could any thing deserving the name of conversation be enjoyed. Happily, American women know little of conversation as a *fine art,* and therefore seldom talk for display. Although the just demands of society often call them from their own firesides, may their sweetest, dearest enjoyments be there,—may they ever find *home* a sphere wide enough for sprightly, rational, intellectual conversation, that, whenever they mingle with larger circles, it may be easy, useful, cheerful, and agreeable. (174–75)

Home, then, is the place for pleasures, for a humor that is "cheerful," "agreeable," and above all "useful." Utility and piety combined is the American recipe for "happiness" according to many nineteenth-century moralists, and comedy, then, serves higher ends.

To Catherine Beecher these higher ends were rather obviously utilitarian. She stressed above all that humor was a tonic, provided by God to serve us in our efforts to live useful and ultimately pious lives. In her very popular *A Treatise on Domestic Economy,* Beecher devoted an entire chapter to "domestic amusements" in order to challenge Calvinist asceticism:

> Another resource for family amusement, is, the various games that are played by children, and in which the joining of older members of the family is always a

great advantage to both parties. All medical men unite in declaring, that nothing is more beneficial to health than hearty laughter; and surely our benevolent Creator would not have provided risibles, and made it a source of health and enjoyment to use them, and then have made it a sin so to do. There has been a tendency to asceticism, on this subject, which needs to be removed. (261)

Notice that she refers only to family amusements, telling us quite specifically that home is the appropriate forum for laughter.

As long as laughter remains in the home, Beecher worries little about inappropriate use of laughter and amusement. In her view, the cords of familial affection are the bonds that determine the proper range of "amusements," and a comfortable exercise of domesticity will make all necessary allowances:

> Jokes, laughter, and sports, when used in such a degree as tends only to promote health, social feeling, and happiness, are neither vain, foolish, nor "not convenient." It is the excess of these things, and not the moderate use of them, that Scripture forbids. The prevailing temper of the mind, should be cheerful, yet serious; but there are times, when relaxation and laughter are proper for all. There is nothing better for this end, than that parents and older persons should join in the sports of childhood (262)

Here we see, then, that split in "temper of the mind" that suggests the public world should be serious, albeit cheerful, but the home is a legitimate place for regression into childlike laughter and enthusiasm. The regressive nature of American humor on which so many commentators remark, then, is not so much a function of comedy per se as it is a function of the proscription of comedy from adult duties but the allowance of it in the domestic sphere. Thus Irving's man who acts like a child in "Rip Van Winkle" and Mark Twain's efforts to treat serious issues comically by describing them through the eyes of a child in *Huckleberry Finn*, or through the retrospective eyes of nostalgia in works too numerous to mention, are just some of the manifestations of American definitions of humor as a domestic exercise.

Similarly, it was as a domestic amusement calculated to inculcate moral habits of mind that belles lettres snuck into American culture in spite of Puritan distrust of fiction. Or more accurately, as Catherine Beecher's remarks again suggest, America came to accept fiction in an effort to ameliorate the harshness of Calvinism. As she put it in *Common Sense Applied to Religion*, Beecher was driven to virtual despair over her father's doctrines of innate depravity and election. "It was at such times I understood for what the love of the comic was implanted, and if all Christians should feel as I do, what might be the legitimate use of works of fiction, the drama and the dance. In such a case, and properly regulated, they would be needful and only beneficial alternatives" to despair and atheism (xxx). Beecher sees the comic and literature as fundamentally linked, as parts of a useful exercise of the imagination. Yet her emphasis on proper regulation, along with her insistence that fiction be *used* legitimately, establishes humor in a hierarchical position vis-à-vis morality and salvation while it implies a system of regulation.

To the proper regulation of a taste in fiction many moralists of the day devoted considerable attention. Tuthill, in discoursing on the virtues and dangers of the imagination, warns young women who discover in themselves too strong an imagination, evinced by a propensity to "imagine yourself a heroine, and exult in your airbuilt castles" (34) to "[r]ead books of sound reasoning or sober fact; abjure novels, and deny yourself, for a time, the luxury of poetry of a sentimental character" (35). Only when, says Tuthill, the imagination is well regulated should her readers develop a knowledge of English literature by beginning with Shakespeare's *Merchant of Venice,* which should be read along with an appropriate guide: "Mrs. Jameson's splendid development of this character [Portia] in her Characteristics of Woman will assist you to understand and appreciate it." Then more Shakespeare, Milton, and finally, "You may think yourself happy if you have been denied the perusal of the Waverley novels until your judgment is mature; for now you can read them for their perfect delineations of human character. When read too early, they are very imperfectly understood" (36). But when perfectly understood, proper literature "cannot fail to give pleasure to a cultivated mind, to improve the taste, and correct the imagination" (36–37).

Other moralists had other lists and other means to "perfect understanding"; if they hadn't, literary criticism as a profession might never have been born. But nineteenth-century American moralists, especially as the century progressed, did share agreement that literature, including comic literature, had value. The universally shared object in teaching the young to read imaginative literature was to exercise and cultivate taste without overtaxing intellectual faculties or overstimulating the imagination. This was primarily an Enlightenment agenda, with the ideal of exercising all of the faculties in accordance with practical morality. However, the point of this exercise, according to those Christian moralists who adopted it in opposition to their Calvinist past, was to bring the morally developed person to gradual salvation.

Such moralizing was confined neither to the midcentury nor to explicitly didactic works. William Dean Howells's *The Rise of Silas Lapham* for instance, developed an ethics of reading for moral content rather than for models of false heroism. For boys, girls, women, and men, with different emphases depending on the moralist, fine literature was designed for the home as the province of moral elevation. Humor was granted the lowest rung on the ladder of sentiments, but as a branch of belles lettres, it was assigned an honored position in the didactic, as well as in the recreational, aspect of domesticity.

Again, the impact of these definitions of the proper range and function of humor on the comedians I have discussed throughout this book should be apparent. Mark Twain turned to serious moralizing in *The Gilded Age* partly because he and Charles Dudley Warner were challenged by their wives to write a better novel than the ones they complained were corrupting young women though false notions of heroism. And in *Adventures of Huckleberry Finn,* Mark Twain turns savagely on Tom Sawyer's "misreading" of fiction, as I pointed out earlier. In this kind of moralizing, Twain followed the cultural commonplaces of domestic ideology, using humor to promote "correct" taste, even as his use of vernacular English challenged many of the particular standards common to his day.

Among the particular uses of literature that Twain might have challenged was the idea that the moral use of literature helped readers on the road to salvation. But it was as a vehicle to salvation that liberal Christianity was able to use literature to relax a rigid Calvinism in the first place; it was not a purpose quickly surrendered. Such a purpose, though, had a profound impact on the social practice of humor in that the ideas of cheerfulness and amiability, so fundamentally a part of the definition of acceptable comedy, are closely connected to the idea of Christian perseverance in the face of suffering. I suspect, then, that the critical commonplace that humor is displaced suffering is in fact a historical residue of the shift from an ascetic Christianity to a Christianity that promoted a didactic aesthetic.

I have already cited Beecher's justification of comedy as an alternative to religious despair. She cites her own case history to point out that too serious a devotion to religious thought will lead not to salvation, but rather to doubt and despair or anger. In her *Treatise on Domestic Economy* she explains in a didactic mode what she suggests in *Common Sense* in a confessional mode, that "any such attention to religion, as prevents the performance of daily duties and needful relaxation, is dangerous, as tending to produce such a state of the brain as makes it impossible to feel or judge correctly" (*Treatise* 189). She does not here renounce the idea of self-renunciation; she only a suggests that the brain needs an occasional time-out to develop proper balance. The bulk of Beecher's book encourages each person to undertake "a course of self-denying benevolence" (193). As she developed the virtue of self-denying benevolence in *Common Sense*, "as self-denial always involves more or less pain, it becomes a fact that happiness is to be gained only by more or less *suffering*" (37). In this worldview, humor becomes merely an interlude in a rigorous life of suffering, though it is a necessary interlude in that it is a buttress against despair. The close connection, then, between humor and pain arises out of this strange conjunction between the Enlightenment rhetoric of happiness and the Christian rhetoric of suffering.

Tuthill's volume is perhaps more suggestive of this connection. Her volume works to a climax in three chapters linked by the common title "Christian Duty" and differentiated by their respective subtitles: "Cheerfulness," "Forgiveness and Forbearance, Self-Denial, Self-Government, Prayer," and "Christian Usefulness." She begins this series of chapters by describing life in this world as a course of painful shocks. After three lurid pages about death, disease, and disappointment, she says, "Yet after this terrible array of possible and probable trials, we should assert that uniform cheerfulness is imperatively a Christian duty. The worldling may turn away from trouble; the philosopher look upon it with calmness; but the Christian only can smile upon it" (305). Such smiling comes from the telos of salvation, "a habit of looking forward to our brighter inheritance [which] is the greatest solace amidst the cares of our present condition"

(309). Such a solace requires a comic double vision, the double vision that Emerson sees in "The Comic" as an aid to transcendence.

But to commentators like Tuthill, such a conjunction of good spirits with transcendence does not entail a condescending rejection of the world in the prospect of salvation; it is, rather, an exercise of a worldly compassion. To liberal Christians of Tuthill's stripe, "[t]he spirit of love should beam forth from their countenances, and display itself in their actions, in a kind word to the old, or a smile of encouragement to the child. Contradict, then, by your daily walk and conversation, the erroneous idea, that piety is too gloomy for the bright period of youth" (310). The parallel between Tuthill's description of Christian cheerfulness and the commonplace description of amiable humor is not accidental; the development of each went hand in glove with the other. In the eyes of many they were the same thing: a disposition to spread joy through a generosity of spirit in spite of apparent differences of social position or spiritual elevation.

I do not mean to suggest that this blurring of humor and faith is peculiar to American uses of comedy. The passage from Kierkegaard that I cited in chapter 1 refers to comedy in much the same spirit. Indeed, Kierkegaard goes so far as to call humor an experience of pain with a telos toward relief in Christian faith, suggesting that tragedy and comedy are nearly the same animal:

> The tragic and the comic are the same, in so far as both are based on contradiction; but *the tragic is the suffering contradiction, the comical, the painless contradiction.*
> . . . The difference between the tragic and the comic lies in the relationship between the contradiction and the controlling idea. The comic apprehension evokes the contradiction or makes it manifest by having in mind the way out, which is why the contradiction is painless. The tragic apprehension sees the contradiction and despairs of a way out. . . . Humor has its justification precisely in its tragic side, in the fact that it reconciles itself to . . . pain. (459–64)

Whether or not it is stripped of its Christian context, this formulation is so much a commonplace of modern criticism that I needn't recapitulate its variations here; nor do I need to recapitulate my objections. That this idea is so widely held is merely a cultural accident by which the cultural forms through which our comedy has been channeled for so long have developed humor as a tool in service of a teleology of happiness through suffering, a worldview in which suffering gives life meaning. This is perhaps the most formidable and effective way that Western culture has circumscribed not only the range but the meaning of humor, because rather than allowing humor the luxury of purposelessness, the serious mind, in the Enlightenment rendition of Christian perfectionism, insists that humor always *have* a telos.

Thus, most of the humorists I treat confront, either directly or by implication, the idea of Christian faith without either wanting to or being able to challenge the terms by which that faith is described. Certainly Stowe's entire collection of humorous stories is an effort to assert, through the double vision of comedy, the possibility of spirit in a physical world. Fern and Irving both require the idea of humor as compensation in order to use it as leverage against despair. Even Harris's anti-Christian Sut Lovingood can do no more than assert humanity's fundamental barbarism and thus the hypocrisy of all believers in salvation, without being able to *postulate* an alternative view of creativity or happiness. That the raw energy and verve of Harris's writing manages in spite of Harris's overt ideas to suggest some hint of a world not given value by definitions of suffering attests to the deep power of humor.

The two authors I discuss here who seem to have directly confronted this narrowing of humor to a rendition of suffering are Melville and Freeman. Melville, exercising humor's power to uncover assumptions, sees faith itself as a manifestation of will rather than as a kind of knowledge. Freeman rather than seeing suffering as the only possible category that gives meaning to life, sees suffering as potentially absurd. To choose what meaning to give to suffering is to choose kinds of faith; faith in a narrow doctrine, or faith in the plenitude of human possibilities.

## VI. Humor as Haven

Thus nineteenth-century American culture tried to control humor not only through the usual mode of satire, but also by sanctioning amiable humor within the ideology of domesticity and ostensibly in service of Enlightenment didacticism and Christian "cheerfulness" in suffering. Even though such a combination very effectively controlled comedy for the most part, the question remains whether humor as social practice could perform for nineteenth-century America the same kind of work it can perform for individuals. If the massive popularity of humorous literature from about 1830–1900 (Blair "Popularity") suggests anything, the answer is a qualified yes. Granted, much of America's "humor" was satire that took the political sphere as its realm. Granted, too, much of America's humor was relegated to other separate spheres, such as the sphere of "gentlemen" readers of the New York *Spirit of the Times* who consumed much southwestern humor as an exercise in their own class superiority. In such cases, belle lettres as the art of the gentleman, like domestic humor itself, was supposed to be antipolitical in that it was supposed to eschew party politics, but it was political in that it cultivated an elitist idea of gentility. Yet the frontier experience, "humorized" for this audience, allowed a significant wedge of creativity and liberalizing via this medium. This subject deserves a book in its own right.

And granted, belle lettres, defined as a domestic art, "faminized" humor. Cut off from much of its intellectual power by standards of taste and decorum and by standards of home as haven, forced into a role as child's play, humor was still given an important role in family life. Given that family life was held to be the center of republican civilization, humor had real leverage if not on cultural values themselves, at least on how cultural values were experienced by individual Americans.

I don't want to elevate humor to a position of seriousness that it cannot bear, but neither do I want to diminish its actual role in American culture. Ideas of freedom and equality, the ideas essential to America's new democratic ideology, were sources of both tension and pleasure. Freedom as a kind of license conferred anxiety, but as an alternative to tyranny it was a source of pride; equality as experienced in a mobile society yielded anxiety for those who feared cultural debasement in "leveling," and generated pleasure in the idea of upward mobility. The paradoxical implications of these terms as translated into personal behavior or political action vexed American culture from the beginning. As long as domesticity was the ideological center of American culture, the political problems of this new democracy were left substantially to domesticity to solve. Such a serious business, still the food of much American political rhetoric, was by necessity the subject matter of the humor that was allowed in the domestic sphere.

In the humor of the home, with all of the hedges against satire and aggression that "humor" implied, nineteenth-century America allowed humor much of its creative energy precisely because such play was safe by definition. Home was to be a place of learning, a place of controlled freedom, precisely the conditions under which humor as a mode of discovering alternatives could thrive. The destructive side of humor followed as a matter of course, hidden the while by the sunny side of humor as an avenue of compassion. I've detailed some of this journey in the preceding pages, trying to give a sense both of how humor was culturally circumscribed and how widely it was able to range notwithstanding, giving, in the extra political realm of belles lettres, a creative space that enabled readers to accommodate the monumental changes that swirled around them.

Thus, humor was indeed the haven in the nineteenth-century's ideological heartlessness. The dominant ideologies were remorselessly serious and rigid in their seriousness, and they demanded the impossible by insisting on the supreme value of opposites. And domestic ideology was at the center of all of these paradoxes. In an urbanizing, modernizing, middle-class culture that demanded that marriages be based on love, men were being increasingly forced to spend six days a week, twelve hours a day at work, ostensibly for their wives and children, but alienated from them as a source of emotional satisfaction. Women, declared equal partners, were increasingly denied access to the economic productivity that would make that equality real. Children, freed from the stigma of original sin, were held in even tighter check than before to make sure they would remain "pure." This recapitulation of the paradoxes and repressions of nineteenth-century middle-class culture could be stretched for pages. Anyone who took seriously these conflicting admonitions was in danger of losing sanity, of losing a grip on meaning. Not surprisingly, a rich humor developed in the period to help put some human flexibility into this newly constructed idea of home. Given how highly Americans came to value this new idea of home, their humor was a necessity. Humor was not only the haven, it was the heart.

# *Appendix*

A New System of English Grammar, by John Phoenix

I have often thought that the adjectives of the English language were not sufficiently definite for the purposes of description. They have but three degrees
of comparison—a very insufficient number, certainly, when we consider that
they are to be applied to a thousand objects, which, though of the same general class or quality, differ from each other by a thousand different shades or
degrees of the same peculiarity. Thus, though there are three hundred and
sixty-five days in a year, all of which must, from the nature of things, differ
from each other in the matter of climate,—we have but half a dozen expressions to convey to one another our ideas of this inequality. We say—"It is a
fine day"; "it is a *very* fine day;" "it is the *finest* day we have seen"; or "It is an
unpleasant day"; "a *very* unpleasant day"; "the *most* unpleasant day we ever
saw." But it is plain, that none of these expressions give an *exact* idea of the
nature of the day; and the two superlative expressions are generally untrue. I
once heard a gentleman remark, on a rainy, snowy, windy and (in the ordinary English language) indescribable day, that it was "most preposterous
weather." He came nearer to giving a correct idea of it, than he could have

done by any ordinary mode of expression; but his description was not sufficiently definite.

Again:—we say of a lady—"She is beautiful"; "She is *very* beautiful"; or "She
is *perfectly* beautiful";—descriptions, which, to one who never saw her, are no
descriptions at all, for among thousands of women he has seen, probably no
two are equally beautiful; and as to a *perfectly* beautiful woman, he knows that
no such being was ever created—unless by G.P.R. James, for one of the two
horsemen to fall in love with, and marry at the end of the second volume.

If I meet Smith in the street, and ask him, as I am pretty sure to do—"how
he does?" he infallibly replies—"*Tolerable*, thank you," which gives me no *exact*
idea of Smith's health—for he has made the same reply to me on a hundred different occasions—on every one of which there *must* have been some slight
shade of difference in his physical economy, and of course a corresponding
change in his feelings.

To a man of a mathematical turn of mind—to a student and lover of the
exact sciences these inaccuracies of expression—this inability to understand
*exactly* how things are, must be a constant source of annoyance; and to one
who like myself, unites this turn of mind to an ardent love of truth, for its own
sake—the reflection that the English language does not enable us to speak the
truth with exactness, is peculiarly painful. For this reason I have, with some
trouble, made myself acquainted with every ancient and modern language, in
the hope that I might find some one of them that would enable me to express
precisely my ideas; but the same insufficiency of adjectives exist in all except
that of the Flathead Indian of Puget Sound, which consists of but forty-six
words, mostly nouns; but to the constant use of which exists the objection, that
nobody but that tribe can understand it. And as their literary and scientific ad-
vancement is not such as to make a residence among them, for a man of my disposition, desirable, I have abandoned the use of their language, in the belief
that for me it is *hyas. cultus.*, or as the Spaniard hath it, *no me vale nada*.

※    ※

Despairing, therefore, of making new discoveries in foreign languages, I have
set myself seriously to work to reform our own; and have, I think made an important discovery, which, when developed into a system and universally
adopted, will give a precision of expression, and a consequent clearness of idea,
that will leave little to be desired, and will, I modestly hope, immortalize my
humble name as the promulgator of truth and the benefactor of the human
race.

Before entering upon my system I will give you an account of its discovery
(which, perhaps I might with more modesty term an adaptation and enlarge-
ment of the idea of another), which will surprise you by its simplicity, and like
the method of standing eggs on end, of Columbus, the inventions of printing,
gunpowder and the mariner's compass—prove another exemplification of the
truth of Hannah More's beautifully expressed sentiment:

Large streams from little fountains flow
Large aches from little toe-corns grow.

During the past week my attention was attracted by a large placard embellishing the corners of our streets, headed in mighty capitals, with the word "PHRENOLOGY" and illustrated by a map of a man's head, closely shaven, and laid off in lots, duly numbered from one to forty-seven. Beneath this edifying illustration appeared a legend, informing the inhabitants of San Diego and vicinity that Professor Dodge had arrived and taken rooms at the Gyascutus House, where he would be happy to examine and furnish them with a chart of their heads, showing the moral and intellectual endowments, at the low price of three dollars each.

Always gratified with an opportunity of spending my money and making scientific researches, I immediately had my hair cut and carefully combed, and hastened to present myself and my head to the Professor's notice. I found him a tall and thin Professor, in a suit of rusty, not to say seedy black, with a closely buttoned vest, and no perceptible shirtcollar or wristbands. His nose was red, his spectacles were blue, and he wore a brown wig, beneath which, as I subsequently ascertained, his bald head was laid off in lots, marked and numbered with Indian ink, after the manner of the diagram upon his advertisement. Upon a small table lay many little books with yellow covers, several of the placards, pen and ink, a pair of iron callipers with brass knobs, and six dollars in silver. Having explained the object of my visit and increased the pile of silver by six half-dollars from my pocket—whereat he smiled, and I observed he wore false teeth—(scientific men always do; they love to encourage art) the Professor placed me in a chair, and rapidly manipulating my head, after the manner of a *sham pooh* (I am not certain as to the orthography of this expression), said that my temperament was "lymphatic, nervous, bilious." I remarked that "I thought myself dyspeptic," but he made no reply. Then seizing on the callipers, he embraced with them my head in various places, and made notes upon a small card that lay near him on the table. He then stated that my "hair was getting very thin on the top," placed in my hand one of the yellow-covered books, which I found to be an almanac containing anecdotes about the virtues of Dodge's Hair Invigorator, and recommending it to my perusal, he remarked that he was agent for the sale of this wonderful fluid, and urged me to purchase a bottle—price two dollars. Stating my willingness to do so, the Professor produced it from a hair trunk that stood in a corner of the room, which he stated, by the way, was originally an ordinary pine box on which the hair had grown since "the Invigorator" had been placed in it—(a singular fact) and recommended me to be cautious in wearing gloves while rubbing it upon my head, as unhappy accidents had occurred—the hair growing freely from the ends of the fingers, if used with the bare hand. He then seated himself at the table, and rapidly filling up what appeared to me a blank certificate, he soon handed over the following singular document.

PHRENOLOGICAL CHART OF THE HEAD OF M. JOHN PHOENIX, BY FLATBROKE B. DODGE, Professor of Phrenology, and inventor and proprietor of Dodge's celebrated Hair Invigorator, Stimulator of the Conscience, and Arouser of the Mental Faculties:

Temperament,—*Lymphatic, Nervous, Bilious*

| | |
|---|---|
| Size of Head, 11. | Imitation, 11. |
| Amativeness, 11 ½. | Self-Esteem, ½. |
| Caution, 3. | Benevolence, 12. |
| Combativeness, 2 ½. | Mirth, 1. |
| Credulity, 1. | Language, 12. |
| Causality, 12. | Firmness, 2. |
| Conscientiousness, 12. | Veneration, 12. |
| Destructiveness, 9. | Philoprogenitiveness, 0. |
| Hope, 10. | |

Having gazed on this for a few moments in mute astonishment—during which the Professor took a glass of brandy and water, and afterwards a mouthful of tobacco—I turned to him and requested an explanation.

"Why," said he, "it's very simple; the number 12 is the maximum, 1 the minimum; for instance, you are as benevolent as a man can be—therefore I mark you, Benevolence, 12. You have little or no self-esteem—hence I place you, Self-esteem, ½. You've scarcely any credulity—don't you see?"

*I did see!* This was my discovery. I saw at a flash how the English language was susceptible of improvement, and, fired with the glorious idea, I rushed from the room and the house; heedless of the Professor's request that I would buy more of his Invigorator; heedless of his alarmed cry that I would pay for the bottle I'd got; heedless that I tripped on the last step of the Gyascutus House, and mashed there the precious fluid (the step has now a growth of four inches of hair on it, and the people use it as a door-mat); I rushed home, and never grew calm till with pen, ink and paper before me, I commenced the development of my system.

This system—shall I say this great system—is exceedingly simple, and easily explained in a few words. In the first place, "*figures won't lie.*" Let us then represent by the number 100, the maximum, the *ne plus ultra* of every human quality—grace, beauty, courage, strength, wisdom, learning—every thing. Let *perfection*, I say, be represented by 100, and an absolute minimum of all qualities by the number 1. Then by applying the numbers between, to the adjectives used in conversation, we shall be able to arrive at a very close approximation to the idea we wish to convey; in other words, we shall be enabled to speak the truth. Glorious, soul-inspiring idea! For instance, the most ordinary question asked of you is "How do you do?" To this, instead of replying, "Pretty well," "Very well," "Quite well," or the like absurdities—after running through your mind that *perfection* of health is 100, no health at all, 1—you say, with a graceful bow, "Thank you, I'm 52 today;" or, feeling poorly, "I'm 13, I'm obliged to you," or "I'm 68," or "75," or 87 ½," as the case may be! Do you see how very close in this way you may approximate to the truth, and how clearly your questioner will understand what he so anxiously wishes to arrive at—your *exact* state of health?

Let this system be adopted into our elements of grammar, our conversation, our literature, and we become at once an exact, precise, mathematical, truth-telling people. It will apply to every thing but politics; there, truth being of no account, the system is useless. But in literature, how admirable! Take an example:

As a 19 young and 76 beautiful lady was 52 gaily tripping down the sidewalk of our 84 frequented street, she accidently came in contact—100 (this shows that she came in close contact) with a 73 fat, but 87 good-humored-looking gentleman, who was 93 (i.e., intently) gazing into the window of a toy-shop. Gracefully 56 extricating herself, she received the excuses of the 96 embarrassed Falstaff with a 68 bland smile, and continued on her way. But hardly—7—had she reached the corner of the block, ere she was overtaken by a 24 young man, 32 poorly dressed, but of an 85 expression of countenance; 91 hastily touching her 54 beautifully rounded arm, he said, to her 67 surprise—

"Madam, at the window of the toy-shop yonder, you dropped this bracelet, which I had the 71 good fortune to observe, and now have the 94 happiness to hand to you." (Of course the expression "94 happiness" is merely the young man's polite hyperbole.)

Blushing with 76 modesty, the lovely (76, as before, of course), lady took the bracelet   which was a 24 magnificent diamond clasp (24 *magnificent*, playfully sarcastic; it was probably *not* one of Tucker's) from the young man's hand, and 84 hesitatingly drew from her beautifully 38 embroidered reticule a 67 port-monnaie. The young man noticed the action, and 73 proudly drawing back, added—

"Do not thank me; the pleasure of gazing for an instant at those 100 eyes (perhaps too exaggerated a compliment), has already more than compensated me for any trouble that I might have had."

She thanked him, however, and with a 67 deep blush and a 48 pensive air, turned from him, and pursued with a 33 slow step her promenade.

Of course you see that this is but the commencement of a pretty little tale, which I might throw off, if I had a mind to, showing in two volumes, or forty-eight chapters of thrilling interest, how the young man sought the girl's acquaintance, how the interest first excited, deepened into love, how they suffered much from the opposition of parents (her parents of course), and how, after much trouble, annoyance, and many perilous adventures, they were finally married—their happiness, of course, being represented by 100. But I trust that I have said enough to recommend my system to the good and truthful of the literary world; and besides, just at present I have something of more immediate importance to attend to.

You would hardly believe it, but that everlasting (100) scamp of a Professor has brought a suit against me for stealing a bottle of his disgusting Invigorator; and as the suit comes off before a Justice of the Peace, whose only principle of law is to find guilty and fine any accused person whom he thinks has any money—(because if he don't he has to take his costs in County Scrip,) it behooves me to "take time by the fore-lock." So, for the present, adieu. Should my system succeed to the extent of my hopes and expectation, I shall publish my new grammar early in the ensuing month, with suitable dedication and preface; and should you, with your well known liberality, publish my prospectus, and give me a handsome literary notice, I shall be pleased to furnish a presentation copy to each of the little Pioneer children.

P.S. I regret to add that having just read this article to Mrs. Phoenix, and asked her opinion thereon, she replied that "if a first-rate magazine article were represented by 100, she should judge this to be about 13; or if the quintessence of stupidity were 100, she should take this to be in the neighborhood of 96." This, as a criticism is perhaps a little discouraging, but as an exemplification of the merits of my system it is exceedingly flattering. How could she, I should like to know, in ordinary language, have given so *exact* and truthful an idea—how expressed so forcibly her opinion (which, of course, differs from mine) on the subject?

As Dr. Samuel Johnson learnedly remarked to James Boswell, Lord of Auchinleck, on a certain occasion—

"Sir, the proof of the pudding is in the eating thereof."

# Notes

Chapter 1

1. This list of critics who specifically treat "women's humor" is not long. The ones I have consulted include Zita Dresner and Nancy Walker, who coedited an important anthology of women's humor, *Redressing the Balance: American Women's Literary Humor from Colonial Times to the 1980s;* June Sochen, editor of and contributor to *Women's Comic Visions;* Linda A. Morris, author of the only book-length study of Frances Miriam Whitcher, *Women's Humor in the Age of Gentility;* Emily Toth, author of "A Laughter of Their Own: Women's Humor in the United States"; theorists Lisa Merrill and Regina Barreca; Kate H. Winter, the biographer of Marietta Holley; and Shirley Marchalonis, who reminds us of the humor in Mary Wilkins Freeman's work.

2. It may seem strange to collapse the positivist materialist philosopher Hobbes with the poststructuralist Foucault since their methodologies seem so antagonistic, but I look to their first principles for my comparison. Hobbes begins his analysis of the human condition by describing it as the war of each against all. Foucault's argument for rejecting structuralism has a familiar ring:

> One's point of reference should not be to the great model of language (*langue*) and signs, but to that of war and battle. This history which bears and determines us has the form of a war rather than that of a language: relations of power, not re-

lations of meaning. History has no "meaning," though this is not to say that it is absurd or incoherent. On the contrary it is intelligible and should be susceptible of analysis down to the smallest detail—but this in accordance with the intelligibility of struggles, of strategies and tactics. (14)

3. The preceding discussion tries to capture a consensus built on over twenty years of scholarship. See Ann Douglas, *The Feminization of American Culture*; Christopher Lasch, *Haven in a Heartless World*; Nancy Cott, *The Bonds of Womanhood*; Barbara Welter, *Dimity Convictions*; Jane Tompkins, "Sentimental Power"; Gregg Camfield, "The Moral Aesthetics of Sentimentality: A Missing Key to Uncle Tom's Cabin"; Elizabeth Ammons, "Stowe's Dream of the Mother-Savior"; Katheryn Kish Sklar, *Catherine Beecher: A Study in Domesticity*; Jay Fliegelman, *Prodigals and Pilgrims*; G. M. Goshgarian, *To Kiss the Chastening Rod: Domestic Fiction and Sexual Ideology in the American Renaissance*; Mary Kelley, *Private Woman, Public Stage: Literary Domesticity in Nineteenth-Century America*, etc.

4. The two poles in this argument were formulated by Douglas's history of the impact of sentimental religion on American literary culture and by Tompkins's response. The extent to which these two critics dominate current criticism can be see by looking at the essays in Shirley Samuels, ed., *The Culture of Sentiment*.

5. That Americans followed the Hutchesonian model more closely than did European nations is attested to by Tocqueville, who was astounded at how free American women were before marriage, yet how constrained they were by domesticity afterward. Like Hutcheson, Tocqueville found this to have positive political value.

6. This battle plays itself out today in the fragmentation of nuclear families into single-parent families. Of course, when "'til death do us part" didn't necessarily mean very long, divorce was not as important an ingredient in the pursuit of individual freedom, though agitation for divorce was an early part of the program of Americans such as Victoria Claflin Woodhull who wished to reform marriage laws.

7. Yet in stating this idea so baldly, I, of course, overstate it substantially, as Karen Lystra's new book *Searching the Heart* makes amply and admirably clear. Romantic ideas of heterosexual love included the idea that *mutual* passion was sanctified by marriage. Lystra's careful reconstruction of Victorian attitudes about love and marriage does much to complicate the kind of categorical picture I give here. But it is the categorical extreme that humor attacks. Indeed, Lystra's research into the letters of married couples shows how often humor was a tool men and women used to communicate their mutual sexual desires in spite of Victorian prudery. See especially chapter 3, "'Lie Still and Think of Empire': Sexuality in Victorian Courtship and Marriage" (56–87), and chapter 4, "Secrecy, Sin, and Sexual Enticement: The Integration of Public and Private Life Worlds" (88–120).

8. This anxiety about Mormonism obsessed Holley, as she returned to it in an extended comic treatment in *My Wayward Pardner* and also wrote a serious "exposé" of Mormonism, a book-length poem entitled *The Lament of the Mormon Wife*. Both were published in 1880.

9. See T. J. Jackson Lears, *No Place of Grace*, and G. M. Goshgarian, *To Kiss the Chastening Rod: Domestic Fiction and Sexual Ideology in the American Renaissance* for discussions of the nineteenth-century attack on masturbation in medical literature, advice books, etc.

10. I think John Bryant has done the best job in *Melville and Repose*.

11. I draw substantially here for my understanding of the distinctions between "wit"

and "humor" on Stuart M. Tave's *The Amiable Humorist: A Study in the Comic Theory and Criticism of the Eighteenth and Early Nineteenth Centuries* for a full history of "conventions of comic theory and criticism" in England. From Tave's introduction:

> In Restoration theory of comedy, largely a derivative and a reduction of Renaissance theory, it was a commonplace that the function of comedy is to copy the foolish and knavish originals of the age and to expose, ridicule and satirize them. By the middle of the nineteenth century, it was a commonplace that the best comic works present amiable originals, often models of good nature, whose little peculiarities are not satirically instructive, but objects of delight and love. The first part of the book tries to describe how the benevolent virtues of "good nature" and "good humor" helped to bring about this change: how these virtues promoted the values of cheerfulness and innocent mirth; and how they restrained raillery, satire and ridicule, the several expressions of "ill-natured" wit. The second part describes the benevolent solution of the problem presented by laughter: the reaction against "Hobbesian" laughter and the substitution of a more congenial theory, based on incongruity; and then the development of an ideal of free, kindly "natural" laughter. The third and main part describes how the seventeenth-century concept of humor as an aberration demanding satiric attack was essentially reversed . . . The final part describes some of the ways in which the development of an amiable humor was itself advanced by, and in turn helped to advance, close interrelationships of jest with earnest: with tragedy, tears, and melancholy; with sympathy; with pathos. Humor in this sense was a historical event with a beginning and an end. This study follows it only until it was well established, but the end was, I believe, around 1914. (viii–ix)

The history Tave writes is applicable to American culture, especially given the influence in America of the Scottish Common Sense philosophers, who were so influential in promulgating sentimental moral philosophy (see my "Moral Aesthetics of Sentimentality"), including the idea that "humor" is not only a sense, but a socially useful sensibility. The persistent power of puritanism in America did, however, keep "humor" from being valued as highly in America as in England.

12. One can get a sense of how important these new ideas about laughter were when one realizes that Hutcheson, a Scots-Irish clergyman who published his observations on laughter in *Hibernicus's Letters*, a Dublin periodical, over the years 1725–27, was elected to the chair of moral philosophy of Glasgow University in 1729 for having written about laughter. Adam Smith was one of his pupils, and he was a correspondent of David Hume. In 1745, he was offered a chair at the more prestigious University of Edinburgh, but he declined it. All this for three essays on laughter.

13. Tave, *Amiable Humorist*, passim, and Neil Schmitz, *Of Huck and Alice* (4–5).

14. Perhaps Kierkegaard is correct about irony, and thus is right to draw not only a taxonomical but a moral distinction between satire and humor.

## Chapter 2

1. For overviews of Irving's career and criticism of Irving's work, see Henry A. Pochman, "Washington Irving," and "Washington Irving: Amateur or Professional?"; Lewis Leary, "Washington Irving;" William L. Hedges, *Washington Irving;* and the extensive scholarly biography by Stanley T. Williams. For a specific treatment of Irving's political conservatism, see Allen Guttman. For his humor, see Hedges, "Washington Irv-

ing: Nonsense, the Fat of the Land, and the Dream of Indolence" John Seelye, and, particularly Martin Roth, whose work is fully informed by the historical context of Irving's humor, though he willfully, I think, downplays Irving's early satire. For treatment of *The Sketch Book,* see Hedges, "Washington Irving: *The Sketch Book of Geoffrey Crayon, Gent."* For recent trends in reading Irving's work as representative of his Americanness, as opposed to his Anglophilic conservatism, see Jeffrey Rubin-Dorsky and Jane D. Eberwein. Most published criticism deals primarily with Irving's two most famous tales, "Rip Van Winkle" and "The Legend of Sleepy Hollow."

2. See Kenneth Lynn, *Mark Twain and Southwestern Humor* for a history of the satire of the Old Southwest as it arose from courtly European models and was translated into the American realm by William Byrd. Lynn may not use the distinction between humor and satire that I insist on in discussing American comedy, but his history of the satiric and conservative political origins of the frame narrator is accurate.

3. See the first section of Lynn's *Mark Twain and Southwestern Humor* for a more detailed history of this use of frame.

4. See Albert J. von Frank's excellent reading of "The Legend of Sleepy Hollow" as an attack on all that Ichabod represents. For a slightly different opinion, see Seelye's "Root and Branch," which argues that Irving's geniality prevented him from developing the disturbing ramifications of his indictment of capitalism. It would take his literary heirs to uncover the dark side of the humor against progress that Irving's tale initiated.

5. Irving was not the only domestic humorist whose sketches express distaste for American mobility in the effort to better one's self. Caroline Kirkland, for instance, wrote:

> The possession of a large number of acres is esteemed a great good, though it makes but little difference in the owner's mode of living. Comforts do not seem to abound in proportion to landed increase, but often, on the contrary, are really diminished for the sake of it; and the habit of selling out so frequently, makes the *home*-feeling, which is so large an ingredient in happiness elsewhere, almost a nonentity in Michigan. The man who holds himself ready to accept the first advantageous offer, will not be very solicitous to provide those minor accommodations, which, though essential to domestic comfort, will not add to the moneyed value of his farm, which he considers merely an article of trade, and which he knows his successor will look upon in the same light. I have sometimes thought that our neighbors forget that "the days of man's life are three score years and ten," since they spend all their lives in getting ready to begin. (36)

6. For a typical criticism of Irving's minor status by twentieth-century standards, see Stanley T. Williams's essay on Irving in *Literary History of the United States,* Williams says, "To us halfway through the twentieth century, all the virtues of *The Sketch Book* seem pallid" at best, because "[t]he gossamer loveliness of these sketches suffers under precise interpretations," and because "we can endure but not applaud . . . the sickly pathos" (247). Hedges, in "Irving, Hawthorne, and the Image of the Wife," a very insightful effort to talk about the impact of Irving's vision of women on the work of Hawthorne, feels compelled to distance himself from the sentimental subject that so interests him. "No one, of course, wants to equate the two writers as sentimentalists" (22), he says, with the "of course" speaking the consensus opinion of Irving's value. In further self-defense he says, "Almost no one today reads 'The Wife,' except graduate students dutifully covering Irving" (23). By the time he finishes defending his credentials as an

antisentimentalist, Hedges has almost eliminated the value of Irving as a subject of discussion. Perhaps more directly, Hedges says in his 1973 article "Nonsense, the Fat of the Land, and the Dream of Indolence:"

> There is something slightly false about Irving's position as a writer from *The Sketch Book* on. He has lost the freedom to speak out bluntly on anything he chooses. Too often now he says things that he thinks readers want him to say. He becomes more of a sentimentalist, for instance, more committed to titillating female readers with stories of broken hearts and lost loves, than he perhaps intended. (151)

Such blatant disregard for women as readers and as a significant part of American culture cries out for replies; the only question is whether the criticism or Irving is to be the target.

For a feminist assault on Irving, see Judith Fetterley's rejection of Irving, which I discuss at length below. Not all feminist critics are so ruthless in their treatment of Irving, though. For Annette Kolodny, Irving's pastoral treatment of the land as mother is superior to the commonplace nineteenth-century treatment of the land as something to rape:

> The endless appeal of Rip resides in his mythic quality as *puer aeternas*, a comic innocent who manages to escape the rest of America's growing pains by sleeping for twenty years in a womb-like "hollow, like a small amphitheatre." The postscript to the tale gives away the pastoral yearning behind its composition by identifying the "Catskill Mountains" as a "region full of fable," reputed by the Indians to be "ruled over by an old squaw spirit, said to be their mother." . . . Irving succeeded in preserving, intact, the maternal image of American pastoral at a time when the aggressive, sexually assertive aspect of the impulse was coming more and more to dominate. (68–69)

Another recent approach, in Laura Plummer and Michael Nelson's "'Girls Can Take Care of Themselves,'" is to read Irving against himself, to find Irving unintentionally undercutting his own political beliefs: "Irving's conservatism subverts itself, since conservation of the existing power structure means the continuance of a female (though certainly not feminist) hierarchy" (176). Still, all of these approaches take Irving seriously. The following discussion will present a different way of looking at these conflicts.

7. For an absolutely opposite, and very compelling reading, see William P. Dawson, "'Rip Van Winkle' as Bawdy Satire." Dawson argues that Dame Van Winkle is set up as the parallel not to Franklinian individualism, but as the parallel to monarchical government, and that Rip is a revolutionary who prefers sexual license as an adjunct to political liberty. Irving's story, says Dawson, satirizes the libertine as well as the liberal impulse as immoral. Dawson runs into difficulty at the end when he sees that Irving does, finally, have some sympathy for Rip. The ambiguity he sees at the tale's end baffles his satiric reading, leading him to the weak conclusion that after drafting such a powerful satire, Irving decided that maybe democratic politics are not so completely heinous after all. My account, by putting the story in the realm of humor, will, I hope, provide balance between the Fetterley and Dawson extremes of interpretation by accounting for the ambiguity.

8. Even though many critics do take into account the humorous distancing of Rip from the both the author and the reader by a double framing inside of two narrators, many do not. For instance, in his otherwise fine article on Irving's political conser-

vatism, Guttman begs the question with one of those critical "of courses" that is so coercive: "Irving's sympathy for Rip is so clear that none needs dispute it" (170). Not surprisingly, few do. Or see Marvin E. Mengeling, "Structure and Tone in 'Rip Van Winkle,'" which greatly sympathizes with Irving's Rip, who cannot "escape the carpings of his shrewish Dame, Irving's caricature of 'all those unpleasant pressures which depreciate and lash out at the unpractical and the imaginative'" (458).

But not all who take Rip seriously as a straightforward representation of Irving's psyche agree with Irving's supposed message. Among the critics who take Rip's plight seriously by neglecting the implications of the author's comic distance from his creation are Fetterley's allies in trashing the story for its ultimately immoral support of Rip's puerile escape from sexuality. Leslie Fiedler, for instance, deliberately equates Irving and Rip in one section of his essay ("The Basic Myths, I" 54) and a few pages later attacks Irving for trying to use humor to cover up his real purposes: "His telling of the tale is, to begin with, disconcertingly comic in tone, undercut by the apologetic wit characteristic of overconscious mythmakers. All the most disturbing implications of Irving's tale, what it seems to *want* to mean despite him, are qualified by the irony proper to a demirebel who only playfully mocks the institutions he is afraid seriously to challenge" (58). Philip Young, too, blames Irving for being blind to the implications of his own work. Incidentally, his essay may explain some of the heat of Fetterley's attack when she relies on Young's essay in much of her own. Young, for all of his assault on Irving's escape from sexuality, assumes that archetypal patterns are all masculine. Perhaps the problem stems from reading Irving so seriously, from dismissing the consequences of comedy in what is so certainly a comic story.

From a different point of view, several critics have set up a sustained counterargument to remind readers that the entire image of Irving as Geoffrey Crayon is inaccurate because it forgets that Irving had another persona of an entirely different kind. Dawson's article may be the best of these essays, but see also Mengeling's "The Crass Humor of Irving's Diedrich Knickerbocker," which argues that Irving cannot be fully understood without first taking into account his earthy side. The complexity of Irving requires us to read his personae as the conscious creations of a craftsman, not the accidents of a literary dabbler.

9. Again, see Seelye, who notes that this melancholy over change is a marker of American character, even in those whose political attitudes are progressive and whose behavior brings about change.

10. I will address these assertions in some detail in the last chapter.

11. This 1852 letter is quoted on page 4 of Joyce W. Warren's recent biography of Fanny Fern, one of very few published pieces of recent criticism on Fern. The paucity of material on Fern is by itself remarkable considering that Nina Baym called attention to Fern's work in her groundbreaking *Woman's Fiction* in 1978 and that Mary Kelley made Fern one of her main subjects in the equally groundbreaking and important *Private Woman, Public Stage* in 1984. Less surprising is the fact that those who have discussed Fern's work talk little about its humor, though Nancy Walker in particular discusses its satire, and Walker, as I mentioned in chapter 1, does not accept the nineteenth-century distinction between humor and satire. This scarcity of commentary on women's humor is true for all of the women authors I treat in this book. Stowe's work has an extensive current bibliography, but it covers almost exclusively *Uncle Tom's Cabin,* with some reference to *The Minister's Wooing.* The MLA Bibliography online lists *no* work on Stowe's Oldtown books, and nothing on Stowe as a humorist, though references do appear in surveys of humor (such as three passing references in Cameron C. Nickels's *New En-*

*gland Humor*), and in studies of New England literature (such as an insightful and fairly substantial segment on Stowe in Lawrence Buell's *New England Literary Culture*). Mary Wilkins Freeman has a substantial bibliography, but almost none of the current work acknowledges Freeman's dry sense of humor. Holley's situation is even worse—as an author who billed herself exclusively as a humorist, she has received next to no attention (one biography and a small handful of articles) even though she was explicitly and delightfully a feminist, and a very well known and successful feminist at that. Given the amount of feminist criticism and teaching of the last decade, it astounds me that the rich, witty, politically self-conscious and sophisticated, and altogether delightful early novels of Holley remain stuck in rare-book rooms. I wonder if Holley's ghost is able to laugh at that irony?

12. Both Walker (*Fanny Fern* 20) and Warren argue that Fern became less sentimental and more satirical as her career progressed. While this may be true, even her satire, as I argue below, stems from her acceptance of, not her condemnation of, sentimental values.

13. Probably a reference to Mormonism.

14. See also "A House without a Baby" in *Fresh Leaves*, in which she speaks of "old Maids" as "vinegar and icicles."

15. For a compatible argument with a different focus about the reason for Parton's multivocality, though limited to a discussion of the single novel *Ruth Hall*, see Susan K. Harris, "Inscribing and Defining: The Many Voices of Fanny Fern's Ruth Hall." I agree with Harris's use of Bakhtin's idea of the dialogics of the novel, but it is important to see Fern's sentimental side not merely as a capitulation to market forces, but as a dominant facet of her weltanschauung. And it is equally important to see that sentimentalism is not intrinsically opposed to humor and laughter. In other words, the dialogics can be within an author's own psyche rather than between an author's progressive intentions and the regressive demands of the marketplace. The same goes for Walker's recognition of Fern's "two different voices: one which mouthed the sentimental platitudes of the period, and another, increasingly dominant as her career progressed, that attacked satirically the very origins of naive sentimentality" (*Fanny Fern* 3).

16. This is why Warren's selection of newspaper pieces in her anthology *Ruth Hall and Other Writings* in many ways inaccurately represents Fern's work. Warren for instance reprints, "A Call to Be a Husband" without reprinting the companion piece, "A Call to Be a Wife." One gets the impression that Parton merely attacks men in their hypocritical abuse of power while she exonerates women. Nothing could be further from the truth.

17. I had a German student in one of my classes on nineteenth-century American comedy. He failed to find the humor in all of this preaching, even when it was mock preaching, as in Sut Lovingood, Simon Suggs, Mark Twain, etc. My American students, on the other hand, could find all of this comic sermonizing funny. This is suggestive to me of the close affinities between satire and an attraction to the object satirized.

18. See Linda Huf, for instance, who sees all of Fern's comic pieces as satires (28), or see Walker's treatment of Fern in *A Very Serious Thing*, or see Walker and Dresner's selections of Fern's writings in *Redressing the Balance*. For a more balanced treatment of the conflicted nature of Parton's attitudes to both literature and to domesticity, see Mary Kelley, "The Literary Domestics" and *Private Woman, Public Stage:*

> For the most part these women writers have been dubbed the "sentimentalists" or the "scribbling women." But those terms have a pejorative and ahistorical quality

about them, calling to mind maudlin, unthinking celebrants of a cloyingly inti-
mate and blissful homelife. That has in turn primarily served to raise the question
of whether such creatures of emotion could ever have written books, or, in fact,
whether they even existed. . . . As if to counter that tack, a few critics have
portrayed these women as subversives, as promulgators of quasi-revolutionary
manifestos with the expressed purpose of liberating women from their domestic
captivity. Rather than paper dolls, we have paper tigers. But in either case the
portrayal is static and one-dimensional, leaving us with cardboard cutouts. The
result has been . . . to place them outside of history. (viii)

## Chapter 3

1. Lawrence Buell's chapter on Yankee humor in *New England Literary Culture* is not
only the best, but perhaps the only treatment of Stowe's Sam Lawson as humorist in
modern criticism. He, rightly I think, sees Lawson's character broadly as an escape valve
from all kinds of Yankee repression. While Stowe's humor may not have received much
critical attention in recent years, her domesticity has been at the center of the debates
about the critical and ethical value of nineteenth-century women's fiction. Especially
pertinent to this study is Mary Kelley's "At War with Herself," in which Kelley describes
the disjunction between Stowe's domestic ideology and her experiences of domesticity
in her own life, especially as her husband's sexual drives drove her to illness, both physical as a consequence of childbearing, and psychological. For discussions of both Oldtown books that are insightful and valuable, but clearly dated in their unwillingness to
see the emotional and intellectual significance of domesticity and sentimentalism to
Stowe's work and to American literature in general, see Charles H. Foster's chapters 7
and 8 in *The Rungless Ladder*. For a history of composition and of the stunning popular
success of the Oldtown books, see Forrest Wilson's biography of Stowe, or see the new
biography of Stowe by Joan D. Hedrick. Hedrick, unlike Foster, sees *Oldtown Folks* as
"lack[ing] the energy and life of her best work" (345), but Hedrick allows her interest in
Stowe's serious politics to completely obscure the view of Stowe's humor; she says virtually nothing about *Sam Lawson's Oldtown Fireside Stories*.

2. See Hedrick's biography, chapter 25, for an astute discussion of the political allegory between Stowe's depiction of postrevolutionary America and Reconstruction
America.

3. According to Ann Janine Morey, who also quotes some of this passage, "Stowe
takes up this theme of the cruelty of man-made theological systems so extensively and
consistently in her writing that if there is anything to be identified as her province beyond her spectacular testimony against slavery, this is it" (747).

4. Morey sees less joy and more pain in what she calls Stowe's vision of the "confine-
ment" of domesticity (749–50 and passim), perhaps because Morey does not see Stowe
as a humorist at all.

5. Mather a grandmother? Perhaps Benjamin Franklin would have called Cotton
Mather a grandmother, but I doubt he would have meant it as a compliment.

6. See, for instance, William L. Alden's "Mr. Simpkins's Downfall."

7. Ann Douglas is virtually the only critic to look at the ideology of domesticity as one of Melville's significant subjects (see Bertani Vozar Newman for an
overview of the criticism of Melville's short fiction). Carl Schaffer's recent article on "I
and My Chimney" follows Douglas's direction in analyzing domesticity as a trap, as a

limitation of free will. Scott Harshbarger follows a different path suggested by Douglas in arguing that the transcendental elements of "The Apple-Tree Table" are meant to be taken straight since Melville was trying to woo his magazine audience.

8. John Bryant's provocative new book, *Melville and Repose,* argues both that Melville never fully subscribed to an aesthetics of geniality, and, more important, that he never fully rejected it toward the end of his career. Bryant sees Melville continuing to use the tropes of amiable humor right into *The Confidence-Man.* While Bryant does not discuss the stories I treat here, his study treats much more fully Melville's humor.

9. I am aware that Melville's own home life was troubled to say the least, that his mental illness included his abuse, at least mentally if not physically, of his wife and children, as Elizabeth Renker argues. That Melville's humor in writing was not strong enough to solve the real problems of his daily behavior, or even strong enough to break him out of the nineteenth-century obsession to "strike through the mask" in search of absolute truth, shows him to be much closer to Stowe than I otherwise suggest in this chapter.

10. Douglas also sees the importance of reading the narrators of Melville's pieces rather than seeing them, as Warner Berthoff or Michael Paul Rogin do, as simple expressions of the author's real experiences. Where Douglas and I differ, though, is in characterizing the emotional valences of these tales. She insists that Melville expresses rage from behind the narrative mask. Particularly, she sees Melville outraged that his writing has been "feminized" by a sentimental culture, and that he therefore could not tell the truth except by indirection. I do not disagree with this interpretation of Melville's career as a whole, but Melville's vision of life was tortured in part because it was so contradictory. I sense that when Melville turned to sentimental magazine sketches, the form and feel, rather than constraining him and eliciting rage, liberated the side of him that admired and indulged humor. Rather than mastered by the form, Melville was temporarily its master, using it to find access to the humor that was so much a part of his greatest work, but that he increasing lost a grip on, as irony, in its relentless abstraction into egotistical nihilism, took over. In other words, I do not blame domesticity for Melville's madness; all social systems have their crazy-making contradictions. But Melville's approach to those contradictions shifted from work to work, and the ironic approach partly caused his rage, whereas the humor of these magazine sketches allowed him at least temporary respite from his madness.

11. The sexual implications of the farmer's agricultural metaphor, especially given the narrator's suggestion of vegetative, "druidical" powers in the chimney, are fairly obvious. In fact, once one gets started on the sexual innuendos in this piece, they appear everywhere. It serves no purpose to comment on every one.

12. Which before it receives its new top appears to have a "wax nose"; is that an allusion to a cosmetic effort to hide the ravages of syphilis?

13. For a more strenuously antitranscendental reading, see Joseph Rosenblum, who sees Melville as energetically mocking Thoreau by having the bird simply die.

## Chapter 4

1. I am indebted to James M. Cox's work on humor and on Mark Twain for much of what follows in this chapter.

2. See my *Sentimental Twain.*

3. Perhaps this explains in part Holley's remarkable neglect even at the hands of

recent critics. The bulk of the work done on Holley has been done by Kate H. Winter and published by Syracuse University Press, which intends to recover New York state writers. The few other recent discussions of Holley—see Melody Graulich, Cheri Ross, Emily Toth, and Nancy Walker—spend most of their energy simply describing Holley's work in order to bring it to light. The most provocative, though still scant, treatment of Holley's work remains Walter Blair's discussion in *Horse-Sense in American Humor*. Like most recent critics of Holley, Blair basically sees the Samantha novels as successful satire, in which Holley's main character directly and unabashedly speaks common sense in the faces of various fools who stand as straw targets to Samantha's assaults. He does, however, suggest that the contrasts between spinster Holley and married Samantha might speak to Holley's own ambivalences about her circumstances: "No one has made public enough about the life of Miss Holley to settle the point, but we cannot help wondering whether her Samantha did not gain a great deal of vitality because a certain amount of envy and admiration entered into her creation" (239). Winter has now given us the biography that allows us to address that speculation, as I will try to do in the pages that follow. Throughout this discussion I rely on Winter for biographical data.

4. And see *My Opinions* for an example of Samantha using the metaphor of horses on women.

5. So as not to give an unbalanced view of Holley's ideas of gender, I should note that she wrote a similar poem from a man's point of view. Yet note that the male speaker of "The Sea Captain's Wooing" is much older than the woman he woos, and while he holds himself unworthy of her love, he promises her his strength, etc.

> Put the crown of your love on my forehead,
>     Its sweet links clasped with a kiss,
> And all the great monarchs of England
>     Never wore such a gem as this.
> Give me your hand, little maiden,
>     That sceptre so pearly white,
> And I'll envy not the kingliest wand
>     That ever waved in might.
>
> I know 'tis like asking a morning cloud
>     With a grim old mountain to stay,
> But your love would soften its ruggedness,
>     And melt its roughness away.
> I have seen a delicate rosy cloud,
>     A rough, gray cliff enfold,
> Till his heart was warmed by its loveliness,
>     And his brow was tinged with its gold.
>
> Oh, poor and mean does my life show
>     Compared with the beauty of thine,
> Like a diamond embedded in granite
>     Your life would be set in mine;
> But a faithful love should guard you,
>     And shelter you from life's storm,
> The rock must be shivered to atoms
>     Ere its treasure should come to harm.

How your sweet face has shone on me
    From the tropics' midnight sea,
When sailors slept, and I kept watch
    Alone with my God and thee.
I know your heart is relenting,
    The tender look in your eyes
Seems like that sky's soft splendor
    When the sun was beginning to rise.

You need not veil their glorious light
    With your eyelids' cloud of snow,
A tell-tale bird with a crimson wing
    On your cheek flies to and fro;
And whispers to me such blissful hope
    That my foolish tears will start,
Ah, little bird! your fluttering wing
    Is folded on my heart. (*Poems* 128–29)

6. The dedication of the book of poems is rather interesting in that it seems to be a last tribute to her mother as she developed the confidence to leave the old homestead:

WHEN I WROTE MANY OF THESE VERSES I WAS MUCH YOUNGER THAN I AM NOW, AND THE "SWEETEST EYES IN THE WORLD" WOULD BRIGHTEN OVER THEM, THROUGH THE READER'S LOVE FOR ME. I DEDICATE THEM TO HER MEMORY—THE MEMORY OF

MY MOTHER

## Chapter 5

1. Though in at least one of the tales, "Mrs. McCloud's Mare," Harris's anti-Yankee sentiments erupt into a patently political attack.

2. Though Twain was a Harris fan.

3. It is difficult to find in *Sut Lovingood's Yarns* much real elitism, as Harris probably was not really very committed to exalting a class to which he never belonged, but the racism is very real and is now probably the greatest impediment, not excepting the opaque language, to reading these tales. The degree to which Harris reflects aristocratic values is one of the points of contention in the scholarship, with some critics, like Louis J. Budd, Lorne Fienberg, and Kenneth Lynn, seeing that the frame and the original forum (Porter's *Spirit of the Times*) pushed the stories in an elitist direction. But other critics, such as David C. Estes and Milton Rickels, see the stories as antithetical to any kind of hierarchical order.

4. Significant exceptions are the tales that reveal Sut's and by extension Harris's racism, such as "Sut Assisting at a Negro Night-Meeting," or "A Snake-Bit Irishman." Still, Sut's act of racist malice proves almost as disruptive of the slave-owning class as it does of the slaves themselves, and one wonders if the clergy and the landed gentry aren't a substantial part of Sut's target in the first place. See Estes's account of Sut's attack on the "Night-Meeting."

5. In another story, Sut makes the connection between faith and wealth much more explicit:

Suckit-riders am surjestif things tu me. They preaches agin me, an' I hes no chance tu preach back at them. Ef I cud, I'd make the institushun behave hitself bettur nur hit dus. They hes sum wunderful pints, George. Thar am two things nobody never seed: wun am a dead muel, an' tuther is a suckit-rider's grave. Kaze why, the he mules all turn into old field school-masters, an' the she ones into strong minded wimen, an' then when thar time cums, they dies sorter like uther folks. An' the suckit-riders ride ontil they marry; ef they marrys money, they turns intu store-keepers, swaps hosses, an' stays away ove collickshun Sundays. Them what marrys, an' by sum orful mistake *misses the money,* jis' turns intu poler-tishuns, sells "ile well stock," an' dies sorter in the human way too. (89)

6. The editors of *The Norton Anthology of American Literature* call Sut the quintessential male chauvinist, probably because he says in "Sicily Burns's Wedding," "Men wer made a-purpus jis' tu eat, drink, an' fur stayin awake in the yearly part ove the nites: an' wimen wer made tu cook the vittils, mix the sperits, an' help the men du the stayin awake. That's all, an' nuthin more, onless hits fur the wimen tu raise the devil atwix meals, an' knit socks atwix drams, an' the men tu play short kerds, swap hosses wif fools, an' fite fur exersise, at odd spells" (88). Indeed, when it comes to seeing women as servants, Sut is as sexist as can be. There is, though, a kind of lowest common denominator equality in Sut's vision that does not partake of the usual hypocrisies in describing the differences between men and women, the hypocrisies that enable sexism to be masked as moral reformism.

7. In Sut's philosophy, any idealistic distinction between love and lust is nonsense. Consider the beginning of "Taurus in Lynchburg Market": "Eatin allers goes jis' afore luv. 'Less a feller hes his belly stretched wif vittils, he can't luv tu much pupus, that's so. Vittils, whisky, an' the spring ove the year, is what makes luv; an' yu jis' bring em all tu bar tugether, an' yu'll see luv tu sum pupus, I'm durn'd if yu don't. Did yu ever try hit, wif a purty gal sot on steel springs wif injun rubber heels, an cinamint ile smell tu help yu?" (123).

8. At story's end Sut says that he "may turn human sum day, that is sorter human, enuf tu be a Squire ur school cummisiner" (97).

9. "Glimmers ove the sun"? "Play'd a silver shine"? It is difficult to imagine that this is the same Sut who made fun of George setting a scene with elaborate, yet trite, description. Sut is so captivated that he forgets how to "talk hit all off in English" (116).

10. Sut is quite outspoken about his shame over his father and preference for his mother, as when in the last story he is embarrassed to have the "respectable" churchgoing Squire Hanley break in on his family's tomfoolery: "A appertite tu run began tu gnaw my stumick, an' I felt my face a-swellin wif shame. I wer shamed ove dad, shamed ove mam's bar laigs an' open collar, shamed ove mysef, an' dam, if I minds right, if I warn't a mossel shamed ove the pup. But when I seed the squar, blazin look mam met him wif, I made up my mine ef she cud stan the storm, I cud, an' so I didn't run that time—nara durn'd step" (286).

11. A few other current critical works do mention Freeman's comedy. Lawrence Buell's *New England Literary Culture from Revolution through Renaissance* has a chapter on New England's "Comic Grotesque" that includes brief mention of Freeman. Emily Toth (not to be confused with Susan A. Toth, whom I quote below) mentions Freeman in passing in her "A Laughter of Their Own: Women's Humor in the United States," 204–5. The wide focus of the essay, of course, allows no more than passing mention of any of the dozens of women writers of comedy. Toth insists that women's

humor is pointedly satiric, refusing to draw a distinction between humor and satire. A few other critics see Freeman's use of irony, but without seeing irony as a component of a rich comedy. See note 13 below.

12. While most recent criticism does focus on Freeman's realism and on her politics, some critics are willing to see the ambiguities and indeterminacies in Freeman's work. But even while ambiguity is a primary source of comedy, such critics seem to miss the forest for the trees, as is the case in Elizabeth Meese's "Signs of Undecidability: Reconsidering the Stories of Mary Wilkins Freeman." She rightly sees Freeman's play with ambiguity as the playground of choices: "exploring the tensions between autonomy and compromise, Freeman places a certain value on these acts of will; without them life and character would be bland, unprincipled" (167). Thus, Freeman herself as a writer wrote texts that resist simple readings in order to continue to assert the writer's will: "Freeman, in a necessary strategy, outwits us all. She anticipates us, encouraging and demanding our differences of view by encoding them within her fictions. She constructs us as she did her characters, particularly in her refusal to write an easy solution to the problematics of gender. Through her insistence on this complexity, she stages the text's resistance to temporality" (167).

Thus does Meese enjoy the "subversion" of the endless play of signifiers, yet she finds such play ultimately tragic because it finally refuses to assert a feminist resistance in the place of a merely textual one:

> But returning for a moment to Barthes' view of the tragic, I cannot deny the relationship between Freeman's renunciation of "The Revolt of 'Mother'" and the characters in a Greek play who limit their understanding of what they hear and say as they stage the text's misunderstandings. . . . [Freeman] retreats from her own feminist moment and plays the "woman," exposing her personal inability to escape temporality. The price of denial is great. . . . (174)

To use Meese's last words against her, the price of denial is great when one denies humor. Not only was Freeman's "renunciation" "tongue-in-cheek" (Marchalonis, "Introduction" to *Critical Essays* 10), Meese's serious insistence that play is tragic makes it impossible for her to acknowledge that ironic play can be liberating, rather than the sign of impending doom. It all depends on awareness, and Freeman, I would argue, was acutely aware of comic potentials.

Nor must irony be nihilistic and cynical, as Alice Glarden Brand postulates in her influential "Mary Wilkins Freeman: Misanthropy as Propaganda." Brand's refusal to see anything but derision and vituperation in comedy and irony may very well have scared off later critics who, rightly I believe, see in Freeman an optimistic, joyful, and creative writer.

13. Indeed, a dominant line of historical criticism of American humor suggests that even the tall tale serves America's "horse sense" realism. See Walter Blair's extensive work on American humor. But if one sees that Freeman had an uncomfortable relationship to realism, that she had a strong affinity for symbolistic fiction, it is a bit easier to see her humor as working against a realistic point of view. Perhaps the best way to see Freeman's resistance to realism is through her ghost stories. As Beth Wynne Fiskin points out in her study of Freeman's ghost stories, Freeman wrote various confessional letters in which she both decried and exposed her tendency away from realism: "I do not care much about that story, and do not approve of this mystical vein I am apt to slide into if I don't take care," she wrote in 1889. By 1919, though, she was confessing that

realism per se was unsatisfying to her: "Most of my own work, is not really the kind I my-self like. I want more symbolism, more mysticism. I left that out, because it struck me people did not want it, and I was forced to consider selling qualities" (41–42). Fiskin quotes these letters in the context of Freeman's ghost stories, but they seem equally ap-plicable to the humorous stories I treat here, stories that can be marketed as realism, but that nonetheless, through their subtle humor, open the stories to an ironic symbolism.

14. Whether or not the other names have such transparently religious meanings, "Alma Way" must be accounted for. *Alma* is Spanish for "soul" or "spirit". Are we to make it possessive and turn the name into "the soul's way"? That, at least, is what Mary R. Reichardt does in her reading of the story (*Web 149*). Or are we to use it as the Latin adjective for "nurturing" or "generous"?

15. According to Brent L. Kendrick, "Mellin's Food was a commercially prepared brand of baby food."

16. This letter is an undated fragment that, on the basis of internal evidence, Kendrick dates as "before April 28, 1886" (68).

17. Again, the realism of the tale is violated by the meaningful names. In this case, the meaning of Woodman is obvious; what is evocative but indeterminate is the name George Elliot given to a young man.

18. One example should suffice to make the point:

*Little Libbie*

One more little spirit to Heaven has flown,
    To dwell in that mansion above,
Where dear little angels, together roam,
    In God's everlasting love.

One little flower has withered and died,
    A bud near ready to bloom,
Its life on earth is marked with pride;
    Oh, sad it should die so soon.

Sweet little Libbie, that precious flower
    Was a pride in her parents' home,
They miss their little girl every hour,
    Those friends that are left to mourn.

Her sweet silvery voice no more is heard
    In the home where she once roamed;
Her place is vacant around the hearth,
    Where her fiends are mourning lone.

They are mourning the loss of a little girl,
    With black eyes and auburn hair,
She was a treasure to them in this world,
    This beautiful child so fair.

One morning in April, a short time ago,
    Libbie was active and gay;
Her Saviour called her, she had to go,
    E're the close of that pleasant day.

While eating dinner, this dear little child
    Was choked on a piece of beef.
Doctors came, tried their skill awhile,
    But none could give relief.

She was ten years of age, I am told,
    And in school stood very high.
Her little form now the earth enfolds,
    In her embrace it must ever lie.

Her friends and schoolmates will not forget
    Little Libbie that is no more;
She is waiting on the shining step,
    To welcome home friends once more.

19. The name is "Dole" not only because she writes about doleful subjects, but because she doles out her verse in generous portions, her speed at composition another indicator of her lack of aesthetic polish.

20. See my *Sentimental Twain: Samuel Clemens in the Maze of Moral Philosophy*, and my "'I Wouldn't Be As Ignorant As You for Wages': Huck Talks Back to His Conscience."

21. After all, in the Grangerford chapters, Twain has the Sheperdsons and Grangerfords, both obsessively cultivating feelings of hurt from some dimly remembered past, wipe one another out, whereas Harney Shepherdson and Sophia Grangerford, who look forward to building a future, get away. Still, Twain indulges the satirist's double standard. He gets to contemplate death all the time while blaming those who do for being morbid and retrogressive.

22. After Betsey writes the poem, having avoided eating the entire day, she finally gets up to prepare a scant evening meal. When she rose, "[t]here were red spots on Betsey's cheeks; her knees were unsteady when she walked" (148). The red spots are symptoms of the tuberculosis that she allows to kill her at tale's end when she finds that her verse has been judged to be poor by the educated clergyman/poet who is her pastor.

23. Until recently, critics assumed that Freeman was mocking New England neuroses in the character of Louisa. For the best statement of this point of view see David H. Hirsch, "Subdued Meaning in 'A New England Nun.'" Recent critics argue strenuously against this belief in the neurosis of Louisa in particular and the centrality of repression in Freeman's stories more generally. Ann Romines, in *The Home Plot*, counters with the apt observation that Louisa is also described as a queen, suggesting that Freeman felt ambivalent about the choices available to women and felt that celibacy was a way for a woman to maintain self-control. Some critics go further, suggesting that Freeman showed no ambivalence because there is no negative imagery in the characterization of Louisa. According to Marjorie Pryse, for instance, Louisa is not neurotic so much as heroic in her defiance of masculine penetration ("An Uncloistered 'New England Nun'"). All of this argument is contingent on the belief that Freeman was a realist and that therefore she is describing women's reality. But shift the argument to the grounds of humor, and extremity is not so much illness or heroism as exaggeration for the sake of both clarity and fun. Truths about heroism and social constraint and freedom, and excessive will, and love are all still accessible, but because they are removed from immediate identification, they are accessible safely. Thus, many of the points I make in the fol-

lowing section find their correlates in the critical literature, but since all of the others take these points in a context of high seriousness, they miss the significance in missing the tone.

24. The sale of her birthright for a mess of pottage is a reference to Genesis 25:21–34, in which Esau, the older of twin sons of Isaac, sells his birthright as first son to his younger brother, Jacob, for a pottage of lentils. The gloss on the story is that the elder son, a hunter rather than farmer, lived for the day and was improvident of his future. The Hebrew belief that spiritual destiny is acted out in the physical world leads to the implication that Esau sells not only his superior inheritance and his political preeminence, but that he sells out the spiritual future as well by paying too much attention to immediate concerns while undervaluing his posterity. In this context, Louisa is more concerned with the day than with the future, and is less spiritual because of it (see Romines). Such a spiritual judgment would be reinforced by Freeman's readers' anti-Catholic bias.

## Chapter 6

1. See, for instance, Daniel E. Berlyne, "Humor and Its Kin" (44–45).

2. See Paul E. McGhee and Jeffrey H. Goldstein, citing Berlyne, page 245 of *The Psychology of Humor*, or McGhee and Goldstein, citing Goldstein, Suls, and Anthony, page 253 of the same book for discussions of those aspects of Freudian neuroanatomy that are outdated.

3. See Constance Rourke's *American Humor*, and Walter Blair's *Native American Humor* and *Horse-Sense in American Humor*.

4. Also true of rhymes—they seem playful and therefore inappropriate to regular conversation, but the real problem is that they suggest connections by sound when logic alone dictates no connection should exist. To make rhyme and reason connect—that is an intellectual pleasure deeply akin to the pleasure one takes in comedy.

5. Along the way here, I am assuming a model of mind that I will elaborate in the next section. I realize that the model I implicitly advance here is not universally accepted.

6. Compare with Evelyn Fox-Keller's argument that the "masculinist" obsession with hierarchical models of the cell blinded cell biologists to the interactive process of cell functioning until fairly recently. The idea of DNA as the "master molecule" is a metaphor that restricts understanding as much as it facilitates it.

7. This is a very compelling explanation of what I first heard about when, as a graduate student at Berkeley in the mid-1980s, I heard of the work of Berkeley researcher Marian Diamond, who proved that the mass of a brain frequently used actually increases as compared to a brain deprived of stimulation. While her studies were of rats, she had no hesitation in applying her findings to human beings, admonishing Berkeley students that what was true of their bodies was true of their brains: "use it, or lose it." Her remarks about her research struck me not only as funny but also as fascinating because I had been raised on the hundred-year-old consensus that brain cells were anatomically fixed and ceased to grow by the end of puberty. The anatomy class I took as a senior in college in 1980 did little to dispel my belief in the structural rigidity of the brain, as Paul Bach-y-Rita explains that it has only been recently that neurological science has slowly come out of the shadow of Paul Broca's work of the 1860s. Such "knowledge" even worked its way down to the pop-cultural level in the movie *Young Frankenstein*, in

which Dr. Frankenstein says, with comic unction, that "once a nerve fiber is severed, there is no way in heaven or on earth to regenerate life back into it."

But observations of patients who recovered substantial function after catastrophic nerve damage challenged older models of neuronal rigidity, and recently, work on neuronal plasticity has exploded. The database I most recently consulted lists over a thousand items on neuronal plasticity published between 1990 and March of 1994. Besides the articles and books I cite elsewhere, I have found Michael M. Merzenich and Koichi Sameshima's "Cortical Plasticity and Memory" a useful confirmation of Edelman's theories, as their article reviews a substantial amount of the recent work on the brain's ability to restructure itself before providing a provisional theory of the nature of memory as a function of cortical plasticity.

8. Edelman's theories presented me first with both the evidence to support my theory and the largest single impediment to it. If changes in conceptualization require neuronal plasticity and humor is a value on which plasticity is encouraged, then humor must be able to induce structural changes in the brain, or at least *enable* structural changes in the brain, very quickly. As Bach-y-Rita puts it, "plasticity" can be defined to encompass almost all aspects of mental functioning, but, in the way the term is most commonly used, plasticity is the ability of the central nervous system to "modify its own organization and function" (548). Plasticity is considered "to be one of the two fundamental properties of the nervous system: It permits enduring functional changes to take place" (548). The other property is "excitability, which relates to rapid changes leaving no trace in the nervous system." Obviously, according to Edelman's theory, the epiphenomenon of excitability is one of the causes of plasticity, as Bach-y-Rita also suggests (548). Thus, humor as an epiphenomenon of excitability can easily work as an agent of adaptation, as I suggest. But it would make my theory more plausible if it could be shown that structural changes in neurons take place rapidly enough to be readily correlated with something as ephemeral as humor. Some recent research lends itself to such conclusions. According to Charles D. Gilbert's study of cortical changes in visual perception, such changes can happen very rapidly:

> Though the underlying mechanisms of short-term cortical plasticity are as yet unknown, they must involve in some way a change in the synaptic weight of existing connections, altering the patterns of activation of intrinsic circuits. It now seems quite likely that mutability of receptive fields and cortical architectures is associated with normal sensory experience, not just peripheral lesions, and that these changes can take place on a time scale of minutes, if not seconds. (102)

Gilbert describes in very interesting detail a range of possible mechanisms for these changes, and, most interestingly from my point of view, speculates on the implications of his research for more complex learning and for conceptual functioning:

> The functional implications of adult cortical plasticity depend centrally on the time course over which the alterations in receptive field properties take place. The longest term changes may be useful for recovery of function after lesions of the central nervous system, but would be less important for normal processing of sensory information. The shorter term changes take on an entirely different importance. Changes taking place over minutes are useful for adapting to changes in the sensory environment and, in the case of the motor cortex reorganization,

postural changes. In visual perception, an ongoing process of seeing any attribute, such as position, depth, curvature, brightness, color or size, could require a repeated normalization, through which the system calibrates itself. Any value would be interpreted in terms of the spatial and temporal context within which that value is measured. One could think of the cortex as constantly expanding and contracting the representation of various aspects of the sensory environment in response to the amount of input it receives of particular sets of stimuli. It is tempting, albeit highly speculative at this point, to relate the adaptational changes in primary sensory cortex to the process of learning complex images in higher cortical areas. (101)

Edelman would not have such reservations about being speculative, I suspect, as he sees the patterns of brain function as similar from the simplest levels of primary perception to the highest levels of symbolic conceptualization. If Edelman is right, then Gilbert's work would suggest that neural changes can take place quickly enough for my theory of humor to be plausible.

The other question, then, is whether or not any research suggests that humor is correlated with mental plasticity. The answer is yes. As Fry puts it in his overview article, "The Physiologic Effects of Humor, Mirth, and Laughter," "[t]he exact effect of humor on the central nervous system is not fully known, but it is theorized that increased catecholamine levels are responsible for the beneficial effects humor has on mental functions, including increasing interpersonal responsiveness, alertness, and memory" (1857). Increased ability to remember suggests that humor increases the kind of neuronal plasticity that Edelman's theory requires. Thus, it does seem as though humor leads to mental adaptability. In fact, while I have found no study that confirms that catecholamines cause neuronal plasticity, many studies correlate catecholamine production and neuronal plasticity. See J. H. Cai et al., J. P. Huston et al., H. Nishino et al., L. Iacovitti et al., and especially L. Iacovitti.

9. Thus, the many theorists of comedy, such as Santayana, who categorize it under aesthetics may be in touch with one of comedy's real components.

10. Which explains, in part, why a joke repeated can remain funny. More important, though, the impulse toward suspended acceptance of a given idea can recur with as much pleasure in its repeated indulgence as in its initial indulgence. Incongruity remains incongruous whether it surprises or not. When incongruity causes laughter it does so not when the puzzle it raises is resolved but because its puzzle is unresolvable.

11. Tristram Potter Coffin and Hennig Cohen list several of these in their *Folklore from the Working Folk of America*, though at least some of the variants they cite tame the rhymes to some extent. For instance:

Little Willie had a mirror
And he licked the back off,
Thinking in his childish error
It would cure the whooping cough.

At the funeral Willie's mother
Softly said to Mrs. Brown,
'Twas a chilly day for Willie
When the mercury went down. (127)

Perhaps, however, the "softly" is merely mother's characteristic composure in the face of disaster, as in:

Little Willie, mean as hell,
Pushed his sister in the well.
Said his ma while drawing water:
"Gee, it's hard to raise a daughter." (127)

12. See John Bryant, *Melville and Repose,* especially pages 41–51, for an excellent treatment of nineteenth-century America's understandings of comic forms and purposes.

# Bibliography

Addison, Joseph, and Richard Steele. *Selections from the Tatler and the Spectator*. Ed. Robert J. Allen. 2nd ed. New York: Holt, Rinehart and Winston, 1970.

Alden, William L. "Mr. Simpkins's Downfall." *Mark Twain's Library of Humor*. New York: Webster & Company, 1888.

Ammons, Elizabeth. "Stowe's Dream of the Mother-Savior: *Uncle Tom's Cabin* and American Women Writers before the 1920s." *New Essays on Uncle Tom's Cabin*. Ed. Eric J. Sundquist. Cambridge: Cambridge UP, 1986.

Bach-y-Rita, Paul. "Brain Plasticity as a Basis for Recovery of Function in Humans." *Neuropsychologia* 28.6 (1990): 547–54.

Bacon, Francis. *Novum Organum*. 1620.

Bader, Julia. "The Dissolving Vision: Realism in Jewett, Freeman, and Gilman." *American Realism, New Essays*. Ed. Eric J. Sundquist. Baltimore: Johns Hopkins UP, 1982.

Bakhtin, Mikhail. *Rabelais and His World*. Trans. Helene Iswolsky. 1965. Bloomington: Indiana UP, 1984.

Banks, Jenifer S. "Washington Irving, the Nineteenth-Century American Bachelor." *Critical Essays on Washington Irving*. Ed. Ralph M. Aderman. Boston: G. K. Hall, 1990.

Barnstone, Aliki "Houses within Houses: Emily Dickinson and Mary Wilkins Freeman's 'A New England Nun.'" *Centennial Review* 28.2 (1984): 129–45.

Barreca, Regina. Introduction. *Last Laughs: Perspectives on Women and Comedy*. Ed. Regina Barreca. London: Gordon and Breach, 1988.

Baym, Nina. *Woman's Fiction: A Guide to Novels by and about Women in America, 1820–1870*. Ithaca, NY: Cornell UP, 1978.

Beecher, Catherine. *Common Sense Applied to Religion; or, the Bible and the People*. New York: Harper & Brothers, 1857.

———. *A Treatise on Domestic Economy*. 1841. Rpt. New York: Schocken, 1977.

Bergson, Henri. *Laughter: An Essay on the Meaning of the Comic*. Trans. Cloudesley Brereton and Fred Rothwell. New York: Macmillan, 1911.

Berlant, Lauren. "Fanny Fern." *The Culture of Sentiment*. Ed. Shirley Samuels. New York: Oxford UP, 1992.

Berlyne, Daniel E. "Humor and Its Kin." *The Psychology of Humor: Theoretical Perspectives and Empirical Issues*. Ed. Jeffrey H. Goldstein and Paul E. McGhee. New York: Academic, 1972.

Berry, Wendell. "Writer and Region." *What Are People For?* San Francisco: North Point, 1990.

Berthoff, Warner. Introduction and Headnotes to *Great Short Works of Herman Melville*. New York: Harper/ Perrenial, 1969.

Bierce, Ambrose. *The Devil's Dictionary. The Collected Writings of Ambrose Bierce*. New York: Citadel, 1946.

Blair, Walter. *Horse-Sense in American Humor*. Chicago: U of Chicago P, 1942.

———. "Introduction to the Sweet Singer of Michigan: the Collected Poems of Julia A. Moore." *Essays on American Humor*. Madison: U of Wisconsin P, 1993.

———. *Mark Twain and Huck Finn*. Berkeley: U of California P, 1960.

———. *Native American Humor*. New York: American Book Company, 1937.

———. "The Popularity of Nineteenth-Century American Humorists." *Essays on American Humor*. Madison: U of Wisconsin P, 1993.

Boskin, Joseph. "The Complicity of Humor: The Life and Death of Sambo." *The Philosophy of Laughter and Humor*. Ed. John Morreall. Albany: State U of New York P, 1987.

Brackenridge, Hugh Henry. *Modern Chivalry*. 1805.

Brand, Alice Glarden. "Mary Wilkins Freeman: Misanthropy as Propaganda." *New England Quarterly* 50 (1977): 83–100.

Brown, Carolyn S. "Sut Lovingood: A Nat'ral Born Durn'd Yarnspinner." *The Tall Tale in American Folklore and Literature*. Knoxville: U of Tennessee P, 1987.

Brown, Gillian. "Getting in the Kitchen with Dinah: Domestic Politics in *Uncle Tom's Cabin*." *American Quarterly* 36 (1984): 503–23.

Brown, Lynda. "Anderson's Wing Biddlebaum and Freeman's Louisa Ellis." *Studies in Short Fiction* 27.3 (1990): 413–14.

Browne, Charles Farrar. *Artemus Ward: His Book*. New York: Carleton, 1862.

Bryant, John. *Melville and Repose: The Rhetoric of Humor in the American Renaissance*. New York: Oxford UP, 1993.

Budd, Louis J. "Gentlemanly Humorists of the Old South." *Critical Essays on American Humor*. Ed. W. Craig Turner and Bedford Clark. Boston: G. K. Hall, 1984.

Buell, Lawrence. "Chapter 15: Comic Grotesque." *New England Literary Culture from Revolution through Renaissance*. Cambridge: Cambridge UP, 1986.

Burdett, Robert J. "She Had to Take Her Things Along." *Mark Twain's Library of Humor*. New York: Webster & Co., 1888.

Burgh, James. *Rules for the Conduct of Life*. Philadelphia: Thomas Stokes, 1846.

Butler, William Allen. *Nothing to Wear: An Episode of City Life*. New York: Rudd & Carleton, 1857.

Byrd, William. "The History of the Dividing Line." *The Prose Works of William Byrd of Westover: Narratives of a Colonial Virginian*. Ed. Louis B. Wright. Cambridge, MA: Harvard UP, Belknap Press, 1966.

———. "The Secret History of the Line." *The Prose Works of William Byrd of Westover: Narratives of a Colonial Virginian*. Ed. Louis B. Wright. Cambridge, MA: Harvard UP, Belknap Press, 1966.

Cai, J. H., et al. "Reserpine Impairs Spatial Working Memory Performance in Monkeys: Reversal by the Alpha 2-Adrenergic Agonist Clonidine." *Brain Research* 614.1–2 (1993): 191–96.

Camfield, Gregg. "'I Wouldn't Be As Ignorant As You for Wages': Huck Talks Back to His Conscience." *Studies in American Fiction* 21 (1992): 169–72.

———. "The Moral Aesthetics of Sentimentality: A Missing Key to *Uncle Tom's Cabin*." *Nineteenth-Century Literature* 43 (1988): 319–45.

———. *Sentimental Twain: Samuel Clemens in the Maze of Moral Philosophy*. Philadelphia: U of Pennsylvania P, 1994.

Celnart, Mme. *The Gentleman and Lady's Book of Politeness and Propriety of Deportment*. Boston: William D. Ticknor, 1837.

Chomsky, Noam. *Cartesian Linguistics*. New York: Harper & Row, 1966.

Church, Joseph. "Reconstructing Woman's Place in Freeman's 'The Revolt of Mother.'" *Colby Library Quarterly* 26.3 (1990): 195–200.

Churchland, Patricia. *Neurophilosophy: Toward a Unified Science of the Mind-Brain*. Cambridge, MA: MIT P, 1986.

Cixous, Hélène. "The Laugh of the Medusa." Trans. Keith Cohen and Paula Cohen. *The Signs Reader: Women, Gender & Scholarship*. Ed. Elizabeth Abel and Emily K. Abel. Chicago: U of Chicago P, 1983.

Clemens, Samuel. *Adventures of Huckleberry Finn*. Berkeley: U of California P, 1988.

———. *The Adventures of Tom Sawyer*. Berkeley: U of California P, 1980.

———. "Advice to Youth." *Mark Twain: Collected Tales, Sketches, Speeches and Essays, 1852–1890*. Ed. Louis J. Budd. New York: Library of America, 1992.

———. "A Cat-Tale." *Letters from the Earth*. Ed. Bernard DeVoto. New York: Harper & Row, 1962.

———. "Chronicle of Young Satan." *Mark Twain's Mysterious Stranger Manuscripts*. Ed. William M. Gibson. Berkeley: U of California P, 1969.

———. *A Connecticut Yankee in King Arthur's Court*. Berkeley: U of California P, 1979.

———. "Female Suffrage: Another Letter from Mark Twain." *Collected Tales, Sketches, Speeches and Essays, 1852–90*. New York: Library of America, 1992.

———. *The Innocents Abroad*. Hartford, CT: American Publishing Company, 1869.

———. "The Man That Corrupted Hadleyburg." *The Man That Corrupted Hadleyburg and Other Stories*. New York: Harpers, 1900.

———. *Roughing It*. Hartford, CT: American Publishing Company, 1872.

———. "Three Statements of the Eighties." *What Is Man? and Other Philosophical Writings*. Ed. Paul Baender. Berkeley: U of California P, 1973.

———. "Votes for Women." *Mark Twain's Speeches*. Ed. William Dean Howells. New York: Harper & Brothers, 1910.

Clemens, Samuel, and Charles Dudley Warner. *The Gilded Age*. Hartford, CT: American Publishing Company, 1873.

Coffin, Tristram Potter, and Hennig Cohen, eds. *Folklore from the Working Folk of America*. Garden City, NY: Anchor/Doubleday, 1973.

Cogan, Rosemary, et al. "Effects of Laughter and Relaxation on Discomfort Thresholds." *Journal of Behavioral Medicine* 10.2 (1987): 139–44.

Cott, Nancy. *The Bonds of Womanhood: "Woman's Sphere" in New England, 1780–1835*. New Haven, CT: Yale UP, 1977.

Cousins, Norman. *Anatomy of an Illness as Perceived by the Patient: Reflections on Healing and Regeneration*. New York: W. W. Norton, 1979.

Cox, James M. "Humor and America: The Southwestern Bear Hunt, Mrs. Stowe and Mark Twain." *Sewanee Review* 83 (1975): 573–601.

———. *Mark Twain: The Fate of Humor*. Princeton, NJ: Princeton UP, 1966.

Current-Garcia, Eugene. "Sut Lovingood's Rare Ripe Southern Garden." *Studies in Short Fiction* 9 (1972): 117–29.

Curtis, George William. "Our New Livery." *The Potiphar Papers*. New York: G. P. Putnam, 1853.

Cutter, Martha J. "Frontiers of Language: Engendering Discourse in 'The Revolt of Mother.'" *American Literature* 63 (1991): 279–91.

———. "Mary E. Wilkins Freeman's Two New England Nuns." *Colby Library Quarterly* 26.4 (1990): 213–25.

Daigrepont, Lloyd M. "Ichabod Crane: Inglorious Man of Letters." *Early American Literature* 19 (1984): 68–81.

Danzer, A., J. A. Dale, and H. L. Klions. "Effect of Exposure to Humorous Stimuli on Induced Depression." *Psychological Reports* 66.3, part 1 (Jun 1990): 1027–36.

Dawson, William P. "'Rip Van Winkle' as Bawdy Satire: The Rascal and the Revolution." *Emerson Society Quarterly* 27 (1981): 198–206.

Dennet, Daniel C. *Consciousness Explained*. Boston: Little, Brown, 1991.

deSousa, Ronald. "When Is It Wrong to Laugh?" *The Philosophy of Laughter and Humor*. Ed. John Morreall. Albany: State U of New York P, 1987.

Diamond, M. C., et al. "Plasticity in the 904-Day-Old Male Rat Cerebral Cortex." *Experimental Neurology* 87.2 (Feb 1985): 309–17.

———. "Rat Cortical Morphology Following Crowded-Enriched Living Conditions." *Experimental Neurology* 96.2 (May 1987): 241–47.

Donovan, Josephine. "Silence or Capitulation: Prepatriarchal 'Mothers' Gardens' in Jewett and Freeman." *Studies in Short Fiction* 23.1 (1986): 43–48.

Douglas, Ann. *The Feminization of American Culture*. New York: Alfred A. Knopf, 1977.

Douglass, Frederick. *My Bondage and My Freedom*. 1855. Rpt. New York: Dover.

Dresner, Zita, and Nancy Walker, eds. *Redressing the Balance: American Women's Literary Humor from Colonial Times to the 1980s*. Jackson, MS: UP of Mississippi, 1988.

Dundes, Alan. *Cracking Jokes: Studies of Sick Humor Cycles and Stereotypes*. Berkeley, CA: Ten Speed, 1987.

Eberwein, Jane D. "Transatlantic Contrast in Irving's *Sketch Book*." *College Literature* 15 (1988): 151–70.

Edelman, Gerald M. *Bright Air, Brilliant Fire: On the Matter of the Mind*. New York: Basic, 1992.

———. *Neural Darwinism: The Theory of Neuronal Group Selection*. New York: Basic, 1987.

———. *The Remembered Present: A Biological Theory of Consciousness*. New York: Basic, 1989.

Eliot, T. S. Introduction. *Adventures of Huckleberry Finn*. New York: Chanticleer, 1950.

Emerson, Ralph Waldo. "The Comic." *Letters and Social Aims*. Ed. James E. Cabot. Boston: Houghton Mifflin, Riverside, 1903.

English, James. "Humor, Politics, Community." *Comic Transactions*. Ithaca, NY: Cornell UP, 1994.

Estes, David C. "Sut Lovingood at the Camp Meeting: A Practical Joker among the Backwoods Believers." *Southern Quarterly* 25.2 (1987): 53–65.

Fern, Fanny [Sara Willis Parton]. *Fern Leaves from Fanny's Port Folio*. Auburn, NY: Derby and Miller, 1853.

———. *Fern Leaves, Second Series*. Auburn, NY: Miller, Orton, and Mulligan, 1854.

———. *Fresh Leaves*. New York: Mason Brothers, 1857.

———. *Ruth Hall and Other Writings*. Ed. Joyce W. Warren. New Brunswick, NJ: Rutgers UP, 1986.

Fetterley, Judith. *The Resisting Reader: A Feminist Approach to American Fiction*. Bloomington: Indiana UP, 1978.

Fiedler, Leslie A. "The Basic Myths, I: The End of Petticoat Government." *The Return of the Vanishing American*. New York: Stein and Day, 1968.

———. "Come Back to the Raft Ag'in, Huck Honey!" *Partisan Review* 15 (Jun 1948): 664–71.

Fienberg, Lorne. "Colonel Noland of the *Spirit:* The Voices of a Gentleman in Southwest Humor." *On Humor: The Best from American Literature*. Ed. Edwin H. Cady, and Louis J. Budd. Durham: Duke UP, 1992.

———. "Mary E. Wilkins Freeman's 'Soft Diurnal Commotion': Women's Work and Strategies of Containment." *New England Quarterly* 62.4 (Dec 1989): 483–504.

Fiske, John. *A Century of Science and Other Essays*. Boston: Houghton Mifflin, 1900.

———. "Charles Darwin." *Atlantic Monthly*. 49 (1882): 835–45.

Fisken, Beth Wynne. "The 'Faces of Children That Had Never Been': Ghost Stories by Mary Wilkins Freeman." *Haunting the House of Fiction: Feminist Perspectives on Ghost Stories by American Women*. Ed. Lynette Carpenter and Wendy Kolmar. Knoxville: U of Tennessee P, 1991.

Fliegelman, Jay. *Prodigals and Pilgrims: The American Revolution against Patriarchal Authority, 1750–1800*. Cambridge: Cambridge UP, 1982.

Foster, Charles H. *The Rungless Ladder: Harriet Beecher Stowe and New England Puritanism*. Durham, NC: Duke UP, 1954.

Foster, Edward. *Mary Wilkins Freeman*. New York: Hendricks House, 1956.

Foucault, Michel. *Power/Knowledge: Selected Interviews and Other Writings, 1972–1977*. Trans. Colin Gordon, Leo Marshall, John Mepham, and Kate Soper. Ed. Colin Gordon. New York: Pantheon, 1980.

Frank, Albert J. von. "The Man That Corrupted Sleepy Hollow." *Studies in American Fiction* 15 (1987): 129–43.

Franklin, Benjamin. "Dogood Papers." *Benjamin Franklin: Writings*. New York: Library of America, 1987.

Franz, Marie-Louise von. *Patterns of Creativity Mirrored in Creation Myths*. Zurich: Spring Publications, 1972.

Freeman, Mary E. Wilkins. "A Conflict Ended." *A Humble Romance and Other Stories*. New York: Harper & Brothers, 1887.

———. *The Infant Sphinx: Collected Letters of Mary E. Wilkins Freeman.* Ed. Brent L. Kendrick. Metuchen, NJ: Scarecrow, 1985.

———. "A Modern Dragon." *A Humble Romance and Other Stories.* New York: Harper & Brothers, 1887.

———. "A New England Nun." *A New England Nun and Other Stories.* New York: Harper & Brothers, 1891.

———. "A Poetess." *A New England Nun and Other Stories.* New York: Harper & Brothers, 1891.

———. "A Village Singer." *A New England Nun and Other Stories.* New York: Harper & Brothers, 1891.

Freud, Sigmund. "Humor." *The Philosophy of Laughter and Humor.* Ed. John Morreall. Albany: State U of New York P, 1987.

———. *Jokes and Their Relation to the Unconscious.* Trans. James Strachey. New York: W. W. Norton, 1963.

Fry, William F. "The Biology of Humor." *Humor: International Journal of Humor Research* 7 (1994): 111–26.

———. "The Physiologic Effects of Humor, Mirth, and Laughter." *Journal of the American Medical Association* 267.13 (April 1992): 1857–58.

Gardiner, Elaine. "Sut Lovingood: Backwoods Existentialist." *Southern Studies: An Interdisciplinary Journal of the South* 22.2 (1983): 177–89.

Gardner, Kate. "The Subversion of Genre in the Short Stories of Mary Wilkins Freeman." *New England Quarterly* 65.3 (1992): 447–68.

Gilbert, Charles D. "Rapid Dynamic Changes in Adult Cerebral Cortex." *Current Opinion in Neurobiology* 3.1 (Feb 1993): 100–103.

Glasser, Leah Blatt. "Legacy Profile: Mary E. Wilkins Freeman (1852–1930)." *Legacy: A Journal of Nineteenth-Century American Women Writers* 4.1 (1987): 37–45.

———. "Mary E. Wilkins Freeman: The Stranger in the Mirror." *Massachusetts Review* 25.2 (1984): 323–39.

Goffman, Erving. *The Presentation of Self in Everyday Life.* Edinburgh: U of Edinburgh Social Sciences Research Centre, 1956.

Goshgarian, G. M. *To Kiss the Chastening Rod: Domestic Fiction and Sexual Ideology in the American Renaissance.* Ithaca, NY: Cornell UP, 1992.

Graulich, Melody. "'Women Is My Theme, and Also Josiah': The Forgotten Humor of Marietta Holley." *American Transcendental Quarterly* 47–48 (1980): 187–98.

Grotjahn, Martin. *Beyond Laughter.* New York: McGraw-Hill, 1957.

Groves, D. F. "'A Merry Heart Doeth Good Like a Medicine . . . .'" *Holistic Nursing Practice* 5.4 (Jul 1991): 49–56.

Guttman, Allen. "Washington Irving and the Conservative Imagination." *American Literature* 36 (1964): 165–73.

Haig, Robin Andrew. *The Anatomy of Humor: Biopsychosocial and Therapeutic Perspectives.* Springfield, IL: Charles C. Thomas, 1988.

Harris, George W. *Sut Lovingood: Yarns Spun by a "Nat'ral Born Durn'd Fool."* New York: Fitzgerald, 1867.

Harris, Susan K. "'But Is It Any Good?': Evaluating Nineteenth-Century American Women's Fiction." *American Literature* 63 (1991): 43–61.

———. "Inscribing and Defining: The Many Voices of Fanny Fern's Ruth Hall." *Style* 22.4 (1988): 612–27.

Harshbarger, Scott. "Bugs and Butterflies: Conflict and Transcendence in 'The Artist of he Beautiful' and 'The Apple-Tree Table.'" *Studies in Short Fiction* 26 (1989): 86–89.

Hart, James D. *The Popular Book in America*. New York: Oxford UP, 1950.

Hawthorne, Nathaniel. *The Blithedale Romance*. 1852. Rpt. New York: W. W. Norton, 1978.

Hedges, William L. "Irving, Hawthorne, and the Image of the Wife." *American Transcendental Quarterly* 5 (1970):

———. *Washington Irving: An American Study, 1802–1832*. Baltimore: Johns Hopkins UP, 1965.

———. "Washington Irving: Nonsense, the Fat of the Land, and the Dream of Indolence." *The Chief Glory of Every People*. Ed. Matthew J. Bruccoli. Carbondale: Southern Illinois UP, 1973.

———. "Washington Irving: The Sketch Book of Geoffrey Crayon, Gent." *Landmarks of American Writing*. New York: Basic, 1969.

Hedrick, Joan D. *Harriet Beecher Stowe: A Life*. New York: Oxford UP, 1994.

Hemingway, Ernest. *The Green Hills of Africa*. New York: Charles Scribner's Sons, 1953.

Hirsch, David H. "Subdued Meaning in 'A New England Nun.'" *Studies in Short Fiction* 2 (1965): 124–36.

Holland, Norman N. *Laughing: A Psychology of Humor*. Ithaca, NY: Cornell UP, 1982.

Holley, Marietta. *Josiah Allen's Wife as a P.A. and P.I.: Samantha at the Centennial*. Hartford, CT: American Publishing Company, 1877.

———. *The Lament of a Mormon Wife*. Hartford, CT: American Publishing Company, 1880.

———. *My Opinions and Betsey Bobbet's*. Hartford, CT: American Publishing Company, 1872.

———. *My Wayward Pardner; or, My Trials with Josiah, America, The Widow Bump, and Etcetery*. Hartford, CT: American Publishing Company, 1880.

———. *Poems, by Josiah Allen's Wife*. New York: Funk & Wagnalls, 1887.

———. *Samantha among the Brethren*. New York: Funk & Wagnalls, 1890.

———. *Samantha at Saratoga; or, "Flirtin' with Fashion."* Philadelphia: Hubbard Brothers, 1887.

———. *Samantha on Children's Rights*. New York: G. W. Dillingham Company, 1909.

Howells, William Dean. *The Rise of Silas Lapham*. Boston: Ticknor, 1885.

Huf, Linda. "Ruth Hall (1855): The Devil and Fanny Fern." *A Portrait of the Artist as a Young Woman*. New York: Ungar, 1983.

Huston, J. P., et al. "The Basal Ganglia-Orofacial System: Studies on Neurobehavioral Plasticity and Sensory-Motor Tuning." *Neuroscience Biobehavioral Review* 14 (1990): 433–46.

Hutcheson, Francis. "Reflections on Laughter." *The Philosophy of Laughter and Humor*. Ed. John Morreall. Albany: State U of New York P, 1987.

———. *A System of Moral Philosophy*. Glasgow: R. and A. Foulis, 1755.

Iacovitti, L. "Effects of a Novel Differentiation Factor on the Development of Catecholamine Traits in Noncatecholamine Neurons." *Journal of Neuroscience* 11.8 (1991): 2403–9.

Iacovitti, L., et al. "Expression of Tyrosine Hydroxylase in Neurons of Cultured Cerebral Cortex: Evidence for Phenotypic Plasticity in Neurons of the CNS." *Journal of Neuroscience* 7 (1987): 1264–70.

Irving, Washington. *Bracebridge Hall*. 1822.

———. *Knickerbocker's History of New York*. 1809.

———. *The Sketch Book of Geoffrey Crayon*. 1820; rpt. New York: New American Library, 1961.

Jackson, Herbert G., Jr. *The Spirit Rappers*. Garden City, NY: Doubleday, 1972.

James, William. *The Meaning of Truth* . Excerpted in *The Writings of William James*, ed. John J. McDermott. New York: Random House, 1967.

———. *Pragmatism*. New York, 1907.

———. "Remarks on Spencer's Definition of Mind as Correspondence." *William James: The Essential Writings*. Ed. Bruce W. Wilshire. Albany: State U of New York P, 1984.

———. "The Sentiment of Rationality." *The Writings of William James*. Ed, John J. McDermott. New York: Random House, 1967.

Jameson, Frederic. *The Political Unconscious: Narrative as a Socially Symbolic Act*. Ithaca, NY: Cornell UP, 1981.

Jaynes, Julian. *The Origin of Consciousness in the Breakdown of the Bicameral Mind*. Boston: Houghton Mifflin, 1976.

Kauffman, Stuart A. *The Origins of Order: Self-Organization and Selection in Evolution*. New York: Oxford UP, 1993.

Keller, Evelyn Fox. "Feminism and Science." *The Signs Reader: Women, Gender & Scholarship*. Ed. Elizabeth Abel and Emily K. Abel. Chicago: U of Chicago P, 1983.

Kelley, Mary. "At War with Herself: Harriet Beecher Stowe as Woman in Conflict within the Home." *American Studies* 19.2 (1978): 23–40.

———. "The Literary Domestics: Private Women on a Public Stage." *Ideas in America's Cultures: From Republic to Mass Society*. Ed. Hamilton Cravens. Ames: Iowa State UP, 1982.

———. *Private Woman, Public Stage: Literary Domesticity in Nineteenth-Century America*. New York: Oxford UP, 1984.

Kierkegaard, Soren. *The Concept of Irony*. Trans. Lee M. Capel. Bloomington: Indiana UP, 1965.

———. *Concluding Unscientific Postscript*. Trans. David F. Swenson and Walter Lowrie. Princeton, NJ: Princeton UP, 1968.

Kirkland, Caroline. *A New Home, Who'll Follow?* 1839; rpt., New Brunswick: Rutgers UP, 1990.

Kolodny, Annette. *The Lay of the Land: Metaphor as Experience and History in American Life and Letters*. Chapel Hill: U of North Carolina P, 1975.

Koppelman, Susan. "About 'Two Friends' and Mary Eleanor Wilkins Freeman." *American Literary Realism* 21.1 (1988): 43–57.

Langer, Susanne K. "The Cultural Importance of Art." *Philosophical Sketches*. Baltimore: Johns Hopkins UP, 1962.

Langevin, Ronald, and H. I. Day. "Physiological Correlates of Humor." *The Psychology of Humor*. Ed. Jeffrey H. Goldstein and Paul E. McGhee. New York: Academic, 1972.

Lasch, Christopher. *Haven in a Heartless World: The Family Besieged*. New York: Basic Books, 1977.

Leach, Maria, ed. *Funk & Wagnalls Standard Dictionary of Folklore, Mythology, and Legend*. San Francisco: Harper & Row, 1972.

Lears, T. J. Jackson. *No Place of Grace: Antimodernism and the Transformation of American Culture, 1880–1920*. New York: Pantheon, 1981.

Leary, Lewis. "Washington Irving." *Six Classic American Writers: An Introduction*. Minneapolis: U of Minnesota P, 1963.

Lecky, William E. H. *History of European Morals*. New York: D. Appleton, 1874.

Lopez, Barry. *Giving Birth to Thunder, Sleeping with His Daughter: Coyote Builds North America*. New York: Avon, 1990.

Lynn, Kenneth. *Mark Twain and Southwestern Humor*. Boston: Little, Brown, 1959.

Lystra, Karen. *Searching the Heart: Women, Men, and Romantic Love in Nineteenth-Century America*. New York: Oxford UP, 1989.

Maik, Thomas A. "Dissent and Affirmation: Conflicting Voices of Female Roles in Selected Stories by Mary Wilkins Freeman." *Colby Library Quarterly* 26.1 (1990): 59–68.

Marchalonis, Shirley. "The Sharp-Edged Humor of Mary Wilkins Freeman: The Jamesons—and Other Stories." *Critical Essays on Mary Wilkins Freeman*. Ed. Shirley Marchalonis. Boston: G. K. Hall, 1991.

———, ed. *Critical Essays on Mary Wilkins Freeman*. Boston: G. K. Hall, 1991.

May, Henry F. "The Didactic Enlightenment." *The Enlightenment in America*. New York: Oxford UP, 1976.

McClary, Ben Harris. "George Washington Harris's 'Special Vision': His Yarns as Historical Sourcebook." *No Fairer Land: Studies in Southern Literature before 1900*. Ed. J. Lasley Dameron, and James W. Matthews. Troy, NY: Whitston, 1986.

McGhee, Paul E., and Jeffrey H. Goldstein. "Advances toward an Understanding of Humor: Implications for the Future." *The Psychology of Humor*. Ed. Jeffrey H. Goldstein and Paul E. McGhee. New York: Academic, 1972.

Meese, Elizabeth. "Signs of Undecidability: Reconsidering the Stories of Mary Wilkins Freeman." *Critical Essays on Mary Wilkins Freeman*. Ed. Shirley Marchalonis. Boston: G. K. Hall, 1991.

Melville, Herman. "The Apple-Tree Table, or Original Spiritual Manifestations." *The Piazza Tales and Other Prose Pieces, 1839–1860*. Evanston, IL, and Chicago: Northwestern UP and Newberry Library, 1987.

———. "Cock-a-Doodle-Doo! or, The Crowing of the Noble Cock Beneventano." *The Piazza Tales and Other Prose Pieces, 1839–1860*. Evanston, IL, and Chicago: Northwestern UP and the Newberry Library, 1987.

———. *The Confidence-Man. Herman Melville: Pierre; Israel Potter; The Piazza Tales; The Confidence-Man; Uncollected Prose; Billy Budd, Sailor*. New York: Library of America, 1984.

———. "I and My Chimney." *The Piazza Tales and Other Prose Pieces, 1839–1860*. Evanston, IL, and Chicago: Northwestern UP and Newberry Library, 1987.

———. *Moby Dick*. Evanston, IL, and Chicago: Northwestern UP and Newberry Library, 1987.

Mencken, H. L. "The Burden of Humor." *Mark Twain: The Critical Heritage*. Ed. Frederick Anderson. New York: Barnes & Noble, 1971.

Mengeling, Marvin E. "The Crass Humor of Irving's Deidrich Knickerbocker." *Studies in American Humor* 1 (1974): 66–72.

———. "Structure and Tone in 'Rip Van Winkle': The Irony of Silence." *Discourse: A Review of the Liberal Arts* 9 (1966): 457–63.

Merrill, Lisa. "Feminist Humor: Rebellious and Self-Affirming." *Last Laughs: Perspectives on Women and Comedy*. Ed. Regina Barreca. London: Gordon and Breach, 1988.

Merzenich, Michael M., and Koichi Sameshima. "Cortical Plasticity and Memory." *Current Opinion in Neurobiology* 3 (1993): 187–96.

Moore, Julia A. "Little Libbie." *The Sentimental Song Book*. Cleveland: J. F. Ryder, 1876.

Morey, Ann Janine. "American Myth and Biblical Interpretation in the Fiction of Harriet Beecher Stowe and Mary E. Wilkins Freeman." *Journal of the American Academy of Religion* 55.4 (1987): 741–63.

Morreal, John. *The Philosophy of Laughter and Humor*. Albany: SUNY Press, 1987.

Morris, Linda A. *Women's Humor in the Age of Gentility: The Life and Works of Frances Miriam Whitcher.* Syracuse, NY: Syracuse UP, 1992.

Mushabac, Jane. *Melville's Humor.* Hamden, CT: Archon, 1981.

Neal, Joseph C. "'Tis Only My Husband." *Neal's Charcoal Sketches, Three Books Complete in One. Etc.* Philadelphia: T. B. Peterson & Brothers, 1865.

Newman, Bertani Vozar. *A Reader's Guide to the Short Stories of Herman Melville.* Boston: G. K. Hall, 1986.

Nickels, Cameron C. *New England Humor from the Revolutionary War to the Civil War.* Knoxville: U of Tennessee P, 1993.

Nishino, H., et al. "Phenotypic Plasticity of Grafted Catecholaminergic Cells in the Dopamine-Depleted Caudate Nucleus in the Rat." *Neuroscience Research Supplement* 13 (1990): S54-60.

Oaks, Susan. "The Haunting Will: The Ghost Stories of Mary Wilkins Freeman." *Colby Library Quarterly* 21.4 (1985): 208–20.

Pattee, Fred Lewis. *The Feminine Fifties.* New York: D. Appleton, 1940.

Pennell, Melissa McFarland. "The Liberating Will: Freedom of Choice in the Fiction of Mary Wilkins Freeman." *Critical Essays on Mary Wilkins Freeman.* Boston: G. K. Hall, 1991.

Petry, Alice Hall. "Freeman's New England Elegy." *Studies in Short Fiction* 21.1 (1984): 68–70.

Phoenix, John [George Derby]. "A New System of English Grammar." *Phoenixiana; or, Sketches and Burlesques.* 1855. Rpt. New York: AMS, 1973.

———. "Sewing Machine—Feline Attachment." *The Squibob Papers.* New York: Carleton, 1865.

Plummer, Laura and Michael Nelson. "'Girls Can Take Care of Themselves': Gender and Storytelling in Washington Irving's 'The Legend of Sleepy Hollow.'" *Studies in Short Fiction* 30 (1993): 175–84.

Pochmann, Henry A. "Washington Irving: Amateur or Professional?" *Essays on American Literature in Honor of Jay B. Hubbell.* Durham, NC: Duke UP, 1967.

———. "Washington Irving." *Fifteen American Authors before 1900.* Madison: U of Wisconsin P, 1971.

Pribek, Thomas. "Between Democritus and Cotton Mather: Narrative Irony in 'The Apple-Tree Table.'" *Studies in the American Renaissance* (1989): 241–55.

Pryse, Marjorie. "The Humanity of Women in Freeman's 'A Village Singer'." *Colby Library Quarterly* 19.2 (1983): 69–77.

———. "An Uncloistered 'New England Nun.'" *Studies in Short Fiction* 20.4 (Fall 1983): 289–95.

Rapp, Albert. "A Phylogenetic Theory of Wit and Humor." *Journal of Social Psychology* 30 (1949): 81–96.

Reed, Kenneth T. "Oh These Women! These Women!: Irving's Shrews and Coquettes." *American Notes and Queries* 8 (June 1970): 147–50.

Reichardt, Mary R. "Mary Wilkins Freeman: One Hundred Years of Criticism." *Legacy: A Journal of Nineteenth-Century American Women Writers* 4.2 (1987): 31–44.

———. *A Web of Relationship: Women in the Short Stories of Mary Wilkins Freeman.* Jackson: U of Mississippi P, 1992.

Renker, Elizabeth. "Herman Melville, Wife Beating, and the Written Page." *American Literature* 66 (1994): 123–50.

Rickels, Milton. "The Grotesque Body of Southwestern Humor." *Critical Essays on American Humor.* Ed. W. Craig Turner and William Bedford Clark. Boston: G. K. Hall, 1984.

Rogin, Michael Paul. *Subversive Genealogy*. Berkeley: U of California P, 1979.

Romines, Ann. *The Home Plot: Women, Writing and Domestic Ritual*. Amherst: U of Massachusetts P, 1992.

Rorty, Richard. *Philosophy and the Mirror of Nature*. Princeton, NJ: Princeton UP, 1979.

Rosenblum, Joseph. "A Cock Fight between Melville and Thoreau." *Studies in Short Fiction* 23 (1986): 159–67.

Ross, Cheri L. "Nineteenth-Century American Feminist Humor: Marietta Holley's 'Samantha Novels.'" *Journal of the Midwest Modern Language Association* 22.2 (1989): 12–25.

Roth, Martin. *Comedy and America: The Lost World of Washington Irving*. Port Washington, NY: Kennikat, 1976.

Rourke, Constance. *American Humor, a Study of National Character*. New York: Harcourt, Brace, 1931.

Rubin-Dorsky, Jeffrey. *Adrift in the Old World*. Chicago: U of Chicago P, 1988.

Samuels, Shirley, ed. *The Culture of Sentiment: Race, Gender, and Sentimentality in Nineteenth-Century America*. New York: Oxford UP, 1992.

Santayana, George. "The Genteel Tradition in American Philosophy." *The Genteel Tradition, Nine Essays*. Ed. Douglas L. Wilson. Cambridge, MA: Harvard UP, 1967.

———. *The Sense of Beauty: Being the Outlines of Aesthetic Theory*. 1986. Rpt. Cambridge, MA: MII, 1986.

Schaffer, Carl. "Unadmitted Impediments: Meville's 'Bartleby' and 'I and My Chimney.'" *Studies in Short Fiction* 24 (1987): 93–101.

Schmitz, Neil. *Of Huck and Alice: Humorous Writing in American Literature*. Minneapolis: U of Minnesota P, 1983.

Schopenhauer, Arthur. "Book I, section 13." *The World as Will and Idea*. Trans. R. B. Haldane and J. Kemp. New York: AMS, 1977.

Sedgwick, Catherine. *A New England Tale*. New York: E. Bliss and E. White, 1822.

Seelye, John. "Root and Branch: Washington Irving and American Humor." *Nineteenth-Century Fiction* 38 (1984): 415–25.

Shear, Walter. "Time in 'Rip Van Winkle' and 'The Legend of Sleepy Hollow.'" *Midwest Quarterly* 17 (1976): 158–72.

Sklar, Katheryn Kish. *Catherine Beecher: A Study in American Domesticity*. New York: W. W. Norton, 1976.

Smith, Henry Nash. *Mark Twain: The Development of a Writer*. Cambridge, MA: Harvard UP, 1962.

Snow, C. P. *The Two Cultures and the Scientific Revolution*. New York: Cambridge UP, 1959.

Sochen, June, ed. *Women's Comic Visions*. Detroit: Wayne State UP, 1991.

Spencer, Herbert. *The Data of Ethics*. New York: Hurst, 1879(?).

Springer, Haskell. *Washington Irving: A Reference Guide*. Boston: G. K. Hall, 1976.

Stearns, Frederic R. *Laughing: Physiology, Pathophysiology, Psychology, Pathopsychology, and Development*. Springfield, IL: Charles C. Thomas, 1972.

Stowe, Harriet Beecher. *The Minister's Wooing. Stowe: Three Novels*. New York: Library of America, 1982.

———. *Oldtown Folks and Sam Lawson's Oldtown Fireside Stories*. 2 Vols. New York: AMS, 1967.

———. *Uncle Tom's Cabin. Stowe: Three Novels*. New York: Library of America, 1982.

Sumner, William Graham. *What Social Classes Owe to Each Other*. 1883. Rpt. New York: Arno, 1972.

Tave, Stuart M. *The Amiable Humorist: A Study in the Comic Theory and Criticism of the Eighteenth and Early Nineteenth Centuries*. Chicago: U of Chicago P, 1960.

Tenney, Tabitha. *Female Quixotism*. New York: Oxford UP, 1992.

Thoreau, Henry David. *Walden*. 2d ed. New York: W. W. Norton, 1992.

Tocqueville, Alexis de. *Democracy in America*. New York: Vintage, 1945.

Toelken, Barre. Foreword to Barry Lopez, *Giving Birth to Thunder, Sleeping with His Daughter: Coyote Builds North America*. New York: Avon, 1990.

Tompkins, Jane P. "Sentimental Power: *Uncle Tom's Cabin* and Politics of Literary History." *Sensational Designs: The Cultural Work of American Fiction, 1790–1860*. New York: Oxford UP, 1985.

Toth, Emily. "A Laughter of Their Own: Women's Humor in the United States." *Critical Essays on American Humor*. Ed. William Bedford Clark and W. Craig Turner. Boston: G. K. Hall, 1984.

Toth, Susan A. "A Defiant Light: A Positive View of Mary Wilkins Freeman." *New England Quarterly* 46 (1973): 82–93.

———. "'The Rarest and Most Peculiar Grape': Versions of the New England Woman in Nineteenth-Century Local Color Literature." *Regionalism and the Female Imagination: A Collection of Essays*. Ed. Emily Toth. New York: Human Sciences, 1985.

———. "Mary Wilkins Freeman's Parable of Wasted Life." *American Literature* 42 (1971): 564–67.

Tuthill, Louisa C. *The Young Lady's Home*. Boston: William J. Reynolds, 1847.

Veblen, Thorstein. *The Theory of the Leisure Class*. New York: Macmillan, 1899.

Walker, Katherine Kent Child. "The Total Depravity of Inanimate Things." *Atlantic Monthly*, Sept 1864.

Walker, Nancy A. *Fanny Fern*. New York: Twayne, 1993.

———. *A Very Serious Thing: Women's Humor and American Culture*. Minneapolis: U of Minnesota P, 1988.

Walker, Nancy, and Zita Dresner, eds. *Redressing the Balance: American Women's Literary Humor from Colonial Times to the 1980s*. Jackson: UP of Mississippi, 1988.

Warren, Joyce W. *Fanny Fern: An Independent Woman*. New Brunswick, NJ: Rutgers UP, 1992.

Weatherspoon, M. A. "1815–1819: Prelude to Irving's Sketch Book." *American Literature* 41 (1970): 566–71.

Welter, Barbara. *Dimity Convictions*. Athens, OH: Ohio State UP, 1976.

Wenke, John. "Sut Lovingood's Yarns and the Politics of Performance." *Studies in American Fiction* 15.2 (1987): 199–210.

Westbrook, Perry D. *Mary Wilkins Freeman*. Boston: Twayne, 1988.

Whitcher, Frances Miriam. *The Widow Bedott Papers*. New York: Derby & Jackson, 1855.

Williams, Stanley T. *The Life of Washington Irving*. 2 vols. New York: Oxford UP, 1935.

———. "Washington Irving." *Literary History of the United States: Third Edition*. Ed. Robert E. Spiller et al. Third Edition, Revised. New York: Macmillan, 1963.

Wilson, Edmund. *Patriotic Gore*. New York: Oxford UP, 1962.

Wilson, Forrest. *Crusader in Crinoline*. Philadelphia: J. B. Lippincott, 1941.

Winter, Kate H. *Marietta Holley: Life with "Josiah Allen's Wife."* Syracuse, NY: Syracuse UP, 1984.

Wood, Ann Douglas. "The Literature of Impoverishment: The Women Local Colorists in America 1865–1914." *Women's Studies* 1 (1972): 3–40.

Young, Philip. "Fallen from Time: The Mythic Rip Van Winkle." *Kenyon Review* 22 (1960): 547–73.

Yovetich, N. A., J. A. Dale, and M. A. Hudak. "Benefits of Humor in Reduction of Threat-Induced Anxiety." *Psychological Reports* 66.1 (Feb 1990): 51–58.

# Index